Organizational Cognition
Computation and Interpretation

LEA's Organization and Management Series
Arthur Brief and James P. Walsh, Series Editors

Ashforth • Role Transitions in Organizational Life: An Identity-Based Perspective

Beach • Image Theory: Theoretical and Empirical Foundations

Garud/Karnoe • Path Dependence and Creation

Lant/Shapira • Organizational Cognition: Computation and Interpretation

Thompson/Levine/Messick • Shared Cognition in Organizations: The Management of Knowledge

Organizational Cognition
Computation and Interpretation

Edited by

Theresa K. Lant
and
Zur Shapira

LAWRENCE ERLBAUM ASSOCIATES, PUBLISHERS
2001   Mahwah, New Jersey   London

Lawrence Erlbaum Associates, Inc., Publishers
10 Industrial Avenue
Mahwah, NJ 07430

Cover design by Kathryn Houghtaling Lacey

Library of Congress Cataloging-in-Publication Data

Organizational cognition : computation and interpretation / edited
by Theresa K. Lant and Zur Shapira.

p. cm.

Includes bibliographical references and index.
ISBN 0-8058-3333-1 (cloth : alk. paper)
1. Knowledge management. 2. Decision making. I. Lant, Theresa K.
II. Shapira, Zur.   III. Series.
HD30.2C626   2000
658.4'03 —dc21   00-047155
                                                    CIP

Printed in the United States of America
10 9 8 7 6 5 4 3 2 1

About the Editors

Theresa Lant is Associate Professor of Management at the Stern School of Business, New York University. She received her PhD from Stanford University in 1987 and her AB from the University of Michigan in 1981. She is Senior Editor of *Organization Science*, which is an international journal of the Institute for Operations Research and the Management Sciences. Professor Lant's research focuses on the processes of managerial decision making, organizational learning , and strategic adaptation. Currently, she is studying the emergence of the new media sectors in New York City. Her publications have appeared in the *Strategic Management Journal, Advances in Strategic Management, Organization Science, Management Science, and the Journal of Management.*

Zur Shapira is Research Professor of Management at the Stern School of Business, New York University. He was born in Tel Aviv in 1945, raised and educated in Jerusalem, and graduated from the Hebrew University in Jerusalem. He received his PhD in Psychology and Management from the University of Rochester and has taught at the University of Rochester, Hebrew University, Carnegie-Mellon University, University of California at Berkeley, and the University of Chicago before joining New York University in 1988. He has been a Research Fellow at the International Institute of Management in Berlin and a Visiting Scholar at the Russell Sage Foundation.

Professor Shapira is best know professionally for his work on risk taking and organizational decision making. Among his publications are the books, *Risk Taking: A Managerial Perspective* (1995), *Organizational Decision Making* (1996) and *Technological Learning: Oversights and Firefights* (1997). He has been a speaker at major academic and private institutions and professional associations such as the Israeli Management Center, The Academy of Management, The Institute for Quantitative Research in Finance, and Arthur Andersen. He appeared on BBC Worldwide and on CNBC.

Professor Shapira has been a consultant to various business firms, governmental agencies, and nonprofit organizations including: Arthur Andersen, The Electronics Corporation of Israel, El Al-Israel Airlines, bank of Israel, Bank of Leumi, Intel, Teva Pharmaceutical Co., The Center for strategic studies (Tel Aviv), The National institute of Defense (Israel), Daimler-Benz Aerospace Company, and the Thomas Register Company.

Contents

Series Editor Foreword

We are editing the "LEA Series in Organization and Management" because we want to provide a home for promising scholarship that either opens up new avenues of inquiry or redirects contemporary research in some meaningful way. The work collected here by Theresa Lant and Zur Shapira meets our aspirations. The past 50 years have been witness to two revolutions. Land, labor, and capital are no longer the key factors of production that they once were. Knowledge is now the prime source of competitive advantage. In this light, it may come as no surprise to learn that 50 years ago, decisions supplanted hierarchy as the key unit of analysis for organization theory. The knowledge revolution in productive enterprises and the decision-making revolution in organization theory emerged hand-in-hand. Lant and Shapira take stock of the history of work on the cognitive aspects of decision making and discover that those working within the computational, information-processing paradigm have not yet come to terms with the work of those laboring within the interpretive meaning-making paradigm ... and vice-versa. The collection of work in this volume is not an attempt to integrate the two perspectives per se, but rather an attempt to clarify the contributions and limits of each others point of view.

Lant and Shapira's hope is that the clarification we find in this book will facilitate a fruitful integration of these perspectives someday soon. We hope that his integration will in turn help organizations as they grapple with the implications of the knowledge revolution. We are very pleased to bring this book to you. Enjoy.

—*James P. Walsh*
—*Arthur Brief*

Preface

The genesis of this book was a conference held at New York University in the spring of 1998. The conference attracted a wide range of young and established scholars from around the world. We chose a subset of the best papers and asked the authors from the United States, Canada, England, France, Italy, and India. Authors range from eminent scholars such as Jim March to doctoral students. The type of work includes theoretical models and empirical studies, both qualitative and quantitative.

We would like to thank a number of people who helped make the conference a success and helped us with the editing of the book. First, we are very grateful to Greg Udell at the Berkley Center for Entrepreneurial Studies for sponsoring the conference. The center's administrative staff, Loretta Poole and Patricia Edwards, helped immensely with the organization and running of the conference, and we are deeply indebted to them for making it such a pleasant experience. We would also like to thank the Management Department at New York University's Stern School of Business for cosponsoring the conference. Several staff members have helped us pull the book together, namely Berna Sifonte and Karen Angelilo. We are also most grateful to our work-study student, Emily Fernandez, who has put in endless hours formatting, proofreading, and creating the index for the book. Of course, the book might never have been conceived without the encouragement of Anne Duffy from LEA. We also appreciate the encouragement, editorial feedback, and friendship of the LEA Management series editors, Art Brief and Jim Walsh.

Introduction: Foundations of Research on Cognition in Organizations

Theresa K. Lant
Zur Shapira
New York University

Research on managerial and organizational cognition has increased dramatically since the 1980s. The importance of cognition research to management theorists is indicated by the increase in articles on cognition in the major management journals as well as the creation and institutionalization of a cognition interest group in the major professional association of management scholars, The Academy of Management. This increased interest in cognitive phenomena might have been influenced by research in other fields such as information systems and biology, in which the 1990s was called "the decade of the brain" by former President George Bush. One may be tempted to think that this line of inquiry in management is a recent phenomenon. However, research on cognition in management goes back at least 50 years to the time Herbert Simon published the first edition of *Administrative Behavior* (Simon, 1947). One of the most influential publications in the field of management, March and Simon's (1958) *Organizations* set the tone in arguing that decision making is a major explanatory variable in organization theory. Reflecting on some 35 years of research in the field, March and Simon (1993) commented:

The central unifying construct of the present book is not hierarchy but decision making, and the flow of information within organizations that instructs, informs, and supports decision making processes. The idea of "decision" can also be elusive, of course. Defining what a decision is, when it is made, and who makes it have all, at times, turned out to be problematic. Nevertheless, the concept seems to have serves us reasonably well. (p. 3)

March and Simon (1958) viewed organizations as information processing systems consisting of embedded routines through which information is stored and enacted. Some researchers have taken this to mean that organizations are systems that process and code information in a *computational* manner. That is, the problem that organizations face is one of searching and processing relevant information when such search is costly and decision makers are boundedly rational. Other researchers interpreted March and Simon to mean that organizations are social entities that enact their world. Some see in these words the elements of collective mind (Garud & Porac, 1999; Sandelands & Stablein, 1987). These two views separated in the last decade into two distinct branches of cognition research in organizations: the computational approach and the interpretive approach. The computational stream of research examines the processes by which managers and organizations *process information* and make decisions. The interpretive approach investigates how *meaning* is created around information in a social context.

THE COMPUTATIONAL PERSPECTIVE

The cognitive revolution received a big push in the mid-1950s. In particular, in 1954 the metaphor of the computer as a model for human information processing emerged, and cognitive research started to focus on information processing. Most of the work in this tradition is consistent with the computational–symbolic representational model of human cognition and information processing (Thagard, 1996). One of the most intriguing articles in this era was Miller's (1956) account of the limitations on short-term memory, which he claimed is seven plus or minus two items. Simon and his colleagues started to work on the general problem solver paradigm (Newell, Shaw, & Simon, 1958) and pushed cognitive research further into the domain of artificial intelligence. Critique of the Simonian approach surfaced only in the mid-1960s when the RAND Corporation decided to solicit an independent evaluation of the merit of artificial intelligence. Dreyfus' (1965) working paper, later published as a book (1972), titled *What Computers Cannot Do* provided a critique of the artificial intelligence approach that continues today (see also Dreyfus & Dreyfus, 1986).

At the individual level of analysis, a long duel is raging between those researchers who advocate rational models and those who advocate behavioral models to describe human decision making. Psychologists have criticized the rational model (cf. Von Neumann & Morgenstern, 1944) for not accurately describing how individuals make judgments. In contrast, they have developed a behavioral perspective on judgment and choice. The original work initiated in the 1950s by Edwards (1954) on probability estimation, Meehl (1954) on information integration, and Simon (1955) on heuristic search led to the emergence of a new field called behavioral decision theory. This field has developed descriptive models of human information processing (see Kahneman, Slovic, & Tversky, 1982) and choice under risk (Kahneman & Tversky, 1979). Although this field studies how human actors process information and make choices, it is equally concerned with how actors form preferences and how the context or framing of situations influences their choices.

The early 20th century also saw the development of behaviorism, which focused on the relationship between stimuli and behavior and criticized any reference to consciousness, introspection, or cognitive processes (Skinner, 1953; Watson, 1913). Many researchers since the 1950s have questioned the generalizability of behaviorism. In response, these researchers suggested that cognition mediates stimulus–response (e.g., Neisser, 1967). Since then, a flood of work ensued on how humans process information and how information processing guides behavior (Fiske & Taylor, 1984; Lord & Maher, 1991; Nisbett & Ross, 1980). Subsequently, researchers found evidence that information processing involves categorization processes, in which information is filtered by existing knowledge structures and schemas. These knowledge structures have been called cognitive maps. These maps have been shown to influence how individuals interpret information and make decisions.

THE INTERPRETIVE PERSPECTIVE

The origin of the computational approach in organizational cognition was influenced primarily by developments in psychology. The interpretive approach has its roots in sociology and, in particular, in the sociology of knowledge. Following the tradition of the Frankfurt school, Berger and Luckman's (1966) treatise on the social construction of reality became the basis on which the interpretive approach has flourished. One of the major contributors to this approach in the organizational literature has been Karl Weick, whose 1969's text on the social psychology of organizing became a classic. Other researchers such as Gioia (chap. 18, this volume) have also been strong advocates of the interpretive approach.

Bruner (1990) gave an illuminating account of the relations between the computational and the interpretive approaches, in which he tells the story of the cognitive revolution in psychology. In his words, "The cognitive revolution as originally conceived virtually required that psychology join forces with anthropology and linguistics, philosophy and history, even with the discipline of law" (p. 3). He commented that the efforts "were not to 'reform' behaviorism but to replace it." However, it appears that the computational approach was making strong headway into cognitive psychology. As Bruner commented,

> Very early on, for example, emphasis began shifting from *meaning* to *information*, from the *construction* of meaning to the *processing* of information. These are profoundly different matters. The key factor in the shift was the introduction of computation as the ruling metaphor. (p. 4)

For Bruner (1990), this was the wrong turn of events because he equated cognition with the construction of meaning and claimed that "Information is indifferent with regard to meaning" (p. 4).

At a higher level of analysis, however, the question of how collectives process and store information and the concept of cognitive maps proved to be problematic (Walsh, 1995). Daft and Weick (1984) viewed organizations as interpretation systems that "encode cues from the environment, make sense of these cues using existing stocks of knowledge, and incorporate the resulting interpretations into organizational practices and routines." Weick and Roberts (1993) suggested that interpretation goes on in the interactions among actors. As Garud and Porac (1999) pointed out—this view of organizational cognition involves all of an organization's systems and structures. Walsh (1995) noted that collectives can serve as a repository of organized knowledge that acts as a template for interpretation and action.

Once the question was raised about how collectives of individuals think, the concept of *collective mind* followed (Sandelands & Stablein, 1987). The notion of collective mind was not new. Durkheim (1895) wrote about the social origins of individual behavior. John Dewey's (1938) words echo the same sentiment:

> Experience does not go on simply inside a person. We live from birth to death in a world of persons and things which is in large measure what it is because of what has been done and transmitted from previous human activities. (p. 39)

The essentials of the argument are that human thought, cognition, or knowledge is situated within a cultural system, including artifacts and practices, which is itself made up of prior thoughts and knowledge. Knowledge is embedded in these systems, which reach out across time and space, and our own thoughts are enabled and constrained by this embedded knowledge (Pea, 1993; Vygotsky, 1929; Wundt, 1921). For the most part, however, these ideas have been soundly rejected by most psychologists and even organization theorists. As early as 1924, Allport (1924) claimed that discussing such a concept as collective mind leaves one in a "state of mystical confusion." Douglas (1986), in her book about how institutions think, dismissed the idea as "repugnant."

COMPUTATION OR INTERPRETATION?

Are the computational and the interpretive approaches branches of the same tree describing human cognition or do they make assumptions that cannot be reconciled? There are some fundamental assumptions that push the two approaches away from each other. One major issue is the way reality is conceived: If reality is only socially constructed, as some interpretivists claim, then one true reality doesn't exist. If researchers take this ontological assumption to its extreme, it would suggest that there are no real criteria against which human information processing can be compared. There would be no way of assessing the accuracy or efficacy of decisions. The emphasis in computational research on error and accuracy would be meaningless to interpretivists who believe that all criteria are socially constructed, and therefore, none is more real or more important than the other. In approaching an interpretivist colleague with a question on examples of criticism of the interpretivist approach, he answered, "The interpretivist approach cannot be criticized."

Researchers in the computational camp soundly disagree with this assumption. At the extreme, these researchers take the view that cognition research should focus entirely on the "processing structures of the brain and the symbolic representations of the mind" (Norman, 1993, p. 3). Simon and others argued that all thought and behavior can be represented in symbolic models (cf. Vera & Simon, 1993). This perspective suggests that down to the most complex social interaction, symbolic models can represent the real nature of this interaction. Other researchers who take a situated cognition perspective argue that by attributing all cognitive activity to symbolic processing, the "question of how people use symbols to create and communicate meaning seems to have disappeared" (Greeno & Moore, 1993, p. 51).

We believe there is a common ground that can be discovered between the two approaches. We argue that extreme positions on either side are unlikely to produce progress in our understanding of cognitive processes in organizations. We suggest that both information processing and meaning making are simultaneous, ongoing processes in organizations. With this book, we hope to discover some of the boundary conditions under which one process is more prevalent than the other, as well as those instances in which they complement each other.

Our goal in editing this volume is to foster a dialogue and cross-pollination among researchers who may see their work as falling into one or the other camp. We believe that at this point in the history of cognition research as applied to organizations, such integration is necessary for this field to progress. To that end, we assembled chapters that illustrate both perspectives and some that have roots in both camps. We have woven these chapters together in an attempt to allow the readers to consider the different perspectives and form their own judgment about the overlapping versus the distinctive features of each approach.

THE STRUCTURE OF THE BOOK

At this stage of the field of organizational cognition, for progress to be made, we need to increase the level of dialogue among researchers with different perspectives. This book does not represent a single dominant paradigm that has been accepted; rather, it offers a wide variety of studies. All the chapters help foster a dialogue about the computation–interpretation debate. Many of these chapters illustrate how integration of the two perspectives is the best way to make progress.

Although we have designed the book to highlight variance on a number of dimensions, we have set certain boundaries. We are interested specifically in cognition in organizational contexts. The chapters all highlight the importance of the actor–system interface. A variety of approaches are used in these chapters but all are relevant to the issues associated with the cognition of actors in complex systems. By recognizing organizational systems as a level of analysis and considering the complex, unstructured nature of problems in organizations, we are able to see things that we would not if we just focused on individual cognitive processes or even managerial cognition in the absence of a context within which it is embedded. We learn from these chapters that the social and technical context characterized by organizations is not "beside the point" to the study of cognition but "is the point."

Part II of this book places several theoretical stakes in the ground concerning computational and interpretive processes and their roles in organizational intelligence. These theoretical positions serve as foundation ideas from which the ideas in the subsequent chapters can be reflected. Dhar's chapter (chap. 2, this volume) analyzes learning processes in organizations based on the computational approach. He argues that machine learning methods can produce models that promote human dialog and exploration that does not otherwise occur in routine organizational activity. However, Dhar does not ignore or negate the importance of interpretation. Rather, he examines the actor–machine interface in organizations and suggests a set of boundary conditions under which computational approaches are feasible and desirable and can replace human judgment and when they can merely serve as support systems.

Ocasio's chapter (chap. 3, this volume) develops a theoretical perspective on how organizations think. He articulates the elements and processes of cognition at the individual, social, and organizational level. He shows how both the computational and the interpretive perspectives are crucial to an understanding of cognition at the organizational level of analysis. Organizations are viewed as dynamic social systems that structure and regulate the cognition of organizational participants.

March's chapter (chap. 4, this volume) provides a rich and compelling narrative about the pursuit of intelligence in organizations. He outlines the two critical problems in this pursuit. The first, *ignorance*, is essentially a problem of *computation*. Intelligent action requires information and prediction. In a world where information is difficult and costly to obtain and future states are uncertain, intelligent action is problematic. However, as Dhar (chap. 2) points out, given sufficient data, theories about cause and effect, and a well defined payoff matrix associated with uncertain outcomes, this problem boils down to one of computation. The second problem, *ambiguity*, is a problem of *interpretation*. To assess intelligence, one has to know what outcomes are desired and know when outcomes have been achieved. The definition of preferences turns out to be a very sticky problem and one that, in organizations, is played out in a social domain. To make progress in the pursuit of organizational intelligence, it is necessary to develop our knowledge about both computation and interpretation and to work on an integration of the two perspectives. Sitkin's commentary provides a discussion of the chapters in light of the balancing act that organizations undertake with respect to managing ignorance and ambiguity.

Part III is devoted to empirical examinations of knowledge, learning, and framing in organizational settings. These studies concern the influence of organizational structures, routines, and processes on the distribution, transmission, and interpretation of information in organizations. Rulke and Zaheer (chap. 5, this volume) explore the cognitive maps of managers across subunits of an organization to assess the use of learning channels and the degree and use of transactive knowledge. The study concerns the location of an organization's self-knowledge (knowing what you know) and resource knowledge (knowing who knows what) throughout an organization and how and through what means such knowledge is disseminated. The issue of where knowledge is located is essentially the organizational equivalent of mental representations that guide information retrieval and processing. They find that both types of knowledge matter to performance, thus speaking to the question of how organizations can reduce their ignorance, in March's (chap. 4, this volume) terms. Paul-Chowdhury (chap. 6, this volume) also tackles the issue of the location and dissemination of knowledge in an organization. She reports on an exploratory field study in three major banks where she finds that the transfer of lessons learned from performance feedback is inhibited due to barriers such as organizational structures, promotion and reward systems, and pressures toward conformity. Leadership of bank executives was an important mechanism for disseminating lessons through the organization.

The Murphy, Mezias, and Chen chapter (chap. 7, this volume) tackles the ambiguity issue raised by March (chap. 4) as opposed to the ignorance question. These authors argue that the setting of goals is a decision that frames performance feedback as either positive or negative, thus influencing the interpretation of performance information. They use data from the quarterly performance reports of a large American corporation to examine the question whether the framing of performance feedback as success or failure relative to previous aspiration can be expected to have an effect on the adaptation of aspirations over time. They show how simple decision rules, such as how aspirations adapt in response to feedback, can have a powerful effect on the goals that are set by organizations. Sutcliffe provides an integrative summary of these three empirical chapters. She raises questions regarding four issues that are central to advancing theory in this area: culture, performance pressures, learning costs, and attribution framing.

Part IV provides four empirical studies on managerial thinking and decision-making processes. Tamuz (chap. 8, this volume) examines how the managerial cognition of ambiguous events, encoded in varying definitions of aircraft near accidents, influences the processes of filtering, interpretation, and knowledge generation. She shows how the categorization of ambiguous events (an interpretation process) influences if and how knowledge about these events is generated. Thus, interpretations influence the computational process of gathering information. She finds that who the decision makers are affects how they will interpret and categorize ambiguous events. Categorization differs depending on past experience, goals, and position.

Bennett and Anthony (chap. 9, this volume) investigate the way cognitive and experiential differences between inside and outside members of boards of directors may impact the nature of their personal contributions to board deliberations. Like Tamuz (chap. 8), they find that who the directors are influences how they categorize and interpret events. Nair (chap. 10, this volume) also examines how managers deal with ambiguous, complex situations. He presents an empirical study on the relation between the structure of cognitive maps of managers and their effectiveness in solving complex problems.

Vidaillet (chap. 11, this volume) provides a fine-grained view of the decision-making processes surrounding a highly complex and ill-structured problem—a hazardous material incident that occurred in France. She finds that before information about the incident could be processed, the actors needed to frame and categorize the incident. Each set of actors constructed a representation of the crisis and then processed information and acted accordingly. The context of the actors—their background, job, and physical location—all influenced their framing of the incident. These four chapters illustrate how important the interpretive process of framing and categorization are to actors faced with ambiguous issues. In all these examples, this interpretive process is a precursor to information processing. The interpretations of managers are influenced by their context—their prior experiences, their social context, and their location in time and space. If we only examine decision making after goals, preferences, and problem definitions have been set, we will see decision making as largely a computational, information-processing exercise. To do so, however, misses half of the story. Defining problems and determining preferred outcomes are interpretive processes that serve to reduce ambiguity and allow information search, retrieval, and processing to ensue. Dukerich (this volume) discusses the key issues that arise when managers deal with ambiguous, unstructured problems. She shows how in these four papers, ill-structured problems allow for multiple interpretations of the problem, of the relevance of information, and the appropriateness of various actions.

Part V deals explicitly with the social embeddedness of managerial and organizational cognition. The chapters cover three different levels of analysis from interorganizational to organizational to intraorganizational. Odoroci and Lomi (chap. 12, this volume) explore the ways in which competitors categorize each other into strategic groups. This categorization process is the result of interaction and interpretation and frames subsequent decisions and actions by the competitors. They examine water treatment plants in Italy to address questions about the origins and implications of perceptions of strategic similarity among competitors.

Oldfield (chap. 13, this volume) shows that large-scale projects often fail because the framing of problems associated with these projects systematically excludes information that would help assess project risk. She finds that in organizational and project failures, there is evidence that the relevant information for predicting negative outcomes is available within the project team; however, the available knowledge is not shared effectively. This occurs because the interests of certain stakeholders are routinely excluded, resulting in an overly narrow definition of problems.

Brooks, Kimble, and Hildreth construct an interpretive framework based on structuration theory (Giddens, 1986) to explore the processes by which an information technology is created, used, and institutionalized within an organization. They show how technologies are not just used by actors in an organization but, rather, are created and institutionalized by the process of actors using technologies. At all three levels of analysis, we can see the role of the interaction of actors in creating the interpretations of situations that guide action. In all three cases, we see how features of organizational life that on one hand seem to lend themselves especially well to computational–representational approaches—the definition of strategic groups, assessment of risk, and application of technology—are all guided by interpretive processes. Gioia (this volume) joyfully summarizes these studies by arguing that strategy essentially boils down to social cognition.

Starbuck's chapter (chapter 15, this volume) opens the final section with a historical account of the development of cognitive research in psychology. In comparing the behaviorist and cognitive approaches, he concludes that behaviorist theories can explain phenomena that cognitive theories cannot, and cognitive theories can explain phenomena that behaviorist theories cannot. He argues that although an integration of the two perspectives is the correct long-term goal, there is value in facilitating debate that clarifies the concepts and assumptions of the perspectives. We have a similar goal for this book. Although we seek integration of the computational and interpretive perspectives in the long run, we encourage variance, contrast, and debate at this stage of the game. In our final chapter, Lant and Shapira (chap. 16, this volume) look back at the research reported in this volume and summarize the major trajectories, commenting on methodological issues, and provide some conjectures for future research in managerial and organizational cognition. We hope you find our approach useful in your own endeavors toward understanding cognition in organizations.

REFERENCES

Allport, F. H. (1924). *Social psychology*. Boston: Houghton Mifflin.
Berger, P., & Luckman, T. (1966). *The social construction of reality*. Garden City, NY: Doubleday.
Bruner, J. (1990). *Acts of meaning*. Cambridge, MA: Harvard University Press.
Daft, R. L. & Weick, K. E. (1984). Toward a model of organizations as interpretation systems. *Academy of Management Review, 9*, 284–295.
Dewey, J. (1938). *Experience and education*. New York: Macmillan.

Douglas, M. (1986). *How institutions think*. Syracuse, NY: Syracuse University Press.

Dreyfus H. (1965). *Alchemy and artificial intelligence*. Rand Corporation paper P-3244.

Dreyfus, H. (1972). *What computers cannot do: A critique of artificial reason*. New York: Harper & Row.

Dreyfus, H., & Dreyfus, S. (1986). *Man over machine: The power of human intuition and expertise in the era of the computer*. Cambridge, MA: Basil Blackwell.

Durkheim, E. (1895). *The rules of sociological method*. New York: The Free Press.

Edwards, W. (1954). The theory of decision making. *Psychological Bulletin, 51*, 380–417.

Fiske, S. T., & Taylor, S. E. (1984). *Social cognition*. Reading, MA: Addison-Wesley.

Garud, R., & Porac, J. F. (1999). Kognition. In R. Garud & J. F. Porac (Eds.), *Advances in managerial cognition and organizational information processing* (Vol. 6, pp. ix–xxi). Greenwich, CT: JAI.

Giddens, A. (1986). *Central problems in social theory: Action, structure, and contradiction social analysis*. Berkeley, CA: University of California Press.

Greeno, J. G., & Moore, J. L. (1993). Situativity and symbols: Response to Vera and Simon. *Cognitive Science, 17*, 49–60.

Kahneman, D., Slovic, P., & Tversky, A. (1982). *Judgment under uncertainty: Heuristics and biases*. New York: Cambridge University Press.

Kahneman, D., & Tversky, A. (1979). Prospect theory: An analysis of choice under risk. *Econometrica, 47*, 263–291.

Lord & Maher, K. J. (1991). Cognitive theory in industrial and organizational psychology. In M. D. Dunnette & L. M. Hough (Eds.), *Handbook of industrial and organizational psychology*, (Vol. 2, 2nd ed., pp.1–62). Palo Alto, CA: Consulting Psychologist Press.

March, J. G., & Simon, H. (1958). *Organizations*. New York: Wiley.

March, J. G., & Simon, H. (1993). *Organizations* (2nd ed.). Cambridge, MA: Basil Blackwell.

Meehl, P. (1954). *Clinical versus statistical prediction*. Minneapolis, MN: University of Minnesota Press.

Miller, G. (1956). The magical number seven plus or minus two: Some limits on our capacity for processing information. *Psychological Review, 63*, 81–97.

Neisser, U. (1967). *Cognitive psychology*. New York: Appleton-Century-Crofts.

Newell, A., Shaw, J., & Simon, H. (1958). Elements of a theory of human problem solving. *Psychological Review, 65*, 151–166.

Nisbett, R., & Ross, L. (1980). *Human inference: Strategies and shortcomings of social judgment*. Englewood Cliffs, NJ: Prentice-Hall.

Norman, D. (1993). Cognition in the head and in the world: An introduction to the special issue on situated action. *Cognitive Science, 17*, 1–6.

Pea, R. D. (1993). Practices of distributed intelligence and designs for education. In G. Solomon (Ed.), *Distributed cognitions: Psychological and educational considerations* (pp. 47–87). Cambridge, England: Cambridge University Press.

Sandelands, L. E., & Stablein, R. E. (1987). The concept of organization mind. In *Research in the sociology of organizations*, (Vol. 5, pp. 135–161). Greenwich, CT: JAI.

Simon, H. A. (1947). *Administrative behavior*. New York: The Free Press.

Simon, H. A. (1955). A behavioral model of rational choice. *Quarterly Journal of Economics, 69*, 99–118.

Skinner, B. F. (1953). *Science and human behavior*. New York: The Free Press.

Thagard, P. (1996). *Mind: Introduction to cognitive science*. Cambridge, MA: MIT Press.

Vera, A. H., & Simon, H. A. (1993). Situated action: A symbolic interpretation. *Cognitive Science, 17*, 7–48.

Von Neumman, J., & Morgenstern, O. (1944). *Theory of games and economic behavior*. Princeton, NJ: Princeton University Press.

Vygotsky, L. S. (1929). The problem of cultural development of the child. *Journal of Genetic Psychology, 36,* 415–434.

Walsh, J. P. (1995). Managerial and organizational cognition: Notes from a trip down memory lane. *Organization Science, 6,* 280–319.

Watson, J. B. (1913). Psychology as the behaviorist views it. *Psychological Review, 20,* 158–177.

Weick, K. (1969). *The social psychology of organizing.* Reading, MA: Addison-Wesley.

Weick, K., & Roberts, K. H. (1993). Collective mind in organizations: Heedful interrelating on flight decks. *Administrative Science Quarterly, 38,* 357–381.

Wundt, W. (1921). *Elements of folk psychology.* London: Allen & Unwin.

I

Theoretical Foundations

2

The Role of Machine Learning in Organizational Learning

Vasant Dhar
New York University

> The individual human being is unpredictable, but the reaction of human mobs, Seldon found, could be treated statistically. The larger the mob, the greater the accuracy that could be achieved.
>
> —Isaac Asimov, The Foundation Series

There is extensive literature on organizational learning and on machine learning but virtually no connection between the two. There are several reasons for this. First, the disciplinary foundations of the two areas are different. But perhaps more importantly, the lack of a connection is due to the fact that until recently, information technologies have played a predominantly transaction processing role. The primary purpose of information technologies has been to support accounting and audit, as opposed to facilitating core business processes such as customer–supplier interactions, supply chain management, and so on. This situation has changed rapidly in the last few years with the maturation of information technologies and their increasing importance as enablers of business processes.

Figure 2.1 shows roughly how core information technologies such as networks, databases, interfaces, and artificial intelligence have matured in the last few years. The figure also illustrates to some extent why some early predictions of intelligent systems in organizations proved to be false, or at least premature: The enabling technologies were simply not mature enough to

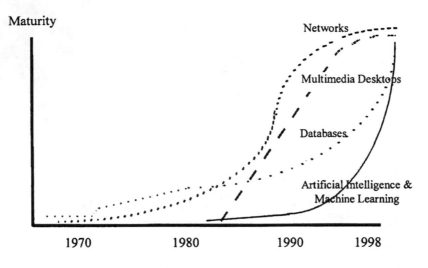

FIG. 2.1   From *Seven Methods for Transforming Corporate Data into Business Intelligence*, by V. Dhar and R. Stein, Prentice Hall, 1997.

support information-intensive commerce in a reliable and scalable manner. The maturation of these enabling technologies has been particularly dramatic in the last two years with the explosion of the Internet, which has fueled the power of desktops, search engines, and databases. It is estimated that since the late 1990s, the data in electronic databases has been roughly doubling each year. This trend is likely to accelerate.

Most organizations struggle to extract meaningful information from their deluge of data. There are several reasons for this, two of which are readily observable in organizations. The first has to do with not recording history carefully. In most organizations, much of the data comes in from one end and goes out of the other. Apart from recording transactions, the focus is on current events such as news, economic indicators, last week's sales, and so on. Hardly any of these data, what I call *history*, are retained at all, let alone recorded systematically. The further back in time we go, the availability and reliability of information declines rapidly. The lack of accurate historical information makes it impossible to generate and test hypotheses about past behaviors of events, customers, and markets, and to compare them with the present. This effectively limits human deliberation and the ability of organizations to learn from their history.

The second reason is that the speed with which new insights are derived from exploration is usually much too slow. The human effort and expense is incurred now and the benefits are potentially spread out over time at best.

There is little motivation to expend resources to explore the data. The net result is that data continue to accumulate and archive and little value is realized.

The first observation implies that the yield that organizations derive from data diminishes dramatically with time. For example, in the financial industry, all participants have roughly equal access to current data (and often react to it similarly, sometimes as a herd) but their abilities to extract meaningful information from historical data vary dramatically. It is not surprising that organizations are now beginning to deploy significant resources toward their data resource, specifically, toward enterprise wide data warehousing. A major motivation is to get away from developing expensive one-time applications to gather and analyze data each time a business hypothesis needs to be verified.

The second observation implies that even if organizations collect and warehouse their data meticulously, there is still the obstacle of speed, of generating useful insights quickly enough to satisfy managers. The challenge is to compress the period required to generate useful results to the point that managers realize that their ideas can be discussed, tested, refined, and implemented within days or weeks instead of months or years.

This chapter describes how organizations can dramatically increase their ability to better understand and exploit history. I draw on my personal experience as a manager of an advanced technology group in a large financial organization that used machine learning methods to enable the organization to better harness its data resource and improve customer management, sales, and investment decisions. Several decision support systems were developed as a result of this work that have been in regular use for almost 3 years. It is reasonable to point to them at least anecdotally as successes of data-driven learning. My objective in this chapter is to highlight the major lessons learned and, more broadly, to claim that in this information intensive-age, data-driven information systems are a critical part of organizational learning.

I shall use three small vignettes from core problems in the financial industry as running examples. The first involves learning from transaction data, where a transaction is a trade that specifies a product was bought or sold by a customer on a particular date and time through a particular salesperson. Thousands of such transactions are conducted daily, providing a rich source of data that link customers, products, and the sales process. The organizational objective is to learn about how to serve existing customers better, to improve the sales process, and to increase overall profitability.

The second vignette involves the assessment of credit risk for retail customers, namely, the likelihood of a customer defaulting on borrowed funds.

Retail banks are exposed to significant levels of risk in this area, and cutting down losses through fraud prevention and better customer management is a major business objective.

The third vignette involves learning about financial equity markets, specifically, how prices of equities are affected by various types of data that flow into the market on an ongoing basis. The data consist of earnings announcements (or surprises), analyst projections or revisions about earnings relating to companies or industry sectors, quarterly balance sheet or income statement disclosures by companies, and so on. The objective is to learn about the relations among these variables and incorporate these insights into profitable trading and risk management. The ability to trade intelligently is one of the most important problems facing securities firms. This problem is a particularly challenging one because many of the relationships among problem variables are ephemeral or difficult even for an expert to specify precisely. Whether markets are efficient or not, they are all about information, and investment professionals devote considerable effort to gathering and interpreting data.

ORGANIZATIONAL LEARNING: MECHANISMS AND IMPEDIMENTS

Levitt and March (1988) provided the following definition of *organization learning*: "organizations are seen as learning by encoding inferences from history into routines that guide behavior ... " This is a descriptive view of learning, viewing it as a process that guides behavior. If we were to take a normative view, we would replace the term *guide* by *improve*. March characterized organizational activity broadly into *exploration* and *exploitation* (March, 1991). Developing new knowledge requires exploration. Using previously acquired knowledge is exploitation.

Another view of learning that is somewhat more normative is that of Argyris and Schon (1978), which emphasized that learning takes place through a questioning of existing beliefs, norms, and evaluation criteria. Argyris refers to this as "double loop" learning. The "inner" loop is simply a comparison of goals with actuals using some evaluation criteria to make decisions or to modify the inputs. This is similar to the notion of feedback in the cybernetic sense. The "outer" loop, which occurs less often, is about questioning and modifying the evaluation criteria themselves (Lant & Mezias, 1992).

In the remainder of this section, the two major approaches to learning and the impediments associated with them are discussed. This is followed by a discussion of machine learning methods and how they can be used to address these impediments. My intention is not to cover all the nuances of organizational learning because these have been discussed at length by a number of authors such as Argyris and Schon (1978), March (1999), and many others. Accordingly, I keep this section as brief as possible.

LEARNING BY DOING

There is considerable agreement in the literature on the various mechanisms through which organizations learn as well as the impediments to learning (Levitt & March, 1988). The first mechanism is "learning by doing," that is, from direct experience.

For example, a sales manager in the asset gathering division of an investment bank discovered the following relationship over time. His commission revenues tended to be much higher when he focused on executing large transactions for a small number of clients instead of pursuing a large number of clients at the same time. He explained this success by saying that the former required him to spend a lot less time on the phone, which gave him more time to read research reports and better understand his products in terms of performance and risk characteristics. This in turn led to large sales and a high hit rate. He was interested in verifying his hypothesis and institutionalizing this learning if appropriate.

It turned out that the sales manager's hypothesis was in fact correct, but only for specific account types, namely institutional as opposed to retail customers. This was, in effect, a nonlinear relationship, a point returned to shortly. This affirmed piece of knowledge was used subsequently in mentoring the sales force and, more importantly, to monitor and analyze other possible exceptions to the rule. Significant counterexamples to the rule might suggest other nonlinearities, or that the rule was not particularly robust after all, or that the marketplace was changing.

There are several limitations to this type of learning that have been noted in the literature. The first arises due to the selective ways that histories play out and hence data get recorded. Histories are usually produced only for those actions that are taken and not for ones that are not. Alternatives that are rejected or not even considered do not get a chance to play out. No information is generated about them. Over time, organizations are therefore more likely to learn by rejecting bad alternatives than by discovering good ones unless the perceived worth of making an effort to explore is significant. If the perceived costs of exploration are high, which is often the case, there is a systematic bias against exploration. In effect, there is a self-correcting bias toward Type I errors (the selection of bad alternatives) and not toward Type II errors (the rejection of good alternatives) (March, 1991).

Another potential side effect of the selective recording of routine activity is that there may be little memory of the decision process, including partial solutions or rejected alternatives. For example, organizations spend large amounts of money redeveloping commonly used pieces of software. Large software projects cry out for some coherent form of historical capture of software development, especially because of the high turnover of programmers. A major research effort at the Microelectronics and Computer Corporation in the early 1980s (Conklin & Begeman, 1988; Curtis, Krasner, & Iscoe, 1988; Ramesh & Dhar, 1992) focused on tools for the systematic capture and retrieval of memory. Other similar efforts have been reported by some major Japanese corporations (Cusamano, 1991; Nonaka, 1994). Andersen Consulting also spent a lot of effort building libraries (video and text) of past engagements (Slator & Riesbeck, 1991) for purposes of knowledge capture and sharing. It is probably fair to say that these efforts met with mixed success. The common problems reported at the time were high cost, lack of incentives for people entering information into a system, the lack of good business processes, and high task complexity that made it difficult to specify good reusable components.

More recently, however, there have been some notable successes in creating and accessing memory at the organizational level, particularly in organizations that have service-intensive operations such as Compaq, Dell, and Microsoft. Compaq, for example, pioneered the use of "case based reasoning" techniques (Schank, 1986) in capturing information from customers and making this knowledge, suitably cleaned up, accessible to its entire sales force (Dhar & Stein, 1997). The major reason for this success was the fact that the problem complexity is low, and there is a solid business process in place for dealing with customers. The information flowing into the system about customers' problems does not depend on individuals' memories but on a structured interaction with the customer. By maintaining a highly structured case base of ongoing customer interactions and having easy access to the knowledge contained in it, the organization continues to learn about problems with its products. Compaq is now beginning to use this knowledge to improve its manufacturing and testing processes.

Finally, a limitation of learning by doing is simply the limited generation of experience of decision makers. People become competent at things that happen as a by-product of this limited experience. If a learned strategy was successful in the past, it is likely to be exploited, shutting out exploration of other, possibly better routines. In terms of March's (Leventhal & March, 1993; Levitt & March, 1988) notion of exploration and exploitation, pure exploitation in the absence of exploration leads to "competency traps" and obsolescence. These traps might also arise because of sunk costs in the existing way of doing things, where changes to an existing process might be too hard to implement and the benefits hard to evaluate with certainty.

LEARNING THROUGH INTERPRETATION

The second major mechanism for learning is through an *interpretation* of history. For example, financial market economists and analysts often draw analogies to previous periods and how these are similar or different from the current. Likewise, traders often point to past formations of economic indicators such as prices, volatilities, and volumes, and what these imply for the future.

The most obvious drawback of this type of learning is that it often suffers from small sample size, that is, there aren't enough events from which to draw reliable conclusions. Sometimes, the small sample size is inherent to the problem, where there are simply not enough similar events from which to learn. Strategic decisions such as whether to enter a market or make an acquisition fall into this category. However, the problem of small sample size arises not only because of limited data but because of lack of access to the relevant data. In the latter situation, decision makers may not recognize similar events that have indeed occurred in the past.

Even when the relevant data are available, humans often make systematic errors in data interpretation. They also exhibit asymmetric behavior toward risk aversion and risk taking depending on the size of rewards and penalties (Kahneman & Tversky, 1982). Also, perceptions of risk and, hence, behavior depend on whether an individual is seeking to avoid drawbacks or aspiring to achieve ambitious objectives (Shapira, 1995).

Finally, human biases are often compounded by goal and outcome ambiguity. For example, how successful had the sales manager's strategies really been in the past? Verifying this objectively is hard not only because of lack of objective data about outcomes but because of the ambiguity of success itself (Levitt & March, 1988) and the time lag between when actions are taken and outcomes are observed.

The previously mentioned impediments are also related to Argyris' notions of single and double loop learning. For example, if the sales manager's strategy of maximizing commission revenue is routinized as the norm, is it in fact the right way of evaluating salespeople? Or might it be wiser to question sales revenue as a yardstick for success and focus instead on what types of sales strategies are better at keeping the customer happy even at the expense of commission revenue? It might be that these alternative strategies will lead to more loyal customers in the long run who are more reticent to move their assets elsewhere for reasons such as cheaper trade execution. A fair amount of literature on organizational learning (Senge, 1994) exhorts managers to question their measures and processes periodically, arguing that true learning occurs in this manner, that is, as double loop learning.

A SUMMARY OF THE IMPEDIMENTS
TO ORGANIZATIONAL LEARNING

Table 2.1 summarizes the discussion thus far. The first set of impediments is associated with why new knowledge is not discovered. The second set explains why new knowledge, even when potentially beneficial, can be ignored.

Discovery is inhibited for a number of reasons. The most obvious one is that the phenomenon is too complex, involving nonlinear interactions among variables. In these problems, it is the interactions among the variables rather than individual variables that need to be understood (Holland, 1975). Even relatively simple problems such as that of sales performance mentioned earlier involve nonlinearities that may not be apparent to reasoned decision makers. Financial markets are full of such problems and are often characterized in terms of interactions between variables such as earnings, supply, demand, and so on. These variables may be described using concepts such as *trends*, *volatilities*, and *momenta*. Volatilities of prices, for example, tend to cluster, where periods of high and low volatility persist. Tran-

TABLE 2.1
Impediments to Organizational Learning

Impediments	Reasons
Knowledge is not discovered.	Nonlinearities–discontinuities.
	Hypothesis testing is too slow.
	Time lag between actions and outcomes.
	Type II errors are not handled.
	Interpretation biases.
	No memory and access to it.
	Phenomenon is too infrequent.
Knowledge is ignored.	Competency traps.
	Sunk costs.
	Structural impediments.
	Interpretation biases.

sitions in volatility take place smoothly, like changes in seasons. Price trends, on the other hand, tend to be more sporadic and occur less often but they do persist occasionally for varying lengths of time. Finding relations among these variables is difficult. Understanding them is even harder. Explaining them to users is harder still.

Discovery is also expensive in terms of cost and time. For a senior manager, finding answers to simple questions such as which customers were in the top 20 in terms of commission revenue for 3 years in a row is cumbersome. Harder still are questions such as what is common or different about customers who were in the top 20 for 3 years in a row. Such requirements are typically passed on to information technology professionals or controllers, and the answers can take weeks or months. The more the intermediaries, the more the structural impediments, and the less the exploration and discovery.

Time pressure also limits how much "doing" can occur realistically in organizations and what can be learned from it. This phenomenon is illustrated using the well known bandit problem, where a subject armed with a certain amount of money is exposed to an array of slot machines with different payoffs and the goal is to maximize winnings within a specific duration (March, 1998). The shorter the duration, the sooner the subject must commit to some subset of slot machines to exploit, and the more limited the search. In reality, the payoff function changes over time, making it even more difficult to balance the effort required in gathering information versus exploiting it. But organizational reality is characterized by yet another undesirable version of the bandit problem: the information about the goodness of different slot machines, the outcomes, is not available instantly! In other words, there is usually a significant time lag between the time an experiment is conceptualized (such as the payoff function of a slot machine) and the time when results can be observed. This is a major inhibitor against exploration.

Fourthly, Type I errors are self-correcting because we recognize when bad decisions turn out to be bad. There is no such information about good decisions that were not recognized or exercised because of the time and cost of discovery and experimentation. In other words, the impediments to discovery are doubly penalizing—not only because of managers' reticence to pose hypotheses but because the answers they have are restricted to what they already do.

A fifth factor inhibiting discovery is interpretation bias. Humans exhibit considerable biases in interpreting statistical phenomena and a wide variance in their judgment of and adoption of risk depending on their objectives. Shapira (1995), for example, described how managers may under or over estimate true risk depending on whether they are trying to achieve relatively easy objectives or to break out to new levels of performance. Fischhof (1975) showed how interpretation of data is shaped by individuals' values and frames of reference.

A sixth impediment to knowledge discovery is the lack of a process for the systematic recording of events. Unless experiences are recorded systematically, they cannot be compared, which means that no general conclusions can be drawn from them. There are all kinds of examples of this phenomena: software being built from scratch each time, similar service calls from customers being handled without knowledge of the prior encounter, similar market conditions not being recognized, and so on. Sometimes the problem is that of task complexity, as with software, where previously coded routines do not completely solve the problem at hand and the effort of modifying the software can exceed that of writing it from scratch; or the sheer volume of data is huge, as with financial market data, which requires an extensive information technology infrastructure and skilled staff.

The last factor inhibiting discovery is that certain types of phenomena simply suffer from small sample size. They just do not occur often enough to provide adequate data from which reliable inferences can be drawn. Business strategy formulation is typical of this—there are usually not enough prior data points from which to learn.

But even when improvements are discovered, they can be ignored. The first reason is competency traps, where an existing way of doing things works fine. In particular, when successes occur, the current procedures are associated with successful outcomes although there may be no direct linkage. Improvements are also ignored because of sunk costs in an existing way of doing things and the cost of instituting change. This is a major factor inhibiting organizational learning. Indeed, there are extensive case studies (Kearns & Nadler, 1992) demonstrating that large-scale organizational change is extremely costly and difficult to manage.

Structural impediments can also prevent knowledge from being disseminated effectively. Paul-Chowdhry (1998), for example, found repeated instances of loan losses caused by poor credit assessment, where lessons from previous decisions should have transferred to the new situation but did not. She explained these observations in terms of *structural impediments*, which consist mainly of lack of communication among line, credit, and risk management functions of the banks.

Finally, interpretation biases also play a role in ignoring information. Milliken and Lant (1991) pointed to cases where managers ignored vital information because they were looking for confirmatory rather than disconfirmatory information. This behavior has been observed in a number of other areas ranging from medical diagnosis to financial trading.

In the next section, I introduce the basic concept and capability of machine learning and demonstrate through focused real-world examples why it is a powerful facilitator of organizational learning. I specifically consider how and to what extent it helps us in dealing with the impediments in Table 2.1. My primary goal is to address the issue of why knowledge is not discovered as opposed to why it is ignored. Accordingly, I limit my discussion to issues of discovery.

THE ROLE OF MACHINE LEARNING

The traditional way of thinking about extracting useful information from data is via queries that say "What data match the pattern expressed by this query?". The retrieved data are then analyzed and interpreted. Traditional information systems work in this manner.

Machine learning algorithms turn the process of discovery around, to answer the question "What patterns match this data?". By turning the question this way, machine learning methods effectively automate one creative aspect of theory formation, namely the generation of hypotheses. They also automate the evaluation of hypotheses. The process of generating and evaluating hypotheses creatively is in the spirit of Tukey's (1977) "exploratory data analysis." High-powered search algorithms and computing power are instrumental in turning Tukey's notions of exploratory data analysis into a practical reality capable of dealing with large volumes of data. For a survey of the major approaches to machine learning, see Dhar and Stein (1997).

Turning the query around, into a process of hypothesis testing, is powerful as long as the right hypotheses are generated. The reason for focusing the search is simple: With any real sized database, the number of potential hypotheses that can be generated is combinatorial. For example, even with a small database of 20 attributes having 10 values each, the number of hypotheses is 10^{20}, too large to be explored exhaustively. From a Bayesian perspective, the number of priors and posteriors to be computed is 10^{20}. Even if there were enough data to generate the priors, it is computationally infeasible to do so.

Automating hypothesis testing gives us a much better chance of reverse engineering whatever process it is that might have generated the data (Pinker, 1997). The difficulty in a reverse engineering exercise is that the problem is underspecified; there are usually many degrees of freedom involved. For example, if a sales manager observes sales decrease dramatically in a quarter, he might construct several hypotheses, such as price reductions, increased advertising by competitors, a drop in market size, and so on to account for the observation. Because there can be many hypotheses that are consistent with the observation, the trick is to generate the more plausible ones and refine them. Machine learning algorithms help in achieving this objective. By automating hypothesis generation and testing, they iterate through this process to get to the more interesting distributions of outcomes quickly. With current technology, large-scale data analyses can be done in days or weeks rather than months or years.

Figure 2.2 shows where machine learning fits into the larger cycle of learning. It characterizes learning as occurring in two loops. The inner loop is the machine learning cycle. The outer loop is reflection, dialog, and an agenda definition for the inner loop. This is where the results from the inner loop are analyzed, interpreted, and discussed. The process is similar in spirit to Argyris' double loop learning.

Placing an upper bound on the frequency of the outer loop has important implications for learning. In most ongoing projects where senior managers are actively probing into some aspect of the business, unless they see interesting new results on a regular basis, their memories about previous dialogs are hazy and cumulative learning is low. Although there is no hard evidence about the optimal frequency for reviewing intermediate results, my experience with data mining projects has been that the elapsed time between reviews in the outer loop should not exceed 2 or 3 weeks. This upper bound of 2 to 3 weeks places a heavy burden on the inner loop. In fact, this is what makes machine learning a practical necessity. It speeds up hypothesis generation and testing by enabling analysis to proceed with an initially rough specification of the problem without requiring any assumptions about the form of the relation among the variables. Indeed, the relation emerges after several cycles of the outer loop.

What do we mean by the form of the relationship? In traditional hypothesis testing, the null hypothesis is stated as a statistical relation (or lack of

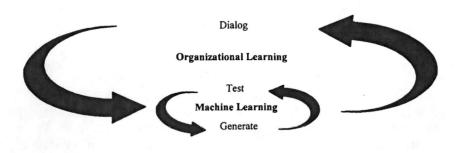

FIG. 2.2   Machine Learning Forms A Loop Within
the Organizational Learning Cycle.

one) among problem variables. For example, that income and default are inversely correlated. This relation might be stated as $d = k_1 - k_2 * i$ where d is the default rate, i is income, and k_1 and k_2 are constants usually determined by a regression.

But what if the relation is not linear? For example, default usually decreases at a decreasing rate with rising income. Also, after a certain level of income, the probability of default flattens out. Although nonlinear, the relation is monotonic: Default does not increase at any point with increasing income. Economic theory is full of such relations. For such problems, linear regression methods do a fairly good job of capturing the relation in certain ranges of the independent variables.

Financial markets are full of nonlinearities and they are often not monotonic or continuous. In the sales example, the sales strategy hypothesized by the managers held only for certain types of customers. In other words, it was nonlinear. As another example from the investment arena, the maxim the trend is your friend is commonly used by momentum-based investors. There is indeed evidence that trending situations develop and persist. However, suppose that the longer a trend persists, so does the hazard that it is likely to end. This is a U-shaped relation for a momentum-based investor. It isn't monotonic.

In addition, nonlinearities can also arise as discontinuities. The sales example demonstrated one type of discontinuity, where the relationship between two variables changed dramatically when the customer type changed from retail to institutional. Another type of nonlinearity arises when the relation holds only in certain ranges, such as at the tails of distributions. For example, a commonly tested null hypothesis in the accounting arena and the investment management community is the following: Positive earnings surprise is associated with an increase in price.

Suppose that this effect occurs only in the tails of the distribution of earnings surprise? That is, it holds only when the surprise is more than, say, one standard deviation from the consensus mean earnings estimate. Otherwise, the effect is nonexistent. What this says, in effect, is that most of the cases, those within one standard deviation, are essentially noise, whereas the signal is located in selected areas, namely, the tails. Figure 2.3 shows this phenomenon.

We can as easily construct examples where the effect might occur everywhere except toward the tails and so on (the default vs. income example above being one such example). The point is that the signal is located only in certain selected areas and the challenge is to find these areas.

The effect can also occur due to the interaction of two or more variables. For example, the earnings surprise effect might hold only when the funda-

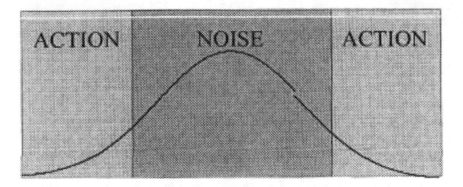

Degree of Earnings Surprise

FIG. 2.3   Earnings surprises more than + X standard deviations from the
consensus mean lead to positive returns over the next N days.

mentals of the company, measured in terms of variables such as price–earnings ratios, are strong. Such interaction effects are, in effect, nonlinear.
Finding them is a combinatorial search problem.

Machine learning techniques are able to find complex patterns quite effectively. They accomplish this by asking: "Under what conditions does X
hold" instead of "Does X hold?". The search finds the conditions. In the
credit example, it would look for ranges of variables where the relation is the
strongest. Similarly, in the investment example, it would attempt to find
variables and their ranges that best explain performance. It does so by sampling the data appropriately into learning, test, and production sets and testing patterns against these data. In effect, it creates hypotheses and backtests
them on the data. The trick is to help it formulate and refine its hypotheses
intelligently, which is what machine learning methods are good at doing.

The ability to create and backtest hypotheses provides the ability to simulate what would have happened if the hypothesized action had been taken
(Dhar, 1998). For example, we can compute the profits from a hypothesized
trading strategy. The top part of Figure 2.4, for example, shows the monthly
returns from a hypothesized earnings-surprise-driven investment strategy
of the type described earlier. The strategy is to buy when the earnings surprise is highly positive and sell when it is highly negative.[1] The bottom part
shows a benchmark strategy, namely, returns from investing in the S&P500

---

[1]A few additional conditions were used as part of the strategy. These are not relevant to this discussion.

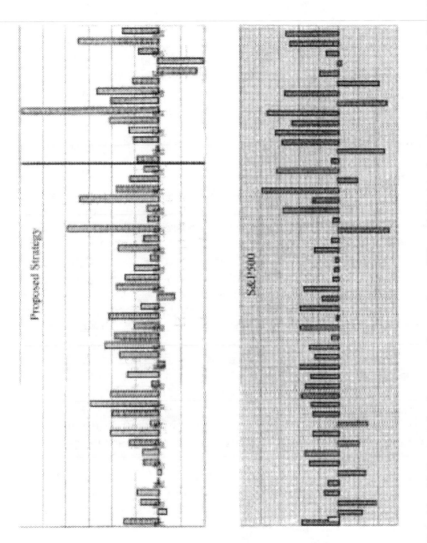

FIG. 2.4   Monthly Returns of an Investment Strategy Learned Through Machine Learning Compared to the S&P 500.

29

index. As it turns out, for the period under consideration, this was a difficult benchmark to beat.[2]

The revenue impacts of taking hypothesized actions on credit card customers can be modeled similarly. For example, we could test the revenue impact of denying further credit to customers who develop a certain profile characterized by specific levels of accelerating debt and deteriorating payment history. This strategy could be compared with a baseline (such as *no action*) to assess its effectiveness. More complex interventions such as *working with the customer* rather than denying credit completely are harder to simulate but can still be approximated, especially if data or reasonable expert estimates on these interventions are available. In general, however, as the precision of the evaluation function declines, so does the quality of the hypotheses and, consequently, the chances of developing a robust theory about the problem domain.

Automating the generate and test activity via backtesting addresses a number of impediments to learning. For some problems, it addresses the small sample size problem by creating data points. It also addresses to some degree the Type II error problem because the outcomes of a large number of actions are actually evaluated in the backtesting. In this sense, the process is an adaptive simulation, where the search has the intelligence to figure out which actions are worth simulating based on results of prior experiments.

The outputs of machine learning also help provide transparency into the problem. When the outputs are easy to interpret, such as rules or conditional distributions of outcomes, they can be used to test prior assumptions or to flesh them out. In the earlier example involving the interaction of earnings surprise and company fundamentals (i.e., value orientation) , the results might show an earnings-growth-driven investor the conditions under which a value orientation works or vice versa. For example, it might say that the one standard deviation surprise rule is a good predictive model only when the fundamentals of a company are strong. Similarly, in the example of the sales manager earlier, the hypothesis that a small number of larger orders as more profitable led to a discussion among the management committee about the possible underlying reasons for the effect. One explanation was that it provided more time to prepare a better sales story. Another was that the larger orders were generated by the more experienced salespeople and it was, therefore, experience that influenced profitability not better preparation afforded by fewer sales calls. Yet another explanation was that only a few customers provided large orders and the more profitable salespeople just happened to be assigned to them. The proponents of the last hypothesis sug-

---

[2]Only 8% of mutual funds performed better than the S&P500 during this period.

gested that removing these customers from the analysis would provide different results. When the machine learning uncovered the fact that the relationship held more strongly for institutional customers, some managers pondered whether doing one's research before approaching prospects was more important for sophisticated (equated with institutional) customers.

In all of these cases, the results from the machine learning exercise nudge further human dialog along a number of useful directions. In terms of Fig. 2.3, the dialog about sales effectiveness generated at least three hypotheses. These hypotheses, in turn, focused the machine learning loop. That is, the outer loop provides the basis for setting up the next series of experiments, for testing the credibility of the alternative hypotheses, which were not existent in the initial experiment. In this way, the process of learning is distributed cyclically between humans and the machine, where the human dialog defines the search space for the machine, and the machine, in turn, drives the human dialog into more relevant areas. The net effect is that machine learning speeds up and focuses the process of exploration and assumption surfacing, thereby providing actionable results in a realistic time frame.

Finally, organizations struggle with the memory problem, of not keeping an adequate memory of events. Because experiences are not recorded systematically, they are difficult to group into useful clusters or patterns, to retrieve, and to use. We referred in the earlier section about how service-oriented organizations such as Compaq are beginning to exploit case-based search methods for finding relevant information about past experiences. Other organizations such as Morgan Stanley are combining numerically oriented exception-based analysis with qualitative methods for finding historical information relating to customers and salespeople. For example, a tree induction algorithm reveals groupings of customers that are exceptions along some criteria such as revenues. A sales manager can then zoom in on this grouping and find all the call reports that salespeople from across the organization might have put into the system about this set of customers. Differences between this grouping and those of the lower revenue customers can lead to more effective sales strategies or product offerings.

Useful groupings or patterns of this type are an important element of the learning process. By maintaining a memory of past events and providing powerful access mechanisms, systems are able to overcome a major impediment to learning at the level of the organization.

Table 2.3 summarizes the discussion thus far. It lists some of the impediments from Table 2.2 and how machine learning methods contribute toward addressing them. The contributions should be interpreted literally, as contributions, and not as complete solutions. For example, automated hypothesis generation and backtesting will not compensate for bad data or the lack

TABLE 2.2

Impediments to Organizational Learning Addressable
Through Machine Learning

Impediment	Contribution of Machine Learning Methods
Nonlinearities–Task complexity.	Provide better signal–noise ratio.
Information gathering or hypothesis testing is too slow.	Speeds up pattern discovery through automated generate and test.
Type II error handling.	Automated hypothesize and backtesting surfaces otherwise overlooked actions.
Frames, assumptions, etc.	Provide explainable models (transparency) capable of challenging or confirming assumptions.
Inadequate organizational memory.	Data warehousing and recording of cases.
	Better access methods to data and case bases.

of a good evaluation function. It is also worth noting that such methods do not address several of the impediments to learning such as human biases in data interpretation. If anything, the need to interpret the outputs from machine learning algorithms correctly is critical, especially about the confidence intervals associated with the outcome distributions and the sensitivity of these results to minor changes in inputs.

AUTOMATION VERSUS SUPPORT

If models that are learned from machine learning and human deliberation can be crafted to make high quality decisions, what is to stop us from eliminating the decision maker from the loop entirely? By high quality decisions, I mean decisions that on average are better than those that would be taken otherwise.

In *The New Science of Management Decision*, Simon (1965) conjectured that because much of middle management dealt with fairly structured decision making (programmed decision making) that could be made by machines, this layer of management was likely to be replaced by information systems within the next decade or two. Senior managers, on the other hand, dealt with nonprogrammed decision making that would be harder to automate.

A number of explanations can be advanced as to why Simon's conjecture did not materialize in the 1970s or 1980s. One is that the technology simply

TABLE 2.3

Conditions Under Which Decisions Should be Made
by Computer Versus Human

		Payoff Well Defined?	
		Yes	No
Theory formation?	Yes	Automate	Support
	No	Support	Support

did not mature rapidly enough and that the conjecture will in fact materialize in time. Another is that middle managers do more than making structured decisions and exercise judgment that cannot be automated. Yet another is that a lot of middle management consists of authorization and verification, a function that is risky to eliminate. Finally, we can view the insights from the man–machine interaction as an endless learning loop, where we are seldom comfortable enough that we have learned enough to abdicate decision making to the machine. Other explanations, from social and political perspectives on organizations can be provided.

Regardless of the accuracy of the conjecture, Simon's classification of decision making provided the basis for several other frameworks describing the role of information systems in decision making (Gorry & Scott-Morton, 1971; Keen, 1978). The basic reasoning was that problem complexity determines whether decision making can be automated. Factories are automated because the decisions involved can be specified algorithmically. Management decisions require judgment and are therefore not automated. This is the raison d'etre for decision support systems: They provide the analytics for support of decision making where human judgment is ultimately required. This reasoning makes intuitive sense. After all, it is usually more cost effective or reliable, or both, to automate routine decisions and too risky to automate the complex ones.

However, consider the following alternative reasoning. Exploration is a theory-building exercise. Building theory requires testing. And testing a theory that is driven ground up from the data must be tested particularly rigorously. Specifically, if the learned model involves decision making, then this model must be tested without human intervention, otherwise it is impossible to separate the contribution of the human from that of the machine-learning-based model.

This point poses an interesting paradox. If we're using machine learning methods to uncover patterns in complex nonlinear situations where the output of the model is a decision, then we must be particularly careful in ensuring that it is the learned model that is separating the noise from signal and not the decision maker. Otherwise, we don't know whether the learned model captures the true structure of the underlying problem or whether human judgment is compensating for a poor model.

Consider the earnings surprise example. The top part of Fig. 2.4 shows the returns assuming a completely systematic or automated implementation of a particular model. The part to the left of the heavy vertical bar shows the performance of the automated implementation based on historical data. If the model is any good, or alternatively, if it truly captures the underlying structure of the problem that is reflected in the data, we would expect the performance of the model to be good on data it has never seen before. The part to the right of the bar shows the performance of the model in reality, or out of sample. These results can be compared to benchmarks, critiqued by experts and others to evaluate the model. But if the results were achieved through human intervention, we would not know whether our learned model captured a real effect in the data or whether the decision maker steered it right when it made bad decisions or in the wrong directions when it made good decisions.

This counterintuitive point is that even highly complex nonprogrammed decision situations may require completely automated solutions to test the model. In the example mentioned previously, where a theory about market behavior is being tested, the precision with which the payoff function is defined has more of an impact on whether a decision is automated or supported than problem complexity. Although the decision is a complex one, the payoff function is precise: the profit or loss on a trade. Automation provides a clean and rigorous way to test the theory.

The same reasoning applies to the example of credit risk estimation for a retail bank. The impact of denying or continuing to provide credit can also be specified quite precisely in terms of the monetary amount lost as a consequence of failing to detect signs of delinquency. Fraud problems are also similar: The degree of loss can be computed as a function of the relative proportion and costs of Type I and Type II errors. All of these problems are complex, requiring human judgment. Yet, if our objective is to form a rigorous theory of behavior, it makes sense to automate decision making to be able to test the learned model.

Ironically, however, the flip side of the coin is that simple problems may not be easy or practical to automate. In the example about the sales manager's conjecture about profitable sales strategies, coming up with a precise function relating actions and payoffs is difficult. The discovered relationship and the conjecture that better prepared salespeople make bigger sales is more of an explanation after the fact, where several alternative reasons are conjectured, including pure chance, and discussed to explain the data. The conjectures are difficult to test because of the lack of adequate data, historical and future; historical in the sense that there is unlikely to be available data on time spent by salespeople researching their products before approaching customers and future in the sense that it is not practical to obtain such data going forward.

Table 2.3 summarizes the discussion in this section indicating automation or support, depending on the precision of the payoff function and theoretical objectives. The upper left quadrant, exemplified by the trading example, is one where automation makes sense. In this quadrant, the relevant data for theory formation are available, and the payoff function is well defined. When either of these do not apply, as in the other three quadrants, only support is feasible. This more commonly occurring situation explains the relative preponderance of systems that support rather than automate much of managerial decision making.

CONCLUDING REMARKS

A quantitative analyst at a large bank once remarked that he was appalled by the paucity of information that went into decisions that have multimillion dollar impacts. One would expect that decision makers would learn from such decisions and improve over time, especially when they are repetitive. However, the reality is that it is difficult for organizations to learn from prior decisions. Some of the reasons have to do with the poorly understood link between actions and outcomes. Other impediments have do to organizational structure and interpretation biases.

In this chapter, I argue that machine learning can enable organizations to better understand the link between potential actions and outcomes. The motivation for this argument is the observation that organizations are beginning to collect vast amounts of data as a by-product of electronic commerce. These data represent collections of large numbers of events, making it possible to test assumptions and hypotheses statistically for many types of problems, especially those where decisions are repetitive. I assert that for such problems, organizations underestimate the wealth of knowledge they can uncover directly or indirectly from their databases. They can learn from their data. In particular, they can use machine learning methods to mitigate Type II errors by better relating potential actions to outcomes (Dhar, 1998).

But uncovering useful knowledge is an exploratory exercise. Given the systematic bias against exploration, it is not surprising that the data resource often remains largely untapped for purposes of decision making. The purpose of this chapter is to show how some of the major impediments to organizational learning can be addressed when machine learning is an integral part of a business process. By asking the question, "What patterns emerge from the data?", machine learning provides managers with a powerful attention directing and learning mechanism.

The incorporation of machine learning into managerial decision making is a lot more than more analysis or more rational decision making. At times, it is about rigorous hypothesis testing and theory building. At other times, it is an efficient attention directing mechanism for identifying exceptions or tail-oriented phenomena and acting on them. Sometimes it is about validating deeply held beliefs or refuting them. The upshot is that it leads to dialog among decision makers that would not occur otherwise, which leads to raising better questions, collecting better data, and obtaining better insight into the problem domain.

Whereas some of the literature on organizational learning points to structural impediments, I have also observed that machine learning methods are capable of producing systems that can eliminate some of these impediments. For example, the decision support system that resulted from analysis of the sales data enabled the sales manager to circumvent his usual process of obtaining information. Instead of relying on assistant and controllers and waiting several weeks for information, the fact that he could test his hypotheses instantly resulted in the elimination of the intermediary functions. In other words, not only did the machine learning exercise help him better relate actions to outcomes but perhaps even more significantly, it made the process of information gathering more efficient. The cost savings were significant.

One simple way of summarizing the impacts of information technology in general and machine learning in particular on organizations is that it increases the knowledge yield from an organization's information systems. But realizing this benefit requires a process where senior managers periodically question their assumptions and business objectives and determine the extent to which these assumptions and objectives can be substantiated, refined, refuted, or fleshed out by the data. My objective in this chapter is to show why and how this can be done by integrating machine learning into organizational learning, enabling organizations to achieve higher levels of knowledge about themselves.

REFERENCES

Argyris, C., & Schon, D. (1978). *Organizational learning.* Reading, MA: Addison-Wesley.
Conklin, J., & Begeman, M. (1988). gIBIS: A hypertext tool for exploratory policy discussion. *ACM Transactions on Office Information Systems, 6,* 4.
Curtis, B., Krasner, H., & Iscoe, N. (1988). A field study of the software design process for large systems. *Communications of the ACM, 31,* 11.

Cusamano, M. (1991). *Japan's software factories: A challenge to U. S. management.* New York: Oxford University Press.

Dhar, V. (1998). Data mining in finance: using counterfactuals to generate knowledge from organizational information systems. *Information Systems, 23,* 7.

Dhar, V., & Stein, R. (1997). *Seven methods for transforming corporate data into business intelligence.* Englewood Cliffs, NJ: Prentice-Hall.

Fischhof, B. (1975). Hindsight = / = foresight: the effect of outcome knowledge on judgement under uncertainty. *J. Experimental Psychology: Human Perception and Performance, 1.*

Gorry, A., & Scott-Morton, M. S. (1971). A framework for management information systems. *Sloan Management Review, 13,* 1.

Holland, J. H. (1975). *Adaptation in natural and artificial systems.* Ann Arbor, MI: University of Michigan Press.

Kahneman, D., & Tversky, A. (1982). Intuitive prediction: Biases and corrective procedures. In D. Kahneman, P. Slovic, & A. Tversky (Eds.), *Judgement under uncertainty: Heuristics and biases.* Cambridge, England: Cambridge University Press.

Kearns, D., & Nadler, D. (1992). *Prophets in the dark.* Harper Business.

Keen, P. (1978). *Decision support systems.* Reading, MA: Addison-Wesley.

Lant, T. K., & Mezias, S. J. (1992). An organizational learning model of convergence and reorientation. *Organization Science, 3,* 1.

Leventhal, D., & March, J. G. (1993). The myopia of learning. *Strategic Management Journal, 14.*

Levitt, B., & March, J. G. (1988). Organizational learning. *Annual Review of Psychology, 14.*

March, J. G. (1991). Exploration and exploitation in organizational learning. *Organization Science, 2,* 1.

March, J. G. (1998). The pursuit of intelligence in organizations. In T. Lant & Z. Shapira (Eds.), *Managerial and organizational cognition.* Hillsdale, NJ: Lawrence Erlbaum Associates.

Milliken, F. J., & Lant, T. K. (1991). The effect of an organization's recent performance history on strategic persistence and change: The role of managerial interpretations. In P. Shrivastava, A. Huff, & J. Dutton (Eds.), *Advances in strategic management* (pp. 129–156). Greenwich, CT: JAI.

Nonaka, I. (1994). A dynamic theory of organizational knowledge creation. *Organization Science, 5,* 1.

Paul-Chowdhry, C. (1998). Internal dissemination of learning from load loss crisis. In T. Lant & Z. Shapira (Eds.), *Managerial and organizational cognition.* Hillsdale, NJ: Lawrence Erlbaum Associates.

Pinker, S. (1997). *How the mind works.* New York: Norton.

Ramesh, B., & Dhar, V. (1992). Process knowledge-based group support for requirements engineering. *IEEE Transactions on Software Engineering, 18,* 6.

Schank, R. (1986). *Explanation patterns: Understanding mechanically and creatively.* Hillsdale, NJ: Lawrence Erlbaum Associates.

Senge, P. (1994). *The fifth discipline: Strategies and tools for building a learning organization.* Garden City, NY: Doubleday.

Shapira, Z. (1995). *Risk taking: A managerial perspective.* NY: Russell Sage.

Slator, B., & Riesbeck, C. (1991, October). TAXOPS: *Giving expert advice to experts* (The Institute for the Learning Sciences, Working Paper). Evanston, IL: Northwestern University.

Simon, H. A. (1965). *The new science of management decision.* New York: Harper & Row.

Tukey, J. W. (1977). *Exploratory data analysis.* Reading, MA: Addison-Wesley.

CHAPTER

3

How Do Organizations Think?

William Ocasio
Northwestern University

How do organizations think? Take the example of a typical research university in the United States. From football and food halls to fraternities and fund-raising, aerospace engineering and anthropology to women's studies and zoology, the admissions office and board of trustees to the faculty senate and student government, universities, similar to other complex organizations, are characterized by multiple interactions between individuals and groups with inconsistent interests and identities rather than by the independent action of any single decision maker or group of individuals (March, 1997). Given this complex system of interacting individuals and groups, in what way, if any, can researchers say that a university thinks?

One possible answer is to say that they cannot, that only individuals think—universities do not think, only its professors and perhaps its administrators, alumni, staff, and students do. Whereas thinking may take place in university settings, thinking, according to this perspective, is a purely psychological activity of individuals, not of organizations. Consistent with this view, some organizational psychologists criticize the term *organizational cognition*, the same way they criticize the term *organizational behavior* (Weick, 1979). Whenever organizations think or behave, people think or behave. Therefore, how is it meaningful to talk of organizations thinking or behaving?

Traditionally, theories of organizational cognition have responded by examining how the organization shapes the symbolic representations, knowledge structures, or schemas used by individuals (Walsh, 1995). Whereas thinking may be an individual-level activity, the sources of schemas and knowledge structures that shape individual cognition come from social groups, organizations, and institutions. Various theories from institutional analysis (Douglas, 1986), organizational culture (Schein, 1985), and organizational identity theory (Albert & Whetten, 1985) share this view. Two variants are particularly common in studies of organizational cognition: the shared cognition perspective and top management cognition perspective.

According to the first perspective, organizations think in terms of their shared assumptions and beliefs, their common organizational culture and identity (Albert & Whetten, 1985; Dutton & Dukerich, 1991; Schein, 1985). For example, there are distinct differences in organizational cultures among universities, so that researchers explain how Harvard, MIT, University of Chicago, or Northwestern thinks in terms of their respective cultures and organizational identities. But this viewpoint, although important, does not take into account the fragmented nature of organizational cultures (Martin, 1992), or the decentralized nature of thinking or information processing that takes place in organizations (Radner, 1997). It also does not take into account the commonalties of thinking across different organizations.

A second perspective on organizational thinking focuses on the thinking of top managers (e.g., Fligstein, 1990; Hambrick & Mason, 1984). Building on demographic theories of organization (Pfeffer, 1983), political coalition views (Cyert & March, 1963), and theories of information processing in organizations, top management perspectives (Hambrick & Mason, 1984) highlight the power and control of the top echelon group or team in shaping organizational action or cognition. Here, not only the CEO but the top management coalition shapes how organizations think and act. Whereas in certain organizations with powerful chief executives or top managers this perspective may be useful, it does not account for the diversity of interacting groups and individuals in organizations, the organizational division of labor, or the lack of consensus with top management beliefs. Although universities are typically organizations where the cognition of top management is of secondary importance, even for-profit organizations with powerful CEOs and top management teams are subject to differentiation and fragmentation in information processing (Lawrence & Lorsch, 1967).

Given the limitation of theories of shared cognition or managerial cognition, what, then, does it mean to talk about organizational cognition? To what extent, then, can one argue that organizational cognition is more than shared cognition or different from the cognition of its individuals or groups, particularly its top managers? Providing an answer to these questions is the challenge of this chapter. This chapter will argue that yes, it is meaningful to talk about an organization thinking in ways that cannot be reduced to the thinking of its individual members. This is true even for the relatively decentralized thinking that occurs in organizational settings. For example, what and how students think in a master's power and politics elective at Northwestern University is a result not just of their own individual cognition, or even of the professor's, but also of where they are thinking (the classroom setting at the Kellogg Graduate School of Management), what other issues they are thinking about (recruiting, student activities, and other classes), how they interact among themselves and with the teacher in the classroom, the history of the course at Kellogg, the structure of other power and politics electives, and MBA education more generally in top-ranked U.S. business schools. If organizational thinking is considered in the context of more centralized activity such as tenure and promotion decisions or official responses to excessive drinking in fraternities, the situated and structured nature of organizational thinking becomes even more obvious. How a university thinks about an individual tenure decision or about student drinking is more than the thinking of any individual. To understand how organizations think is therefore to understand not only how individuals think but how thinking is situated in organizations, how situations are structured by organizations, and how thinking and situations are embedded in broader social, economic, political, and cultural environments (Ocasio, 1997). From this perspective, thinking is a cross-level process shaped by individual cognition, by the social psychology of the situation, by the organizational structure, and by the broader social, economic, and cultural environment.

Theories of organizational fragmentation, situated action, and loose coupling (March & Olsen, 1976; Ocasio, 1997; Weick, 1979) provide an alternative to theories of shared and differentiated cognition (Martin, 1992) and serve as a foundation for this chapter. In this chapter, a framework for organizational cognition is presented that takes this perspective and allowing not just for organized anarchy (Cohen, March, & Olsen, 1972) in organizational thought and action but also order, coherent, persistence, and reproducibility of thought and action. The framework suggested is an architectural work in progress that builds on existing knowledge and understanding of individual information processing (Thagard, 1996), situated action and cognition (Hutchins, 1995; Ocasio, 1997), social and cultural structures (Granovetter, 1985; Zukin & DiMaggio, 1990), and social systems (Luhmann, 1992). The objective is to develop a coherent cross-level perspective consistent with both the understanding of human cognition and the knowledge and understanding of organizations, social action, and social systems. Note that the objective is not to develop a full-fledged theory of organizational cognition. No specific propositions or hypothesis will be presented. The goal, instead, is to begin to formulate a unifying framework for organizational-level cognition and to present a set of issues for further research and theoretical development.

ELEMENTS OF A THEORY
OF ORGANIZATIONAL COGNITION

In developing a framework for explaining and understanding how organizations think, *thinking* and *organizations* must first be defined. Thinking is a concrete activity of individual and groups. Drawing from cognitive science, this chapter defines thinking as a transient, dynamic representation of particular unique situations by human beings (Johnson-Laird, 1983). Individuals make sense and act on their immediate environments by translating external events or situations into internal symbolic representations or mental models. This chapter assumes that all individual thinking occurs through *mental models*. Mental models are working integrated symbolic representations of goals, data, inferences, and plans, which serve to interpret and attend to environmental stimuli, permit inferences, and make decisions (Holyoak & Gordon, 1984; Ocasio, 1995).

To understand organizational cognition, we must also define what we mean by organizations. As March and Simon (1958) stated in their classic treatise, it is easier to give examples of organizations than to define the term. Different perspectives in organization theory provide different definitions of its subject matter (Scott, 1997). In this chapter, *organizations* is defined as social systems of collective action that structure and regulate the actions and cognitions of organizational participants through its rules, resources, and social relations (Ocasio, 1997). The assumption here is that all collective action involves a set of participants, issues, resources, schemas, space, and time. Organizations, at any moment in time, structure and regulate how participants combine and use the repertoire of issues, resources, schemas, and space available to the organization. Consequently, there are three ways in which organizational cognition can be talked about. First, organizational thinking is situated within organizations or takes place within organizational settings. Second, the physical, cultural, economic, and social characteristics of the organizational environment structure and regulate the way in which thinking takes place within organizations. Third, organizational thinking persists even when individual participants change. The persistence of thought and action in organizations despite personnel turnover is indicative of how cognition within organizations is socially structured and constituted at the level of the organization (Weick, 1979).

This chapter presents seven building blocks for a theory of organizational cognition. These building blocks focus on the individual, the social psychological, and the organization levels of analysis and are derived from diverse literatures linking multiple levels of analysis. The organizing assumption is that thinking is a cross-level process, and the seven building blocks were selected to form a coherent synthesis of the process of organizational thinking. At the individual level, they include two core assumptions of individual cognitive psychology: the computational–representational model of cognition (Thagard, 1996) and the limited attention and computational capacity (Pashler, 1998). At the social psychological level, this chapter focuses on the power of the situation and the social construction and control of the situation (Ross & Nisbett, 1991; White, 1992). And at the level of the organization, this chapter emphasizes the view of organizations as social systems, embedded in broader environments, and as processes for organizing collective action and interlocked behaviors (Scott, 1997; Weick, 1979).

The seven building blocks linking multiple levels of analysis are as follows:

1. The enactment selection retention model.
2. Computational–representational model of information processing.
3. Limited attention to issues and schemas.
4. Situated cognition.
5. Dynamic control.
6. Social, cultural, and economic embeddedness.
7. Social systems regulation.

The Situation-Enactment-Retrieval-Selection-Transmission-Storage Model of Human Information Processing

This chapter begins the discussion of the building blocks for the study of organizational cognition with Weick's (1979) enactment-selection-retention model. This model, although emphasizing the social psychology of organizational cognition, provides a linkage to both the individual and the organization, thereby facilitating the object to link multiple levels of analysis. Weick's perspective builds on Campbell's (1965) theory of sociocultural evolutionary processes. A central concept in Weick's model is that of enactment. Weick (1979) provided a distinctive perspective that defines behavior explicitly in terms of processes of attention. For Weick, the central question for explaining organizational behavior is as follows: "How are the processes and contents of attention influenced by the conditions of

task-based interdependency found in those settings we conventionally desig-
nate as organizations?" (pp. 32–33). In outlining an answer to his question,
Weick concentrated on the cognitive and social psychological processes that
lead organizational members to notice and interpret their environment as
they act and to retain certain response repertoires that will be invoked by
them in future noticing and sense making. Perhaps the central contribution of
Weick's perspective is the idea of organizational enactment of its environment. According to Weick, organizations are not passive recipients of environmental stimuli but active creators of the environmental stimuli for action,
which they impose on their actions. "Enactment emphasize(s) that managers
construct, rearrange, single out, and demolish many of the objective features
of their surroundings" (Weick, 1979, p. 164). Enactment is an output of organizing activities, which actively orders the objects of action through the impo-
sition of schemas and causal maps on the objects of action.

Weick (1979) invoked an example of the task of calling balls and strikes to
describe the enactment process. For the clever umpire who correctly under-
stands enactment, a ball or a strike "ain't nothing till I call them" (Weick,
1979, p. 1). The rules of the game, the role of the umpire, and the particular
individual who plays umpire create or enact a ball or a strike. Players in the
ball game then react to this enacted ball or strike rather than to any objective
stimuli. Similarly, managers enact their own stimuli for action: profits, market
share, competitor moves, product quality, customer satisfaction, market
trends, pollution, economic downturns, union demands, government regulations, and so on all "ain't nothing" till they are enacted.

One difficulty in applying Weick's (1979) framework is that the concept
of *enactment* is used in two distinct ways. First, enactment for Weick is the
first stage of the human cognition and action and involves the equivocal understanding and interpretation of the environment. Second, the enacted
environment for Weick is a result of the selection and retention process and
is an outcome rather than an input of human information processing. This
chapter uses the concept of enactment primarily in terms of Weick's first usage. When an umpire is calling a ball a strike, he is selecting among equivocal enactments. To clarify the meaning of enactment, consider the concept
of mental models introduced earlier. Enactment is the triggering and development of mental models in response to the focalization of consciousness of
the human mind. Enactment responds both to the focalization of the current perceptual stimuli or to the retrieval in memory of previous cognitions
or mental models. Any perception or retrieved representation from memory
is processed through mental models. Mental models may, however, be
equivocal, and multiple parallel mental models may be processed of the
same stimuli. Reflexivity (Giddens, 1984) and mindfulness (Langer, 1990)

in human behavior requires the consideration and analysis of alternative mental models for one or more stimuli. Enactment is consequently the process by which alternative, equivocal mental models are triggered.

Selection is the reduction of equivocality in human cognition through the implicit or explicit choice of one among alternative enactments. An individual's communication with another individual involves selection. According to Weick (1979), retention involves both transmission and storage. Because the mechanisms underlying transmission and storage are distinct, they will be treated as two separate cognitive processes. Therefore, this chapter modifies Weick's framework and presents the situation-enactment-retrieval-selection-transmission-storage (SERSTS) as an alternative model of information processing.

This model presents several important characteristics for the study of organizational cognition:

1. Enactment and retrieval, although situated and structured by organizations (Ocasio, 1997), occur primarily at the level of individual cognition and information processing. Selection and transmission, on the other hand, are inherently social processes and involve the symbolic interaction among individual information processors.

2. Retrieval is separated from enactment as complementary inputs into organizational cognition and action. Cognition refers to on-line perception of environmental stimuli. Although direct enactment of the environment is common in manufacturing and operational processes, most administrative processes in organizations are more likely to rely on retrieval of information from organizational memory (Walsh & Ungson, 1991).

3. The model distinguishes the process of transmission from that of storage. Although both aspects affect retention of the enacted environment, transmission refers explicitly to the communication with other organizational participants not involved in the initial process of enactment and selection. Transmission provides opportunities for information dissemination and diffusion (Weick, 1979).

4. Storage occurs at various levels of organization including individual memory, group memory, organizational memory (Walsh & Ungson, 1991), and institutional memory (Douglas, 1986).

5. The dotted line relationship between enactment and storage implies both that (a) enactments may be stored in memory even prior to equivocality reduction of the selection process and (b) not all enactments are stored in memory and many if not most enactments of the environments are lost to the individual and to the organization, not subject to future recall and retrieval.

6. The stimuli for cognition constitute the situation in which human information processing takes place. This includes a set of participants, space, resources, and time. Environmental stimuli include a set of material resources in the environment, a set of participants involved in the process of human information processing, and thinking situated in time and space. This view of environmental stimuli is consistent with the concept of situated action and cognition discussed next. Also, by including participants themselves as part of the situation, the environment is not perceived objectively but is socially enacted by participants in the situation.

7. Thinking in the SERSTS model of human information processing occurs through mental models, and the mental modeling that constitutes thinking is inherent in all the thinking processes: enactment, retrieval, selection, transmission, and storage. The content of these mental models includes issues and schemas. Issues and schemas, as discussed next, are the knowledge representations used by individuals in organizations to characterize situations and to guide actions.

Computational-Representational Model of Human Information Processing

Cognitive scientists have developed the computational–representational model as the dominant understanding of human cognition and information processing (Thagard, 1996). This model assumes that:

1. Individuals have mental representations.
2. Individuals have algorithmic processes that operate on these representations.
3. These algorithmic processes applied to the representations produce organizational cognition and behavior.

Current research on organizational cognition has highlighted the importance of mental representations but has paid relatively little attention to the computational or algorithmic processes employed in human information processing. For example, Walsh's (1995) survey of managerial and organizational cognition emphasized the central importance of knowledge structures or schemas. This chapter also emphasizes the importance of mental models and mental modeling as a critical part of human information processing. Mental models refer to concrete combinations of environmental data, information recalled from memory, schemas or knowledge structures, and organizational actions and behaviors.

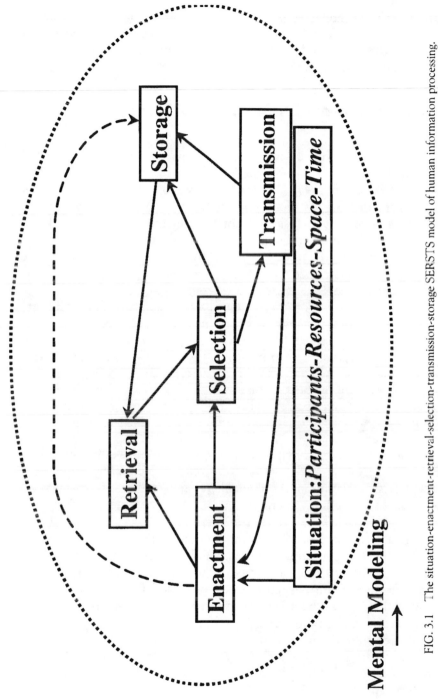

Mental Modeling

FIG. 3.1   The situation-enactment-retrieval-selection-transmission-storage SERSTS model of human information processing.

In the SERSTS model, both schemas and issues are the input and output of mental models used in information processing. Enactment, retrieval, selection, transmission, and storage operate through algorithmic processes that operate on issues, schemas, and mental models.

Limited Attention to Issues and Schemas

A critical aspect of human and organizational cognition is the limited attentional capabilities of individuals and organizations (Ocasio, 1997; Pashler, 1998; Simon, 1947). Attention has two components: selectivity or direction and intensity or effort (Fiske & Taylor, 1991; Kahneman, 1973). *Attention* is thereby defined as the amount of selective cognitive work undertaken by individuals and organizations. With respect to the SERSTS model, attention can be directed toward the various components of the model including enactment, retrieval, selection, and transmission. The impacts of attentional limits on storage are more indirect. At the level of the individual information processing, research suggests that voluntary decisions to ignore a stimulus often prevent a stimulus from being registered in either short-term or long-term memory (Pashler, 1998). Storage in long-term memory is subject to attentional bottlenecks, although the evidence shows little interference with short-term memory. Nevertheless, whereas short-term memory storage is not subject to attentional limitations, it is closely tied to perceptual attention or enactment. Perceptual selection of a stimulus is a necessary condition for short-term storage to occur (Pashler, 1998).

In moving the discussion from attentional limitations of individual information processing to that of organizations, this chapter employs the concept of issues. *Issues* are the available repertoire of categories for making sense of the environment: problems, opportunities, and threats (Ocasio, 1997). Issues constitute the cognitive categories that make up the agenda confronted by the organization and its participants, which are then available to organizational decision makers to respond to or to ignore (Dutton & Jackson, 1987; Jackson & Dutton, 1988). Organizational participants possess a cultural repertoire of possible categories of problems and opportunities that have been encountered in the past, both by the organization and in its environment (Hutchins, 1995; Schein, 1985; Swidler, 1986). As cultural products, issues are reflected in the technology, physical space and arrangements, archives, documents, stories, vocabulary, and narratives that are part of both individual and organizational memory (Walsh & Ungson, 1991).

In applying the principle of limited attention to the SERSTS model of human information processing, this chapter assumes that all aspects of individual and organizational cognition are processed through a limited set of issues and a limited set of schemas. Every cognitive process, therefore, involves a limited attention to issues as issues serve to reduce equivocality in the environment. Cognitive processes also involve selective attention to schemas (Walsh, 1995) as individuals select among alternative knowledge representations to reduce equivocality.

Situated Cognition

The principle of *situated cognition* specifies that human information processing operates in context through individuals' interactions with their physical and social environment (Hutchins, 1995; Lave, 1988; Suchman, 1987). Although this perspective is often viewed as an alternative to the computational–representational understanding of mind (Thagard, 1996), the two views can be reconciled by examining how the physical and social environment shapes the computational and representational processes in the mind. This integrated approach is consistent with the Lewinian perspective in social psychology (Ross & Nisbett, 1991).

In the SERSTS model of human information processing, the principle of situated cognition is represented by the interplay between participants, issues, schemas, resources, space, and time. Participants, resources, space, and time are the social and physical dimensions of the environmental stimuli in which human thinking takes place. As will be discussed next, in examining the process of systems regulation, issues and schemas become associated with the participants, resources, and space that characterize the situation.

Participants, or the individuals physically present and focusing attention on any particular situation, provide the social dimension and composition to situated cognition. Resources are material, nonhuman elements present in any situation. Space is the physical location of any situation. Time is the historical time and duration of any situation. The time dimension of the situation includes a consideration of the past, present, and future of the situation. Time is an irreversible process that results from a history and that anticipates a future.

The situated model of organizational cognition suggests that the allocation of participants, resources, space, and time generates a context in which the social enactment of environmental stimuli takes place. This social and physical enactment itself triggers a retrieval process by which issues and schemas are retrieved from organizational storage. The output of the situated enactment and retrieval is that of organizational selection where equivocality is reduced, alternative mental models are discarded, and new mental models, issues, and schemas are socially constructed for subsequent transmission and storage. This process takes place in any situation whether it is an organization or any other social activity. What is distinctive about organizational thinking is that the situations where cognitions takes place are socially regulated by the organization's system of rules, resources, and relationships. Organizations provide a relatively stable configuration of core participants, issues, resources, schemas, and space over time. Whereas each of these components may vary over time, organizations are systems where a subset of these components remains stable across time periods. The stability in social and organizational systems will be explored below.

Selection and Dynamic Control

Selection is at the heart of both Weick's (1979) model of enactment-selection-retention and the current model of situation-enactment-retrieval-selection-transmission-storage. According to Weick:

> In the formula "How can I know what I think until I see what I say?" selection is seeing. Selection is the organizational process that generates answers to the question "What is going on here?" The selection process selects meaning and interpretations directly and it selects individuals, departments, groups, or goals indirectly. The selection process houses decision-making, but is crucial to remember that decision-making in the organizing model means selecting some interpretation of the world and some set of extrapolations from that interpretation and then using these summaries as constraints on subsequent acting. (p. 175)

Weick's model provides an incomplete specification of how selection takes place. A key component of the process is the reduction of equivocality. The inputs into selection consist of equivocal enactments and cause maps (Weick, 1979, p. 179). In the SERSTS model, both enactment and retrieval provide equivocal inputs to the selection process in the form of alternative schemas, issues, and mental models. Whereas Weick did not offer a complete theory of the selection process, his arguments included a predilection for regularity and unequivocal behavioral orientation, retrospective sense making, and historicizing. According to Weick, equivocality is removed and selection may occur when an enactment is supplied with a history that could have generated it (Weick, 1979, p. 195).

In this chapter, the process of *dynamic control* (White, 1992) is proposed to explain the selection process in organizational cognition. The question is which among alternative schemas, issues, and mental models enacted from the situation or retrieved from storage are to be selected as a guide for subsequent thought and action. The belief that organizational members seek a sense of ontological security (Giddens, 1984) and cognitive balance in the process of reduction of equivocality is posited. Participants seek control of the situation both cognitively and socially, seeking to maintain their sense of identity and position (White, 1992). Consequently, the belief that selection is the result of dynamic control as participants in the situated cognition seek to maintain their cognitive understanding and social, economic, and physical mastery over the situation at hand is posited. Selection is thereby both a cognitive process and a political process as organizational members struggle with the definition of the situation and the resulting choices consistent with the definition. Selection is a form of social discipline as the organization and its social systems exert control over organizational participants as to which thoughts are likely to prevail and take hold. Note that selection in organizational situations occurs both at the level of the individual and the level of the group. In both instances, however, selection results from a set of communications among individuals. Communication serves to reduce equivocality by selecting one among alternative enactments. Only by communicating either verbally, nonverbally, or in writing does selection occur and equivocality is reduced.

Selection (and dynamic control) remains perhaps the most obscure (and theoretically speculative) process in the SERSTS model of human information processing. Selection is motivated and intentional (Searle, 1992); but the intentionality associated with selection is not the property of autonomous individuals but results from the prevailing characteristics of the situation (Ross & Nisbett, 1991). In addition to the motivational mechanisms that shape the selection process of dynamic control, selection results from central processing limitations in decision making (Pashler, 1998). Research on attentional processing suggests that capacity constraints on selection and action are independent of capacity constraints on enactment and perception. At the level of individual information processing, the massive parallelism that occurs at the earlier stages of enactment and retrieval does not seem to extend to the selection of responses (Pashler, 1998, p. 317).

Connectionist perspectives on human information processing provide some suggestive ideas on how selection may occur through computational methods. A theory of explanatory coherence based on methods of activation of prototypes in local distributed networks yields a selection among various alternative models depending on which representation receives the greatest activation (Thagard, 1996). At the social psychological level, selection may operate by constraining enactment to those that yield consistency, provide a sense of ontological order, and minimize cognitive dissonance (Giddens, 1984; Festinger, 1957).

At the level of group selection, the power and control of group participants become a critical determinant of how the selection process occurs. When multiple individuals have a common focus of attention on enacted and retrieved stimuli, the control processes and identifications of organizational members become critical in determining how selection is made. Following White's (1992) theory of identity and control, three alternative models of selection are identified: councils, arenas, and interface. In the council model, selection occurs according to the relative power, reputation, and importance of alternative participants. Organizational participants take into account power differences between actors in selecting among alternative enactments. In the council model, the selected enactments result from negotiation and coalition building between participants with differential power position. As an example, academic senates in universities tend to follow the council model. Participants in the senate are characterized by conflicting interests and identities, with differential levels of power and prestige within the organization. Which enactment is likely to prevail in the deliberations of an academic senate and how these deliberations will shape the construction of university thinking on any particular issue will depend on the relative power of academic senators, the negotiations and shifting political coalitions among members, and the ability of certain factions to structure the agenda and outcomes of political debates.

In the arena model, in contrast, members share a common social identification and selection results from a logic of appropriateness with respect to the common identity (March & Olsen, 1989). Arenas are social groupings that create and enforce socially constructed rules and procedures that represent the social identity of participants and the appropriateness of their activities. Examples of arenas include professional accreditation and licensing boards, functional departments, appellate court systems, and editorial peer review boards. Arenas are a form of discipline, distinct from councils, whose control function resides in their ability to select and exclude the social and material activities of the actors in the discipline in terms of socially negotiated rules of what is or is not the right thing to do. Arenas are characterized by a conversation among a community of participants, one in which the vocabulary of motives is based primarily on normative commitments rather than on material interests. Arena disciplines presuppose a common social identity by participants and shared assumptions regarding the appropriateness of the rules and standards. Otherwise, arena disciplines are likely to break down, and decisions will be based instead on the concrete economic, social, and political networks of relationships of participants within the arena. Arenas place strong reliance on historical precedent to guide their decisions. The rules, standards, and principles that take force within the arena are not fixed but evolve and change with the values and beliefs of their participants (White, 1992).

A third model of sequential selection by individuals produces a social interface where social comparisons among participants seeking status and position shape how individual selection is made. In the interface model of selection, group processes result as status ordering becomes salient and participants establish their position in the social hierarchy (White, 1992). Interface processes are characterized by a common valuation ordering for status and prestige among participants, with status competition becoming the prevalent form of organizational control. Selection in an interface discipline occurs through status competition, social comparison, and differential attention to participants with greater status and prestige in the interface. Examples of interfaces in organizations include researchers competing for status based on publication records, participants in academic seminars and workshops competing for status based on their communications and ideas, and members of nonprofit boards competing for status based on their fund-raising abilities and outcomes.

Which of the three models of social discipline may operate at any point in time may depend on the characteristics of the situation. For example, department meetings may operate as councils, arenas, or interface depending on whether department members are forming coalitions among various factions, invoking superordinate goals and common identities, or competing against each other for status and recognition. Similarly, an admissions office of a university may function as an arena or council. If faced with normatively agreed on rules of admissions, participants in an admissions office may function as an arena discipline, selecting alternative candidates based on the comparison of their qualifications with established admissions criteria. Note that political and social contact may still influence admissions in arena disciplines as established criteria may give preference to families of faculty, alumni, and administration. In the absence of agreed on criteria, admissions processes may function as a council discipline. For example, graduate admissions in an academic department with diverse theoretical and methodological factions is likely to resemble a council discipline, with the various identities and interests represented in the admissions processes negotiating and forging political coalitions to decide on the preferred candidates.

Social, Procedural, Cultural, and Economic Embeddedness

In the SERSTS model, participants, issues, schemas, resources, space, and time are the individual components that contribute to the enactment, retrieval, selection, transmission, and storage of mental models. The principle of *embeddedness* suggests that these individual components are not autonomous but are embedded in broader social, political, cultural, and economic networks and environments outside of the immediate situation (Granovetter, 1985; White, 1992; Zukin & DiMaggio, 1990). Organizations, in the SERSTS model, are decentralized networks of situations, where although each situation is separated from other situations by time and space, the components of the situation are embedded within the broader organizational and supraorganizational environment.

The focus on various forms of embeddedness (Zukin & DiMaggio, 1990) allows for linkages with other components outside the immediate situation. *Social embeddedness* refers to how participants are structurally embedded in a network of social relations among actors (Granovetter, 1985). This implies that individuals' thinking in situation is affected not only by the immediate participants but also by other participants that they are related to. *Procedural embeddedness* refers to how organizational issues are themselves part of issue networks and action channels (Allison, 1971; Bower, 1970) where output of a particular selection process become inputs of subsequent selection efforts. *Cultural embeddedness* (Zukin & DiMaggio, 1990) refers to how schemas used by individual information processors are part of broader culture rule systems and tool kits (Swidler, 1986) both within the organization and the broader environment. *Economic embeddedness* refers to how the resources available in any particular situation are part of a broader resource structure in an organization, with the resulting flow of revenues and costs.

The embeddedness principle suggests that situations are not constructed *de novo* but reflect broader social, political, cultural, and economic structures outside the situation. Furthermore, the embeddedness principle suggests that we most look outside of the immediately available set of participants, issues, schemas, and resources to examine how they are linked through the organizational transmission, retrieval, and storage process to the mental models that shape any particular situation. Embeddedness is not, however, absolute or continuous as situations become decoupled from other situations (March & Olsen, 1976; Weick, 1979) where decoupling allows for the different cognitions in different situations. The relation between embeddedness and decoupling remains, however, unexplored and is subject to additional theorizing and research.

Social Systems Regulation

Organizations as social systems regulate and structure the situated cognition of organizational participants (Ocasio, 1997). Here, this chapter's theory departs from Weick's model where the focus is on the organizing process (Weick, 1979) with limited attention to organizations. For Weick, organizations can be characterized as a system of interlocked behaviors where retention refers to the retention of both enactments and behaviors. Here, the chapter takes a different perspective that views organizations as dynamic, open social systems embedded within their structural, institutional, economic, and cultural environments. Three principles of social systems will be highlighted: reproduction, differentiation, and stratification.

The systems-perspective views organizations as relatively stable subassemblies of individual components (Simon, 1967). Following the SERSTS model, the components of organizational cognition are participants, resources, issues, schemas, space, and time. Whereas time is a nonreproducible component of the situation, all other components are subject to social systems reproduction. Organizations as social systems are, therefore, relatively stable subassemblies of participants, resources, issues, schemas, and space combinations. As subassemblies, the separate subsystems are likely to reproduce themselves over time in relatively stable patterns or combinations. Organizational systems serve to provide stability and order to the organized anarchy (Cohen et al., 1972), limiting the possible combinations of components in organizational situations. For example, over time and across situations, organizational participants are likely to regularly enact, retrieve, select, and transmit certain issue–schema combinations, called a *rule*. Rules, or issue–schema combinations, are subassemblies that are available for organizational thought and action across organizational situations, with the component issue and schema more likely to occur together rather than separately. For another example, certain participants are likely to regularly employ certain schemas about themselves, the situation, the organization, and the environment, and this regular pattern of participant–schema combinations is defined as an *identity*.

Stable subassemblies of organizational systems occur when two or more components or groups of components recur over time. It is beyond the scope of this chapter to fully develop the list of components of organizational subsystems. Table 3.1 lists the available set of organizational subassemblies and provides a vocabulary for the various types.

The following focuses on elementary forms of organizational systems.

The principle of social reproduction suggests that the components that characterize thinking in an organizational situation are likely to recur over

TABLE 3.1

Organizational Subsystems and Their Components

Systems	Components	Examples
Relationships	Participants–issues	Committee and informal tie
Assembly	Participants–space	Department meeting
Outfit	Participants–resources	Cost, revenue, and profit centers
Identity	Participants–schema	Profession, occupation, and work role
Forum	Issues–space	Bulletin board and town hall meeting
Task	Issues–resources	Computing and fund–raising
Rules	Issues–schema	Compensation and promotion policies
Setting	Space–resources	Office, manufacturing plant, and classroom
Design	Space–schema	Logistics and distribution plans
Artifact	Resources–schema	Equipment

time in particular combinations according to the availability and stability of organizational subsystems. Social reproduction serves to structure how organizations think by limiting the set of combinations that are likely at any time and in any place.

According to a second principle of social systems regulation, organizations constitute differentiated subsystems of relationships, assemblies, outfits, identities, forums, tasks, rules, settings, designs, and artifacts. With increased size and variation in situational components, the greater the differentiation in organizational subassemblies (Blau, 1994). Each organizational subsystem structures and channels its components to specific organizational situations and allows for variation in other components. The idea here is that the greater the degree of differentiation among subsystems, the greater the differentiation in mental models. Furthermore, subsystems with common components will have greater commonalties in mental models.

According to a third principle of social systems regulation, organizations create a system of social and economic stratification that distributes power, social status, and position among its members. The components of a social system vary in status and importance according to the organization's stratification system: Participants have distinct status positions, issues, and resources, and schemas vary in their importance in the organization, allowing for differential attention toward those participants, issues, schemas, places, and resources that are most important to the organization (March & Olsen, 1976). Stratification also serves a system of motivation: Organizations provide a set of incentives and rewards that motivates members and focuses their attention and effort. The system of stratification is at the core of selection and dynamic control in the SERSTS model. Stratification serves to structure thinking by organizational participants by motivating their thoughts in ways that enhance the power, status, and social position of organizational participants.

CONCLUSIONS

This chapter develops a framework of organizational cognition by linking multiple levels of analysis and multiple literatures. The framework so far has developed into a set of orienting principles that describe the process by which organizations think. This chapter makes a series of contribution to the literature on organizational cognition. A first contribution is to extend Weick's (1979) model of enactment-selection-retention and to link it to the process of situated cognition, the computational representational understanding of mind, and limited attention to issues and schemas. These ideas are synthesized in the SERSTS model of human information processing. This model highlights how individual cognition is situated and how organizations can be seen as parallel, distributed networks of situations where human thinking takes place. Organizations structure and regulate situations by providing the participants, resources, issues, schemas, and space that constitute the situation. Individual situations are linked in organizations through the processes of retrieval, transmission, and storage.

A second contribution is to propose the principle of dynamic control to explain the selection process. This principle has both a social component and a cognitive component. The social component of selection is based on the idea of social discipline. In determining the effect of the situation, participants must answer the question who are we? Competitors, collaborators, politicians, or a community? In answering this question, constraints on selection are derived from the search for local coherence. This model also involves limited rationality and the sequential attention to issues, schemas, and alternative mental models.

A third contribution of the chapter is to bring a social systems perspective to the understanding of organizational cognition. Participants, issues, schemas, resources, and space in organizational situations are not autonomous components but are themselves embedded in broader social systems. The social system perspective extends the embeddedness principle from a focus on social relationships to other forms of social, procedural, spatial, economic, and cultural embeddedness. For example, how a participant thinks in an organizational situation is embedded in other social relationships, assemblies, outfits, and identities that she belongs to. The sources of schemas and knowledge structures in organization are contained in the identities, rules, designs, and artifacts that constitute an organization's culture. The issues that focus thinking in organization are embedded in the formal and informal set of relationships, forums, tasks, and rules in organizations. The resources available for producing thoughts in organization are economically embedded in the organization's outfits, tasks, settings, and artifacts. And finally, thinking occurs in physical space and the spatial characteristics and connections in organizational assemblies, forums, settings, and designs provide a spatial structure for organizational cognition.

How do organizations think? This chapter gives three interrelated answers. First, organizations think through parallel, decentralized processes of situated enactment, retrieval, selection, transmission, and storage. Organizations think, according to this observation, by organizing the situations in which enactment and selection occurs and by linking the retrieval, transmission, and storage of issues and schemas among situations. Second, organizations think by reducing equivocality through the process of selection and dynamic control. Thinking by individuals and groups in organizations is controlled by the contests for status in organizations, by differential power and prestige of organizational coalitions, and by the logic of appropriateness and common social identification contained in an organization's culture. Finally, organizations think by embedding the components of thinking—the participants, resources, issues, schemas, and space that constitute organizational situations and knowledge structures—into organizational subsystems that regulate the enactment, retrieval, transmission, and storage of the issues, schemas, and mental models that constitute thinking in organizations.

REFERENCES

Albert, S., & Whetten, D. (1985). Organizational identity. In L. L. Cummings & B. M. Staw (Eds.), *Research in organizational behavior* (pp. 263–295). Greenwich, CT: JAI.

Allison, G. T. (1971). *Essence of decision: Explaining the Cuban missile crisis.* Boston: Little, Brown.

Blau, P. M. (1994). *Structural contexts of opportunities.* Chicago: University of Chicago Press.

Bower, J. L. (1970). *Managing the resource allocation process.* Boston: Harvard Business School Press.

Campbell, D. T. (1965). Variation and selective retention in socio-cultural evolution. In H. R. Barringer, G. I. Blankstein, & R. Mack (Eds.), *Social change in developing areas* (pp. 19–49). Cambridge, MA: Schenkman.

Cohen, M. D., March, J. G., & Olsen, J. P. (1972). A garbage can model of organizational choice. *Administrative Science Quarterly, 17,* 1–25.

Cyert, R. M., & March, J. G. (1963). *A behavioral theory of the firm.* Englewood Cliffs, NJ: Prentice-Hall.

Douglas, M. (1986). *How institutions think.* Syracuse, NY: Syracuse University Press.

Dutton, J. E., & Dukerich, J. (1991). Keeping an eye on the mirror: Image and identity in organizational adaptation. *Academy of Management Journal, 34*(3), 517–554.

Dutton, J. E., & Jackson, S. E. (1987). Categorizing strategic issues: Links to organizational action. *Academy of Management Review, 12,* 76–90.

Festinger, L. (1957). *A theory of cognitive dissonance.* Evanston, IL: Row, Peterson.

Fiske, S. T., & Taylor, S. (1991). *Social cognition* (2nd ed.). New York: Random House.

Fligstein, N. (1990). *The transformation of corporate control.* Cambridge, MA: Harvard University Press.

Giddens, A. (1984). *The constitution of society.* Berkeley, CA: University of California Press.

Granovetter, M. (1985). Economic action and social structure: The problem of embeddedness. *American Journal of Sociology, 91,* 481–510.

Hambrick D. C., & Mason, P. A. (1984). Upper-echelons: The organization as a reflection of its top managers. *Academy of Management Review, 9,* 193–206.

Holyoak, K. J., & Gordon, P. C. (1984). Information processing and social cognition. In R. S. Wyer & T. K. Srull (Eds.), *Handbook of social cognition* (Vol. 1, pp. 39–70). Hillsdale, NJ: Lawrence Erlbaum Associates.

Hutchins, E. (1995). *Cognition in the wild.* Cambridge, MA: MIT Press.

Jackson, S. E., & Dutton, J. E. (1988). Discerning threats and opportunities. *Administrative Science Quarterly, 33,* 370–387.

Johnson-Laird, P. N. (1983). *Mental models.* Cambridge, MA: MIT Press.

Kahneman, D. (1973). *Attention and effort.* Englewood Cliffs, NJ: Prentice-Hall.

Langer, E. J. (1990). *Mindfulness.* Reading, MA: Addison-Wesley.

Lave, J. (1988). *Cognition in Practice.* Cambridge, England: Cambridge University Press.

Lawrence, P.R. & Lorsch, J.W. (1967). *Organization and environment.* Homewood, IL: Irwin.

Luhmann, N. (1992). *Social systems.* Stanford, CA: Stanford University Press.

March, J. G. (1997). Understanding how decisions happen in organizations. In Z. Shapira (Ed.), *Organizational decision making* (pp. 9–32). Cambridge, England: Cambridge University Press.

March, J. G., & Olsen J. P. (1976). *Ambiguity and choice in organizations.* Bergen, Norway: Universitetsforlaget.

March, J. G., & Olsen J. P. (1989). *Rediscovering institutions: The organizational basis of politics.* New York: The Free Press.

March, J. G., & Simon H. A. (1958). *Organizations.* New York: Wiley.

Martin, J. (1992). *Cultures in organizations.* New York: Oxford University Press.

Ocasio, W. (1995). The enactment of economic adversity: A reconciliation of theories of failure-induced change and threat-rigidity. In L. L. Cummings & B. M. Staw (Eds.), *Research in Organizational Behavior* (pp. 287–331). Greenwich, CT: JAI.

Ocasio, W. (1997). Towards an attention-based view of the firm. *Strategic Management Journal, Summer,* 18: 187–206.

Pashler, H. E. (1998). *The psychology of attention.* Cambridge, MA: MIT Press.

Pfeffer, J. (1983). Organizational demography. In L. L. Cummings & B. M. Staw (Eds.), *Research in organizational behavior* (pp. 299–357). Greenwich, CT: JAI.

Radner, R. (1997). Bounded rationality, indeterminacy, and the managerial theory of the firm. In Z. Shapira (Ed.), *Organizational decision making* (pp. 324–352). Cambridge, England: Cambridge University Press.

Ross, L., & Nisbett R. E. (1991). *The person and the situation: Perspectives of social psychology.* New York: McGraw-Hill.

Schein, E. (1985). *Organizational culture and leadership.* San Francisco: Jossey-Bass.

Scott, W. R. (1997). *Organizations: Rational, natural, and open systems,* (3rd ed.). Englewood Cliffs, NJ: Prentice-Hall.

Searle, J. (1992) *The rediscovery of the mind*. Cambridge, MA: MIT Press.

Simon, H. (1947). *Administrative behavior: A study of decision-making processes in administrative organizations*. New York: Macmillan.

Simon, H. (1967). The architecture of complexity. In H. Simon (Ed.), *The science of the artificial* (pp. 84–118). Cambridge, MA: MIT Press.

Suchman, L. (1987). *Plans and situated actions: The problem of human–machine communication*. Cambridge, England: Cambridge University Press.

Swidler, A. (1986). Culture in action: Symbols and strategies. *American Sociological Review, 51*, 273–286.

Thagard, P. (1996). *Mind: Introduction to cognitive science*. Cambridge, MA: Bradford Books.

Walsh, J. P. (1995). Managerial and organizational cognition: Notes from a trip down memory lane. *Organization Science, 6*:280–321.

Walsh, J. P., & Ungson G. R. (1991). Organizational memory. *Academy of Management Review, 16*, 57–91.

Weick, K. M. (1979). *The social psychology of organizing* (2nd ed.). New York: Random House.

White, H. C. (1992). *Identity and control: A structural theory of social action*. Princeton, NJ: Princeton University Press.

Zukin, S., & DiMaggio, P. (1990). *Structures of capital: The social organization of the economy*. Cambridge, England: Cambridge University Press.

4

The Pursuit of Intelligence in Organizations

James G. March
Stanford University

Organizations pursue intelligence. In that pursuit, they process information, formulate plans and aspirations, interpret environments, generate strategies and decisions, monitor experiences and learn from them, and imitate others as they do the same. Organizations seek to serve their interests and conceptions of self, imposing coherence when they can and exploiting the advantages of confusion, chaos, and ambiguity when the opportunity arises. These efforts are disciplined by the presence of other organizations that, in similar pursuit of their own interests and self-conceptions, provides elements of competition and objects for emulation.

This pursuit of intelligence in organizations is never completely successful. To be sure, organizations sometimes manage to achieve impressive attributions of intelligence, but organizational intelligence can also be equivocal, ephemeral, and chimerical. Despite all the paraphernalia of intelligence available to them and powerful incentives to avoid errors, organizations often pursue courses that adversely affect some of the interests represented in an organizational coalition. They routinely make blunders, sometimes huge ones. They often fail to survive very long. They frequently discover that actions they thought were unusually clever have subsequently been seen as prelude to disaster. History is filled with organizational stupidity as well as organizational brilliance.

There are reasons for the failures. The pursuit of organizational intelligence appears quite straightforward but it is not. The difficulties begin with complications in the concept of intelligence itself. In a general way, intelligence refers to the ability to achieve outcomes that fulfill desires as much as possible. We assess the intelligence of a particular decision procedure by evaluating the outcomes resulting from its use in terms of organizational desires. An intelligent organization is one that adopts procedures that consistently do well (in the organization's own terms) in the face of constraints imposed by such things as scarce resources and competition.

The assessment of organizational intelligence in such terms is a classical case of social construction and it is particularly complicated by the fact that desires, actions, and outcomes are all distributed across space and time and connected with each other in intricate ways. Organizations seek intelligence in the name of multiple, nested actors over multiple, nested time periods. As a result, any assessment of intelligence, even within a community of shared meanings, is conditional on the time and place perspective chosen. What is intelligent from the point of view of one group's desires over one time period may be quite unintelligent from the perspective of another time and set of desires. And what is intelligent from the point of view of preferences activated when action is taken may be quite unintelligent from the point of view of preferences activated later, particularly after preferences adjust to subsequent experience.

If these conceptual problems were not enough, pursuing organizational intelligence, once defined, is made particularly elusive by two elementary problems: The first problem is the problem of *ignorance*. Not everything is known. The future is uncertain. The consequences of taking one action or another are difficult to anticipate precisely. Sometimes, they are difficult to anticipate at all. The future depends in part on the actions of many actors, each of whom is simultaneously trying to anticipate the others. Many of the contingencies can be given probabilistic estimates, but such estimates leave considerable range in the possible futures. Moreover, different people in an organization often anticipate dramatically different futures.

The past is also uncertain. It is not uncertain because it still remains to be realized but because it is dimly, inaccurately, or differently recalled. The past is experienced in ways that affect both its interpretation and the memories that are retained about it. History is a story, and the storytellers of the past appear to be as variable as the storytellers of the future. Ignorance about the future and the past is organized around ignorance about the causal structure of the world. Interpretations of why things happen in and to organizations are predominately *post hoc* explanations that seem to shift with changing fashions in interpretation and may provide only weak aids to comprehending a future that will reflect new changes.

The second problem is the problem of *ambiguity* in the evaluative bases of action. Intelligence presumes some accomplishment of what is desired. The desires may take the form of preferences defined over possible outcomes. They may take the form of conceptions of self that are to be fulfilled. The preferences to be pursued or the identities to be enacted are usually assumed to be clear, stable, and exogenous. In organizations, in fact, they are typically neither clear, nor stable, nor exogenous. Preferences and identities are defined ambiguously and measured crudely. They are not stable. They are likely to change between the time action is taken and the time that its outcomes are realized, so that there is a predictable difference between the intelligence of an action *ex ante* and its intelligence *ex post*. Moreover, preferences and identities not only change but are likely to change as a result of the process of trying to act intelligently. As a result, the evaluative bases of action—the criteria of intelligence—are ambiguous.

In the face of these problems, organizations adopt various practices and procedures for taking action. To arrive at good procedures, they experiment with alternatives, copy the practices of others, consult decision theorists, and hire consultants. They try to adopt practices that make credible claims of leading to intelligent actions and defend actions that lead to disasters as reflecting unfortunate outcomes of good decisions. A claim of intelligence for an action, in these terms, is a claim that it resulted from an intelligent procedure. A claim of intelligence for any particular procedure is a claim that the procedure will, in general, lead to favorable outcomes and that there are no systematic features of the procedure itself that confound the achievement of a sense of intelligence.

Thus, for example, the claim that rational action is intelligent is a claim that estimating the future consequences of possible current actions and choosing the one with the highest expected value will generally lead to outcomes that are evaluated as desirable in the long run. The credibility of the claim is supported primarily by indirect arguments. It can be shown that in a specific abstractly specified world and structure of meaning, a specific rational decision procedure will yield (on average) the best decisions as defined in a particular way. The demonstrations are in many ways persuasive, but they tend to beg two obvious questions: First, does the abstract world adequately represent the real world? Second, do real organizations when attempting to follow rational procedures in real situations produce equivalently favorable results?

It would be misleading to say that answers to these questions are firmly established by evidence. In general, the idea that intelligence can be achieved by choosing among alternative courses of action on the basis of prior preferences and estimations of likely consequences is widely accepted, but it is also widely questioned. It is not clear that the abstract world of decision theory adequately represents the world as we experience it. There is a substantial body of commentary that notes the difficulties of knowing what alternatives exist, of estimating the future consequences of possible current action, and of establishing valid measures of the values of those consequences. There is also considerable doubt about the way rational action treats future preferences as equivalent to current preferences. Preferences and identities change, and it is future preferences and identities that are relevant to assessing future outcomes.

And when real organizations attempt to follow rational procedures in real situations, it is not clear that their actions can be assured to lead to favorable results. Stories of disasters stemming from actions based on calculations of expected consequences and from efforts to implement particular rational procedures are standard to both folk tales and to research.

Claims of intelligence for procedures based on rule-based action and organizational learning are similarly supported by two kinds of indirect arguments rather than by direct evidence. The first argument is that the processes by which rules are established involve more careful assessments of the collective and long-term consequences of individual action than can be expected from individual actors at a particular time. Specific action occurs under pressures of time and is taken by individuals and organizations with incomplete knowledge and under conditions of compressed attention, thus, it is unlikely to be intelligent. A system of rules allows a separation of the judgments necessary to define intelligent action from the myopic, decentralized, short-term making of decisions by particular actors.

The second observation is that rules reflect the accumulation of knowledge in a way that is impossible for individual calculation. They store past experience—experience that extends over more time, individuals, and situations than any one individual's experience can. Rules retain and extend knowledge through differential survival and growth of organizations using more intelligent rules and they reproduce by spreading from one organization to another.

There is no question that some of the experiences of organizations with learning and rule following have been positive. Organizations have been known to gain reputations for improvement by learning from experience. They have been known to transfer knowledge to and from others. They have been known to accumulate knowledge and develop procedures for storing and retrieving it, particularly in standard procedures and rules. The evidence for the contribution of learning to intelligence is, however, mixed. Organizations learn and remember the wrong things as well as the right things. They are prone to superstitious learning. And learning itself sometimes produces traps for intelligence.

Thus, although they are unquestionably useful, neither rationality nor learning assures favorable outcomes. The point is not simply that outcomes are draws from a probability distribution thus knowable in advance only up to that distribution. The argument is much more that there are systematic features of rational and learning procedures and systematic features of the interaction between those procedures and key features of organizational life and people's interpretations of it that complicate the realization of intelligence. The pursuit of intelligence is frustrated by persistent properties of individuals and organizations, by intrinsic properties of the worlds in which organizations operate, and by unintended traps of adaptive action.

A central feature of the pursuit of intelligence is the way organizations (like other adaptive systems) are plagued by the difficulty of balancing *exploration* and *exploitation*. Exploration means such things as search, discovery, novelty, and innovation. It involves variation, risk taking, and experimentation. It commonly leads to disasters but occasionally leads to important new directions and discoveries. Exploitation means refinement, routinization, production, and implementation of knowledge. It involves choice, efficiency, selection, and reliability. It usually leads to improvement but often is blind to major redirections.

Both exploration and exploitation are essential for adaptation. Exploration cannot realize its occasional gains without exploitation of discoveries. Exploitation becomes obsolescent without exploration of new directions. Finding a good balance between exploration and exploitation is a recurrent problem of theories of adaptation. In theories of rational choice, it takes the form of deciding how much should be allocated to search (rather than execution of the currently best alternative). In learning theories, it takes the form of deciding how much to experiment with new alternatives (rather than increase competence on old ones). In theories of selection, it takes the form of evaluating the rate of generation of new, deviant rules (mutations). Theories of adaptation talk about balancing search and action, balancing efficiency and adaptiveness, balancing variation and selection, balancing change and stability, and balancing diversity and unity.

Balance is a nice word but a cruel concept. Defining an optimum mix of exploration and exploitation is difficult or impossible. It involves trade-offs across time. It also involves trade-offs across people and across levels of a system. The optimum balance may vary from one participant to another. It may vary from an individual to an organization or from an organization to a population of organizations. Although determining the optimal mix of exploration and exploitation is ordinarily beyond comprehension in any realistic situation, some things are known about optimal allocations to exploration and exploitation. For example, in general, the shorter the time horizon and the narrower the domain (the lower the level of integration considered), the more the optimum balance shifts toward exploitation. As that example suggests, however, the optimum is not a simple determination but depends on the time perspective and on the part of the system that is the focus of attention.

Even if it were possible to define an optimum mix of exploitation and exploration, achieving that mix would be difficult or impossible. When costs and benefits extend over time, action tends to be more localized than its effects, and decision makers tend to focus on nearby effects rather than distant ones. Similarly, experiential learning is more responsive to effects that are in the temporal and spatial neighborhood than to effects that are more distant. As a result, ordinary rationality and learning are likely to lead to a level of investment in exploration that subsequently will be judged to have been inadequate. Moreover, adaptation affects subsequent adaptation. As a particular domain is explored, the pool of prospects is likely to be depleted, thus the likelihood of finding a better alternative is likely to decline over time. Competence increases with experience, thus encouraging the status quo. Aspirations change as a result of one's own experience and the experiences of others. Values shift.

Two conspicuous dynamic threats to the exploration–exploitation balance are especially relevant to organizations. The first is the failure trap, a dynamic of excessive exploration. Experiments usually fail. They fail because, on average, new ideas are poor because incompetence with new ideas makes even good new ideas less productive than they might be, and because new ideas are likely to be oversold to be adopted, burdening them with excessive expectations. The result is a cycle of failure and exploration, running through a series of new ideas but failing to persist in any one of them long enough to discover whether it might be good.

The second dynamic threat to the balance is the success (or competency) trap, a dynamic of excessive exploitation. The rewards to exploitation tend to be more certain, nearer in time, and nearer in space than the rewards to exploration. Successful experience leads to more experience, which leads to greater competence, which leads to more success, and so on. The local positive feedback among experience, competence, and success generates traps of distinctive competence and results in inadequate exploration.

Substantial elements of these problems stem from the sequential sampling character of experiential learning. Consider the following stylized process: (a) The realized return from a particular alternative depends on its true (perhaps socially constructed) value but also is subject to random error or risk, thus is a draw from a normal distribution with a mean equal to the expected value of the alternative and a variance that varies from alternative to alternative; (b) As long as the average return from any particular venture is above a target return, the decision maker continues to pursue that venture; (c) If the average return goes below that target, the decision maker chooses a new alternative at random.

To continue with alternatives whose values are believed to be greater than the target and to discard alternatives whose values are believed to be below the target, the process makes estimates of the value of an alternative. However, those estimates are subject to error. In particular, there are two kinds of errors to be avoided if possible—Type I error: continuing with an alternative that has a true value less than the target; and Type II error: Rejecting an alternative that has a true value greater than the target.

It is clear that the more experience one has with an alternative, the better the estimate of its real value, and the less likely an error. Experience is accumulated, however, only by alternatives with average returns above the target. As a result, alternatives that are really poor but appear to be good accumulate additional results that are likely to correct the error. On the other hand, alternatives that are really good but appear to be poor do not accumulate additional results to correct the error. Consequently, Type I errors (accepting poor alternatives) are self-correcting; Type II errors (rejecting good alternatives) are not.

Actual decision situations do not ordinarily conform in all respects to this stylized description but they often contain the elements of sequential sampling that generate the tendency to make Type II errors more often than Type I errors. Experience leads to abandoning good alternatives, particularly good alternatives with high variance in their returns, more often than it does to continuing with bad ones. This suggests that, on average, decision makers who base their decisions on experience with alternatives probably need to have greater patience than they do. By this analysis, stock portfolios, jobs, marriages, favorite restaurants, and favorite auto mechanics should (from a normative point of view) show lower turnover than they typically do when choices are made through sequential experiential learning.

The complications of finding an appropriate balance between exploration and exploitation are legendary. Even if they were not, ignorance, conflict, and ambiguity would combine with a changing world to make efforts to achieve intelligence endlessly challenging. Research over the past few decades has illuminated some important behavioral aspects of the pursuit of organizational intelligence. That research can be organized in four clusters of ideas about relations among organizational situations, actions, and outcomes:

- First, ideas about how decisions happen in organizations, in particular ideas about two major conceptions of the bases of action—ideas of choice and ideas of rule following.

- Second, ideas about organizational learning and other forms of organizational change, the evolution of thinking about social evolution and special features of organizational adaptation, and the complications involved in comprehending a complex world on the basis of small, biased samples of experience.
- Third, ideas about risk taking, experimentation, and innovation in organizations, particularly the roles of knowledge, targets, foolishness, incentives, and identities in generating and sustaining novel ideas.
- Fourth, ideas about the giving and taking of advice in organizations, particularly problems of agency and conflict of interest between advice givers and advice takers.

That past research has been particularly successful in identifying some of the conspicuous problems in the pursuit of intelligence; it has been notably less successful in resolving the dilemmas of intelligence and understanding how organizations act in the face of those dilemmas. It seems likely that future understanding of organizational intelligence will be linked particularly to research on three grand issues of understanding knowledge in organizations.

First, research seeking to understand how knowledge is extracted from experience in organizations can be expected. Researchers have learned a fair amount about the limitations and strengths of human inference making in relatively constrained experimental settings. They know rather less about how history is construed in real organizational situations. They also know rather little about the effects of knowledge on the extraction or generation of further knowledge. It is clear that knowledge cumulates, that prior knowledge is an important ingredient of future knowledge; but it is also clear that knowledge constrains experimentation, that it focuses elaboration of ideas and interferes with novelty. Interference with novelty is, of course, exactly what is meant by knowledge and it is not to be denigrated. Nevertheless, novelty is essential. Consensus and controversy within the knowledge establishment are each important parts of the story.

Second, research seeking to understand how knowledge is extracted or generated from the knowledge of others can be expected. Many ideas about knowledge diffusion adopt variations of epidemiological theories of diffusion. They see the spread of knowledge as following networks of contacts and spreading from one link to another. Such theories are clearly useful but they tend to accept two dubious assumptions. The first is the assumption of reproductive reliability, the idea that knowledge moves from one point in a network to another point without change. Most observations suggest that knowledge transfer usually involves knowledge transformation as well. The second assumption is that of network exogeneity, the idea that the networks of diffusion are given by exogenous forces. Most observations suggest that networks evolve in the process of spreading knowledge.

More generally, theories of knowledge transfer need to deal with a host of complications. They need to elaborate the complementary roles of evocative ambiguity and clarity in the transmission and development of knowledge. They need to develop some adequate treatment of inarticulate knowledge, the transfer of tacit knowledge, and implicit learning. They need to cope with various problems of interactive knowledge accumulation, issues of things such as interactive meaning and absorptive capacity. They need to understand the spread of competing concepts and mutual effects in a world in which everyone is simultaneously learning and teaching.

Third, research seeking to understand the relation between knowledge and action can be expected. How is knowledge linked to its returns? In particular, what is the relation between general causal knowledge and specific contextual detail? What is the relevance of relevance in the transfer and use of knowledge? How does conflict of interest affect the development and transfer of knowledge? One of the oldest trade-offs in politics is the trade-off between confidence (trust) in an advisor and competence in an advisor. More generally, it seems likely that precisely the people from whom one can learn the most (i.e., those with different knowledge) are likely to be the people with whom one is least likely to seek contact and whose knowledge one is least likely to trust (for good reason).

These questions all straddle a deep canyon that divides studies of organizations. On one side of the canyon are found studies trying to understand how things happen in organizations. Why does an organization do what it does? These studies are variously described as descriptive, positive, or behavioral. They try to report organizations as they actually are. On the other side of the canyon are studies devoted to advising how an organization can be induced to produce better outcomes. How can an organization be improved? These studies are variously described as prescriptive, normative, or instructional. They try to shape organizational actions to conform to models of proper decisions.

Unless one presumes that competitive pressures will eliminate all organizations that fail to pursue optimal courses, the two questions are rather different. The first invites the skills and perspectives of behavioral scientists, trying to characterize the way things really are. What are the major phenomena associated with the generation of organizational action? The second invites the skills and perspectives of decision theorists, operations analysts, and economists, trying to show how things might be improved. How can an organization be made more successful or more durable?

The canyon between these two perspectives is deep. A sacred principle of organization studies is the commandment: Thou shalt not confuse behavioral (or descriptive) assertions with normative (or prescriptive) statements. Yet, many writers on organizations straddle this chasm without notable strain. They describe and they advise. And their descriptions slide into their advice (or vice versa) with the ready lubrication of a common terminology, a mixed audience, and a vigorous market for relevance. If the habit of slipping from the language of observers to the language of reformers without changing the words is an academic sin, then academic hell is crowded with students of organization.

Much of the behavioral research on decision making, information processing, and learning in organizations has been carried out primarily from the point of view of describing organizations. It has been executed by academics who see themselves as observing and reporting organizational life, for the most part, not reforming it. Nevertheless, much of that research is also in the spirit of straddling the chasm. It tries to describe how organizations operate but with one eye to how they might be made to operate more intelligently and another eye to the major problems involved in making any assertion about the existence of a guaranteed route to intelligence. Necessarily, such a spirit invites observations of the many ways in which reforms in the name of intelligence may not serve intelligence, of the many possibilities for things that appear obvious to turn out to be misleading or wrong, and of the complexities in establishing that actions, or even outcomes, are desirable.

At the same time, however, the same spirit invites an effort to say something, however tentative, about how things might be better. We ask how to improve the *exploitation* of what is known; how human beings of limited capabilities for inference can confront incomplete and biased data on history and still make some sense of their experiences; how organizations can cope with the complexities of experience, particularly the way the intelligence of a particular course of action depends on the courses of action adopted by others, as well as the whole history of actions and responses to them; how it is possible to deal with sparse, redundant, confusing data generated in part from sources that are not innocent; how the knowledge and actions of others can inform organizational action; and how learning can be retained and spread within an organization.

We ask how organizations can improve the *exploration* of what might come to be known. We examine the proverbial resistance to change in organizations and conclude that knowledge and experience produce systematic biases against exploration, not because of irrational human rigidity or resistance to change but because most new ideas and practices are likely to be inferior to existing ones, particularly in the short run. In the face of this, we ask whether organizations can increase the yield from experimentation with new ideas by improving the average quality of new ideas; how they can increase the quantity of new ideas by stimulating experimentation and the taking of risks; and how they can increase persistence with new ideas by buffering new ideas from adverse feedback or from responding to it. The fundamental dilemma remains, however: The quantity of new ideas and persistence in pursuing them can be increased by changing incentives or by encouraging certain forms of willfulness, ignorance, and fantasy; but increasing the number of good new ideas generally leads at the same time to increasing the number of bad new ideas, and specialists in novelty are generally short lived.

And we ask how greater wisdom can arise from the interaction of advice givers and advice takers in organizations. To a substantial extent, the observations on the giving and taking of advice are built around three themes. The first theme elaborates the idea that understanding is necessarily incomplete, that representing the full complexity of the phenomena associated with organizational intelligence would involve a level of complexity that is inaccessible to human thought or communication. The second theme recognizes the complementarities between general and specific knowledge. It elaborates the idea that intelligent action requires a mixture of knowledge gleaned from an intimate awareness of the fine detail of a specific context and knowledge gleaned from general analytical thinking and that implementing such a mixture requires a high level of self-discipline on the part of both experts and practitioners. The third theme elaborates the idea that both the human spirit and organizational prosperity require commitment and autonomy and that great commitment comes not so much from anticipation of great consequences or the pursuit of self-conscious cleverness as from a profound sense of self and the obligations of identity.

If organizational intelligence were easier, the tale would be shorter and life would be simpler. Or, possibly, the tale would be simpler and life would be shorter. In either case, it is comforting that consideration of topics as utilitarian as decision making, learning, risk taking, and the giving of advice lead to such deep puzzles as the fundamental bases of human action, the connections between stability and change, the nature of history, the role of imagination, and the place of poetry in ordinary life. The comfort is, however, more the comfort of Søren Kierkegaard than that of Jeremy Bentham. If research on the pursuit of intelligence in organizations suggests anything of a general sort, it is that that pursuit is an activity in which knowledge can sometimes produce power and often produces hubris, but any serious understanding more reliably results in humility. We do research on organizational intelligence not in hopes of remarkable gains but because that is what we do.

ACKNOWLEDGMENTS

This chapter is a revised version of one that appeared in James G. March, *The Pursuit of Organizational Intelligence* (Oxford, England: Blackwell Publishers, 1999). It is printed here with the permission of Blackwell Publishers. Some of the ideas are elaborated in other chapters of the Blackwell book, as well as in James G. March, *A Primer on Decision Making: How Decisions Happen* (New York: The Free Press, 1994). Some relevant citations to the literature are provided in *The Pursuit of Organizational Intelligence* as well as in James G. March, *Decisions and Organizations* (Oxford, England: Basil Blackwell, 1988), James G. March and Johan P. Olsen, *Rediscovering Institutions: The Organizational Basis of Politics* (New York: The Free Press, 1989), and James G. March and Johan P. Olsen, *Democratic Governance* (New York: The Free Press, 1995). The research has been supported by the Spencer Foundation.

Commentary: The Theoretical Foundations of Organizational Cognition

Sim B. Sitkin
Duke University

Organizational cognition—even the term raises questions about whether those who study under its rubric are pursuing theory-driven science or metaphorical elaboration. Whether the term *organizational cognition* represents a fad or a lasting framework for scholarship lingers just below the surface of many discussions between scholars who identify with the cognition rubric and those who do not.

This issue cannot be resolved in a volume such as this one. However, it is possible to advance the understanding of what organizational cognition might mean if it were more than just a metaphor for an individual-level process. The chapters in this volume offered by March, Dhar, and Ocasio do just that by helpfully distinguishing individual and organizational cognition in a way that advances researchers' ability to frame the theoretical foundations that can be useful for future work in the area.

The chapters by March, Dhar, and Ocasio make clear that organizational cognition is a potentially important and appropriate construct for organizational scholars to pursue. Specifically, they provide support for the idea that cognition takes place for units of analysis other than the individual and can refer meaningfully to more than the mere aggregation of individual cognitions. Taken together, these three chapters suggest that the cognition tent both is and should be an inclusive one that addresses similarities and differences across multiple levels of analysis.

TYPES OF COGNITIVE PROCESSES

Ideas have existed for some time concerning the need to create variation in order to be able to then selectively focus activity on more effective options. Evolu-

73

tionary biology is based on such ideas. Creative group decision making also exhibits this pattern in its emphasis on the divergent ideas generated by brainstorming, followed by various convergence-forcing techniques. In the organizational design literature, notions of differentiation and integration have long stressed the need for both functions. Notwithstanding this long tradition, there has been a resurgence of interest in this duality in the organizational cognition literature, in part spurred by March's recent work on the exploitation–exploration dichotomy (Levinthal & March, 1993; March, 1991, 1995).

Thus, I found it both useful and striking that the three chapters highlighted this distinction in three very different domains and by tapping three very different theoretical bases. Within the organizational and individual cognition literatures, the distinctions March refers to as *exploitation* and *exploration* have been discussed under a variety of labels: *convergence–divergence, control–learning,* or *high and low mastery orientation* (Cohen & Sproull, 1996). Underlying the various labels is the basic notion that the content, form, or processes underlying cognition can be distinguished based on whether they stress enhancing the level of mastery over the relatively well-known or emphasize the exploration of the relatively unknown. March's chapter (chap. 4) examines this distinction in terms of organizational and individual learning. Dhar (chap. 2) draws on a similar underlying distinction in his discussion of the implementation of more routine computational or machine-based information processes and the enactment of more human-based information processes. Ocasio (chap. 3) also uses a similar distinction is his examination of evolutionary stages, where variance-trimming selection processes are preceded by variance-enhancing enactment processes.

This helpful distinction seems to raise as many questions as it helps to answer—but that is precisely what is useful about how these authors apply the general distinction to specific and diverse problems. The distinction raises questions about whether there is a trade-off between exploration and mastery or whether they can be jointly analyzed in theoretically useful ways—and this issue is addressed in the next section.

BALANCING PROCESSES OF EXPLORATION AND MASTERY

Although Dhar does not directly address the issue of how computational and human cognition might be combined, the issue of balance is directly addressed by both March and Ocasio. March, drawing on some of his prior work with Levinthal (e.g., Levinthal & March, 1993), conceptualizes *intelli-*

gence as balancing that occurs through the creation and institutionalization of procedures that appropriately weight exploration and mastery. The requirements of the situation as well as the organization's capacity to absorb uncertainty and new information all play into how *intelligence* is achieved.

March's treatment of balance is somewhat more static than Ocasio's in that Ocasio's structurational approach to cognition lends itself quite naturally to the idea of sequential balance. Taken together, Ocasio and March highlight how the need to simultaneously examine variation-enhancing and variation-reducing processes can be studied at a point in time and across the life of evolutionary processes. Put differently, although they have complementary areas of emphasis, both March and Ocasio recognize that balance is both a state and an ever-unfolding process.

I would have liked to see another aspect of balance more fully explored: the precise relation between mastery and exploration. In some of my own work with Kathleen Sutcliffe and Larry Browning, for example, we have begun to examine conditions under which mastery-oriented activity and exploratory activity are antithetically, orthogonally, or synergistically related (Sutcliffe, Sitkin, & Browning, 2000). Most work to date—including the chapters here—seems to presume that there is a fixed amount of cognitive resources (attention, etc.) and that mastery and exploration processes compete for those resources in a kind of zero sum game. However, work on innovation by Henderson and Clark (1990), Cardinal (1999), or Brown and Duguid (1991) illustrated how greater levels of incremental (i.e., mastery) innovation can sometimes be synergistic with enhancements in radical (i.e., exploratory) innovation. This work pointed to directions in which future research on the nuances of balance could be more fully developed and studied.

Although Dhar (chap. 2) does not address this issue directly, his chapter contains some of the most useful implications for addressing this issue. Specifically, the distinction between computational routines and human learning highlights the potential for more systematically examining links that have been the focus of research on human–machine interfaces and the social context of computing. These have not been the subject of sustained inquiry within the organizational literature with the exception of work on decision support systems (e.g., Suchman, 1987). However, the potential is great for examining not only Dhar's suggestions about how routine knowledge may be exploited through computational routines and machine learning, but also for building on his argument that such routinization–formalization processes could serve as a springboard for exploratory activities (Sitkin, 1992, 1995; Sitkin, Sutcliffe, & Schroeder, 1994). This work could build on research examining how high reliability organizations learn under severely constrained conditions or how organizations that excel in managing reliability-enhancing control systems (e.g., Total Quality Management (TQM)) can leverage those skill sets to become better and more efficient at exploration (e.g., Sutcliffe et al., 2000; Weick, Sutcliffe, & Obstfeld, 1999).

COGNITION ACROSS LEVELS OF ANALYSIS

Another area in which the chapters make a clear and consistent statement is that organizational cognition can be thought of in several distinct ways. Furthermore, the authors suggest, these are not alternatives but are synthetic and should be treated as necessary elements for theorizing about organizational cognition.

First, they point out that cognition is a rubric under which is included collective, aggregate patterns of individual cognition within organizations (both for the managers and other individual participants in organizational life). This aspect of organizational cognition reflects the value of examining aggregated individual cognition both to see patterns of individual cognition and also to study the patterns as group or organizational level attributes. This broad umbrella stresses the important point that the study of individual thought, group and organizational patterns of beliefs, and information processes are legitimate foci under the rubric of organizational cognition research. This conception treats both the individual and the organization as legitimate *levels of analysis* but stresses individual cognition as the *unit of analysis*.

Second, all three chapters suggest ways that organizations and organizational subunits can engage in cognition distinct from the cognitions of their individual members. For example, information acquisition and processing rules, routines, or devices can be an attribute of the organizational unit or community without individual members even being aware that a particular routine is actually taking place or governing their behavior. This is the essence of the institutional argument that the more institutionalized a set of cognitive or behavioral assumptions are, the less they will be an explicit part of the considerations of individual members. In short, the institutionalists argue the essence of institutionalization is to raise the level of explanation for observed actions or cognitive processes from the individual to the community.

Thirdly, Ocasio (chap. 3) emphasizes how organizations are systems that structure and regulate individual cognition. His view does not examine organizational cognition so much as it is treats organizational attributes as key contextual elements that must be taken into account in any theory of cognition within organizational settings. But the important general point made is that theories of organizational cognition are severely limited to the extent that they fail to take seriously the impact of organizational processes and structures on individual attention, processing, and storage of information.

My first point noted how organizational cognition is significantly influenced by and even composed of individual cognition. In contrast, the third point, raised by Ocasio, highlights how individual cognition is shaped by its context. Taken together, the first and third points thus paint a structuration-like picture of cognition in which individual cognition both shapes and is shaped by its context.

EMBEDDEDNESS AND COGNITION

Ocasio's (chap. 3, this volume) emphasis on a structuration-like approach makes it natural for him to stress the importance of conceptualizing cognition as embedded. The three chapters provide a nice frame for thinking about when cognition as a process or a product of thinking and learning may lend itself to context-free analysis, as well as stressing the degree to which cognition should or must be examined in situ.

Ocasio's approach to embeddedness was especially useful in the way that he relates cognition to a number of situational differences. By recognizing that situational requirements shift as one moves through evolutionary stages (enactment, selection, and retention) or as one moves across cultural or task-related conditions, Ocasio is able to posit how cognitive processes and content will vary. By elaborating on concepts of situated cognition and situated learning (e.g., Lave & Wenger, 1991; Suchman, 1987), Ocasio is thus able to describe the structurational process of dynamic emergence and adaptation between the features of the situation and individual, group, or organizational cognition. Thus, his notion of embeddedness is actually an essential underpinning of the issue of sequential balance discussed previously.

COGNITION AT THE GROUP
AND COMMUNITY LEVEL

Perhaps the most significant omission in the foundations laid by these chapters was inattention to the role of cognition and learning at the group level. Whether one frames this as a group, subunit, or community phenomenon, there has been a significant recent rise in organizational researcher attention to issues of belief, shared understanding, and tacit collective knowledge.

A number of streams of independent scholarship point to the importance of cognitive analysis at the group level. Given the diversity of many formal organizations in terms of task requirements, constituencies, cultures, and so on, it is sensible to think that more proximate social units—such as work groups, occupational sets, and communities of practice—are a more influential antecedent and effect of individual cognition than are more distal and abstract formal organizations. Yet, research on such issues as communities of practice (e.g., Brown & Duguid, 1991; Wenger, 1998) or transactive memory (e.g., Cohen & Bacdayan, 1994) have had only a slight impact on organizational cognition research. The absence of attention to this level of analysis in these chapters, which make only occasional tangential reference to the issue, is thus representative of a significant omission and opportunity for the field (Wong & Sitkin, 1999).

In conclusion, these chapters not only provide several complementary and useful frameworks for examining issues of organizational cognition—but perhaps more importantly—they raise a number of issues that can be mined by cognition researchers for years to come.

ACKNOWLEDGMENT

The preparation of this chapter was partially supported by the National Science Foundation (Grants No. SBR-94-22367 and SBR-95-20461)

REFERENCES

Brown, J. S., & Duguid, P. (1991). Organizational learning and communities of practice: Toward a unified view of working, learning and innovation. *Organization Science, 4*, 40–58.

Cardinal, L. C. (1999). Technological innovation in the pharmaceutical industry: The use of control in managing research and development. Under review.

Cohen, M. D., & Bacdayan, P. (1994). Organizational routines are stored as procedural memory. *Organization Science, 5*(4), 554–568.

Cohen, M. D., & Sproull, L. S. (Eds.). (1996). *Organizational learning.* Thousand Oaks, CA: Sage.

Henderson, R. M., & Clark, K. B. (1990). Architectural innovation: The reconfiguration of existing product technologies and the failure of established firms. *Administrative Science Quarterly, 35*, 9–30.

Lave, J. & Wenger, E. (1991). *Situated learning: Legitimate peripheral participation.* New York: Cambridge University Press.

Levinthal, D. A., & March, J. G. (1993). The myopia of learning. *Strategic Management Journal, 14*, 95–112.

March, J. G. (1991). Exploration and exploitation in organizational learning. *Organization Science, 2*, 71–87.

March, J. G. (1995). The future, disposable organizations, and the rigidities of imagination. *Organization, 2*(3/4), 427–440.

Sitkin, S. B. (1992). Learning through failure: The strategy of small losses. In B. Staw & L. Cummings (Eds.), *Research in Organizational Behavior* (Vol. 14, pp. 231–266). Greenwich, CT: JAI.

Sitkin, S. B. (1995). On the positive effects of legalization on trust. In R. Bies, R. Lewicki, & B. Sheppard (Eds.), *Research on negotiation in organizations* (Vol. 5, pp.185–217). Greenwich, CT: JAI.

Sitkin, S. B., Sutcliffe, K. M., & Schroeder, R. G. (1994). Distinguishing control from learning in total quality management: A contingency perspective. *Academy of Management Review, 19,* 537–564.

Suchman, L. (1987). *Plans and situated actions: The problem of human–machine communications.* New York: Cambridge University Press.

Sutcliffe, K. M., Sitkin, S. B., & Browning, L. D. (in press). Tailoring process management to situational requirements: Beyond the control and exploration dichotomy. In R. Cole & W. R. Scott (Eds.), *The quality movement in America: Lessons for theory and research* (pp. 315–330). Thousand Oaks, CA: Sage.

Weick, K. E., Sutcliffe, K. M., & Obstfeld, D. (1999). Organizing for high reliability: Processes of collective mindfulness. In B. Staw & R. Sutton (Eds.), *Research in organizational behavior* (pp. 81–124). Greenwich, CT: JAI.

Wenger, E. (1998). *Communities of practice: Learning, meaning and identity.* New York: Cambridge University Press.

Wong, S., & Sitkin, S. B. (2000). Shaping collective cognition and behavior through collective learning. Working paper. Duke University.

PART

II

Knowledge and Learning in Organizational Settings

5

Shared and Unshared Transactive Knowledge in Complex Organizations: An Exploratory Study

---

Diane Rulke
Royal Holloway, University of London, UK

Srilata Zaheer
University of Minnesota

Scholars and practitioners have identified the management of organizational knowledge as a key source of competitive advantage, particularly in complex organizations that consist of multiple divisions, products, and units. In particular, distributed local knowledge in an organization becomes organizational knowledge when different parts of the organization possess or know where to acquire this knowledge (Lessard & Zaheer, 1996). The problem of integrating and making distributed knowledge widely available is particularly interesting in the complex organization because pockets of knowledge may exist across organizational boundaries and may even span nations and cultures (Bartlett, 1986; Ghoshal & Bartlett, 1988).

This chapter focuses on the extent of shared and unshared knowledge in a complex, multiunit organization and its antecedents and consequences for organizational performance. It identifies two dimensions of *transactive knowledge*—self-knowledge and resource knowledge—where transactive knowledge is the knowledge required for the effective functioning of a group or collective (Liang, Moreland, & Argote, 1995; Wegner, 1986). It examines different learning channels through which transactive knowledge can be transferred into and across an organization. It then develops propositions on which of these learning channels might be more effective in developing shared resource knowledge within the organization and on the effects of shared and unshared resource knowledge on organizational performance.

In developing the propositions and as a first step toward designing measures and instruments that can be used to empirically test them, the authors drew significantly on an exploratory, qualitative study conducted in one firm in the retail foods industry. They report on this study, which they used to develop the dimensions of self- and resource knowledge and of learning channels through cognitive mapping as well as to inform some of their propositions. They also provide some preliminary exploratory analyses from this study and conclude with a discussion of the implications of their work.

The retail food industry is a traditionally low-margin industry that is seeing increasing competition, rapid technological change, and cross-border investments (Connor, 1994). The presence of multinational investment in what one would expect to be a particularly culturally embedded industry signals that this industry is one in which there are areas of firm-specific knowledge that can be exploited across subunits of an organization (Kogut & Zander, 1993). Furthermore, the retail food industry is currently facing a combination of rapid changes in technology and markets and severe competitive pressures. Making the best use of knowledge, especially within the organization, is thus becoming critical for performance in this industry.

THEORY AND PROPOSITIONS

Self- and Resource Knowledge

The effective retrieval and use of existing knowledge within a firm requires managers to not only understand what knowledge their units need to acquire but also where they can go to find the needed knowledge. The literature on knowledge retrieval in groups suggests that both types of knowledge are important to knowledge transfer. Larson and Christensen (1993) indicated that a precondition for effective knowledge transfer is *meta-knowledge*—knowledge about where knowledge resides within the group. Wegner (1986) also suggested that knowledge about what one knows and about what others know allows groups to locate and retrieve information more accurately and effectively, thus outperforming mere sums of individuals. Empirical studies (Hollingshead, 1998; Liang et al., 1995; Rulke & Rau, forthcoming) found support for Wegner's theory.

Drawing from this literature, it is proposed that a necessary condition for knowledge transfer within the organization is the existence of both knowledge about the strengths and limitations of available expertise at the unit level, or *self- knowledge*, and knowledge about where else expertise resides, or *resource knowledge*, among unit managers in a complex organization. Self-knowledge acts in two ways. The unit may require a certain level of expertise even to receive and absorb knowledge (Cohen & Levinthal, 1990). Second, unit managers need to have some depth of understanding of the expertise that exists in their unit to know in which areas the unit's knowledge may need to be augmented. Self-knowledge as defined here is situated in the manager of a particular organizational unit and is the unit manager's assessment of the knowledge residing in that unit.

As for resource knowledge, units whose managers possess wide knowledge about where expertise is located will be in a stronger position to initiate knowledge transfer. Resource knowledge can further be shared or unshared within the organization. An example of resource knowledge that is shared within an organization, and a particularly institutionalized form of shared resource knowledge, is the *Knowledge Resource Directory* published annually by McKinsey and Company, which is distributed to all of its consultants. This directory lists by function and by business sector individuals in the company who are particularly knowledgeable in specific areas. However, formal resource knowledge of this type, if it exists at all, is likely to be a very small part of the resource knowledge of most firms. In most firms, and particularly in complex organizations, there are likely to be pockets of resource knowledge that remain unshared across the organization, and resource knowledge is likely to be unevenly distributed across subunits.

In a complex organization, the problem of diffusing or sharing resource knowledge can be nontrivial as different parts of the organization are geographically dispersed and there may be little ongoing face-to-face interaction among managers that may be required for the transfer of such knowledge to take place (Nonaka, 1990). Furthermore, the cost of transfer of organizational knowledge can be significant (Teece, 1977). In this situation, the learning channels or processes used within the organization for knowledge transfer become important.

Learning Channels

To understand the types of learning mechanisms that might facilitate the transfer of self- and resource knowledge in complex organizations, the authors draw from the literatures on social networks and group communication. Prior research found that personal relationships and social networks indeed facilitate learning and the transfer of practices (Galaskiewicz & Wasserman, 1989; Huberman, 1983; Liebenz, 1982). Researchers who work in the area of transactive knowledge in groups have suggested that both self- and resource knowledge can be acquired either explicitly through formal mechanisms or, as is more usual, implicitly through interaction between group members (Hollingshead, 1998; Rulke & Rau, 1996). Research in organizations has shown that managers may make deliberate efforts to acquire and disseminate knowledge (Berry, 1994; Holyoak & Spellman, 1993) or to learn about best practices through personal contacts (Holyoak & Spellman, 1993). Thus, two basic types of learning channels are identified in the literature that may be important to the transfer of self- and resource knowledge: purposive learning channels designed to explicitly disseminate or acquire knowledge and relational learning channels that might facilitate informal knowledge transfer. Furthermore, both purposive and relational learning can occur from internal or from external sources.

In a complex organization, it is likely that these learning channels will contribute to the development and transfer of both self- and resource knowledge. Purposive learning channels are often explicitly designed to transmit knowledge. In formal training sessions in a firm, for example, one would expect specific knowledge about key industry practices to be imparted, contributing to self-knowledge. Trade journals often carry stories about best practices. These purposive learning channels allow benchmarking of units and give managers the information they need to assess the capabilities of their units in different areas. Managers can also directly bring the knowledge they acquire through these purposive channels to bear in improving the capabilities of the unit that they manage. Relational learning channels can also provide some direct knowledge of key practices from the contacts that the focal manager maintains whether within or outside the organization.

The transfer of resource knowledge in complex organizations is likely to be both difficult and costly (Kogut & Zander, 1993; Teece, 1977). In particular, the transfer of resource knowledge may require taking it through the tacit-explicit-tacit cycle (Nonaka & Takeuchi, 1995) as resource knowledge is essentially tacit but may have to be made explicit to be communicated across subunits of the organization where it will again be internalized and become tacit. It is suggested that in such a situation, purposive learning channels may be better at taking resource knowledge through the tacit-explicit part of the cycle and therefore lead to effective transmission of resource knowledge across organizational subunits. Examples of such tacit-explicit mechanisms might include the McKinsey *Knowledge Resource Directory* mentioned earlier, computerized databases on resource knowledge, or newsletters from the head office that are often used for the dissemination of resource knowledge. On the other hand, relational learning channels may be better at taking resource knowledge through the explicit-tacit part of the cycle as informal person-to-person contacts may better provide the context and the values that facilitate the internalization of knowledge. This leads to the proposition:

> Proposition 1: Purposive and relational learning channels will both facilitate the transfer of self- and resource knowledge in complex organizations. Purposive channels will facilitate the making of tacit knowledge explicit, whereas relational channels will facilitate the internalization of knowledge.

Shared and Unshared Resource Knowledge

Research in psychology has suggested that shared knowledge about where knowledge is available creates a group memory system that is richer than the sum of individual members' memories (Wegner, 1986). The foundation for this system lies in the fact that team members know about each others' expertise so that the group may pool the knowledge that exists in the group when solving problems or in producing a product (Liang et al., 1995). Resource knowledge that is shared among several members of the group enables the group to retrieve and to implement this knowledge when needed. Drawing parallels from this literature to the level of subunits within an organization, the extent of *shared resource knowledge* in a complex organization is defined as the extent to which resource knowledge is commonly held (i.e., the extent of overlaps in resource knowledge) across subunit managers.

Propositions on which types of learning channels might lead to greater shared resource knowledge are now developed. As suggested earlier, the deliberateness inherent in purposive learning channels may be more effective in the transmission of certain types of knowledge in complex organizations. Thus, for distributed local resource knowledge to become shared organizational resource knowledge, purposive learning channels might be more effective in creating more of a shared knowledge base among subunits. We therefore propose that:

> Proposition 2: The greater the exposure of subunits to purposive learning channels, the greater will be the extent of shared resource knowledge across the subunits of a complex organization.

The authors' exploratory study revealed that there are several dimensions to resource knowledge such as its breadth, in terms of its geographic coverage, and its variety, in terms of the types of sources cited. They suggest that relational learning channels facilitate tacit-to-tacit transfer (Nonaka & Takeuchi, 1995), and hence will lead to more effective transmission of localized or even personal knowledge across subunits. Therefore, it is expected that subunits that are exposed to relational learning channels will be more aware of discrete local pockets of knowledge within and outside the organization that may not be part of the organization's shared resource knowledge. This leads us to hypothesize that:

> Proposition 3: The greater the exposure of a subunit to relational learning channels, the more resource knowledge it will have that is outside the scope of the organization's shared resource knowledge.

Finally, this chapter makes the link between the characteristics of a subunit's resource knowledge—the extensiveness of each subunit's unique or unshared knowledge—and its performance, controlling for exogenous economic factors. The authors distinguish between performance that is static and efficiency driven and innovation performance, which essentially captures the capacity of the organization to change and grow. It is suggested that a higher degree of overlap between a subunit's resource knowledge and the organization's shared resource knowledge indicates greater integration of the subunit into the organization. This integration, in turn, is likely to lead to rapid diffusion of existing best practices within the firm and a greater focus on efficiency, thus contributing to the units' performance in those terms. This leads us to propose that:

> Proposition 4: The greater the extent of overlap between a subunit's resource knowledge and the organization's shared resource knowledge, the better the subunit's performance in terms of efficiency, all else being equal.

In terms of innovation performance, however, the picture is likely to be quite different. Researchers studying group decision making have argued that unshared knowledge (knowledge that is not shared by all group members but only by a few) can provide new innovative ideas in organizations and facilitate group problem solving (Stasser & Titus, 1985). In a parallel vein but from a different discipline, sociologists have argued that being exposed to knowledge that is not shared by an individual's inner circle through weak ties (Granovetter, 1973) can lead to superior information and outcomes. Drawing on these ideas, this chapter suggests that subunits that have resource knowledge that is not widely shared by the rest of the organization will perform better on the innovation dimension than those whose resource knowledge is limited to what is widely shared in the organization. This leads us to an alternative proposition:

> Proposition 5: The more extensive a subunit's unshared resource knowledge is, the better its innovation performance, all else being equal.

The following section describes an exploratory qualitative study that informed the development of these propositions as well as paved the way toward creating measures and methods that could be used to test these propositions.

AN EXPLORATORY STUDY OF RETAIL FOOD STORES

To test propositions on the extent of shared and unique knowledge across subunits, the authors needed to develop robust methods to assess the fairly subtle characteristics of self- and resource knowledge as well as evaluate the measures of subunits' exposure to different learning channels. They also needed to determine how best concepts such as subunit performance or subunit innovation performance could be measured. The rest of this chapter describes an exploratory study used to develop cognitive maps of subunit managers, which were analyzed to determine some of these subunit characteristics. The subunits in the study were all the 11 grocery stores belonging to one regional retail food chain. The subunit general manager's knowledge was used as a proxy for subunit knowledge, which does not pose too much of a problem in this industry context as the store general manager is the only individual in the store with any real decision-making authority.

Data Collection

To develop cognitive maps of the self- and resource knowledge held by subunit general managers, a combination of in-depth semistructured interviews, analyzed using qualitative content analysis techniques was used, as well as factual data collected from both primary and secondary sources. The interview and survey were structured in three parts. In the first part, data was gathered to develop cognitive maps of the store managers' self- and resource knowledge. The concept of resource knowledge was explored by asking them simple, open-ended questions on who does this best about specific areas that were rated as critical to growth and performance in the retail foods industry (e.g., home meal replacements, shelf-space management, etc.). The areas of interest chosen for this analysis were arrived at after extensive pilot interviews at other supermarket chains, discussions with industry experts, visits to trade shows, and material gathered from trade magazines. The depth of self-knowledge was further rated by probing how much the managers knew about these areas in the qualitative analysis and by an assessment in the structured portion of the interview of how the managers rated their stores compared to industry leaders in those areas. The second part of the interview–survey focused on the channels through which the store managers had acquired knowledge. The interview–survey concluded with demographic information on the respondent.

The interviews were taped and transcribed to facilitate the qualitative analysis and typically lasted from 1.5 to 2 hours each. The transcribed interviews ran to more than 200 pages of single-spaced text. The participants were all 11 general managers with overall profit responsibility for their subunit. The researchers had been introduced to each of the general managers by a memo from the Vice President in charge of Strategic Planning at the headquarters of the chain. All interviewees were promised confidentiality. The primary researchers conducted all the interviews, except one.

Factual Measures

For the construct capturing efficiency-driven performance, it was determined that readily available hard performance data such as sales per square foot, number of customers per week, and average transaction size could be used. In the course of discussions, it became clear that a major thrust of the retail foods industry, and one that the industry believes is critical to its success, is the whole area of home-meal replacements or the provision of ready-to-eat dinners that people can grab and go. The criticality of this area to the continued success and survival of this industry is not in doubt as over the past decade, supermarkets have been steadily losing marketshare to restaurants and to fast-food outlets in dollars spent on food by the American consumer (Kinsey & Senauer, 1996). Therefore, researchers created a measure of the percentage of store sales from the deli as a measure of the store's innovation performance because supermarkets all try and increase their sales of value-added food products to the consumer.

From the extensive discussions prior to this study with executives in the industry and from an examination of the literature on learning channels, the researchers had elicited a list of learning channels, including formal as well as informal, social learning channels, to which managers might be exposed. As part of the structured portion of the interview, managers were asked to rate their exposure to 10 different learning channels.

For the cognitive dimensions of a manager's self- and resource knowledge, a qualitative content analysis of the semistructured interviews, accompanied by a brief, personally administered questionnaire was used.

Qualitative Analysis Methodology

The semistructured interviews were analyzed using the QSR NUD.IST 3.0 software for qualitative data analysis (Qualitative Solution and Research, 1995). QSR NUD.IST is a textual analysis software system designed to support and manage qualitative data analysis projects. It allows the analysis of unstructured data and the development of hierarchical trees of concepts and themes from a content analysis of textual material. The transcribed interviews were analyzed with the software by first developing a set of coding categories that reflected aspects of manager's self- and resource knowledge. Each of the two researchers read through the transcribed interviews several times identifying possible categories of self and resource knowledge. They then sat together and discussed the categories identified and arrived at a final list designed to be as extensive and inclusive as possible. The categories identified included measures of the geographic breadth of a manager's resource knowledge and variety in identified sources for resource knowledge. In assessing self-knowledge, the depth of the manager's understanding of specific areas (a measure of judgmental accuracy) as well as their understanding of their store's capabilities relative to industry leaders emerged as key coding categories. Other issues that emerged in the interviews were also coded including the learning channels used as well as what the managers thought of the various best practices that are being discussed in the industry. As mentioned earlier, a list of such practices was developed from earlier pilot interviews with other firms in the industry and from trade publications. In addition, data was collected on the factual characteristics of each store and the demographic characteristics of the general manager. Figure 5.1 shows the hierarchical tree structure used in analyzing the text.

The following describes the categories of resource knowledge, self-knowledge, and learning mechanisms that were coded from the text.

Measures

Resource Knowledge.   With the semistructured interview format, there were many open-ended opportunities for interviewees to talk about their knowledge of where new ideas and good practices were to be found. The breadth of resource knowledge category picked up the number of times the respondent mentioned different cities, U. S. states, and foreign

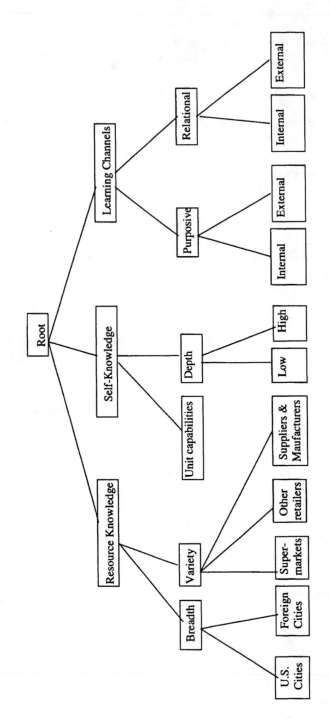

FIG. 5.1 Coding transactive knowledge in the retail food industry.

countries as locations where there were stores that were particularly good at some aspect of the business. To capture the variety of resource knowledge in managers' mindsets, researchers coded the extent to which managers mentioned other supermarket chains, other nonsupermarket retailers, and other industry participants such as manufacturers, wholesalers, suppliers, and trade associations in their discussion.

Self Knowledge.   In reading through the transcripts, it became evident that although self-knowledge in the groups literature (e.g., Liang et al., 1995) can be completely captured by the knowledge possessed by an individual, when trying to measure self-knowledge at the unit or organizational level, it needed to be measured slightly differently. In particular, researchers needed to take into account two elements in measuring unit self-knowledge from interviews with managers: the depth of a unit manager's personal knowledge of different areas of best practice (which can be construed almost as a measure of judgmental accuracy) as well as the manager's assessment of the unit's capabilities in each of those areas. To capture a manager's depth of knowledge in each area of interest, researchers coded high depth by the number of times respondents mentioned the specifics of various practices and used statistics and technical terms in their descriptions of practices. Low depth was coded from their use of language that exhibited confusion and lack of knowledge by the presence of phrases such as "I don't know," "I'm guessing," "What do you mean," and so on. The counts of how many text units (lines of speech) that contained mentions of these concepts was normalized by the total number of text units spoken by each manager (as some were more verbose than others), to get measures for each manager that captured the proportion of their interview they devoted to the concept. These proportions were used in the correlation analyses that follow. To measure the manager's assessment of the capabilities of their unit in each area of interest, researchers used their rating of their units in each of the areas of best practice compared to leaders in the field on a seven-point Likert-type scale that was obtained in the structured questionnaire.

Table 5.1 focuses on the relationships between the emergent dimensions of breadth and variety of resource knowledge and the depth of self-knowledge that appeared in the qualitative analysis. The correlations between the variables that constituted the constructs of breadth, variety and depth are reported in Table 5.1.

The results showed that the two dimensions of geographic breadth were highly correlated. Managers who were aware of innovations in other U. S. cit-

TABLE 5.1

Correlations Among Variables That Make Up the Cognitive Characteristics of a Manager's Knowledge (Values Presented Here are Normalized Scores Multiplied by 1,000)

Construct/Variable	Mean	SD	1	2	3	4	5	6	7	8	9
RESOURCE KNOWLEDGE											
Breadth of cognition											
1 Other U.S. Cities	8.39	5.64	1.00								
2 Foreign locations	0.49	1.62	0.64**	1.00							
Cognitive variety											
3 Other supermarkets	18.30	7.23	0.18	-0.30	1.00						
4 Nongrocery retailers	6.34	4.16	-0.00	-0.01	-0.14	1.00					
5 Manufacturers	1.12	1.37	0.11	-0.00	-0.16	0.22	1.00				
6 Wholesalers	8.47	2.18	0.12	0.05	-0.08	-0.11	0.72**	1.00			
7 Associations	2.94	1.38	0.05	-0.20	0.48*	0.00	-0.02	-0.03	1.00		
SELF-KNOWLEDGE											
9 Low-cognitive depth	34.83	115.23	-0.10	-0.10	-0.01	0.65***	-0.19	-0.52	-0.28	0.12	1.00
10 High-cognitive depth	14.5	37.94	0.42	-0.20	0.46	-0.00	0.57**	0.41	0.13	-0.20	-0.30

*P < 0.5.
**P < 0.01.
***P < 0.001.

94

ies were also aware of innovations that occurred in foreign locations. The number of times a manager mentioned other U. S. cities and foreign locations was averaged to measure geographic breadth. The reliability for this construct is 0.64. Two significant relations emerged among the dimensions of cognitive diversity that were coded (Table 5.1). The first indicated that those managers who were aware of what was going on in other supermarkets were also aware of the activities of industrial associations. Furthermore, managers who were aware of a range of manufacturers' practices were also aware of wholesalers' practices. The number of times a manager mentioned other supermarkets, nongrocery chains, manufacturers, wholesalers, and industrial associations was averaged to measure cognitive variety. The reliability for cognitive variety is about 0.52. Although this is low, as researchers are trying to capture the range of a manager's cognition with this construct, they do not necessarily expect high inter-item correlations (i.e., a manager who is aware of practices at a number of other supermarkets may not also be aware of practices at a similar number of manufacturers, although together these variables reflect the number of different sources the manager is aware of).

Learning Channels. This study focused on two types of learning mechanisms or learning channels—purposive and relational. Purposive learning channels include deliberate efforts to disseminate knowledge and to learn such as formal training programs, internal knowledge dissemination efforts such as newsletters, benchmarking visits to competitors stores, vists to conferences, and trade shows undertaken for the specific purpose of learning. The extent to which managers were exposed to 10 such purposive and relational mechanisms were measured on 7-point Likert-type scales. A factor analysis of these 10 learning mechanisms confirmed the two basic types of channels identified. The reliability (Cronbach's Alpha) of the construct of purposive learning channels, which included exposure to formal training programs, newsletters, visits to competitors stores, conferences, and trade shows, was 0.795. Relational learning channels included more passive chance learning such as that from personal contacts in leading supermarkets, third-party visitors (such as manufacturers, wholesalers, and other suppliers), and contacts with other managers in the firm. The reliability (Cronbach's Alpha) of the construct of relational learning channels was 0.81.

The extent of shared and unique knowledge was also calculated. In this particular firm, there was little variability across subunits on this dimension as the extent of shared knowledge was very high (ranging between 0.95 and

0.99). That is not surprising considering that the stores are all within 2-hour drives from each other and the store general managers visit each other's stores and meet frequently.

RESULTS AND DISCUSSION

As this study is primarily a qualitative study meant to refine the constructs and the methods used to develop measures of cognitive depth, breadth and variety from textual analysis of qualitative data, discussion at this stage is restricted to just the correlations among the major constructs. Even in interpreting these correlations, caution is urged, as the sample is not large enough to make definitive statements. Table 5.2 provides the simple statistics associated with the main constructs. Table 5.3 reports the correlations among the major constructs: the breadth, variety and depth of subunit managers' knowledge, their exposure to purposive and relational learning channels, and measures of store performance and characteristics as well as the years of experience of the store general manager.

Certain relations that emerged among these constructs are quite interesting. Surprisingly, sales per square foot, a traditional measure of store performance, was negatively related to most of the resource knowledge variables, and particularly to the managers' geographic breadth of resource knowledge. From an analysis of the interviews, it became apparent that

TABLE 5.2

Descriptive Statistics of Variables Measured in the Study

Variable	Mean	SD	Minimum	Maximum
Geographic breadth	4.44	3.39	0.67	12.33
Cognitive variety	7.43	2.24	4.04	10.68
Low cognitive depth	34.83	14.50	15.20	66.90
High cognitive depth	115.23	37.94	68.70	209.00
Purposive learning	4.69	1.10	2.83	6.33
Relational learning	4.57	0.87	3.50	6.00
Innovation performance	14.15	4.06	9.70	22.50
Sales per square foot ($)	7.72	1.53	4.74	10.19
Size of store (square feet)	58,454.55	15,474.91	35,000	95,000
Manager's experience (years)	27.27	7.95	16.00	40.00

TABLE 5.3

Correlations Among Characteristics of Knowledge, Learning Channels, and Store Performance

Variable	Geographic Breadth (GB)	Cognitive Variety (CV)	Low Depth (LD)	High Depth (HD)	Purposive Learning (PL)	Relational Learning (RL)	Innovation Performance (IP)	Sales per square foot (SSF)	Size of Store	Manager's Experience (Exp)
GB										
CV	.47									
LD	.15	.36								
HD	.30	.82***	.15							
PL	-.63	-.78**	-.64	-.73*						
RL	-.53	-.48	-.63	-.23	.52					
IP	.18	-.06	-.57*	.03	.05	.45				
SSF	-.67**	-.26	-.11	-.34	.67*	.25	-.25			
Size	-.24	-.08	-.32	.02	.21	.48	-.14	.67		
Exp	.66**	.10	.01	.07	-.12	-.002	.55*	-.80***	-.65	

*P < 0.1.
**P < 0.05.
***P < 0.005.

some of the managers who displayed great breadth of resource knowledge had fairly recently been sent to manage stores that were not performing too well. This suggests that perhaps the reverse relation may in fact be holding—that managers with greater resource knowledge are being sent to turn around poorly performing stores, which results in a negative correlation between sales per square foot and managers' resource knowledge. This reverse hypothesis also receives support from the strong negative relations between experience and sales per square foot.

When the percentage sales from deli were examined, a measure of the innovation performance of the store, there were different results. For one, as might be expected, the more confusion and lack of knowledge a manager expressed (low depth of cognition), the lower his or her store's innovation performance was likely to be. Experience, on the other hand, was associated with improved innovation performance.

As for the purposive and relational learning channels, managers who were involved with purposive learning channels (formal training, active benchmarking, etc.) tended to be located in stores with high sales per square foot. Involvement with purposive learning was uncorrelated with innovation performance, however. Managers with clear and in-depth understanding of practices in the industry (high depth of cognition) tended not to be involved in purposive learning. As for relational learning channels (personal relationships with leading firms or with other managers in the firm), there was a positive but nonsignificant correlation between sales per square foot and relational learning. These results strengthen the belief that the cognition and learning constructs are indeed picking up what they are meant to pick up, based on the textual analysis of the semistructured interviews.

Discussion

In this chapter, the authors introduce the concepts of self- and resource knowledge in a complex organization and develop propositions on the links between the extent of shared and unshared knowledge across subunits and their exposure to relational and purposive learning channels and subunit performance. In a complex organization where knowledge is distributed across multiple subunits (Lessard & Zaheer, 1996), an effective transactive knowledge system in which managers of each unit are aware of their unit's capabilities and of what other units within the corporation know may be a precondition for continuous learning and improvement.

The authors also develop a method of extracting cognitive maps of managers' self- and resource knowledge through formal textual analysis of semistructured interviews. The results indicate that this method of assessing the breadth, depth, and variety of managers' knowledge can yield robust constructs. Knowledge has always been one of the most difficult concepts to measure in an organization. This approach is offered as one possible method of trying to come to grips with this concept.

The concepts of shared and unshared knowledge in complex organizations and their differential impact on efficiency versus innovation performance are also interesting as avenues for research as well as for managers. In brief, the authors suggest that extensive knowledge sharing and knowledge integration within the firm might lead to medium-term efficiency but might lead to killing the golden egg in terms of maintaining the pockets of unshared knowledge that contribute to variety and lead to innovation in the long run. It is suspected, however, that most complex organizations are far from running into the danger of too much internal knowledge sharing, given the cost and difficulty involved in such sharing (Chakravarthy, Zaheer, & Zaheer, 1999). However, it was interesting to find that the particular supermarket chain studied did have this problem, leading to a fair amount of groupthink and an inability to come up with really new and innovative ideas.

REFERENCES

Bartlett, C. (1986). Building and managing the transnational. In M. Porter (Ed.), *Competition in global industries* (pp. 367–404). Boston, MA: HBS Press.

Berry, D. C. (1994). Implicit and explicit learning of complex tasks. In N. Ellis (Ed.), *Implicit and explicit learning of languages* (pp. 147–164). London: Academic Press.

Chakravarthy, B., Zaheer, A., & Zaheer, S. (1999). *Creating value through sharing* (Working Paper). Minneapolis, MN: Strategic Management Research Center, University of Minnesota.

Cohen W. M., & Levinthal, D. A. (1990). Absorptive capacity: A new perspective on learning and innovation. *Administrative Science Quarterly, 35,* 128–152.

Connor, J. M. (1994). *Patterns of foreign direct investment in the 50 states: Focus on the food system.* West Lafayette, IN: Purdue University Agricultural Experiment Station.

Galaskiewicz, J., & Wasserman, S. (1989). Mimetic processes within an interorganizational field: An empirical test. *Administrative Science Quarterly, 28,* 22–39.

Ghoshal, S., & Bartlett, C. (1988). Creation, adoption and diffusion of innovations by subsidiaries of multinational corporations. *Journal of International Business Studies, 19,* 365–388.

Granovetter, M. (1973). The strength of weak ties. *American Journal of Sociology, 78,* 1360–1380.

Hollingshead, A. B. (1998). Retrieval processes in transactive memory systems. *Journal of Personality and Social Psychology, 74*(3), 659–671.

Holyoak, K. J., & Spellman, B. A. (1993). Thinking. *Annual Review of Psychology, 44,* 265–315.

Huberman, A. M. (1983). Improving social practice through the utilization of university-based knowledge. *Higher Education, 12,* 257–272.

Kinsey, J., & Senauer, B. (1996). Consumer trends and changing food retailing formats. *In Changes in retail food delivery: Signals for producers, processors and distributors* (pp. 1–17). (Working Paper #96-03). Minneapolis, MN: The Retail Food Industry Center, University of Minnesota.

Kogut, B., & Zander, U. (1993). Knowledge of the firm and the evolutionary theory of the multinational corporation. *Journal of International Business Studies, 24*(4), 625–645.

Larson, J. R., & Christensen, C. (1993). Groups as problem-solving units: Toward a new meaning of social cognition. *British Journal of Social Psychology, 32*, 5–30.

Lessard, D. R., & Zaheer, S. (1996). Breaking the silos: Distributed knowledge and strategic responsiveness to volatile exchange rates. *Strategic Management Journal, 17*(7), 513–534.

Liang, D. W., Moreland, R., & Argote, L. (1995). Group versus individual training and group performance: The mediating role of transactive memory. *Personality and Social Psychology Bulletin, 21*(4), 384–393.

Liebenz, M. L. (1982). *Transfer of technology: U. S. multinationals and Eastern Europe.* New York: Praeger.

Nonaka, I. (1990). Managing globalization as a self-renewing process: Experiences of Japanese MNCs. In C. A. Bartlett, Y. Doz, & G. Hedlund (Eds.), *Managing the global firm* (pp. 69–94). Boston: Routledge & Kegon Paul.

Nonaka, I., & Takeuchi, H. (1995). *The knowledge creating company.* New York: Oxford University Press.

Qualitative Solutions and Research. (1995). QSR NUD-IST: Qualitative data analysis software for research professionals, guide. Thousand Oaks, CA: Scolari (Sage).

Rulke, D. L., & Rau, D. (in press). Investigating the encoding process of transactive memory development in group training. *Group and Organization Management.*

Stasser, G., & Titus, W. (1985). Pooling of unshared information in group decision making: Biased information sampling during group discussion. Journal of Personality and Social Psychology, 48, 1467–1478.

Teece, D. (1977). Technology transfer by multinational firms: The resource cost of transferring technological know-how. *Economic Journal, 87*, 242–261.

Wegner, D. M. (1986). Transactive memory: A contemporary analysis of the group mind. In G. Mullen & G. Geothals (Eds.), *Theories of group behavior* (pp. 185–208). New York: Springer-Verlag.

6

Internal Dissemination of Learning From Loan Loss Crises

Catherine Paul-Chowdhury
Robert H. Schaffer & Associates

Canada's five major banks have realized inadequate returns in their large corporate lending businesses during the past several business cycles (Paul-Chowdhury, 1995). This lack of profitability over the business cycle is largely due to the banks' history of lending heavily in a few credit-hungry sectors at deteriorating margins and with increasingly lenient loan structures, then showing unexpectedly high levels of problem loans when these sectors experience difficulty. Since 1982, Canadian banks have suffered three episodes of heavy, sector-specific loan losses: in developing country (LDC) debt in the early 1980s, in the energy sector in the early to mid-1980s, and in commercial real estate from 1990 to 1993.

This recurring failure to manage credit risk is not a uniquely Canadian phenomenon. British and Japanese banks experienced serious sector-specific losses during the same time frame (Freeman, 1993), and U.S. banks in particular have shown a repeating loan loss pattern similar to that of Canadian banks (Stevenson & Fadil, 1994). Factors identified as contributing to these events include: lack of pricing discipline as competition intensified, emphasis on short-term earning objectives resulting in aggressive loan growth and high concentrations, and the deterioration in borrower credit quality resulting from disintermediation (Freeman, 1993; Stevenson & Fadil, 1994; "Survey of World Banking," 1992).

The recurring nature of these loan loss crises and the similarities in contributing factors across episodes raise intriguing questions for researchers of organizational learning. How does learning occur after such loan loss events? Why do lessons not seem to be applied effectively to other situations? How are the lessons disseminated, or is their transfer across business units or time blocked in some predictable way? How do the organizations remember what they have learned from lending crises, and why is their memory apparently so short?

This chapter focuses specifically on the dissemination of lessons from loan loss events within each bank. The recurring nature of the sector-specific loan loss events and the apparent similarities across events (deteriorating loan structures, increasingly high levels of risk, and over-concentration in specific companies and industry sectors) would seem to indicate to even a casual observer that the lessons learned after one event were not well disseminated within the banks. This study confirms the observation.

With a few industry-specific additions, the lessons reported from the real estate loan losses bear a striking resemblance to those attributed to the energy sector losses in two of the three banks studied. This similarity did not escape notice within Bank A. The executive charged with leading the bank's efforts to recover money on the troubled real estate loans in Ontario (as he had done in Western Canada a decade before) took the report that explained why the bank had experienced such heavy losses in the energy sector and replaced all references to *energy* with *real estate*. The resulting memo provided as accurate a description of why the bank had lost so much in real estate lending as it had for energy. This incident provides a concise illustration of the point that although Bank A appeared to learn from its losses in the early 1980s, these lessons were not applied to real estate lending in Ontario in the late 1980s and early 1990s. Failure to apply these lessons cost the bank close to $4 billion in loan loss provisions over 2 years. The question addressed in this chapter is why these lessons were not transferred within the banks.

DISSEMINATION OF LEARNING

Interpreting and distributing information are integral parts of the learning process (Huber, 1991). In an organizational setting, these are often interpersonal or social activities (Brown, 1992; Brown & Duguid, 1991; Huber, 1991; Weick, 1979, 1995; Wenger, 1991).

Wenger (1991) and Brown & Duguid (1991) characterized learning as a form of membership that evolves as the individual functions within a community of practice. Communities of practice evolve spontaneously around common tasks and values. This suggests that lessons are naturally disseminated within communities of practice as people bring their ideas and experiences to bear on the tasks at hand. It also suggests that transferring lessons across communities of practice may be as important (and as difficult) as transferring them across boundaries on an organizational chart.

The dissemination of individually learned lessons within and across groups in an organization may be viewed as a process whereby many competing interpretations are whittled down to a single or a few dominant and widely held interpretations. Research suggests that which interpretations finally emerge as dominant is a function of at least four factors. First, the meaning that is socially sustained is likely to be one that is favorable to the organization, promoting self-enhancement, efficacy, and consistency (Weick, 1995). Second, interpretations of past events will be affected by the current situation (Olsen, 1976; Weick, 1995). Third, the interpretation that is socially sustained is likely to be that of a powerful individual or group (Daft & Weick, 1984; Weick, 1992). And finally, interpretation in a cohesive group will also be affected by social desires to maintain the harmony of the group and not rock the boat (Janis, 1972).

After lessons have been disseminated through key decision-making groups and gained support among these people, some of the lessons are then institutionalized in organizational processes, policies, or structures. These institutionalized elements comprise a major and important part of organizational memory (Cyert & March, 1963; Levitt & March, 1988; Nelson & Winter, 1982; Simon, 1976; Walsh & Ungson, 1991). Through their influence on behavior—the rules and routines people follow, whom they work with and talk to—institutionalized lessons continue to be disseminated to people who may not have learned them otherwise and, over time, even after the people who originally learned them have left the organization. However, as repositories for an organization's experience, they are not perfect. Not all of an organization's experience is transformed into policies or processes (Levitt & March, 1988). Even when experience has been captured in an organization's routines, that memory may be lost through lack of use (Nelson & Winter, 1982).

The processes by which experience is institutionalized are not well understood (Levitt & March, 1988). However, the relationship between individual or group power and the dominant interpretation has already been noted (Daft & Weick, 1984; Weick, 1992), suggesting that the lessons learned by senior management are more likely to be disseminated both through social interaction and through institutionalized structures. Changing management is a frequently noted way of introducing a new perspective to a group (e.g., Hedberg, 1981). Research also suggests that there may be a window soon after the loan loss event when dissatisfaction with performance is high and change is most likely (Lant, Milliken, & Batra, 1992; Lant & Montgomery, 1987; Simon, 1976). One might therefore expect that an organization would be more likely to institutionalize its lessons soon after a loan loss event or other financial crisis.

Institutionalized organizational elements are both an evolving result of and a constraint on organizational learning. They function as a mechanism for disseminating lessons but also limit what is transferred and learned. Although they do not necessarily determine actual organizational behaviors (Brown, 1992; Nelson & Winter, 1982), they do act as a guide to what is likely and what is rewarded, and a constraint on what is possible (Nelson & Winter, 1982). In this way, previous organizational learning as it is expressed in processes, policies, structures, and strategy acts as a guide and a constraint on individual- and group-level learning (Hedberg, 1981; Levitt & March, 1988).

In particular, organizational theorists and observers have noted that hierarchical organizational structures inhibit communication among functions and divisions, and that information must flow upward to those who have decision-making authority, then downward through the hierarchy in the form of decisions (Ashkenas, Ulrich, Jick, & Kerr, 1995; Hoskisson & Hitt, 1994; Ostroff & Smith, 1993; West & Meyer, 1997). Until about 1985, the large Canadian banks had enjoyed a relatively stable operating environment. They are organized in a hierarchical structure of control, authority, and communication, with a high degree of task definition and specialization. In short, the banks have evolved as mechanistic structures (Burns & Stalker, 1961). This implies that communication of knowledge will tend to move in an up and down direction, with people higher in the organization having broader access to knowledge than those lower down. It also implies the tendency for work behavior to be governed by the decisions and instructions of more senior people, with relatively little influence from peers, particularly from different organizational functions or groups.

In a rare study of the impediments to the transfer of best practices within the firm, Szulanski (1996) noted that although strategic management research has examined impediments to the transfer of best practices between firms, impediments to transferring capabilities within firms have received little attention. Distilling a quantity of prior research from areas including resource-based competition and technological innovation, Szulanski identified four sets of factors that are likely to increase the difficulty of knowledge transfer. These are: characteristics of the knowledge transferred, characteristics of the source of knowledge, characteristics of the recipient of knowledge, and characteristics of the organizational context. Within each of these factors, salient elements are summarized in Table 6.1. Szulanski's study identified the recipients' lack of absorptive capacity, causal ambiguity, and an arduous relationship between source and recipient as the three most important barriers to the transfer of best practice knowledge.

METHODOLOGY

Data Collection

This chapter is based on an exploratory field study, the purpose of which was to examine the phenomenon of recurring loan loss events to understand how the banks learned from these events. The research was conducted in three major banks selected from the population of Canada's five largest Schedule A banks. This population was chosen because each of the firms experienced, to varying extents, the same three loan loss episodes since 1984:

TABLE 6.1

Factors Likely to Increase the Difficulty of Knowledge Transfer

Characteristics of knowledge transferred
Causal ambiguity
Unprovenness
Characteristics of the source of knowledge
Lack of motivation
Not perceived as reliable
Characteristics of recipient of knowledge
Lack of motivation
Lack of absorptive capacity
Lack of retentive capacity
Characteristics of the context
Barren organizational context
Arduous relationship

Source: Szulanski (1996)

in the LDC, energy, and commercial real estate sectors. That they experienced the same three events allows for both within-bank comparisons of the phenomenon of interest across three episodes and across-bank comparison with respect to any one episode. Drawing cases from within this population also controls for extraneous variation due to environmental and industry conditions, product characteristics, and firm size, and helps to define the limits of generalizability of the findings (Eisenhardt, 1989; Pettigrew, 1990).

A preliminary study of publicly available financial data took a rough cut at measuring bank learning, using performance measures (including Provision for Credit Losses divided by Net Interest Income and Return on Equity as indicators. This study's findings divided the banks into two groups: those that appeared to exhibit some cumulative learning across loan loss episodes and those whose performance did not show evidence of such cumulative learning. Research was conducted in one bank from the first group (C) and two banks from the second group (A and B). This design allowed Bank A to be used as a starting point for addressing the central management problem: why learning did not appear to take place. The other two banks were chosen to provide theoretical replication (Yin, 1984), with Bank B expected to show a similar pattern and reasons for the apparently blocked learning, and Bank C expected to show a different and more effective learning pattern.

Within each bank, semistructured interviews and archival data were used to construct the stories of each of the three sector-specific loan loss events. What were the internal and market conditions leading up to each loan loss event? What lessons were reported as having been learned? How were these lessons disseminated and remembered through changes in structures, policies, processes, and so on following each loan loss episode? Specifically, the research focuses on the rules, structures, and routines governing the corporate credit and related risk management processes before and after each loan loss episode. It seeks to understand what changes occurred as a result of each episode and how these changes came about.

Where possible for each of the three loan loss episodes, interviews were conducted with people representing each of the four key groups involved in large corporate or international credits: line or account management, credit, risk management, and workout.[1] The majority of interviews were with bank executives holding the position of vice president or higher. Interviews were taped and varied in length from approximately 45 to 120 minutes. Archival

---

[1]Today it is not uncommon for the credit granting function to reside in the risk management department and for its employees to be called *risk managers*. For the purposes of this research, however, *risk management* refers to the function that monitors risk, including but not limited to credit risk, at a higher, nontransactional level. *Workout* refers to the group of people who recover or work out a bank's problem loans.

data were gathered on an opportunistic basis from interviewees and from corporate libraries and archives. The amounts and types of archival data available varied considerably across banks. However, each bank yielded unique and rich archival material. In total, 98 interviews across the three banks and more than 600 internal and public documents comprised the data set.

Data Analysis

The general approach to data organization and analysis was to become familiar with each case individually (within-case analysis), then compare and contrast across cases in search of patterns (cross-case analysis) (Eisenhardt, 1989). Interviews were transcribed, then each one was coded twice, once to yield the *what* story and once to yield the *how* story.

The *what* story coding bins included build-up to loan loss event, changes in structure, changes in policy and so on. Augmented by the archival data, the coded interviews were then summarized in a detailed chronological story for each bank, describing what had occurred in the build-up to each loan loss event, reported lessons, and the organization-level changes following the event.

The 4-I theory of organizational learning described in the following section was used as a tool to organize the data and provide a framework for understanding *how* learning had occurred and how it had been disseminated and remembered in the banks. The how story coding bins were drawn from this theory: individual-level learning, individual to group, individual to organization, group to individual, group level learning, group to organization, organization to individual, organization to group, and organization-level learning. Interview data were sorted first according to this framework. Then within each coding bin, data were sorted again into clusters of related points. Archival data were then used to support, augment, or contradict the points made in these clusters. These clusters became the basis for observations regarding each bank's learning pattern.

CONCEPTUAL MODEL

This research uses the 4-I theory of organizational learning (OL) proposed by Crossan, Lane, and White (1999); Crossan, Lane, White, & Djurfeldt, (1995) as a lens through which to examine bank learning—and the dissemination of lessons—from sector-specific credit losses. The theory is framed by the following propositions:

Proposition 1: Organizational learning reveals a tension between assimilating new learning (adaptiveness) and using what has already been learned (adaptation).

Proposition 2: (a) Organizational learning is multilevel: individual, group, and institution.
(b) Learning at one level affects the other levels.

Proposition 3: Processes link the three levels.

Proposition 4: Cognition affects action and vice versa.

Figure 6.1 provides an illustration of the theory, making explicit the three levels at which learning can occur, the impact that lessons learned at one level have on learning at the other levels, the learning processes at each level, and the tension between new learning and old. The boxes along the diagonal represent learning at the individual, group, and organization levels of analysis.

At the individual level, learning is characterized by the processes of intuition and interpretation. At the group level, learning is a function of the processes of interpretation within groups and integration of knowledge across groups. At the organization level, learning is reflected in the process of institutionalization, as lessons are embedded into structures, processes, routines, policies, and so on. Crossan, Lane and White (1999) defined these learning processes as follows:

Intuiting is the preconscious recognition of the pattern or possibilities or both, inherent in a personal stream of experience. This process can affect the intuitive individual's behavior but it only affects others as they attempt to interact with that individual.

Interpreting is the explaining of an insight or idea to one's self and others. This process goes from the preverbal to the verbal and requires the development of language.

Integrating is the process of developing shared understanding amongst individuals and the taking of coordinated action through mutual adjustment. Dialogue and joint action are crucial to the development of shared understanding. This process will initially be ad hoc and informal but if the coordinated action taking is recurring and significant, it will be institutionalized.

Institutionalizing is the process of ensuring that routinized actions occur. Tasks are defined, actions specified, and organizational mechanisms put in place to ensure that certain actions occur. Institutionalizing is the process of embedding learning that has occurred by individuals and groups into the organization including systems, structures, procedures, and strategy.

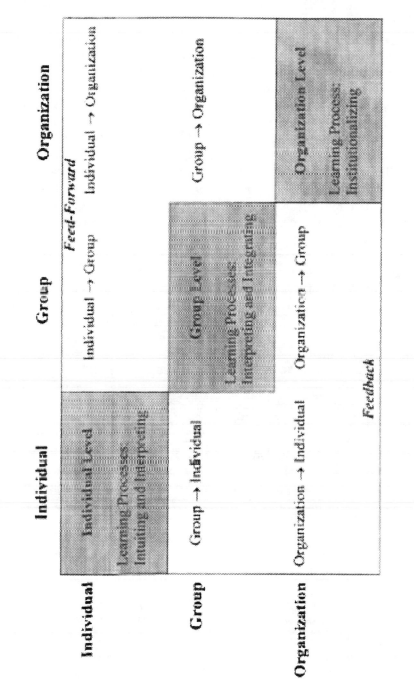

FIG. 6.1 The 4-I framework.

The three boxes in the top right corner of the framework show the feed-forward of learning, from the individual to the group or the organization and from the group to the organization. They are of particular interest as one seeks to understand how lessons from the loan loss episodes were disseminated because they direct one's attention to how lessons learned by an individual are shared with a larger group and how individual and group interpretations of events and lessons are embedded in rules, structures, or procedures. These boxes also represent the assimilation of new learning or the process by which the organization adapts to learning and change.

The three boxes in the lower left corner of the framework illustrate that lessons also feed backward and illustrate a different type of mechanism by which lessons are disseminated. Policies, processes and so on, which are the institutionalized memory of lessons already learned, can direct or constrain learning by individuals or groups. And group-level interpretations can shape what an individual is likely to learn. These boxes also represent the organization's use of the lessons it has already learned. The theory anticipates a tension between feed-forward and feed-back processes, between new learning and old, and between adaptiveness and adaptation.

The theory was chosen to organize the data and guide analysis of how learning occurred because it is the most comprehensive one available, directing the researcher's attention to the key dimensions of organizational learning as it pertained to the phenomenon being studied. In particular, it portrays learning as a dynamic flow—across groups or functions and across the individual, group, and organization levels of analysis. The question of how lessons move dynamically across people and groups over time is central to the study of learning from experience. Much of the OL literature focuses on one of three levels of analysis: the individual, the group, or the organization (see Crossan, Lane, White, & Djurfeldt, 1995; Crossan, Lane, White, & Rush, 1994). However, a number of researchers have taken a more integrated approach, arguing that to understand the OL process, one needs to recognize all three levels (Crossan, Lane, White, & Rush, 1994; Hedberg, 1981; Huber, 1991; Shrivastava, 1983) and develop a better understanding of the flow and tensions among levels (Crossan, Lane, White, & Djurfeldt, 1995; Hedberg, 1981). This theory recognizes the unique contributions and characteristics of learning at each level to the OL phenomenon.

In the 4-I learning theory, the dissemination or knowledge transfer is seen as occurring within the feed-forward learning loop through the processes of integration and institutionalization. The theory anticipates that a certain amount of learning will be shared across groups and institutionalized but that other lessons will be lost due to imperfect integration and institutionalization processes and the ever-present tension between new lessons and previous ones. It also sees knowledge as being disseminated within a feed-back loop as institutionalized lessons are passed on to individuals and groups through policies, processes, and structures. In its explicit recognition of both the feed-forward and feed-backward transfer of learning, the theory reflected the process of learning evident in the banks' handling of the loan loss events, especially their use of credit processes and policies to capture and transmit the lessons learned.

Two things should be noted, however. First, the 4-I theory is still in an early stage of its development. Its propositions delineate the boundaries of the organizational learning phenomenon, identify the key factors that need to be considered, and reflect a theoretical justification for how they are related and why. However, they are quite general and high level in nature. A great deal of empirical work remains to be done for researchers to understand in more detail how organizations learn. Second, the theory was developed to explain organizational adaptation or renewal, which is viewed as a learning process. This research uses it somewhat differently, to help us understand how organizations learn from infrequently occurring crisis events. Although there is nothing inherently contradictory in these two perspectives, they highlight different aspects of the OL phenomenon that may be reflected in different tensions and dynamics. This research should therefore be considered exploratory, despite its use of the 4-I theory as an organizing framework and lens through which to view the problem.

FINDINGS

The methodology section describes how data were coded and sorted into clusters of related points, then supported, augmented, or contradicted with archival data. Finally, these clusters were sorted again into related groups (e.g., all the clusters pertaining to working out the loans and the learning that was reported as occurring in the workout units), each of which was summarized as a key discussion point. In this way, each of the discussion points highlighted in this section emerged inductively from the data through a process of coding and sorting interview and archival data, then grouping related clusters. But, each discussion point also reflects the underlying 4-I theory of organizational learning as it was used to structure the analysis of the data.

This study offers four key findings regarding the dissemination of lessons learned from major sector-specific loan loss events. These findings are discussed in the following sections.

Lack of Direct Horizontal Communication

Lessons learned by individuals or groups do not necessarily find their way into groups that would benefit from them. There is very little direct horizontal communication of lessons learned from a major sector-specific loan loss event, particularly across industry-specialized line units. A number of factors contribute to this failure, including pressure on account managers to generate revenues, the prevalence of interpretations supporting market growth, reluctance to discuss loan losses for fear of embarrassment, and structures that separate the people with the knowledge from those who could use it.

Lessons learned by individuals after loan loss events frequently do not find their way to people who might have benefitted or be expected to benefit from them. The primary explanation for this is that in all three banks studied, there was very little direct horizontal communication of lessons learned across different groups. This is illustrated in Table 6.2, which summarizes the patterns of horizontal communication. It shows the amount of communication within a function (e.g., line-line(L), credit-credit, etc. boxes) as well as the amount of communication found across the functions that played a part in the loan loss episode (e.g., line(L)-risk management). For example, Table 6.2 shows that all three banks experienced a lot of communication between the line and credit functions but low or low–medium amounts of communication between line and risk management.

This is not to say that no communication occurred. It did but it occurred largely at senior levels (senior vice-president) between executives with management and often boundary-spanning responsibilities. But, communication rarely occurred at the front line levels between the people dealing directly with the client companies. This was particularly true across industry-specialized line units (e.g., from real estate lenders to telecommunications industry lenders). But it also held for communication between line and workout, line and risk management, credit and workout, and credit and risk management. Where there was some communication across these units, it was typically when individuals with different backgrounds came together to work on a specific transaction.

The group that consistently deviated from this pattern was head office credit (i.e., the group approving the largest corporate loans). In all three banks, there was ongoing communication between line and credit people concerning specific transactions. This communication was, in each case, a function of the bank's credit granting process. Furthermore, the level of communication seemed to have increased over the 1980–1999 study period. During that period, each of the banks overhauled its credit process

TABLE 6.2

Communication Within and Across Functions

	Bank A				Bank B				Bank C			
	Line (L)	Credit (C)	Workout (W)	Risk Management (R)	Line	Credit	Workout	Risk Management	Line	Credit	Workout	Risk Management
L	Low	High	Low	Low	Low	High	Low	Low	Low	High	Low	Low-Medium
C		High	Low	Medium		High	Low	Medium		High	Low	Medium
W			N/A	Low			N/A	Low			N/A	Low-Medium
R				N/A				N/A				N/A

113

once (Banks A and B in the early 1990s, Bank C in the early 1980s), and in each case, one of the changes was to try and increase the amount and quality of communication between line and credit functions.

The head office credit functions also reported more communication internally between people with responsibilities for different industries. So, it was more likely that lessons would have been transferred horizontally across industry groups within the credit function than within the line function. One reason may have been the relatively small numbers of head office credit people compared to account managers and their close physical proximity to each other. In each bank, these people were located in the same office space with only a few who were responsible for approving loans in any one industry. So, cross-industry discussion was common as credit officers sought answers to transaction-specific questions and in the course of daily social interaction.

In contrast, all three banks reported very little communication among account managers from different industries. In Bank A, this appeared to be exacerbated by its geographically divided organizational structure, but the other banks showed the same tendency with different structures (less geographic division and more industry specialization). All the banks reported the pressure for growth as a very strong force behind each loan loss episode. In every case, this pressure was cited as an important factor contributing to looser deal structures, lower pricing, and less attention to risk. This pressure also inhibited the communication between account managers. They explained that they had difficult growth targets to meet and they did not want to hear anything that might prevent them from doing as much business as they could to reach those targets. The typical response to unwelcome information was, "What do you know about this industry? It's different." Communication between account managers and workout people was also minimal and explained using the same rationale.

A few executives also discussed the unwillingness to embarrass anybody as a reason that specific loan losses were not officially discussed more thoroughly and shared more widely across business lines. This sentiment was echoed by middle-level bankers when explaining why information on specific loan losses was not widely available and why much of their discussions of loan losses were based on rumor and speculation. And particularly in Bank B, many interviewees also became uncomfortable and less communicative when discussing loan losses that were widely attributed to decisions of top bank executives.

This observation supports the 4-I theory's contention that tension exists between new and previous learning (proposition 1), and illustrates what this tension might look like. Account managers experienced the banks' earlier learning as strategy, compensation and reward systems, and structures (e.g., industry specialization) that encouraged them to lend aggressively in a particular industry and discount information that might compromise their ability to do so. The new lessons from the most recent loan loss event seemed to contradict the messages sent by these institutionalized artifacts and it was not in account managers' best interests to heed them. Furthermore, because horizontal communication involves discussion among peers rather than top-down mandates, account managers did not have to listen to the lessons learned by others.

This finding also gives us insight into the process of integration, which the 4-I model posits as a key learning process at the group level. It shows that within-group integration is much easier and more likely than across-group integration, suggesting that as the theory is developed further, making a distinction between the two may be beneficial. It also illustrates how across-group integration may be significantly inhibited by a number of organization-level factors (i.e., a feedback loop) that may make receiving new knowledge threatening or dangerous to some people.

Institutionalized Boundary-Spanning Mechanisms

The lack of direct communication of learning across groups may be offset by institutionalized mechanisms by which lessons go up to a boundary-spanning function then come down again across a wider range of groups through changes in policy, process, the type of decision being made, or the type of questions being asked.

Although there was little direct horizontal communication across front line groups, some of the lessons learned from loan loss events were transferred in an up-then-down pattern. These lessons would go up from the originating group to a boundary-spanning function, then come down again across other groups.

Typically, the originating groups were workout, line, or credit people who had been involved in the workout or top management. The boundary-spanning function most commonly used to transmit lessons across groups was risk management, which, among other things, controlled the authoring of credit policies. To varying extents across the three banks, risk management also provided a policing function, overseeing the credit process. Another key boundary-spanning function was senior management. The role of this group in disseminating lessons will be explored in the following section.

The common mechanisms by which lessons were transferred to other groups included changes in structure, policy, process, credit approval decisions, and training. The systematic use of boundary-spanning mechanisms to disseminate learning from loan losses was observed most strongly in Bank C. The reason was that Bank C created a strong risk management department (the Risk Management Policy Unit) in the mid-1980s as part of its credit process overhaul. This department controlled the authoring and changing of bank policies, oversaw the credit process, reviewed transactions, oversaw credit training and the qualification process, and oversaw the audit process, assessing how each of these interlocking components was performing as markets changed. It had the mandate to monitor these things and propose or make changes as necessary. In other words, learning about what was and was not working (and why) and disseminating lessons to where they were needed was one of the department's central tasks. The lessons were disseminated primarily through institutionalized changes but also through the input of the senior risk management executive on key committees. As well as having the mandate to learn and transmit its learning, Bank C's risk management department had the teeth to institutionalize changes and enforce them.

In contrast, the other two banks used boundary-spanning mechanisms to transmit learning in a much more haphazard way. Neither of these banks had a culture that placed much emphasis on policies. The policies being used in these banks prior to the real estate loan losses in the early 1990s were commonly viewed by employees as being out of date and not very useful, so they were treated quite casually. They were not rigorously followed, and there was not a systematic process for assessing and changing them to reflect new knowledge or market conditions. So, where policies were used as a tool for transmitting lessons in Bank C during the 1980s and early 1990s, Banks A and B lacked the infrastucture and the culture to use them in the same way at that time.

Prior to the real estate loan losses, Banks A and B also lacked powerful risk management departments. The Risk Policy Group formed by Bank A had several of the same tasks as its counterpart at Bank C. It authored bank policy, reviewed certain credit transactions, and had the mandate to learn about concentration and portfolio management issues—but it did not have the scope nor the power to make and enforce change. In Banks A and B, centralized, independent, fairly powerful risk management departments are a recent development—they were put in place after the real estate losses in the early 1990s.

The previous finding regarding the lack of horizontal communication and this finding regarding the role of boundary-spanning mechanisms are consistent with assertions that hierarchical organizational structures inhibit communication among functions and divisions and that information must flow upward to those who have decision-making authority, then downward through the hierarchy in the form of decisions (Ashkenas, Ulrich, Jick, & Kerr, 1995; Hoskisson & Hitt, 1994; Ostroff & Smith, 1993; West & Meyer, 1997).

The role of institutionalized artifacts in transferring learning across organizational units is predicted by the 4-I theory (proposition 2b). It anticipates a feedback loop whereby changes in process, policy, structure, and so on influence what is learned at the group and individual levels. However, that institutionalized boundary-spanning mechanisms are important because they offset a distinct lack of horizontal communication across groups is not anticipated by the theory.

This observation provides a new insight into how banks learn from loan loss events. It suggests that $Group_1$ Organization $Group_2$ is a more common or likely way for lessons to be transmitted than $Group_1$ $Group_2$. This has a number of implications. First, only people—alone or in a group—can remember why decisions were taken. Only people can remember context (Walsh & Ungson, 1991). When learning is institutionalized in organization-level artifacts, such as policy or structure, the context or the story are filtered out. So, with the $Group_1$ Organization $Group_2$ pattern of dissemination, $Group_2$ learns what but not why. It receives the lesson but not the context. Whereas with the $Group_1$ $Group_2$ pattern, $Group_2$ receives both the lesson and the context. This means that only part of the lessons learned from a loan loss event are disseminated across groups and time. To understand the significance of this observation, one needs to know more about the role of context in learning and remembering lessons.

Role of Executives

Bank executives can play an important role in disseminating lessons through the organization. They do this through their boundary-spanning responsibilities, their leadership of change initiatives, and their decisions with respect to loan approval, policy, strategy, structure, and process.

This research found that lessons were more widely disseminated within the bank when they had been learned and their dissemination had been championed by senior executives. These executives transferred learning through their sponsorship of incremental changes that reached beyond the affected sector in their scope (first order changes) and through initiating and leading major transformations that reflected fundamental changes in the bank's attitudes toward credit and risk (second order changes).

But executives also transferred lessons through their organizations in other ways. They shared lessons across groups through formal and informal discussion when their responsibilities crossed group boundaries or involved their participation in key decision-making committees. In Banks A and B, for example, both credit and risk management functions reported to the senior risk management executive. In Bank C, the executive in charge of the workout group was also responsible for project finance. At Banks B and C, a committee of senior line, credit, risk management, and sometimes workout executives met regularly to approve (or not) very large or exceptional corporate loans. Their interpretations of risks and opportunities were systematically reflected in their decisions with respect to loan approval and changes in policy, strategy, structure or processes.

Senior executives also performed an important storytelling function. Through informal conversations as well as speeches delivered inside and outside the banks, executives told the loan-loss stories—what had gone wrong and why and what the bank had changed to prevent a recurrence of such an event. Like any storyteller, they decided which points to highlight and which to gloss over: which contributing factors they would talk about, which lessons they would emphasize, whether they would give an in-depth accounting of the past, or whether they would skim over it and focus on the future.

Storytelling was also an integral part of the three second-order change initiatives observed in the banks (Bank A's credit reengineering program in the early to mid-1990s, and Bank C's credit process overhaul in the early to mid-1980s and its integrated risk management initiative in the early to mid-1990s). Because each of these events entailed a profound change in the way the bank understood and managed credit or portfolio risk, or both, they were accompanied by intensive communication efforts. The executive behind each of these initiatives and a few key members of the group managing the change traveled through the organizations, meeting with people at all levels and telling powerful, consistent, compelling stories about why the changes had to occur. These storytelling blitzes in support of major change initiatives each lasted for 2 to 3 years, longer in the case of Bank C's credit process overhaul.

Research in the field of social psychology has thoroughly documented the pressures toward uniformity experienced by people in organizations (reviewed in Nemeth & Staw, 1989). In particular, "persons who hold positions of power or who are viewed as higher in status are powerful sources of influence, and agreement is often achieved by adopting the positions they propose" (Nemeth & Staw, 1989, p.180). Pressures to agree with those in positions of authority, combined with a lack of widely available competing interpretations, mean that through their communication of the loan loss stories, bank executives exercised considerable power in determining what their organizations would remember about the loan loss events and what context would be widely available to support (or undermine) institutionalized changes.

This observation supports the 4-I theory's propositions that individual learning can influence what is learned at the group and organization levels (proposition 2) and that cognition affects action and vice versa (proposition 4). However, it reveals that learning on the part of senior executives is much more likely to have such an influence than learning by lowerlevel individuals. This observation suggests that the theory may need to differentiate between senior executives and others as its conceptualization of feed-forward mechanisms is further developed.

Although in discussion of the 4-I theory, (Crossan, Lane, White and Djarfeldt, 1995; Crossan, Lane, & White, 1999) identify storytelling as an important part of the integration process, they focus on the type of evolving, mutually negotiated stories associated with communities of practice. These stories evolve to reflect the interpretations of many group members. In contrast, the stories discussed in this section are told by senior executives to employees and external stakeholders. If they reflect or are subject to any negotiation, it is among a very small and elite group within the organization. This suggests that to better understand the integration process that characterizes learning at the group level, researchers need to consider different types of stories, how they evolve, and who tells them.

Role of Training

Training is another tool banks may use to disseminate learning through the organization. However, training programs tend to transfer the lessons from sector-specific loan loss events in very general terms. And, the effectiveness of training depends to a great extent on its degree of alignment with organizational culture, strategy, reward systems, and processes.

Training is a formal and systematic means of communicating an organization's knowledge to newcomers. Lessons from the loan loss events were incorporated into account manager training programs in a number of ways. When a policy or procedure was discussed that reflected lessons learned—for example, a policy regarding concentration limits—the loan loss event was cited as the reason that the policy was in place. Lessons were sometimes referred to when a representative of the workout group, or credit, or risk management, or portfolio management addressed the class. For those people who specialized in lending to specific industries, short training programs were sometimes offered. Overall, the emphasis in the banks' training programs was in using the loan loss episode as necessary to illustrate or support a discussion of the bank's lending and risk management practices.

None of the banks focused on the loan loss event itself as a starting point and engaged in an in-depth discussion of "what did we learn?" One respondent explained that his bank was trying to offer a general training program that would be useful to all the account managers in the class. This meant that the work performed by specialized groups was covered in general terms, not in detail. It was assumed that an account manager who found himself in such a group would learn the details on the job. Specialized groups included the workout unit and also industry-specialized line units—in other words, the groups that would have specific interest in or use finer grained lessons from the loan loss events. Going into a lot of detail about events and lessons that were perceived as pertaining only to a specialized group was not considered a good use of training time. The other two banks did not seem to differ materially in their philosophies.

Overall, it appears that the banks' training programs transferred the what part of the major, generalizable lessons learned. For example, follow the rules much of the time; understand that we won't let you hold more than a certain amount of a single company or industry debt; if you want to lend more than this, you will need to sell off some of the debt; make sure you consider cash flows when filling out a loan application, and so on. However, they typically did not include the context, the story of the loan loss events.

The effectiveness of training depends to a great extent on its degree of alignment with organizational culture, strategy, reward systems, and processes. At Bank C, training was tightly linked to the qualification process that determined what each account manager's credit limit would be. Qualification limits were increased based on success in the required training programs for that level as well as audits showing the success of account managers' portfolios and lending track records. The risk management department oversaw both the qualification process and credit training and met regularly with trainers to decide on changes to the curriculum based on trends it had identified through its various monitoring processes. So, training at Bank C was consistent and integrated with the bank's credit culture, promotion systems, and so on.

Bank A also had a comprehensive training program for account managers. This program involved periods of time in class alternating with internships in the bank's branches. Although respondents seemed satisfied with the contents of the training program, some expressed frustration with the outcome. They felt that the right things were being taught but that these lessons and messages were being undermined by the trainees' experiences in the branches where they got the message, "Okay, what you learned is fine, but this is how we really do things, this is what we really get rewarded for." In contrast with Bank C, Bank A's training program was not consistent with many of its other elements including culture and reward systems.

This finding supports the 4-I theory's assertion that inherent in organizational learning is the tension between old lessons and new (proposition 1). It is also consistent with the proposition that learning at one level will influence the lessons learned at other levels (proposition 2b). In particular, it provides researchers with insight into the feedback loop, in which lessons already learned and institutionalized are transmitted to individuals and groups. It suggests that there is not just one feedback loop—there are many. And when the messages sent in the various feedback loops (by different institutionalized artifacts) are conflicting, then some of the lessons get lost.

CONCLUSION

This study yields quite different results from Szulanski's (1996) research on internal stickiness. Szulanski's study identified recipients' lack of absorptive capacity, causal ambiguity, and an arduous relationship between source and recipient as the three most important barriers to the transfer of best practice knowledge. In contrast, this research finds that strategic and structural factors—referred to as institutionalized organization-level elements in the 4-I model—and the patterns of motivation engendered by these structural factors play a major role in preventing the dissemination of lessons from loan loss events. Many factors inhibited the natural dissemination of lessons from loan loss events across business units, the most important of which were the barriers imposed by organizational structures, promotion and reward systems that discouraged the acquisition of potentially awkward information, and social pressures toward conformity. This is consistent with the work of Burns and Stalker (1961) and other researchers of organizational structure.

A possible explanation for the different results is that the data in Szulanski's (1996) study was based on transfers of knowledge that actually happened, although with varying degrees of success or difficulty, whereas this research includes both transfers that took place and those that did not. It is possible that a data set that includes potential transfers of knowledge that never actually materialized would show a much stronger influence of structural and motivational factors. This suggests that the exploration of internal stickiness would benefit from a more comprehensive set of factors describing organizational context. It also suggests that the factors inhibiting the flow of knowledge in an organization vary depending on the extent to which dissemination has already occurred.

This research also shows that executives played (or had the potential to play) a crucial role in ensuring that lessons were disseminated beyond the affected sector. Executives were able to transfer lessons across organizational boundaries, or facilitate their transfer in a number of ways. Senior executives and occasionally their handpicked deputies played a key role in guiding the interpretation of loan loss events, market signals and so on. They were particularly influential through their storytelling activities, boundary-spanning responsibilities, and leadership of change initiatives. Furthermore, the lessons they learned were systematically reflected across organizational boundaries when they authored policy, approved or refused changes to policy, changed organizational structures and processes, or articulated the strategy for a business. The important role of executives in the dissemination of learning is anticipated by research that suggests that powerful people will exert significant control over interpretation (Daft & Weick, 1984; see Nemeth & Staw, 1989, for a review of the social control literature). It suggests a potentially rich avenue for future research in the area of organizational learning.

REFERENCES

Ashkenas, R., Jick, T., Ulrich, D., & Kerr, S. (1996). *The boundaryless organization*. San Francisco: Jossey-Bass.

Ashkenas, R., Ulrich, D., Jick, T., & Kerr, S. (1995). *The boundaryless organization*. San Francisco: Jossey-Bass.

Brown, J. S. (1992). Presentation by John Seely Brown. In M. Crossan, M. Lane, R. White, & J. Rush (Eds.), *Learning in organizations* (pp.89–99). London, Ontario: University of Western Ontario.

Brown, J. S., & Duguid, P. (1991). Organizational learning and communities of practice: Toward a unified view of working, learning and innovation. *Organization Science, 2*(1), 40–56.

Burns, T., & Stalker, G. M. (1961). *The management of innovation*. London: Tavistock Publications.

Crossan, M. M., H. W. Lane, & R. E. White (1999). An organizational learning framework: From intuition to institution. *Academy of Management Review, 24*(3).

Crossan, M., Lane, H. W., White, R. E., & Djurfeldt, L. (1995). Organizational learning: Dimensions for a theory. *International Journal of Organizational Analysis, 3*(4), 337–360.

Crossan, M., Lane, H. W., White, R. E., & Rush, J. C. (1994). *Learning within organization* (Working Paper No. 94-06) Ontario, CN: University of Western Ontario.

Cyert, R. M., & March, J. G. (1963). *A behavioral theory of the firm*. Englewood Cliffs, NJ: Prentice-Hall.

Daft, R. L., & Weick, K. E. (1984). Toward a model of organizations as interpretation systems. *Academy of Management Review, 9*(2), 284–295.

Eisenhardt, K. M. (1989). Building theories from case research. *Academy of Management Review, 14*, 532–550.

Freeman, A. (1993, April 10). Survey of international banking . *The Economist.*

Hedberg, B. (1981). How organizations learn and unlearn. In P. C. Nystrom & W. H. Starbuck (Eds.), *Handbook of Organizational Design*. New York: Oxford University Press.

Huber, G. P. (1991). Organizational learning: The contributing processes and the literatures. *Organization Science*, 2(1), 88–115.

Janis, I. L. (1972). *Victims of groupthink*. Boston: Houghton Mifflin.

Lant, T. K., Milliken, F. J., & Batra, B. (1992). The role of managerial learning and interpretation in strategic persistence and reorientation: An empirical exploration. *Strategic Management Journal*, 13, 585–608.

Lant, T. K., & Montgomery D. B. (1987). Learning from strategic success and failure. *Journal of Business Research*, 15, 503–517.

Levitt, B., & March, J. G. (1988). Organizational learning. *Annual Review of Sociology*, 14.

Nelson, R. R., & Winter, S. G. (1982). *An evolutionary theory of economic change*. Cambridge, MA: Harvard University Press, Belknap Press.

Nemeth, C. J., & Staw, B. M. (1989). The tradeoffs of social control and innovation in groups and organizations. In L. Berkowitz (Ed.), *Advances in experimental social psychology*, Vol. 22, pp. 175–210. New York: Academic Press.

Olsen, J. P. (1976). The process of interpreting organizational history. In J. G. March & J. P. Olsen (Eds.), *Ambiguity and choice in organizations*. Bergen: Universitetsforlaget.

Ostroff, F. & Smith, D. (1993). *Redesigning the organization*. New York: McKinsey.

Paul-Chowdhury, C. (1995). *Bank of Montreal (A): A Vision for the future*. (Richard Ivey School of Business Case, 9-95-M012). Ontario, CN: University of Western Ontario.

Pettigrew, A. M. (1990). Longitudinal field research on change. *Organization Science*, 1, 267–292.

Shrivastava, P. (1983). A typology of organizational learning systems. *Journal of Management Studies*, 20, 7–28.

Simon, H. (1976). *Administrative behavior* (3rd ed.). New York: The Free Press.

Stevenson, B., & Fadil, M. (1994). Research report ... why lending crises occur so frequently. *Journal of Commercial Lending*, November, 43–49.

Survey of world banking (1992, May 2). *The Economist*.

Szulanski, G. (1996). Exploring internal stickiness: Impediments to the transfer of best practices within the firm. *Strategic Management Journal*, 17, 27–43.

Walsh, J. P., & Ungson, G. R. (1991). Organizational memory. *Academy of Management Review*, 16, 57–91.

Weick, K. E. (1979). *The social psychology of organizing*. Reading, MA: Addison-Wesley.

Weick, K. E. (1992). Conceptual options in the study of organizational learning. In Crossan et al (Eds.), *Learning in organizations* (pp. 25–41).

Weick, K. E. (1995). *Sensemaking in organizations*. Thousand Oaks, CA: Sage.

Wenger, E. (1991). Communities of practice: Where learning happens. *Benchmark*, Fall, 6–8.

West, G. P., & Meyer, G. D. (1997). Communicated knowledge as a burning foundation. *International Journal of Organizational Analysis*, 5(1), 25–58.

Yin, R. K. (1984). *Case study research*. Beverly Hills, CA: Sage.

Adapting Aspirations to Feedback: The Role of Success and Failure

Patrice R. Murphy
Robert H. Shaffer & Associates

Stephen J. Mezias
Ya Ru Chen
New York University

Goals are a primary construct in theories of organization at virtually all levels of analysis. Goalsetting (Locke, Shaw, Saari, & Latham, 1981) and its formalization in programs of management by objectives is one of the oldest traditions at the individual and group levels of analysis. Managers are exhorted to provide goals that are specific, measurable, challenging, reasonable, and timely. Goals are also a key factor linking effort and performance in expectancy theories of motivation (Vroom, 1964). Goals are implicit in the concept of desirable behavior, which is important in theories of organization behavior such as reinforcement theory (Skinner, 1938) and organization behavior modification (Luthans & Kreitner, 1985). Strategic management with its focus on mission statements, corporate goals, tactical plans, and operational goals clearly emphasizes the goal as a key concept. Traditionally, managers have been urged to define the organization's purpose in a mission and to support this mission with corporate goals; strategies serve as comprehensive road maps to how goals can be achieved (Mintzberg & Waters, 1985). Theories of organization have a long history of focusing on goals as a fundamental concept, with a rich vocabulary—interests, norms, criteria, norms, standards, and subgoals—and elaborate structures such as means-end chains (March & Simon, 1958).

At the organizational level, the behavioral theory of the firm (Cyert & March, 1963) takes as one of its key assumptions the view that organizations set goals and adjust behavior in accordance with simple decision rules. Cyert & March (1963) argued that "most organization objectives take the form of an aspiration level rather than an imperative to 'maximize' or 'minimize'" (p. 28). In the behavioral theory of the firm, goals are a critical element in the cognitive processes leading to organization-level search, action, and subsequent trial and error learning.

Behavioral models of managerial choice and action in the face of incomplete information have similarly pointed to the importance of targets and aspiration levels as critical focal values that direct managerial attention. They provide a concrete link to specific actions and simplify decision making (Lant, 1992; March & Simon, 1958; Morecroft, 1985). Aspiration level is assumed to divide subjective success from subjective failure: Performance higher than aspiration level is perceived as success and performance lower than aspiration level is perceived as failure. Positive and negative decision frames have been found to influence behavioral change (Greve, 1998; Lant, Milliken, & Batra, 1992), attributions for performance (Clapham & Schwenk, 1991; Milliken & Lant, 1991), perceptions of the environment (Kiesler & Sproull, 1982; Starbuck & Milliken, 1988), and risk taking (Kahneman & Tversky, 1979; March, 1988; March & Shapira, 1992).

Despite the importance of aspiration formation to many areas of organizational research, much of the scholarship to date has focused on theory development (Cyert & March, 1963; Levinthal & March, 1981, 1988; March, 1991; Mezias & Glynn, 1993), experiment (e.g., Glynn, Lant, & Mezias, 1991), or simulation in a classroom setting (e.g., Lant, 1992). An important empirical exploration of the validity of three distinct models of aspiration adaptation is found in Lant's (1992) study using MBA students and executives to simulate top management team decision making. Behavioral theories of aspiration adaptation were tested using an attainment discrepancy model (Lewin, Dembo, Festinger, & Sears, 1944) and Levinthal and March's (1981, 1988) weighted average model. Noting the long history in the economics literature of models of adaptive expectations, Lant also tested Muth's (1961) rational expectations model of expectation adaptation, a conceptually distinct but potentially predictive model for aspiration adaptation. Results suggest that the attainment discrepancy model provides the most robust description of aspiration formation; this finding was confirmed in a field study in the domestic operations of a large American multinational corporation (Mezias & Murphy, 1998). However, there must be considerably more research to test the robustness of these theories in organizational settings.

In comparison, there have been many empirical studies of the motivational effects of goalsetting as a managerial technique (Locke & Latham, 1990). This work has been primarily concerned with the effect of goals after they have been determined and assigned. By contrast, the aspiration formation literature explores the actual processes by which goals are determined. Although aspiration level theory and goalsetting theory make different assumptions about the origin and adaptation of aspirations in organizations (Shapira, 1989), both assume some level of goal commitment and a cognitive evaluation of performance in the context of the goal that has been set or accepted. Extensive empirical research, mainly in North America, supports the basic tenets of goal theory: that specific and difficult goals lead to high performance levels if accepted by the individual and if feedback is provided (Locke & Latham, 1990). Because goals are assumed to be assigned, goal commitment is shown to have a stronger motivational power than the assigned goal alone. The theory is thus cognitive in nature and tends to focus on the individual's goals, self-efficacy, valences and performance rather than situational factors (Earley & Lituchy, 1991; Eden, 1988; Garland, 1985).

Recent work has pursued the concept of goals as frames and related psychological effects (Heath, Larrick, & Wu, 1998; Larrick, Heath, & Wu, 1998). This builds on earlier research on individual decision making that showed that preferences for an outcome can shift depending on how a problem is framed relative to a neutral reference point (Tversky & Kahneman, 1981). Prospect theory suggests that risky outcomes are evaluated by individuals as positive or negative relative to some neutral reference point that can be the status quo, aspiration level, or some other psychologically significant point (Tversky & Kahneman, 1981). More recently, Heath et al., (1998) confirmed in a series of psychological experiments the motivational effect of mere goals as psychological stimuli, confirming both their status as reference points and the phenomenon of loss aversion.

It is our intent to integrate the literature on the process of aspiration level formation in organizations with the literature that emphasizes aspiration level as a critical construct mediating perceptions of success and failure. This requires that one explicitly recognizes two functions that aspiration levels serve in organizations. First, the selection and public announcement of an organizational goal, or aspiration, can be thought of as a form of organizational decision making; this is the aspiration as decision function. Second, behavioral theories focus on aspiration level as the critical value partitioning success from failure (Cyert & March, 1963; March, 1988; Kahneman, 1992; March & Shapira, 1992); this is the aspiration as neutral reference point function. Putting these two ideas together suggests the possibility that interpretations of past performance as either a success or failure creates a positive or negative decision frame for the formation of subsequent aspiration level. The question explored here is whether the framing of performance feedback as success or failure relative to previous aspiration can be expected to have an effect on the adaptation of aspirations over time. Drawing on the powerful lessons of goals as reference points, this chapter modifies a behavioral model of organizational aspiration formation to allow for the possibility of a framing effect on organizational goal formation.

TARGETS AS DECISION: SETTING ASPIRATIONS

The existing empirical research on the effect of feedback on aspiration formation over time has generally modeled the relationship as a linear function (e.g., Lant, 1992; Mezias & Murphy, 1998). The possibility of an effect on this relationship depending on whether the decision context is positive or negative has not been considered. This chapter returns to the underlying theoretical question of how goals themselves adapt over time in the context of performance feedback that is framed relative to a neutral reference point. How might positive and negative decision frames influence the aspiration formation process itself?

There is considerable empirical evidence that positive and negative frames affect the evaluation of outcomes and individual choice in a range of decision contexts. Kahneman, Knetsch, and Thaler (1986) found that individuals' perceptions of fairness in labor market contracts were strongly influenced by whether actions were framed as imposing losses or reducing gains. Levin and Gaeth (1988) found that positive and negative framing affected consumers' response to product attributes. Mezias (1988) showed that the forecast error, operationalized as deviations between forecast returns and actual returns, is valued differently by participants in the stock market depending on whether its sign was negative or positive. Maheswaran and Meyers-Levy (1990) found that positive and negative framing affected the persuasiveness of health-related messages. Gregory, Lichtenstein, and MacGregor (1993) studied the role of past states in determining reference points for public policy decisions. They found that presenting a proposed change as the restoration of a prior loss rather than as a gain from the status quo had a significant effect on the evaluation of environmental and health policy decisions. A program framed in terms of returning to an earlier, better status was evaluated more favorably than an otherwise identical program framed around the current status.

Similar questions have arisen in the domain of managerial and organizational cognition, where research has investigated the effect of heuristics and framing on managers' strategic decision-making processes (e.g., Milliken & Lant, 1991). The framing of performance outcomes as success versus failure has been shown to influence attributions for performance (Fiske & Taylor, 1984; Staw, McKechnie, & Puffer, 1983), vigilance in environmental scanning (Kiesler & Sproull, 1982; Milliken, 1990), and willingness to search for alternative strategies (Levitt & March, 1988). The psychological and inertial forces favoring persistence with an existing strategy are considerable (Milliken & Lant, 1991). They can be strong enough to prevent the perception of failure from stimulating learning as predicted by simple reinforcement models of behavior (Bandura, 1977; Cyert & March, 1963) and can even lead to threat rigidity (Staw, Sandelands, & Dutton, 1981) and escalating commitment (Staw, 1981; Staw & Ross, 1978).

The importance of framing in these domains suggests that the process by which aspirations are adjusted might also be impacted by the framing of a given level of performance as higher or lower than target, success or failure, desirable or undesirable. If equivalent gaps between performance and aspiration are evaluated differently depending on whether they are positive or negative, we would expect to observe a different rate of aspiration adaptation in response to that feedback. How this difference might manifest itself in the adjustment of aspirations to performance feedback is the topic of the remainder of this chapter.

ASPIRATIONS, SUCCESS, AND FAILURE

This chapter develops hypotheses about aspiration formation reflecting four generic forms of a behavioral model of aspiration formation, implying different assumptions about how feedback of success and failure might affect the process. The key concept underlying all of these models is the idea that performance is interpreted as signaling either success or failure depending on whether it is higher or lower than the target or aspiration level. Thus, an important construct for all of these models is the variable attainment discrepancy (AD), which is defined as follows:

$$AD_{i,t} = P_{i,t} - AL_{i,t}$$

where $AL_{i,t}$ is aspiration level for the ith person or unit and $P_{i,t}$ is the same entity's performance in the same period. Attainment discrepancy is important because at values more than zero, the claim is that performance will be interpreted as success, whereas at values less than zero, performance will be interpreted as failure. Using the concept of attainment discrepancy, this chapter develops different models of how the aspiration level updating process might be affected by whether performance is interpreted as a success or a failure. Then, it uses some empirical data from an American organization to answer the question of which of these models has the best fit with the data.

The Attainment Discrepancy Model

The attainment discrepancy model predicts that aspiration levels will be a function of at least two variables: previous aspiration level and actual performance during the previous period. Previous research findings (Glynn, et al., 1991; Lant, 1992; Mezias, Chen, & Murphy, 1997), suggest that a specific functional form provides the best description of aspiration level adaptation. It models aspiration level as a function of previous aspiration level and attainment discrepancy with a single period lag in the following functional form:

$$ALi,t = \beta_0 + \beta_1 ALi,t\text{-}1 + \beta_2 ADi,t\text{-}1$$

This model is consistent with the claim that the relationship between attainment discrepancy and subsequent aspirations is continuous. It has been assumed that the same relationship holds between attainment discrepancy and subsequent aspiration regardless of whether the former is positive or negative. A graphical representation of this model is presented in Fig. 7.1.

Results from simulation in a classroom setting (Lant, 1992), experiments with graduate and undergraduate students (Glynn, et al., 1991), and field data (Mezias, et al., 1997) suggest that the following three results should be found in estimating the attainment discrepancy model. First, the constant should have a value greater than zero. Although not a direct prediction of the original attainment discrepancy model (Lewin et al., 1944), the finding of a positive constant has been a robust result of the previous empirical research (Glynn, et al., 1991; Lant, 1992; Mezias, et al., 1997). Lant (1992) described this upward pressure on aspiration levels as optimism.

Hypothesis 1: The constant will be significantly greater than zero.

Second, it is predicted that aspiration levels will change incrementally. This implies that aspiration levels in the previous time period will have a

AL $_t$

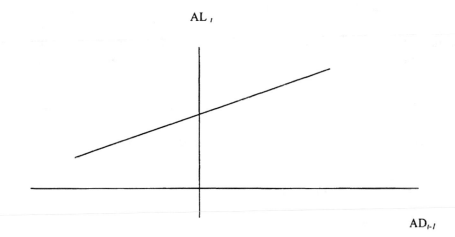

AD$_{t-1}$

FIG 7.1 Constant slope model.

positive effect on aspiration levels in the current time period. Hence we would expect to estimate a value for β_1 that is greater than zero.

Hypothesis 2: The coefficient for goal in the previous period will be significantly greater than zero.

Third, it is predicted that aspiration levels will not be fixed but will adapt in response to performance feedback. The attainment discrepancy model of Cyert & March (1963) suggested that the difference between actual performance and aspiration in the previous period will have a positive effect on subsequent aspiration level. It is predicted that if performance is greater than aspiration level, aspiration in the following period will adjust upward and downward if performance is less than aspiration level. This implies that the coefficient on attainment discrepancy will be greater than zero.

Hypothesis 3: The coefficient on attainment discrepancy in the previous period will be significantly greater than zero.

A Categorical Response Model

The second model considered is similar to what Greve (1998) called the categorical response to success or failure. This model assumes that decision makers' categorization of feedback into a simple signal of success versus failure impacts an otherwise constant response to performance feedback. In other words, the effect of the interpretation of performance as signaling either success or failure results in some shift in the subsequent aspiration. The assumption is that success and failure are noticed but receive a fairly simple cognitive response (Greve, 1998), resulting only in a constant shift of an otherwise unaffected relationship between attainment discrepancy and subsequent aspiration. This is depicted in Fig. 7.2.

As depicted in Fig 7.2, we predict a downward shift in the intercept when the decision context is negative. Accordingly, it is expected that subsequent aspiration will be uniformly higher when the organization's previous performance has exceeded target than when the decision context is negative. For estimation purposes, a dummy variable to reflect the negative feedback signal can be included in the equation:

$$ALi,t = \beta_0 + \beta_1 ALi,t\text{-}1 + \beta_2 ADi,t\text{-}1 + \beta_3 DN$$

where DN is set equal to one when attainment discrepancy is negative and otherwise set to zero. In this form of the equation, the intercept will equal β_0 when feedback is positive and $\beta_0 + \beta_3$ when feedback is negative. It is expected that any shift would be toward a lower goal being assigned in the failure condition, where attainment discrepancy is less than zero:

Hypothesis 4: The intercept when attainment discrepancy is negative will be significantly less than the intercept when attainment discrepancy is positive.

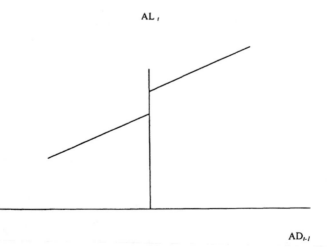

AL $_t$

AD$_{t\text{-}1}$

FIG. 7.2   The categorical response mode.

Support for this model will be indicated if the coefficient for the dummy variable, called negative feedback, is significant and negative.

A Changing-Slope Response Model

A changing-slope response model shares the assumption that managers notice whether the attainment discrepancy signal indicates performance or success. However, this model assumes greater cognitive complexity in the managerial response to performance feedback. Based on the robust finding that losses loom larger than gains, it is expected that framing feedback as negative increases the salience of the feedback. Hence, the slope of the function is predicted to be steeper in the domain of negative feedback than the domain of positive feedback. This is depicted in Fig. 7.3.

For estimation purposes, the validity of this model can be tested by including a variable, called Interaction, which equals the signal of negative feedback (coded as equal to one for failure and zero for success) times attainment discrepancy:

$$ALi,t = \beta_0 + \beta_1 ALi,t\text{-}1 + \beta_2 ADi,t\text{-}1 + \beta_4 DN*ADi,t\text{-}l$$

In this form of the equation, the coefficient on Attainment Discrepancy will equal β_1 when performance is above target and $\beta_1 + \beta_4$ when it is below target. If losses are felt more keenly than gains of an equivalent amount, then the slope of the function will be significantly steeper in the negative domain.

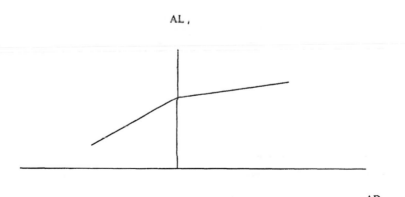

FIG. 7.3   Changing slope response.

Hypothesis 5: The coefficient on negative values of attainment discrepancy will be larger than the coefficient on positive values.

The prediction of a steeper slope for negative values of attainment discrepancy will be supported if $\beta_1 + \beta_4 > \beta_1$. Hence, the model predicts that $\beta4$ will be significant and positive.

The Categorical and Shifting Slope Model

The final possibility considered in this study is that there may be a shift in the constant and a different value for the coefficients on attainment discrepancy in the domain of positive and negative values; that is, a combination of the second and third models. Graphically, the model is shown in Fig. 7.4.

To test the validity of this model, we require an estimation equation including variables that allow for both the intercept and the coefficient on attainment discrepancy to differ in the domains of positive and negative feedback:

$$AL_{i,t} = \beta_0 + \beta_1 AL_{i,t-1} + \beta_2 AD_{i,t-1} + \beta_3 DN + \beta_4 DN*AD_{i,t-1}$$

Support for this model requires both Hypotheses 4 and 5 to be supported in the estimation of the previous equation above: consistent with Hypothesis 4, it is predicted that β_3 will be significant and negative, and consistent with Hypothesis 5, it is predicted that β_4 will be significant and positive.

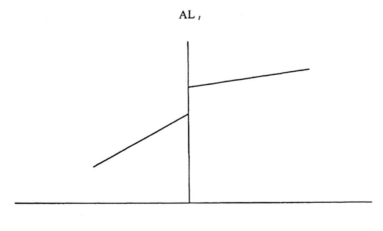

FIG. 7.4   Categorical and changing slope model.

THE FIELD DATA

This study uses data from the quarterly performance reports of a large American financial services organization. The basic attainment discrepancy model rests on a number of assumptions regarding the availability and processing of feedback about performance, any of which might reasonably be violated in a field setting. First, and fundamental to the model under discussion, is the assumption that feedback is available to the decision makers who determine aspiration levels. For this to be true, the people who set performance goals must be provided with performance information from earlier periods. This is mentioned merely to highlight the potential, in field settings, for goals to be set by managers and other employees in the absence of performance feedback. The availability of data on actual performance in an organization does not necessarily mean that accurate feedback is made available to those responsible for goal setting. In the present field study, the parties who set goals for unit (i.e., branch) performance are provided with performance feedback relating to that branch as well as the performance of other branches in the sample.

Second, feedback is assumed to be timely. Specifically, the attainment discrepancy model assumes that decision makers have immediate feedback about performance in the current period in enough time for the information to be used to determine an aspiration level for the next period. In organizational settings, the assumption of a single period lag will be violated if performance feedback is unavailable at the time that aspirations are being formed. For example, budget planning cycles can begin well in advance, with managers setting cost and revenue goals before performance in the current period is complete. In such circumstances, it might be hypothesized that managers rely on complete performance feedback from the last period for which it is available. In the context of the present field data, complete performance feedback is available from period $t-1$ prior to the setting of goals for period t.

A third and related assumption is that only performance feedback from the most recent period is informative about subsequent changes in aspiration level. A reasonable alternative hypothesis is that managers attend to feedback from multiple periods. To test the proposition, separate lagged variables could be included in the attainment discrepancy model for increasingly lagged periods (i.e., t-1, t-2, t-3, and so on). Various models might be hypothesized in different field settings. For example, in the case of data displaying annual seasonality measured quarterly, aspirations might be determined by reference to aspiration at time t-1, attainment discrepancy at t-1, and performance at time t-5. Alternatively, in the context of a turbulent environment and large fluctuations in periodic measures of performance, managers may adapt their aspirations by reference to previous aspiration and the attainment discrepancy of multiple periods, either averaged or weighted to reflect the diminishing salience of older performance feedback. Specific hypotheses incorporating multiperiod feedback on performance should be grounded in the field context: Data for the present study suggests neither annual seasonality nor environmental turbulence.

The data for this study was derived from quarterly reports by 94 retail units (henceforth, branches) of a large financial services organization in two states of the United States during the period 1995 to 1998. Data on aspiration level (stated in terms of a branch goal) and achieved performance (stated as the actual branch result) was gathered for savings account balances. The data was then used to determine the discrepancy between goal and actual performance in each period.

In addition to these elements of the basic model, this study controls for the possible effect of branch size, branch age, the prior experience of branch managers in the process of goal setting, and the effect of branches showing extremely large shifts in aspiration level over one period. The rationale for the first three of these control variables is as follows: Goals for branch performance on various measures are determined by branch managers and their immediate superior through a process of negotiation within the organizational entity's dominant coalition (Cyert & March, 1963). In this respect, branch goals are the result of a "continuous bargaining-learning process" (Cyert & March, 1963, p. 28). Moreover, they reflect a specific, satisficing aspiration rather than a general goal to maximize performance on the relevant measure. Larger and older branches as well as those that have more experienced managers may participate in this process in a manner that yields different aspiration levels over time compared with branches that are smaller, younger, or have less experienced managers.

Accordingly, appropriate controls for such effects have been included. The control for branch size was operationalized using a measure of assets under management; it is called branch size in the analyses. The control for the age of the branch was operationalized as the number of quarters since the branch's establishment; it is called branch age in the analyses. The control for branch manager experience was operationalized as the time in quarters since the appointment of the branch manager to the organization; it is called manager tenure in the analyses. Missing data on branch manager tenure was handled by substituting mean branch manager tenure.

An extremely large movement in aspiration level in a period was controlled using a variable called *Outlier*, constructed as follows. First, the difference between previous goal and current aspiration was calculated as a fraction of previous goal. The distribution of this difference term was then examined. Allowing for a small number of extreme left-tail values, all observations with a difference value greater or less than two SDs from the mean were controlled using a binary variable called Outlier. When a branch experienced an unusually large or small movement in aspiration in one period, it was assigned a value for Outlier equal to 1, otherwise zero. On this basis, 67 observations (8.3% of the data set) were controlled using the Outlier variable.

RESULTS

Results reported here relate to an important measure of retail branch performance: balances held in savings accounts.[1] Because some of the branches were closed or opened during the study period, they had missing observations for this dependent variable. After allowing for all missing data, analysis was conducted on data from 81 branches over 10 quarters. Descriptive statistics are reported in Table 7.1, and a correlation matrix for all of the variables included in any of our regression analyses are reported in Table 7.2.

To test the hypotheses and estimate the effects of the control variables, five models were estimated. The regression results for each are shown in Table 7.3. In the first model, the basic attainment discrepancy model predicted that current aspiration level will be a function of previous goal and previous attainment discrepancy. Hypothesis 1 suggested that the constant will be positive, reflecting an upward drift in aspiration levels. In Model 1, the constant was positive but not significant, failing to support Hypothesis 1. Hypothesis 2 suggested that the goal in the previous period will have a positive effect on current aspiration level. This effect was measured by the variable previous goal, which was significant ($p < .001$) and positive as predicted. Similarly, Hypothesis 3 suggested that the discrepancy between target and actual performance in the previous period will be positively related to current aspiration level. This effect was measured using the variable attainment discrepancy, which was significant ($p < .001$) and positive as predicted.

Model 2 introduced four controls to the basic model. In the estimation of this model, the constant was now negative and not significant, contrary to Hypothesis 1. Previous goal and attainment discrepancy remained significant (both at $p < .001$) and positive, supporting Hypotheses 2 and 3 of the

---

[1]Space limitations in this chapter prevented the report of results for analyses on two other financial products that were gathered concurrently. Results were consistent with those reported here, except for the following: For balances held in international money market accounts, the coefficient on negative feedback was positive but not significant and for balances held in certificates of deposit, the coefficient on the interaction term was positive but not significant.

TABLE 7.1

Descriptive Statistics

Variable	Mean	S.D.	Minimum	Maximum
Current Goal	5918187	2722689	184450	14915308
Previous Goal	5799350	2705270	158000	14915308
Attainment Discrepancy	-322871	727215	-3232422	3168762
Negative Feedback	.75	.44	0	1.00
Interaction	-454074	508901	-3232422	0
Branch Size	65781216	32566961	11638091	235503548
Branch Age	43.04	13.66	3.00	62.00
Manager Tenure	26.34	18.39	1.00	94.00
Outlier	.08	.28	0	1.00

$N = 810$

control variables. Branch size had a significant negative effect ($p < .05$.) and outliers had a highly significant positive effect ($p < .001$). Branch age and manager tenure were not significant.

The third model tested the possibility of a categorical response to performance information by introducing the dummy variable Negative Feedback to distinguish the positive from the negative domain. In the positive domain, Negative Feedback was set equal to zero and hence had no impact on the function: In the negative domain it was set equal to one. In the estimation of this model, the constant was negative and significant ($p < .10$), failing to support Hypothesis 1. The effects for previous goal and attainment discrepancy remained positive and significant (both at $p < .001$), maintaining the support for Hypotheses 2 and 3. Hypothesis 4 suggested that the coefficient for the signal of negative performance would be negative, resulting in a lower intercept for the function in the negative domain. The coefficient for negative feedback was positive and significant at ($p < .05$), failing to support Hypothesis 4. Of the control variables, branch size remained negative and significant ($p < .05$) and Outlier remained positive ($p < .001$). Again, branch age and manager tenure were not significantly different from zero.

Model 4 tested the possibility that a more complex cognitive reaction to performance feedback occurs, such that the influence of attainment discrepancy information is stronger or weaker depending on the sign of the feedback. The model introduced a variable called interaction, operationalized as the negative feedback dummy variable multiplied by the

TABLE 7.2

Pearson Correlation Coefficients

Variable	1	2	3	4	5	6	7	8
Current Goal								
Previous Goal	.97***							
Attainment Discrepancyt-1	-.38***	-.50***						
Negative Feedback	.19***	.27***	-.67***					
Interaction	.49***	-.59***	.86***	-.52***				
Branch Size	.72***	.72***	-.14***	.00	-.30***			
Branch Age	.30***	.32***	-.22***	.23***	-.10***	.14***		
Manager Tenure	.12***	.10**	.05	-.03	.07**	.08**	.12***	
Outlier	-.02	-.08**	.06*	-.18***	-.09**	-.01	-.12***	-.06*

$N = 810$; *$p < .10$; **$p < .05$; ***$p < .001$

TABLE 7.3

Summary of Results of Regressions of Current Aspiration

Variable	Basic Attainment Discrepancy Model	Basic Model With Controls	Categorial Response	Changing Slope Response	Categorical and Changing Slope Response
Intercept	.8606	-134925	-230454*	-87637	-174757
	(99045)	(113852)	(118521)	(112411)	(117105)
Previous Goal	1.05***	1.07***	1.07***	1.08***	1.08***
	(.01)	(.01)	(.01)	(.01)	(.01)
Attainment Discrepancy$_{t-1}$	.48***	.50***	.56***	.24***	.30***
	(.03)	(.03)	(.04)	(.05)	(.06)
Negative Feedback$_{t-1}$			157099**		141788**
			(54158)		(52945)
Interaction of Feedback & Attainment Discrepancy$_{t-1}$				.47***	.46***
				(.07)	(.07)
Control variables					
Branch Size		-.20E-2**	-.19E-2**	-.14E-2*	-.13E-2
		(.81E-3)	(.81E-3)	(.80E-3)	(.79E-3)
Branch Age		1818	1290	872	414
		(1325)	(1332)	(1302)	(1308)
Manager Tenure		740	754	301	322
		(925)	(921)	(905)	(902)
Outlier		618222***	650965***	742351***	769531***
		(67011)	(67649)	(68202)	(68691)
R-squared	.9648	.9684	.9687	.9700	.9702

*$p < .10$; **$p < .05$; ***$p < .001$

attainment discrepancy variable. In the positive domain, the interaction variable equals zero and has no impact on the function: In the negative domain, it equals the value of the attainment discrepancy variable. Thus, a significant coefficient for interaction results in a change in the slope of the function in the negative domain. In the estimation of this model, the constant remained negative and non-significant, failing to support Hypothesis 1. Previous goal and attainment discrepancy remained positive, both significant at the level $p < .001$. Hypothesis 5 suggested that the effect of information about attainment discrepancy will be stronger when performance feedback is negative, implying a coefficient for the Interaction term that is significant and positive. This hypothesis was supported in the estimation of this model; the coefficient for the variable Interaction was positive and significantly at the level $p < .001$. Branch age and manager tenure remained nonsignificant as previously found. Branch size remained negative ($p < .10$) and the Outlier control remained positive ($p < .001$).

The fifth model tested whether the direct effect examined in Model 3 and the interaction effect examined in Model 4 were evident together. All effects were as previously found. The constant was negative but not significant, previous goal was positive ($p < .001$) and attainment discrepancy was positive ($p < .001$), supporting Hypotheses 2 and 3 and failing to support Hypothesis 1. The dummy for negative feedback caused a positive shift ($p < .05$) in the constant contrary to Hypothesis 4, but the significant ($p < .001$), positive effect for the Interaction term offered support for Hypothesis 5. The effect of branch age, manager tenure, and outliers remained as found previously: Branch size, although still negative, was no longer significant.

DISCUSSION

The most immediate conclusion from these results is the robustness of their support for the attainment discrepancy model of aspiration formation, across all formulations of the model. Contrary to Hypothesis 1, researchers found a value for the constant that was not significantly different from zero or, at best, marginally supportive of a negative effect. This suggests a tendency for aspiration level to remain constant or to fall independent of previous aspiration and previous performance. This is interesting mostly because previous research using pedagogical simulation and experiments has found a positive constant. One possible explanation for this difference derives from the aspiration setting mechanism that operates here as opposed to those settings. In both of those settings, participants set their own goals; in the field setting where this study's data was produced, goals are negotiated in the context of a hierarchical relationship between branch managers and their supervisors. However, this does not explain the difference between the sign of the constant in this study and a previous field study (Mezias, et al., 1997). Clearly, the sign of the constant in the attainment discrepancy formula needs to be studied in future research.

Consistent with Hypothesis 2, previous goal was estimated to have a statistically significant coefficient greater than zero. This means that past aspiration serves as an anchor: In reaching their current aspiration level, branches are influenced by the previous aspiration level, independent of performance. Consistent with Hypothesis 3, we estimated that attainment discrepancy to have a statistically significant coefficient between 0 and 1. This means that aspiration level is also sensitive to past performance.

The results here suggest, however, that this sensitivity to past performance takes a more complex form. First, managers are cognizant of the negative signal and respond by shifting goals slightly upward. Across all of the branches in the sample, the upward shift in aspirations was 141788; stated as a percentage of the mean aspiration level, this amounts to a 2.4 change as a result of performance lower than aspiration. Stated as a percentage of the mean attainment discrepancy in the sample, the upward adjustment to aspiration level when feedback is negative is almost 44% of the attainment discrepancy itself. Given that the data reflects the quarterly adjustment of goals for financial products, this is an interesting result.

Second, the strength of the relationship between attainment discrepancy and subsequent goal is affected by news of negative as opposed to positive feedback about performance. Apparently, managers treat attainment discrepancy and the performance signal encoded in it in a different manner, depending on whether the performance is interpreted as success or failure. When the performance signal is coded as failure, aspirations adjust more rapidly, reflected in a steeper slope for the function in the negative region. Thus, a preliminary conclusion of this study must be that the cognitive response of managers to performance signals as they go about the important business of setting subsequent goals can include both a constant shift and an acceleration of the response to negative performance.

It is important that the preliminary nature of this finding be emphasized. The results reported here are based on a single measure at one organization. Before any systematic conclusions can be made regarding whether managers differentiate between positive and negative performance signals in the subsequent setting of performance goals, much more evidence needs to be gathered. Furthermore, it is likely that considerably more theorizing needs to take place (Murphy, 1998). We began here with a fairly straightforward extrapolation of the attainment discrepancy model. Then they investigated whether the constant or the linear relationship between performance signal and subsequent goal were altered by the interpretation of the signal as either success or failure. Correct specification of the relationship between current aspiration, performance signals, and subsequent goals needs to be developed in considerably more detail.

For example, past research on prospect theory found that the value function describing the evaluation of positive and negative outcomes is distinctly nonlinear (e.g., Kahneman, Knetsch, & Thaler, 1990; Kahneman & Tversky, 1982). In a series of experiments concerning framing effects associated with "mere" goals, Heath et al. (1998) showed that the principle of diminishing sensitivity has implications for individuals' effort near a goal, effort far away from a goal, and risk taking. These findings suggest that feedback framed as success or failure may affect aspiration formation more strongly when performance is very close to previous aspiration. Thus, the function describing aspiration adaptation may be more correctly specified as a power function. More complete theorizing of the possible relations, applications to multiple organizations, and including multiple measures should all be goals of subsequent research.

In addition, the cross-national validity of these simple models of aspiration formation have not been examined. There have been few cross-cultural empirical tests of the theories discussed earlier or of the underlying processes of aspiration adaptation. Both prospect theory and theories of aspiration level formation assume a universality that has yet to be confirmed empirically. Cultural values, norms, and social expectations may influence the selection of the reference outcome against which performance is evaluated, the salience of any attainment discrepancy, and the degree of individual's commitment to the goals promulgated in organizational settings (Murphy, 1998). Investigation of the robustness of models of aspiration formation across cultures is another important avenue for future research.

Having expressed these caveats, it is nonetheless interesting to speculate about possible interpretations of the findings. What we may have observed here is a form of catch up that takes place in managerial cognition of performance signals. When performance is down, rather than lowering the bar for future performance managers may be raising the goal for the next period in an attempt to overcome the cumulative effect of past failure. The steeper slope of the function in the negative domain suggests an even more pronounced cognitive response: The constant shift upward of the function is accompanied by a heightened reaction to each unit of attainment discrepancy. Not only is performance below goal a signal for a tougher goal in the next period, but the rate at which the goal increases is sharper when performance is below par. Interestingly, the results reported here also suggest that good performance is rewarded with a relatively smaller increase in goal, ensuring that branches that exceed their goal do not become victims of their own success.

Finally, the long-run implications of a system where targets are adjusted in this way should be considered. A considerable body of work (Lant & Mezias, 1990, 1992; Levinthal & March, 1981/1988; Mezias & Eisner, 1997; Mezias & Glynn, 1993; Mezias & Lant, 1994) has investigated some of the organizational implications of aspirations that adjust to performance. This study's results indicate that the adjustment process is somewhat more complex than has been assumed in this work. The implications of this different specification of the aspiration level updating process needs to be understood in the context of these models of organizations as systems that learn from experience.

REFERENCES

Bandura, A. (1977). *Social learning theory.* Englewood Cliffs, NJ: Prentice-Hall.

Clapham, S. E., & Schwenk, C. R. (1991). Self-serving attributions, managerial cognition, and company performance. *Strategic Management Journal, 12,* 219–229.

Cyert, R. M., & March, J. G. (1963). *A behavioral theory of the firm.* Englewood Cliffs, NJ: Prentice-Hall.

Earley, P., & Lituchy, T. (1991). Delineating goal and efficacy effects: A test of three models. *Journal of Applied Psychology, 76,* 81–98.

Eden, D. (1988). Pygmalion, goal setting, and expectancy: Compatible ways to boost productivity. *Academy of Management Review, 13,* 639–652.

Fiske, S. T., & Taylor, S. E. (1984). *Social cognition.* Reading, MA: Addison-Wesley.

Garland, H. (1985). A cognitive mediation theory of task goals and human performance. *Motivation and Emotion, 9,* 345–367.

Glynn, M. A., Lant, T., & Mezias, S. J. (1991). Incrementalism, learning and ambiguity: An experimental study of aspiration level updating. In J. L. Wall & L. R. Jauch (Eds.), Best paper proceedings of the *Academy of Management Meetings* (pp. 384–388). Madison, WI: Omnipress.

Gregory, R., Lichtenstein, S., & MacGregor, D. (1993). The role of past states in determining reference points for policy decisions. *Organizational Behavior and Human Decision Processes, 55,* 195–206.

Greve, H. R. (1998). Performance, aspirations and risky organizational change. *Administrative Science Quarterly, 43,* 58–86.

Heath, C., Larrick, R. P., & Wu, G. (1998). *Goals as reference points.* Unpublished manuscript.

Kahneman, D. (1992). Reference points, anchors, norms and mixed feelings. *Organizational Behavior and Human Decision Processes, 51,* 296–312.

Kahneman, D., Knetsch, J., & Thaler, R. (1986). Fairness as a constraint on profit seeking: Entitlements in the market. *American Economic Review, 76,* 728–41.

Kahneman, D., Knetsch, J., & Thaler, R. (1990). Experimental tests of the endowment effect and the coase theorum. *Journal of Political Economy, 98,* 1325–48.

Kahneman, D., & Tversky, A. (1979). Prospect theory: An analysis of decision under risk. *Econometrica, 47,* 263–292.

Kahneman, D., & Tversky, A. (1982). The psychology of preferences. *Scientific American*, 246, 160–173.

Kiesler, S., & Sproull, L. (1982). Managerial responses to changing environments: Perspectives on problem sensing from social cognition. *Administrative Science Quarterly*, 27, 548–570.

Lant, T. K. (1992). Aspiration level updating: An empirical exploration. *Management Science*, 38, 623–644.

Lant, T. K., & Mezias, S. J. (1990). Managing discontinuous change: A simulation study of organizational learning and entrepreneurship. *Strategic Management Journal*, 11, 147–179.

Lant, T. K., & Mezias, S. J. (1992). An organizational learning model of convergence and reorientation. *Organization Science*, 3, 47–71.

Lant, T. K., Milliken, F. J., & Batra, B. (1992). The role of managerial learning and interpretation in strategic persistence and reorientation: An empirical exploration. *Strategic Management Journal*, 13, 585–608.

Larrick, R. P., Heath, C., & Wu, G. (1998). *Multiple reference points: Choice, affect and motivation* (Working Paper) Chicago: University of Chicago Graduate School of Business.

Levin, I. P., & Gaeth, G. J. (1988). How consumers are affected by the framing of attribute information before and after consuming the product. *Journal of Consumer Research*, 15, 374–378.

Levinthal, D. A., & March, J. G. (1988). A model of adaptive organizational search. In J. G. March *Decisions and organizations* (pp. 87–218). Cambridge, MA: Basil Blackwell. (Reprinted from *Journal of Economic Behavior and Organization* (1981), 2, pp. 307–333.)

Levitt, B., & March, J. G. (1988). Organizational learning. *Annual Review of Sociology*, 14, 319–340.

Lewin, K., Dembo, T., Festinger, L., & Sears, P. (1944). Level of aspiration. In Hunt, J. (Ed.), *Personality and the behavior disorders*. New York: The Ronald Press Company.

Locke, E., & Latham, P. (1990). *A theory of goal setting and task performance*. Englewood Cliffs, NJ: Prentice-Hall.

Locke, E. A., Shaw, K. N., Saari, L. M., & Latham, G. P. (1981). Goal setting and task performance: 1969–1980. *Psychological Bulletin*, 90, 123–133.

Luthans, F., & Kreitner, R. (1985). *Organizational behavior modification and beyond. An operant and social learning approach*. Glenview, IL: Scott, Foresman.

Maheswaran, D., & Meyers-Levy, J. (1990). The influence of message framing and issues involvement. *Journal of Marketing Research*, 27, 361–367.

March, J. G. (1988). Variable risk preferences and adaptive aspirations. *Journal of Economic Behavior and Organization*, 9, 5–24.

March, J. G. (1991). Exploration and exploitation in organizational learning. *Organization Science*, 2, 71–87.

March, J. G., & Shapira, Z. (1992). Variable risk preference and the focus of attention. *Psychological Review*, 99, 172–183.

March, J. G., & Simon, H. (1958). *Organizations*. New York: Wiley.

Mezias, S. J. (1988). Aspiration level effects: An empirical investigation. *Journal of Economic Behavior and Organization*, 10, 389–400.

Mezias, S. J., Chen, Y. R., & Murphy, P. R. (1997). *Adaptive aspirations in an American financial services organization: A field study*. Unpublished manuscript.

Mezias, S. J., & Eisner, A. B. (1997). Competition, imitation and innovation: An organizational learning approach. *Advances in Strategic Management*, 14, 261–294.

Mezias, S. J., & Glynn, M. A. (1993). The three faces of corporate renewal: Institution, revolution and evolution. *Strategic Management Journal*, 14, 77–101.

Mezias, S. J., & Lant, T. K. (1994). Mimetic learning and the evolution of organizational populations. In J. Baum & J. Singh (Eds.), *Evolutionary dynamics of organizations* (pp. 179–198). New York: Oxford University Press.

Mezias, S. J., & Murphy, P. R. (1998). Adaptive aspirations in an American financial services organization: A field study. *Academy of Management Proceedings*.

Milliken, F. J. (1990). Perceiving and interpreting environmental change: An examination of college administrators' interpretations of changing demographics. *Academy of Management Journal, 33*, 42–63.

Milliken, F. J., & Lant, T. K. (1991). The effect of an organization's recent performance history on strategic persistence and change: The role of managerial interpretations. In J. Dutton, A. Huff, & P. Shrivastava (Eds.), *Advances in strategic management* (pp. 125–152). Greenwich, CT: JAI.

Mintzberg, H., & Waters, J. A. (1985). Of strategies, deliberate and emergent. *Strategic Management Journal, 6*, 257–272.

Morecroft, J. D. (1985). Rationality in the analysis of behavioral simulation models. *Management Science, 31*, 900–916.

Murphy, P. R. (1998). *Aspiration adaptation: A cross-national study*. Unpublished dissertation proposal, New York University.

Muth, J. F. (1961). Rational expectation and the theory of price movements. *Econometrica, 29*, 315–335.

Shapira, Z. (1989). Task choice and assigned goals as determinants of task motivation and performance. *Organizational Behavior and Human Decision Processes, 44*, 141–165.

Skinner, B. F. (1938). *The behavior of organisms*. New York: Appleton-Century-Crofts.

Starbuck, W. H., & Milliken, F. J. (1988). Executive's perceptual filters: What they notice and how they make sense. In D. Hambrick (Ed.), *the executive effect: Concepts and methods for studying top managers* (pp.35–65). Greenwich, CT: JAI.

Staw, B. (1981). The escalation of commitment to a course of action. *Academy of Management Review, 6*, 577–587.

Staw, B., McKechnie, P. I., & Puffer, S. M. (1983). The justification of organizational performance. *Administrative Science Quarterly, 28*, 582–600.

Staw, B., & Ross, J. (1978). Commitment to a policy decision: A multi theoretical perspective. *Administrative Science Quarterly, 23*, 40–64.

Staw, B., Sandelands, L. E., & Dutton, J. E. (1981). Threat-rigidity effects in organizational behavior: A multi-level analysis. *Administrative Science Quarterly, 26*, 501–524.

Thaler, R. (1992). *The winner's curse: Paradoxes and anomalies of economic life*. New York: The Free Press.

Tversky, A., & Kahneman, D. (1981). The framing of decisions and the psychology of choice. *Science, 211*, 453–458.

Vroom, V. H. (1964). *Work and motivation*. New York: Wiley.

Commentary: Motivational Preconditions and Intraorganizational Barriers to Learning in Organizational Settings

Kathleen M. Sutcliffe
University of Michigan

Early work in cognition generated enthusiasm for the cognitive perspective by focusing on cognition itself. However, as the field has grown, so too has the capacity to address key managerial issues by tying cognitive work to substantive issues in organization studies such as learning and firm performance. The three chapters in this section share a similar interest in the idea that knowledge and learning are fundamental to sustainable competitive advantage. The chapters in this section examine the motivational preconditions and intraorganizational contextual barriers to learning in organizational settings. Moreover, these studies raise interesting issues that can be used to invigorate future work on cognition and learning.

Motivational Preconditions and Barriers to Learning

Diane Rulke and Srilata Zaheer's exploratory study (chap. 5, this volume) begins with the idea that a firm's learning capabilities depend on self-knowledge and resource knowledge. Drawing from the literature on transactive memory (e.g., Wegner, 1986), these authors argue that the effective retrieval and use of knowledge within a firm requires managers to have metaknowledge about existing expertise, about knowledge that is needed, and about where (in the organization) new knowledge can be found. Accumulated prior knowledge increases assimilation and use of new knowledge by increasing the ability to put new knowledge into memory and by increasing the ability to use knowledge because of the self-reinforcing aspect of memory development (Bower & Hilgard, 1981; Cohen & Levinthal, 1990, 129–131). The more objects, patterns, and concepts that are stored in memory, the more readily people acquire new information and the better they are at using the information in new settings. If people do not possess appropriate or sufficient prior knowledge when they acquire knowledge, they may have difficulty making the new knowledge fully intelligible (Lindsay & Norman, 1977, p. 517). The authors test their ideas using archival and interview data gathered from managers in multiple units of a firm in the retail foods industry—traditionally a low-margin industry currently undergoing rapid change in competition, technology, and cross-border investments. Although the propositions are largely unsupported, several interesting findings emerge. Causal maps from interview data show that low depth of self-knowledge is negatively associated with store innovation performance. Surprisingly, however, resource knowledge is negatively associated with store efficiency (i.e., sales per square foot). The authors present a plausible explanation for this puzzling finding by noting that this may reflect the fact that managers with greater resource knowledge recently have been sent to turn around poorly performing stores. Still, this study may be disconcerting to cognition researchers interested in transactive memory and absorptive capacity because the data do not show a straightforward positive link between cognition and results. And, it may challenge the beliefs of many theorists who think that the cognitive inertia arising from long experience makes it hard for decision makers to reconceptualize their mental models, particularly when the material conditions of a marketplace change (e.g., Hodgkinson, 1997).

In contrast to Rulke and Zaheer who investigate preconditions that promote knowledge transfer and learning in organizations, Catherine Paul-Chowdhury investigates learning preconditions from another angle by asking the contrasting question: What impedes the transfer of learning in organizations? Paul-Chowdhury examines loan loss events in a sample of banks to understand not only what was learned after these sector-specific loan loss events but more importantly, how learning was impeded. Using archival data and interview data gathered from people representing four key departments within each of the banks, Paul-Chowdhury finds that learning is blocked by a lack of horizontal communication between units: Knowledge simply is not transferred laterally from one group to another. Knowledge (learning) is blocked also when training is haphazard and not closely aligned with the current organizational culture and context. What happens is that people in subunits resist new information and persist with old beliefs when lessons and messages conveyed in central training efforts conflict with a sub-unit's preexisting normative practices. In coming to understand the factors that impede learning, Paul-Chowdhury discovers factors that promote learning. For example, the lack of direct horizontal communication is offset by the dissemination of new organizational policies and procedures that incorporate previous learning. The process of revising and renegotiating policies and procedures links learning with firm effectiveness and sustainability: By encapsulating new knowledge into new procedures, organizational complacency and rigidity are forestalled. Moreover, knowledge is created and promoted by key executives. Key executives are a conduit of learning lessons and also central in constructing the lessons themselves. Through formal speeches and informal conversations, and through the telling and retelling of stories, executives convert subjective knowledge (e.g., knowledge believed by a few people) into objective knowledge (e.g., knowledge believed by many people). And in this way, knowledge is socially constructed (Czarniawska, 1997).

Although learning is often motivated by feedforward mechanisms as is seen in the Paul-Chowdhury study, it is also motivated by feedback. As Murphy, Mezias, and Chen argue, learning processes often are initiated by feedback about results—particularly by discrepancies in previous performance attainment. Presumably, the divergence between actual performance and goals is a potent force that counteracts strong persistence pressures and instigates learning trials because it calls into question the effectiveness of a prior strategy. The question is to what extent does performance feedback influence the formation of subsequent aspirations in real organizations? This question has been explored previously using computer simulations and laboratory experiments, yet rarely has it been examined in field settings. To remedy this state of affairs, these authors test the ideas using archival data gathered from 94 bank branches over a three-year period. Overall, the story that emerges is that aspiration level is seriously dampened by negative information. Specifically, aspiration level formation is a function of the valence of performance feedback, target achievement in the previous period, and the previous period goal. Moreover, the results show a general downward drift in aspiration levels independent of previous aspiration and previous performance. Together, the results suggest that negative performance feedback may inhibit learning by dissuading managers from engaging in learning trials (e.g., increasing aspiration levels).

Learning Channels

Each of these chapters examines the role of learning channels in facilitating knowledge transfer and learning. For example, Rulke and Zaheer examine two channels: purposive and relational channels. Purposive channels include formal training sessions and other mechanisms, such as internal newsletters and competitive benchmarking efforts, by which explicit and specific knowledge is transmitted. Relational channels, in contrast, include more informal transmission mechanisms such as social contact with peers or others inside and outside the organization. The authors find a strong positive association between purposive channels and efficiency. An interesting possibility is that context specific operational knowledge is better disseminated through more formal mechanisms such as training or active benchmarking. These mechanisms may provide for a more precise transmission of operational knowledge because they help to focus attention to key elements and contextualize the knowledge by tying content specifically to problems experienced by people in the organization. As Paul-Chowdhury finds, the effectiveness of formal training to disseminate specific learning lessons depends both on providing the what to be learned and also on providing sufficient contextual detail so that people can fully grasp and integrate the finer details of the lesson.

Performance monitoring also appears to be a potent learning channel as Murphy, et al. show. This finding is consistent with research on firms in high-velocity industries (Eisenhardt, 1989). Performance monitoring influences organizational learning by affecting the timely sensing of idiosyncratic threats, problems, or trends. A more timely and accurate detection of problems and opportunities improves operational and tactical decision making (Eisenhardt, 1989). Thus, presumably, decision makers can initiate corrective actions before substantial problems materialize.

Invigorating Insights and Implications for Advancing Theory

These studies raise a number of interesting issues and questions that can be used to invigorate and advance future research in this domain. Several are singled out that are central to advancing theory on cognition and learning: culture, performance pressures, learning costs, and attribution framing.

Culture.   Failures are an important precondition to learning in organizations (Sitkin, 1992; Weick, Sutcliffe, & Obstfeld, 1999). Yet, communication about previous failures (i.e., loan losses) was largely inhibited in the sample of banks Paul-Chowdhury studied. As she explains, executives were unwilling to embarrass anybody—especially those top bank executives to whom some loan losses were attributed. These findings suggest the possibility that this sample of organizations had cultures that were unfriendly to discussing and examining failures. Yet, studies of innovation processes, high-risk technologies, and public health show that it is extremely difficult for organizations to sustain high levels of reliability when dealing with highly uncertain, complex problems unless they incorporate mechanisms for sensing and learning from failures, errors, and mistakes. The problem is, few organizational cultures are truly open to honest reporting and examination of errors and failures. And as a result, opportunities for learning are seriously circumscribed. Research examining variation in organizational cultures along this dimension and the underlying mechanisms that shape cultures in this direction may provide a number of new insights into why some organizations are better at learning than others.

Performance Pressures.   Learning from failures and mistakes is tied directly to the ability to perceive and make sense of these adverse events. Yet as the Paul-Chowdhury study suggests, even when threats (i.e., failures, mistakes, etc.) are recognized, people often normalize them. This means they reinterpret deviations within the context of the status quo thereby fitting data to existing expectations and within norms of acceptable performance (Vaughan, 1996). The tendency to incorporate discrepant information into existing belief systems diminishes the importance of the information, increases the likelihood that it will be ignored or overlooked, and decreases its potential to contribute to knowledge. Consequently, learning is curtailed. Paul-Chowdhury finds that managers tend to normalize discrepant information when they are under pressures to produce. Production pressures appear to inhibit communication between account managers, increase their defensiveness to probes and questions from relevant others, and increase their tendency to discount discrepant information. What is ironic is that production pressures both increase the likelihood that strong signals will be ignored and also limit people's ability to interpret or make sense of the signals (Weick et al., 1999) because people's cognitive abilities are taxed. The problem is that as people normalize and create a more simplified picture, there is a higher probability that error signals will accumulate and go undetected possibly with untoward or even disastrous consequences for an organization. Studies examining performance pressure and how it influences sensing and interpretation may provide a number of useful insights into impediments to learning.

Learning Costs. An interesting possibility that follows from Rulke and Zaheer relates to the role of experience in affecting outcomes, seemingly through better sensing and learning capabilities. Recall the finding that managerial experience is positively associated with store innovation but negatively associated with store efficiency. It is hard to decipher these results with certainty, given that longer tenured managers recently may have been transferred to poorer performing stores. However, one possibility is that managers with long experience have better sensing and coping capabilities in that they are able to sense trends more quickly and have better capabilities at recombining existing knowledge, skills, and abilities into novel combinations (Weick et al., 1999). Whether this capability is at odds with achieving efficiency outcomes is unknown. However, this may reflect the recurrent tension between exploration and exploitation (March, 1991) and the idea that learning costs. Future researchers may want to more carefully examine these tensions.

Attribution Framing as a Mediating Process. Murphy et al. suggest that the framing of past performance as either a success or failure creates a positive or negative decision frame for the formation of subsequent aspiration level. And, they find that negative performance strongly dampens aspirations in the next period. Still, an important question left unanswered in this study concerns how managers attribute the performance feedback, particularly with respect to the locus of causality. Managerial attributions of causal locus—whether the cause of an outcome resides in the organization (an internal attribution) or in the environment or situation (an external attribution)—are important because they mediate between performance feedback and managerial actions and subsequent outcomes (Sutcliffe, 1997). In other words, causal inferences guide subsequent courses of action. Although some evidence suggests that managers are biased in their causal interpretation of performance data, the evidence is not universal (see Fiol, 1995; Lant, Milliken, & Batra, 1992). Researchers are coming to realize that decision makers' attributional processes may be shaped in fundamental ways by organizational and institutional structures. Clearly, there is a need for studies that examine both the contextual antecedents of executives' attributions and how attributions channel managerial actions and organizational outcomes.

ACKNOWLEDGEMENT

The preparation of this chapter was partially supported by the National Science Foundation (Grants No. SBR-95-50461 and SBR-94-22367).

REFERENCES

Bower, G. H., & Hilgard, E. R. (1981). *Theories of learning.* Englewood Cliffs, NJ: Prentice-Hall.

Cohen, W. M., & Levinthal, D. A. (1990). Absorptive capacity: A new perspective on learning and innovation. *Administrative Science Quarterly, 35,* 128–152.

Czarniawska, B. (1997). Learning organizing in a changing institutional order. *Management Learning, 28,* 475–495.

Eisenhardt, K. M. (1989). Making fast strategic decisions in high-velocity environments. *Academy of Management Journal, 32,* 543–576.

Fiol, C. M. (1995). Corporate communications: Comparing executives' private and public statements. *Academy of Management Journal, 38,* 522–536.

Hodgkinson, G. P. (1997). Cognitive inertia in a trubulent market: The case of UK residential estate agents. *Journal of Management Studies, 34,* 921–945.

Lant, T. K., Milliken, F. J., & Batra, B. (1992). The role of managerial learning and interpretation in strategic persistence and reorientation: An empirical exploration. *Strategic Management Journal, 13,* 585–608.

Lindsay, P. H., & Norman, D. A. (1977). *Human information processing.* Orlando, FL: Academic Press.

March, J. G. (1991). Exploration and exploitation in organizational learning. *Organization Science, 2,* 71–87.

Sitkin, S. B. (1992). Learning through failure: The strategy of small losses. In B. M. Staw & L. L. Cummings (Eds.), *Research in organizational behavior,* (pp. 231–266. Greenwich, CT: JAI.

Sutcliffe, K. M. (1997). The nuances of learning. In J. Walsh & A. Huff (Eds.), *Advances in strategic management* (pp. 331–336). Greenwich, CT: JAI.

Vaughan, D. (1996). *The Challenger launch decision.* Chicago: University of Chicago Press.

Wegner, D. M. (1986). Transactive memory: A contemporary analysis of the group mind. In G. Mullen & G. Goethels (Eds.), *Theories of group behavior* (pp. 185–208). New York: Springer-Verlag.

Weick, K. E., Sutcliffe, K. M., & Obstfeld, D. (1999). Organizing for high reliability: Processes of collective mindfulness. In R. I. Sutton & B. M. Staw (Eds.), *Research in Organizational Behavior, 21,* 81–124. Greenwich, CT: JAI.

PART

III

---

*Cognition at Work:
Managerial Thinking
and Decision Making*

Defining Away Dangers: A Study in the Influences of Managerial Cognition on Information Systems

Michal Tamuz
University of Texas-Houston

Consider the following event that occurred in the skies over New York's LaGuardia airport on April 3, 1998:

> Under the FAA's rules, the event was not classified as an operational error, a designation used when two planes come closer than aircraft separation standards.
>
> That the two planes were dangerously close is not in dispute. The incident occurred at 8:21 a.m. when Air Canada Flight 703, an Airbus A-320, was cleared for takeoff. At the same time, USAir Flight 920, a DC-9, was preparing to land on an intersecting runway. The controller handling both planes realized that the Airbus was not going to clear the runway by the time the DC-9 landed, and ordered the DC-9 flight to abort the landing. That left both flights climbing.
>
> The controller told investigators the aircraft came within 20 feet of each other. The USAir captain estimated that he was within 85 feet of the Air Canada plane's tail when he passed under it....

Although the event meets the criteria for a near midair collision, it was not classified as an operational error because the controller was responsible for keeping the planes separated by watching them out of the tower. (Adcock, 1998, p. A4)

The categories organizations use to classify potential dangers are important. Some labels call attention to events, warning of possible disaster, whereas others signal that because no harm was done, the events can safely be ignored. Categorization also acts as a toggle switch for organizational information processing routines. If an event is sorted into one category, standard procedures require that the organization collect more information about it. But, if the same event is classified differently, no additional information is gathered.

The categorization of potential dangers guides safety information systems as they scan the environment, gathering data about emergent hazards. These systems use coding categories that reflect how their managers think about and classify potential dangers. The study of environmental scanning systems, such as those in the air transportation industry, provides an opportunity to examine how categories created by managerial cognition affect the interpretation of ambiguous events and the gathering of information that could be used in knowledge generation.

In this chapter, the focus is on the categorization of ambiguous, potentially dangerous encounters in the sky. Drawing on extensive interviews with key participants in safety monitoring systems, the study includes a comparative analysis of these aviation safety information systems (A-SIS) and generates propositions to guide future research. The main argument is that the process of classifying potentially dangerous events affects the allocation of attention and the construction of information processing routines that, in turn, influence the availability of information that the organization can transform into knowledge.

CLASSIFYING POTENTIAL DANGERS

Potential dangers are inherently ambiguous events, subject to definition and interpretation by organizational decision makers. Indeed, managerial decision makers in one safety monitoring system can label the same potentially dangerous event differently than those in another. They can focus on what could have happened, defining an event as a near accident or incident in which no damages or injuries occurred but which under slightly different conditions could have resulted in an accident (National Research Council, 1980). Alternatively, they can concentrate on the details of what actually occurred, determining whether someone strayed from standard procedures.

To illustrate, consider the close encounter over LaGuardia airport, described earlier. From a pilot's perspective, this was clearly a near midair collision. "This was an exceedingly dangerous event, as close as you can get and not have an accident," a representative of the Air Line Pilots Association was quoted as saying (Mustain, 1998, p. 22). Indeed, the pilot of the descending aircraft perceived the event as a near midair collision, reported it to a Federal Aviation Administration (FAA) Flight Standards Office, and his report eventually triggered an investigation, supported by additional data gathering (Adcock, 1998). From the point of view of an air traffic controller: "As far as the FAA reporting there was really nothing to report. There was no incident," explained a representative of the controllers union (Crystal, 1998). Technically, this potentially dangerous event did not even meet the FAA definition of an operational error (e.g., Hutchinson, 1998). If routine procedures permit a controller to maintain distance between aircraft by observing them through the tower window, then there are no minimum separation standards. Because the event was not classified as an operational error, no one in the air traffic control tower reported the event and no information was collected.

Seeking to make sense of tales of encounters with potential dangers, air transportation organizations have developed methods to sift through their own experience and the experience of others. Although members of the aviation community use different expressions to describe potential dangers, they share a common interpretation of them. Their descriptions "emphasize how close the organization came to a disaster, thus the reality of danger in the guise of safety" (March, Sproull, & Tamuz, 1991, p. 10). Near accidents are interpreted as warnings rather than as signs that the system is robust.

Aviation safety information systems (A-SIS) have formalized issue classification methods to simplify the tasks of sorting and triage of safety-related events. They are confronted with two main classification tasks. First, these A-SIS develop categories to differentiate near accidents from accidents on one extreme and from normal operations, including expected component failures, on the other. Second, they sort through the data on possible dangers to identify potentially significant events that may yield knowledge about accident precursors.

CONCEPTUAL FRAMEWORK

Categorization in Organizations

Categorization shapes how decision makers interpret, gather information about, and respond to strategic issues. In a seminal paper, Dutton and

Jackson (1987) applied categorization theory (Rosch, 1975, 1978) to the study of the identification and response to strategic issues in organizations. They argued that strategic issues provide decision makers with ambiguous stimuli, and thus, labeling processes can affect how managers define and respond to strategic issues. Furthermore, they posited that the categorization of strategic issues can "become crystallized in formal routines and programs in organizations" such as "environmental scanning activities that rely on issue classification systems" (Dutton & Jackson, 1987, p. 80). Following Dutton and Jackson, the classification schemes embedded in the aviation safety environmental scanning systems are examined.

Category systems are conceptualized as having a structure, with vertical and horizontal dimensions (Dutton & Jackson, 1987; Rosch, 1978).

> The vertical dimension has three levels, with each higher level being inclusive of the levels below it. The highest, most inclusive level of a category system is the *superordinate* level. Superordinate categories subsume *basic* level categories, which in turn, subsume *subordinate* categories. (Dutton & Jackson, 1987, p. 78)

In this study, the relations between the classification schemes at different vertical levels are explored. Potential dangers constitute the superordinate level of categorization. At the basic level, potential dangers are classified as threats to rule enforcement or opportunities for learning. The subordinate categories include event specifications, such as those defining operational errors and near midair collisions.

Attention Allocation

The allocation of attention affects and is affected by how organizational decision makers interpret the meaning of events, and in turn, shapes how they learn from experience. In developing a behavioral theory of attention allocation, March (1989) argued that the organization of attention is a "central process out of which decisions arise" (March, 1989, p. 3). Weick (1995) noted that as individuals pay attention to events, they initiate a process of retrospective sense making. By focusing attention on some attributes of events and distracting attention from others, the organization reduces the "ambiguity of history" (March & Olsen, 1976). But, as organizations simplify the interpretation of events through categorization and coding, they can also limit and distort the interpretation of their experience.

Proposed Model

Building on Dutton and Jackson (1987) and March (1989), in this study the author examined how safety information systems, scanning the organizational environment for potential dangers, classify ambiguous events and codify their interpretation. Managerial cognition is expressed in the categories that information systems use to classify potentially harmful events, in particular, in the basic classification of potential dangers as threats to rule enforcement or opportunities for learning. Categorization, by channeling attention to some events and away from others, also affects the choice of information processing routines. By guiding the collection, collation, and storage of information, these routines influence the resulting pool of information available for organizational learning and knowledge generation (see Fig. 8.1.).

Whereas the model recognizes that incentives also affect the allocation of attention (March & Shapira, 1987) and the construction of information processing routines (Tamuz, 1987), this study focused on the effects of categorization. The aviation safety information systems gather and classify reports of potential dangers that provide organizational decision makers with information, a raw material for knowledge generation. The actual process by which the organization builds its knowledge base is beyond the purview of the current study.

RESEARCH QUESTIONS

In this study, five questions are examined. Each question explores different relations within or among elements in the conceptual framework. For example, the relations between different levels of classification are explored as part of the general process of categorization. The effects of categorization are also explored at different stages of designing and implementing an A-SIS. The first three questions examine the effects of categorization during the design of a safety information system. The last two questions analyze categorization at different stages of information processing, in particular, at the initial data collection stage and the final information storage stage.

The first question examines the basic level of categorization. It seeks indicators that would support or refute the proposition that aviation safety information systems initially classify potential dangers as threats to rule enforcement or opportunities for learning.

The second question explores the link between managerial cognition and categorization. Specifically, it explores the relation between the construction of the basic categories of threat and opportunity and the composition of

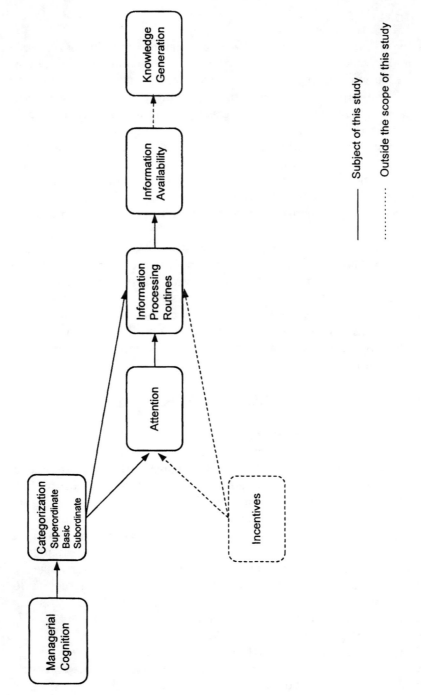

FIG. 8.1. Conceptual framework.

the decision-making teams who constructed the categories. Lacking data that could provide a direct assessment of managerial cognition, the study explores a rough, indirect indicator of managerial cognition: the composition of managerial groups who participated in the design of the aviation safety information systems.

The third question examines the relation between categorization, on a basic level, and the construction of an information processing routine. It asks whether the basic classification of events, in which potential dangers are labeled as threats or opportunities, is associated with the key design choice of a routine for permitting (or preventing) the use of data to justify the enforcement of rule infractions.

The fourth question explores the relation between two levels of categorization, basic and subordinate, and in doing so, explores the relation between categorization and attention. In the process of refining the classification of ambiguous mishaps, the organization focuses attention on some events while ignoring others. Specifically, the fourth question asks whether the basic categorization of potential dangers as a threat to rule maintenance or as a learning opportunity affects the subsequent coding of events, in particular, how precisely an A-SIS defines the subordinate categories it uses to identify and differentiate among potentially dangerous events.

The fifth question examines how categorization, through the allocation of attention, affects the construction of information processing routines. Specifically, it considers if the classification of potential dangers is associated with the choice of information processing routines for the retention and storage of information.

METHODS

Part of a larger research project on safety monitoring systems, the study builds on interviews with key participants in U. S. aviation safety information systems (A-SIS), analyzes reports gathered by these systems, and examines documents for coding the reports. The analysis draws on two rounds of semistructured interviews, the first conducted in 1987 and the second in 1995. Note that the study was not originally designed to interview members of the managerial teams who designed each of the systems. Using qualitative research methods (Miles & Huberman, 1994), categorization processes are examined by observing within and comparing among the A-SIS. Based on an assessment of seven A-SIS, research propositions are developed to guide future research on safety reporting systems operating in other high-hazard industries.

The examination of an aviation safety information system permits the observation of multiple, sequential categorization processes. As A-SIS participants begin to make sense of data gathered from the environment, they sort events into different categories. The process of labeling and sorting events is repeated at different stages, as the data move through the information system, from data gathering to storage.

AVIATION SAFETY INFORMATION SYSTEMS

The aviation safety information systems examined in this study gather descriptions of potentially dangerous events mainly from pilots and air traffic controllers. They collect accounts of potential dangers, excluding reports of accidents, intentional misdeeds, and events related to sabotage and terrorism. These A-SIS monitor potentially damaging events rather than documenting actual damages such as those from accidents and runway incursions or tracking routine aircraft component failures. They provide safety-related information to the industry, including regulators, airlines, aircraft manufacturers, professionals, and accident investigators.

In the United States, multiple forms of aviation safety information systems have emerged (e.g., U. S. Office of Technology Assessment, 1988). Various stakeholder groups have sponsored alternative methods of organizing A-SIS. Some industry-wide systems operate mainly on an interorganizational level, gathering reports from individuals working in various airlines and air traffic control facilities throughout the country. Other airline-based systems function on an organizational level, collecting narratives from employees. Among the A-SIS examined in this study, five operate at the interorganizational level and two at the organizational level (see Table 8.1).

The exploratory study design seeks to include all of the relevant information systems for monitoring potential dangers and thus, seven aviation safety information systems (A-SIS) are examined. Two A-SIS remain outside the scope of the study. The FAA Hotline was excluded because it lacks a computerized database and does not represent a fully developed information system. Although the National Transportation Safety Board operates a complex information system and gathers reports of incidents as well as accidents, it was excluded because the system was primarily designed to collect accident data.

Industry-Wide Aviation Safety Information Systems

As part of the National Airspace Incident Monitoring System (NAIMS), the FAA funds and operates three industry-wide aviation safety information systems. One system monitors operational errors among air traffic controllers (abbreviated here as FAA ATC); a second system tracks pilot deviations from

TABLE 8.1

Aviation Safety Information Systems

Aviation Safety Information System (A-SIS)	Sponsor	Funding	Location	Source of Reports
FAA Operational Error System (FAA ATC)	Federal Aviation Administration (FAA), part of National Airspace Incident Monitoring System (NAIMS)	FAA	Industry-wide and facility-based	Air traffic controllers
FAA Pilot Deviation System (FAA PILOT)	Federal Aviation Administration, part of NAIMS	FAA	Industry-wide	Air traffic controllers
FAA Near Mid-air Collision System (FAA-NMAC)	Federal Aviation Administration, part of NAIMS	FAA	Industry-wide	Pilots
Aviation Safety Reporting System (NASA-ASRS)	National Aeronautics and Space Administration	FAA	Industry-wide	Open to aviation community, pilots file most reports
Air Line Pilots Association (ALPA)	Air Line Pilots Association (ALPA)	ALPA	Industry-wide	Pilots
Airline Safety Action Partnership (ASAP)	Co-Sponsors: FAA Flight Standards, American Airlines, pilot association of American Airlines	American Airlines	Airline-based	American Airlines' pilots
British Airways Safety Information System (BASIS)	An airline, BASIS software supplied by British Airways	An airline	Airline-based	Pilots employed by a particular airline

standards set by controllers (FAA PILOT); and a third system documents near midair collisions reported by pilots (FAA NMAC, pronounced nee-mack).

In an innovative arrangement, the Aviation Safety Reporting System (NASA ASRS) is funded by the FAA, administered under the auspices of NASA, and operated by a contractor (Reynard, Billings, Cheaney, & Hardy, 1986). The NASA ASRS, a nonpunitive industry-wide system, collects voluntary, confidential reports of safety-related events from pilots, air traffic controllers, and other individual members of the aviation community. For example, if the FAA discovers an air traffic violation and the pilots involved can demonstrate that they have voluntarily reported the event to NASA ASRS, the pilots may be granted limited immunity from FAA prosecution.

The AirLine Pilots Association (ALPA) also sponsors an interorganizational safety monitoring system, gathering data from its member pilots. Supported by a network of safety committees located in airlines and airports across the nation, the professional association of pilots employs a team of experts who analyze the safety-related reports and sponsors representatives who lobby for change.

Airline-Based Aviation Safety Information Systems

The study also includes two airline-based systems for monitoring potential dangers: British Airways Safety Information System (BASIS), an innovative program adopted by several U. S. airlines, and the Airline Safety Action Partnership (ASAP), currently operated by American Airlines and under consideration by others. Like BASIS, the ASAP system emphasizes the importance of seeking corrective action, but this unique program has emerged from a distinctly U.S. regulatory environment. Pioneered in American Airlines, it was developed through a cooperative venture joining airline management, the airline-based pilots association, and the Southwest Region of FAA Flight Standards, responsible for enforcing air traffic regulations.

ANALYSIS

Question One: Labeling Potential Dangers as Threats or Opportunities

This study examines whether the initial classification of potential dangers as threats or opportunities is reflected in the design and operation of aviation safety information systems. But, it is difficult to observe directly the use of these basic categories because A-SIS managers do not necessarily use the terms *threat* and *opportunity* to describe potentially damaging events. However, to an external observer, the A-SIS clearly differ in how they label reports of potential dangers.

Four related indicators reflect whether an A-SIS uses the basic categories of threat or opportunity to classify potentially damaging events. They include whether an A-SIS: (a) chooses terms with a negative or neutral connotation to describe potential dangers; (b) focuses on the event or, alternatively, on the reporting of it; (c) seeks to reduce (or augment) the number of safety-related events reported; and (d) evaluates an increase in the volume of events reported as a negative (or positive) performance indicator (see Table 8.2). The choice of terms for describing potential dangers will be described in the next section, followed by an examination of the remaining three indicators.

The terms that an A-SIS uses to describe potentially dangerous events may provide insights into its basic categorization scheme. If an A-SIS classifies events as threats to existing rules and regulations, it may tend to use a term with a negative connotation. Alternatively, if an A-SIS classifies a potential danger as an opportunity for learning, it is more likely to choose a neutral term or one with a positive connotation.

The seven A-SIS vary in the language they use to describe potential dangers, although this indicator does not clearly differentiate among them. Two of the systems use terms with negative connotations. The FAA ATC system uses *operational error* to describe events in which air traffic controllers fail to maintain adequate separation between aircraft; the FAA PILOT uses the term *pilot deviation* if a pilot is held accountable for a similar event. In this context, the words *error* and *deviation* clearly have negative connotations. The FAA NMAC uses *near midair collision*, a nonjudgmental term, to describe the events it monitors. Two A-SIS use terms that have explicitly neutral wording. The NASA ASRS uses several neutral terms to describe the reports it gathers including *incident, safety report,* and *aviation safety hazard* (Reynard, et al., 1986). BASIS uses the terms *incident* and *safety incident,* to describe incidents with accident potential (Holtom, 1991) or near accidents (MacGregor & Hopfl, 1997).

The ASAP uses two contrasting terms. The first is the neutral *incident,* but the second word, *violation,* clearly carries a negative connotation. These terms reflect the stated goals of the ASAP to gather data about general safety concerns as well as possible violations of Federal Aviation Regulations (FAR). The Air Line Pilots Association system does not use a specific term to describe potential dangers, although its database adopts the BASIS terminology.

TABLE 8.2

Basic Categorization of Potential Dangers

Aviation Safety Information System (A-SIS)	Basic Category	Descriptive Term	Focus	Reporting Potential Dangers	Safety Indicator	A-SIS Performance Indicator
FAA Operational Error System (FAA ATC)	Threat to rule enforcement	Negative: operational error	Event	Reduce	Yes	Yes, performance inversely related to reporting
FAA Pilot Deviation System (FAA Pilot)	Threat to rule enforcement	Negative: pilot deviation	Event	Reduce	Yes	No, reflects pilot error
FAA Near Midair Collision System (FAA NMAC)	Threat to rule enforcement	Neutral: near midair collision	Event	Reduce	Yes, but affected by voluntary reporting	Yes, performance inversely related to reporting
Aviation Safety Reporting System (NASA ASRS)	Opportunity for learning	Neutral: incident, safety report	Reporting	Promote	No, affected by voluntary reporting	Yes, performance varies with reporting
Air Line Pilots Association (ALPA)	Opportunity for learning	No specific term	Reporting	Promote	No, affected by voluntary reporting	No
Airline Safety Action Partnership (ASAP)	Opportunity for learning	Mixed, Neutral, and Negative: incident, violation	Reporting	Promote	No, affected by voluntary reporting	Yes, performance varies with reporting
British Airways Safety Information System (BASIS)	Opportunity for learning	Neutral: incident, safety incident	Reporting	Promote	No, affected by voluntary reporting	Yes, performance varies with reporting

168

Consider the aviation safety information systems that categorize potentially dangerous events primarily as a threat to the enforcement of existing rules and regulations. These systems focus on identifying and gathering data on all of the pertinent *events*. By labeling as a *threat* events in which no damages or injuries occurred, the organization lowers the threshold of the definition of danger. Because such events are seen as threats to rule enforcement, the A-SIS seeks to reduce the number of event reports collected. In A-SIS, such as the FAA NMAC, the system for monitoring near midair collisions, managers often reason that by preventing minor incidents they can lessen the frequency of major accidents (U.S. General Accounting Office, 1989). Reduction in the number of potential dangers reported becomes one of the measures by which such an A-SIS assesses its own performance and, to some extent, the safety of air transportation (e.g., Crystal, 1998; U. S. Federal Aviation Administration, 1990).

Conversely, aviation safety information systems may classify potential dangers as an opportunity for learning. These A-SIS concentrate on event *reporting*, the description and explanation of potential dangers, rather than on controlling the events themselves. Although these systems recognize that some potentially dangerous events may also involve rule violations, they primarily categorize the events as learning opportunities. For example, in the Aviation Safety Reporting System, a mishap report is first scrutinized for its instructive potential rather than if it can be classified as a regulatory infraction. The A-SIS seek to increase the reporting of potential dangers because by fostering event reporting, they can enhance the capacity for data analysis and learning. Indeed, an A-SIS, such as the NASA ASRS, gauges its performance, in part, by tracking the volume of near accident reports it receives (e.g., NASA Aviation Safety Reporting System, 1994). Of course, these safety information systems do not seek to increase the incidence of potentially damaging events simply so that they can learn. They advocate increased event reporting based on the assumption that potential dangers are underreported and that fluctuations in the volume of safety-related event reports need not reflect changes in the underlying safety conditions (e.g., Reynard et al., 1986).

Based on a review of these indicators, the findings suggest that three of the seven aviation safety reporting systems tend to categorize potential dangers as a threat to rule enforcement and four of them classify potential dangers as an opportunity to learn (see Table 8.2).

Proposition 1: Safety information systems basically classify potential dangers as *threats* to rule enforcement or *opportunities* for learning.

Question Two: Composition of Management Teams and Basic Event Categorization

The second question explores whether the choice of basic categories for classifying potentially dangerous events varies with the composition of the managerial decision-making teams who participate in A-SIS design. Management team composition serves as a indirect, rough indicator of managerial cognition or how managers think about potential dangers. Specifically, the indicator is the extent of regulator participation in the decision-making team. Because political processes of negotiation may underlie the choice of one set of cognitive assumptions over another, it is assumed that the resulting decisions represent the thinking of the dominant coalition of management team members. Hence, the second question examines whether the involvement of regulators in the decision-making team influences the choice of basic categories for defining potential dangers.

In the following, first, the A-SIS management team composition will be examined; and second, the composition of the management decision-making teams will be compared with the A-SIS choice of basic categories for classifying reports of potential dangers.

Composition of Decision-Making Teams.   The composition of the A-SIS managerial decision-making teams can clearly be sorted into three types depending on the amount of participation by regulators. The first type is composed solely of regulators, albeit from different units of a regulatory agency; the second includes a mix of regulators and representatives of other stakeholders, such as professional associations; and the third excludes regulators (see Table 8.3).

The presence of regulators in the management team provides a key to understanding the cognitive perspective of the decision makers. If managers in a regulatory agency come across an air traffic violation, they may feel duty bound to begin a disciplinary investigation. This attitude surfaced in interviews with FAA representatives, some of whom said that they could not overlook a potential air traffic violation and felt reluctant to refrain from fully exercising their regulatory authority. Based on interviews conducted in this study, regulators tend to think of potential dangers primarily as threats to rule enforcement. But, a 1989 investigation of the FAA NMAC system for monitoring near midair collisions found conflicting perceptions among regulators:

TABLE 8.3

Management Team, Categorization, and Information Processing Routines

Aviation Safety Information System (A-SIS)	Basic Category	Management Team	Information Usage: Regulatory Enforcement	Subordinate Category	Narrative in Database
FAA Operational Error System (FAA ATC)	Threat to rule enforcement	Regulators	Yes	Precisely-measured, specific	No
FAA Pilot Deviation System (FAA Pilot)	Threat to rule enforcement	Regulators	Yes	Precisely measured, specific	No
FAA Near Midair Collision System (FAA NMAC)	Threat to rule enforcement	Regulators	Yes	Mixed: Reports of pilot perceptions, sorted by precise definitions	No
Aviation Safety Reporting System (NASA ASRS)	Opportunity for learning	Multiple stakeholders, including regulators	No	Broad, inclusive	Yes
Air Line Pilots Association (ALPA)	Opportunity for learning	No regulators	No	Broad, inclusive	Some narratives retained
Airline Safety Action Partnership (ASAP)	Opportunity for learning	Multiple stakeholders, including regulators	No	Mixed: Broad, inclusive & specific	Yes
British Airways Safety Information System (BASIS)	Opportunity for learning	No regulators	No	Broad, inclusive	Yes

Some FAA officials maintain that the primary function of the NMAC investigation is to identify the characteristics of the incident and develop corrective actions to prevent future occurrences. Others believe the primary purpose is determining whether pilot error caused the incident and whether FAA regulations were violated. (U. S. General Accounting Office, 1989, p. 17).

For the FAA NMAC, regulators varied in their basic classification of near midair collisions as opportunities for learning "to prevent future occurrences" or threats to the enforcement of FAA regulations. The interview responses reflect the dual mission of the FAA NMAC to reduce the frequency of near collisions and learn how to prevent future NMACs. The differences between the two sets of interviews may reflect differences between the FAA NMAC and regulators working in other FAA systems or it may simply represent variation among individual regulators. Additional research is necessary to assess systematically how regulators think about the monitoring of potential dangers.

Relationship Between Management Team Composition and Categorization.

For the seven A-SIS in this study, the findings suggest that, the composition of the management decision-making team is associated with the construction of basic labels of potential dangers as threats to rule enforcement or opportunities for learning (see Table 8.3). The initial event classification varies with the involvement of regulators in the A-SIS design teams. In managerial decision-making groups comprised only of regulators, the aviation safety information systems labeled potential dangers as threats to rule enforcement. When regulators were kept out of the managerial decision-making team, potential dangers were defined as opportunities for learning. Interestingly, if regulators joined members of other stakeholder groups to participate in a managerial team, the A-SIS classified potential dangers as learning opportunities.

Multiple-stakeholder decision-making teams operate in two safety information systems, the industry-wide NASA ASRS and the airline-based ASAP. In these A-SIS, the FAA, modulating its exercise of authority, limits the extent of punitive sanctions it allots to pilots who can demonstrate that they voluntarily reported air traffic violations. In designing these A-SIS, FAA regulators were able to concede their traditional cognitive categories, in which potential dangers are labeled as threats to rule enforcement, without relinquishing their authority to uphold the air traffic laws. For example, although the FAA is prohibited from prosecuting air traffic violations based on the confidential reports gathered by the NASA ASRS and the ASAP, if regulators discover a potential violation from another source of information, such as from computerized surveillance, the FAA can open an investigation. This illustrates how the composition of management teams, reflecting the cognition of its members, influences the A-SIS classification of potential dangers. It also suggests how the categorization of events may be linked to the distribution of incentives.

> Proposition 2: The basic categorization of potential dangers as threats to rule enforcement or opportunities for learning varies with the composition of the managerial decision-making teams who design the safety information systems. Specifically, the classification varies with the degree of regulator involvement in the A-SIS design teams.

Question Three: Links Between Categorization and an Information Processing Routine

The third question examines the relation between the basic classification of potential dangers and the design of a key information processing routine. The critical design decision involves the choice of a standard operating procedure that permits (or precludes) the use of data for rule enforcement.

If an A-SIS permits the use of its data in rule enforcement, it can provide reports of potential dangers to the authorities, whether among airline managers or regulators, to investigate possible rule or regulatory infractions, adjudicate accountability, and in some cases, take disciplinary action. Note that even when such a rule enforcement capability exists, it is not always exercised in practice, in part, because reports of potentially dangerous events do not always involve air traffic violations. For example, although the FAA can use near midair collision (NMAC) data to enforce federal air traffic regulations, only a small proportion of NMAC reports actually result in FAA enforcement actions against pilots.

In contrast, consider a system where reports of potential dangers cannot be used in rule enforcement actions. The A-SIS safety analysts may discover that rule infringements occurred during a potentially dangerous event but they do not attempt to determine who is to blame. Indeed, the ASAP system actively seeks reports of FAR violations, but the information that the system gathers cannot be used to enforce the rules. Furthermore, safety analysts are free to question the effectiveness of the existing standards and, if necessary, recommend that the rules be changed.

The categorization of potential dangers as a threat to rule enforcement or as an opportunity for learning directly corresponds with the design choice of the key information processing routines among the seven A-SIS (see Table 8.3). All three of the A-SIS in which potential dangers are classified primarily as a threat also provide the data they collect for use in rule enforcement. Similarly, all of the A-SIS that categorize potential dangers as a learning opportunity also do not permit their data to be used in rule enforcement.

Managerial cognition may affect the choice of a key information processing routine either directly, through the initial design of the system, or indirectly, through the conceptualization of basic categories that, in turn, shaped the construction of a critical standard procedure for processing information. In this exploratory study, it is not possible to determine whether the effect of managerial cognition, as roughly indicated by the composition of a managerial decision-making team, affected the choice of information processing routine directly or indirectly, through the decision makers, basic classification of potential dangers as threats or learning opportunities.

Whether managerial cognition had a direct or indirect effect on the A-SIS design choices, in each of the systems, the choice of basic category is consistent with the choice of a standard operating procedure determining the use of data in rule enforcement. If an A-SIS follows this key information processing routine, the repetition of the procedure over time reinforces the initial cognitive classification and perpetuates the managerial cognition of the managerial design team.

The choice of this key information processing routine is also linked to the incentives for reporting potential dangers. For example, pilots may be reluctant to disclose events that involve air traffic violations if they know that the data may be "used against them" (e.g., Tamuz, 1994). In each A-SIS, the basic categorization is tightly linked with the choice of the information processing routine that determines whether data can be used in rule enforcement. Consequently in this sample, it is difficult to untangle the effects of the classification of potential dangers as a threat or opportunity and the design of the key information processing routine. The choice of categories for labeling events as well as the distribution of incentives may exert a combined effect on subsequent stages of information processing, a subject for future research.

> Proposition 3: If the basic classification of reports of potential dangers as a threat or an opportunity is consistent with the choice of a standard operating procedure determining the use of data in rule enforcement, the repetition of the procedure over time will reinforce the initial cognitive classification and maintain it over time.
>
> If the standard operating procedure regarding the use of data in rule enforcement conflicts with the basic classification of potential dangers or if the prescribed information processing standard is not followed in practice, it will undermine the effects of managerial cognition.

Question Four: Channeling Attention Through Basic and Subordinate Categorization

Question four examines how the basic classification of potential dangers as a threat to rule enforcement or as an opportunity for learning influences the subordinate categorization of events. The precision of event definition influences how the A-SIS responds to reports of potential dangers, channeling attention toward the situations that fit its definitions and away from those that do not (see Table 8.3).

The findings indicate that two of the three A-SIS that classify potential dangers as threats also provide specific, precise subordinate definitions. For example, the FAA ATC, the system for monitoring operational errors among air traffic controllers, provides a precise subordinate classification of events. It defines the loss of separation among aircraft, an operational error, according to precisely measured distances prescribed by the FAA (e.g., U. S. Office of Technology Assessment, 1988).

The FAA NMAC, a system that gathers pilot reports of near midair collisions, differs from the other two threat based A-SIS. The FAA NMAC instructs pilots to report near midair collisions as they see them, while simultaneously adopting the FAA definition of a NMAC, described in precise horizontal and vertical measurements. After the pilots report a perceived NMAC, the FAA flight standards investigator determines if the event fits the requirements specified in the definition (e.g., U. S. General Accounting Office, 1989).

Most of the A-SIS that classify reports of potential dangers as an opportunity also construct subordinate definitions that are broad, inclusive, and unspecified. In the Aviation Safety Reporting System, for example, the space for the narrative is entitled simply: "Describe Event/Situation."

In the ASAP system, a cooperative venture between regulators, airline management, and the airline-based pilots association, two subordinate definitions are used. The first subordinate classification consists of a general, inclusive definition, similar to those used by the other three learning-oriented systems. The second is more specific, seeking reports of federal aviation regulations, infractions that rely on precise definitions. But whereas the FAA NMAC applies the precise definition of a near midair collision in sorting all the reports of perceived near midair collisions that it receives, the ASAP system does not use the precise definitions to classify all events. Instead, the ASAP treats reports of suspected regulatory violations as indicators of general safety-related concerns. It tends to broaden the classification of events rather than to seek first to classify them into precise categories.

The findings relate to the two main classification tasks that confront the A-SIS. Aviation safety information systems that label reports of potential dangers as a threat to the enactment of existing rules and regulations concentrate on sorting possible rule infractions from other events. Before a disciplinary authority can establish accountability and allocate blame, it must first determine if a rule violation has occurred. Because the A-SIS uses the reports it receives to determine if the events constitute an air traffic violation, the definitions must clearly differentiate between infractions and other events. To support this sorting process, they construct subordinate categories of events that are precisely defined and readily measured. They write detailed, exact definitions that exclude reports of accidents, on one extreme, and delineate between rule infringements and acceptable variations in normal operations, on the other.

In contrast, in A-SIS that categorize reports of potentially damaging events as a learning opportunity, the safety analysts attempt to identify significant events that may contribute to the discovery of accident precursors. To add to their knowledge base, they seek to construct near accidents from reports of potential dangers. The A-SIS focus attention on finding clues to accident precursors among the expected, mundane mishap reports as well as among those describing unexpected interactions of events. They attend less to the first task of classification, the separation of potential dangers from other events.

To illustrate, consider the NASA ASRS reporting form. It requests a narrative description, encouraging individuals to describe "what you believed caused the problem." It prompts pilots to describe the chain of events leading to the mishap and explore possible causes, especially those related to human performance. It also provides coding checklists to assist in describing the basics, such as the crew, the aircraft, and the airspace. In one sentence, it reminds reporters that criminal activities should not be reported and twice, once on each side of the form, notes that NASA does not collect accident reports. Thus, the bulk of the NASA ASRS reporting form is concerned with describing and explaining how the events unfolded, calling attention to possible causal factors. As its brief statements regarding accidents illustrate, the NASA ASRS does not concentrate on differentiating the safety-related incidents from other types of events.

By using subordinate categories that are intentionally vague and general, the A-SIS can avoid prematurely discarding reports of significant near accidents. Occasionally, safety analysts can immediately recognize the importance of a single report, such as in the case of a dramatic close call (March, et al., 1991). But, often they can make sense of reports only in the process of retrospectively analyzing the unfolding of events and weighing what could have occurred under slightly different circumstances. In seeking to discover previously unknown accident precursors, it is difficult to establish clear categories that would differentiate between those events with potential learning value and other less instructive ones. This is especially problematic in aviation, where complexity and coupling combine to produce unexpected interactions (Perrow, 1984). Under such conditions, as safety analysts recounted in their interviews, well-known events, such as altitude busts, occurring when an aircraft deviates from its assigned altitude, can be produced by an unanticipated interaction of circumstances.

Proposition 4: In safety information systems that classify potential dangers as threats, the subordinate categories are more likely to be exactly defined and precisely measured than in systems that initially classify such mishaps as opportunities for learning.

Question Five: Labeling Events and Storing Data About Them

In question five, the relation between the subordinate classification of potential dangers and information processing routines for data retention and storage is examined. Methods of data storage are especially important because the A-SIS gather and analyze mishap reports in which the full meaning of the events often cannot immediately be deciphered.

The findings indicate that of the seven A-SIS, the three that employ precise definitions of potential dangers also do not store the data in a format conducive to future analysis (see Table 8.3). Although each of these safety information systems maintains a computerized database, the text of the original narratives is not preserved. The FAA NMAC, for example, provides data on the frequency and location of near midair collisions, supported by coded information such as aircraft type and the investigator's final codification of the event according to the precise NMAC definition. The proceedings of the investigation, including the narratives that the pilots originally recounted to the FAA investigators, are filed away, preserved as evidence. But once the case is closed, the text of the original narrative is not stored in an easily accessible computerized format.

In four A-SIS, an emphasis on general definitions is associated with the standard operating procedures for data retention and storage. Among the A-SIS that tend to use broad, inclusive definitions of potentially dangerous events, all retain the original narratives in a computerized database, easily accessible for further analysis. Indeed, the NASA Aviation Safety Reporting System makes portions of its database available for use by other organizations (National Academy of Public Administration, 1994).

If an A-SIS uses a broad category to classify reports of potential dangers, it enhances the availability of information. The inclusive classification method opens up the definition of events, allowing for unanticipated new forms of mishaps. The A-SIS standard routines for narrative storage also permit retrospective sense making, even looking back over several years. For example, after an accident occurs, the NASA ASRS safety analysts routinely conduct a computerized search of the narratives, seeking near accidents similar to the actual one.

The significance of one potential danger report may not be immediately obvious. The meaning of a potentially damaging event may only be revealed in retrospect, for example, after additional near accidents and fatal accidents have occurred in similar conditions (*Application of FAA Wake Vortex Research to Safety*, 1994). If the original narratives are preserved in a readily accessible format, it increases the future availability of information, and, with increased availability, enhances the capacity for organizational learning and knowledge generation.

> Proposition 5: If a safety information system relies on broad, inclusive subordinate definitions of potential dangers, it will also tend to retain and store the original narratives for future review and analysis. If a system uses a precise definition in classifying reports of potential dangers, it will not tend to store narratives in a readily accessible format.

DISCUSSION

Implications for Aviation Safety

The classification of potential dangers as threats to rule enforcement or, alternatively, as opportunities for learning may affect efforts to improve aviation safety.

Categorizing Potential Dangers as Threats.   The categorization of potential dangers as a threat need not improve safety conditions. To illustrate, consider that by reducing the number of potential dangers reported, an A-SIS does not necessarily improve aviation safety. The reduction may be due, in part, to variations in reporting behavior rather than changes in underlying safety conditions (e.g., Reynard et al., 1986; U.S. Federal Aviation Administration, 1990). Furthermore, reducing the number of potential dangers reported is unlikely to lower the

accident rate if the conditions that lead to some near accidents differ systematically from those that result in disaster. Indeed, the reported rate of near midair collisions does not appear to be related to the rate of actual midair crashes (Oster, Strong, & Zorn, 1992).

Similarly, the use of precise definitions to classify potential dangers protects aviation safety by supporting regulatory compliance but it may not assist in generating knowledge about hazards. If an A-SIS gathers data to be used as a basis for rule enforcement, then the events that constitute rule infractions should be clearly defined. But, the application of these precisely specified categories does not necessarily contribute to the identification of accident precursors.

For example, consider an air traffic control center in which controllers monitor the airspace between airports. A controller must maintain a horizontal distance of at least 5 miles between two aircraft when both planes are flying under air traffic control guidance. Should the distance slip to 4 ½ miles, it is considered an operational error that must be reported, although in most conditions, this reduction in the distance separating the aircraft does not significantly heighten the danger.

The categorization of potential dangers as threats can also limit the safety-related information available for analysis. Complications arise when regulators use information that was collected for purposes of rule enforcement in their efforts to learn how to make flying conditions safer (Tamuz, 1994). As in other high-hazard industries, FAA regulators often are confronted with a dual mission. They not only are held responsible for rule enforcement but also are called on to improve aviation safety. The simultaneous demands, to control behavior while learning from it, result in conflicting incentives for gathering information about potential dangers. Moreover, as the present study suggests, the classification of events with threat-based categories in mind can yield inadequate data for gleaning knowledge about why the events occurred.

To illustrate, consider the FAA ATC system for monitoring air traffic controllers. The system was designed primarily to maintain rule enforcement in the local control towers and regional air traffic control centers. But, regulators in the national office also analyze data generated by this system as a basis for identifying emergent problems. The information available to these FAA safety analysts is limited. If an event does not meet the precise definition of an operational error, then the safety information system does not gather or retain information about it. The system uses a categorization scheme that may divert attention from critical events because they do not constitute rule violations, as vividly illustrated by the LaGuardia example.

In the near collision over LaGuardia airport described earlier, two jet air-liners came within about 20 feet of one another, narrowly missing a collision as one attempted to land and the other took off. Yet, this event was not clas-sified as an operational error. When approaching an airport for landing, the regulations permit both pilots and controllers to visually maintain separa-tion between aircraft by looking out the windows of the cockpit and the con-trol tower, respectively. Under this definition, the controller did not break any rules, although the two aircraft narrowly averted a collision. Because the event did not count against the controller, the safety information system did not count the event in its statistics.

These examples illustrate how an A-SIS may discard valuable informa-tion about hazardous circumstances because the reported mishap does not fit into the proper category. To glean knowledge from near accidents, a safety monitoring system should seek to gather data on the full range of potential dangers. If all the possible dangerous interactions of conditions cannot be anticipated and an A-SIS follows a precise categorization scheme, then the system may overlook, discard, or fail to collect data on events constituting accident precursors.

Categorizing Potential Dangers as Learning Opportu-nities.   In an A-SIS in which potential dangers are labeled as learn-ing opportunities, the capacity for knowledge generation can be en-hanced in different ways. First, the use of broad, inclusive categories to define potentially damaging events promotes the gathering of informa-tion about previously unknown or newly emerging conditions. In par-ticular, it enables the A-SIS to collect information about hazards that do not involve rule infractions. For example, in the NASA ASRS, re-peated reports of coffee spills in the cockpit, distracting the pilots' at-tention during takeoffs and landings, gave rise to the enactment of the "sterile cockpit" regulation.

Second, the preservation of the original narratives and their storage in an easily accessible database not only enhances the possibility for future data analysis and knowledge generation but also institutionalizes the concept of retrospective sense making. When analyzing an event as a near accident, an organization considers a range of consequences that could have resulted from only a slight change in the circumstances leading to the mishap. But, as noted earlier, safety analysts cannot always immediately recognize the sig-nificance of a potentially dangerous event. Because of the ambiguities inher-ent in this process, learning from near accidents is not only retrospective but can also develop over time. By retaining the original narrative texts, the system enables analysts to make sense of events by reinterpreting them in a new context. If a first step in knowledge generation is the recognition that we do not know the answers, then an organizational expression of humility is symbolized in the preservation and computerized storage of original narratives in the A-SIS.

Benefitting from Redundancy.   The emergence of multiple aviation safety information systems appears to be redundant, a duplication of efforts among regulators, professional associations, and airlines. But, as in other instances of apparent redundancy among public agencies, the multiple systems can prove beneficial (Bendor, 1985). This study explores how the different perspectives that management teams bring to A-SIS design and operation can produce variations in the sources of safety-related information. The systems differ in the potential dangers that capture their attention and in how they gather and retain information about these events. With safety information systems built on multiple perspectives, the air transportation industry gains variety in information sources. If one system overlooks an accident precursor, a second A-SIS may notice it, gather further information about it, and keep a detailed history of the event for future reference.

To illustrate some of the benefits of maintaining multiple A-SIS, revisit the near collision over LaGuardia. The air traffic controller and his supervisor did not report the dramatic mishap because it did not meet the formal definition of an operational error. Yet, one of the pilots classified it as a near midair collision and reported it to the FAA NMAC system, only to have the report remain unattended in the regional office, apparently due to a paperwork mix-up. The official NMAC report reached FAA headquarters only after it was reported to a third safety monitoring system ("ATC Procedures," 1998). If such a dramatic close call can be defined away, other less striking examples of potential dangers may go unreported or be overlooked. The operation of multiple information systems, managed by decision-making teams with varying cognitive perspectives, can enhance the capacity for knowledge generation on an industry level.

Beyond High-Hazard Industries

Whereas the contents of key attributes of categories and the interpretation of events are specific to organizations operating in high-hazard industries, this study illuminates general processes by which managerial cognition can influence environmental scanning systems. Hence, it may provide insights into more general processes of problem recognition and the identification of strategic issues. For example, the findings from the aviation industry suggest how the influence of managerial cognition can be amplified and maintained when it is encoded in an information system. This exemplifies how managerial cognition can be perpetuated in an organizational culture.

In summary, this study explores how the categorization of potentially dangerous events can channel attention and shape the construction of information processing routines and thus, by constraining the availability of information, indirectly affect the organizational capacity for learning and knowledge accumulation. Based on the study of seven aviation safety information systems, it proposes research propositions to guide the future study of safety monitoring systems in high-hazard industries. It examines how as safety information system participants begin to make sense of ambiguous data gathered from the environment, they sort reports of potential dangers into different categories. Furthermore, it suggests how this labeling process can enhance or inhibit the prospects for making available the information needed to learn how to improve safety in the skies.

ACKNOWLEDGMENTS

I gratefully acknowledge the essential contributions of the anonymous study participants who, drawing on their expertise and experience, patiently explained the A-SIS and described the chock-to-chock operations of the air traffic system. The study benefitted from the skillful research assistance of Matthew C. Mireles and the constructive comments of Lu Ann Aday and Zur Shapira. Valuable support for this research was provided by the National Science Foundation, Decision Risk and Management Sciences Division (Grant SBR-9410749).

REFERENCES

Adcock, S. (1998, June 6). Case of a missed near-miss. *Newsday (New York)*, p. A4.

Application of FAA wake vortex research to safety: Hearings before the Subcommittee on Technology, Environment and Aviation, of the House Committee on Science, Space and Technology, 103rd Cong., 2d Sess. 163 (1994) (testimony of Dr. William Reynard, director, Aviation Safety Reporting System).

ATC procedures questioned after three recent incidents. (1998, June 15). *Air Safety Week*, *12*(24).

Bendor, J. (1985). *Parallel systems: Redundancy in government*. Berkeley, CA: University of California Press.

Crystal, L. (Executive Producer). (1998). *The news hour with Jim Lehrer*. Arlington, VA: Public Broadcasting Service.

Dutton, J., & Jackson, S. (1987). Categorizing strategic issues: Links to organizational action. *Academy of Management Review, 12*(1), 76–90.

Holtom, M. (1991). The basis for safety management. *Focus on Commercial Aviation Safety, 5,* 25.

Hutchinson, B. (1998, June 15). Retraining ordered for air traffic controllers. *Daily News (New York),* p. 36.

MacGregor, C., & Hopfl, H. (1997). The BASIS story: A commitment to change in British Airways and the creation of a global safety superhighway. In *British Airways Safety Information System.* London: British Airways.

March, J. G. (1989). *Decisions and organizations.* Oxford, England: Blackwell.

March, J. G., & Olsen, J. P. (1976). *Ambiguity and choice in organizations.* Bergen, Norway: Universitetsforlaget.

March, J. G., & Shapira, Z. (1987). Managerial perspectives on risk and risk taking. *Management Science, 33,* 1404–1418.

March, J. G., Sproull, L. S., & Tamuz, M. (1991). Learning from samples of one or fewer. *Organization Science, 2*(1), 1–14.

Miles, M. B., & Huberman, A. M. (1994). *Qualitative data analysis: An expanded sourcebook.* Thousand Oaks, CA: Sage.

Mustain, G. (1998, June 28). A spilled coffee led to near miss 1 slip put 2 jets just feet from each other. *Daily News (New York),* p. 22.

NASA Aviation Safety Reporting System. (1994). *Aviation Safety Reporting System program summary.* Moffet Field, CA: Author.

National Academy of Public Administration. (1994). *A review of the Aviation Safety Reporting System.* Washington, DC: Author.

National Research Council, Committee on FAA Airworthiness Certification Procedures. (1980). *Improving aircraft safety: FAA certification of commercial passenger aircraft.* Washington, DC: National Academy of Sciences.

Oster, C. V., Strong, J. S., & Zorn, C. K. (1992). *Why airplanes crash: Aviation safety in a changing world.* New York: Oxford University Press.

Perrow, C. (1984). *Normal accidents.* New York: Basic Books.

Reynard, W. D., Billings, C. E., Cheaney, E. S., & Hardy, R. (1986). *The development of the NASA aviation safety reporting system.* (National Aeronautics and Space Administration, Scientific and Technical Information Branch, NASA Reference Publication 1114). Washington, DC: U.S. Government Printing Office.

Rosch, E. (1975). Cognitive reference points. *Cognitive Psychology, 1,* 532–547.

Rosch, E. (1978). Principles of categorization. In E. Rosch & B. Lloyd (Eds.), *Cognition and categorization* (pp. 27–47). Hillsdale, NJ: Lawrence Erlbaum Associates.

Tamuz, M. (1987). The impact of computer surveillance on air safety reporting. *Columbia Journal of World Business, 22*(1), 69–77.

Tamuz, M. (1994). Developing organizational safety information systems for monitoring potential dangers. In G. E. Apostolakis & J. S. Wu (Eds.), *Proceedings of PSAM II. An international conference devoted to the advancement of system-based methods for the design and operation of technological systems and processes.* (Vol. 2, p. 71 session; pp. 7–12). Los Angeles: University of California.

U.S. Federal Aviation Administration. (1990). *Selected statistics concerning pilot-reported near midair collisions (1985-1988).* Washington, DC: Author.

U.S. General Accounting Office. (1989). *Air traffic control: FAA's interim actions to reduce near mid-air collisions* (GAD/RCED 89-149). Washington, DC: Author.

U.S. Office of Technology Assessment. (1988). *Safe skies for tomorrow: Aviation safety in a competitive environment.* Washington, DC: U.S. Government Printing Office.

Weick, K. E. (1995). *Sense making in organizations.* Thousand Oaks, CA: Sage.

9

Understanding the Role
of Intuition–Tacit Knowledge
and Analysis–Explicit
Knowledge in Bank
Board Deliberations

Robert H. Bennett III
University of South Alabama

William P. Anthony
Florida State University

Boards of directors have emerged as important strategic decision-making bodies over the past several years and are asked by the stockholders of the organization to perform very important corporate governance duties, including acting as a control mechanism on the actions of management (Baysinger & Butler, 1985). They also are expected, however, to provide important input to the strategic deliberations of the company's management and are seen as important resources for the organization (Daily, 1995; Daily & Dalton, 1994; Judge & Zeithaml, 1992). Boards are often relied on by the firm's management to provide decision input, valuable advice, and commentary on the strategic direction of the firm (Baysinger & Hoskisson, 1990; Pearce, 1995; Pearce & Zahra, 1991). Researchers remain unclear, however, as to the dynamics of the deliberation processes performed by corporate boards at the meetings of the board and its committees.

The question that appears insufficiently addressed in the recent literature (e.g., Baysinger & Hoskisson, 1990; Goodstein, Gautam, & Boeker, 1994; Pearce, 1983; Pearce & Zahra, 1992; Rindova, 1994), is: What are the contributions of insiders (employees or former employees of the organization) versus outsiders (non employees) in the decision-related discussions and dynamic deliberations of boards of directors? Researchers have generally speculated through the years on the correct composition of boards of directors (Baysinger & Butler, 1985; Ford, 1988) but very few have looked at the more complex and interesting question of what members actually contribute to the deliberations and thus what influence the members have on the board's and the company's effectiveness.

This study of boards of directors in the banking industry will attempt to determine the importance of using tacit knowledge and intuitive styles (e.g., Agor, 1986; Behling & Eckel, 1991; Sternberg, 1997; Wagner & Sternberg, 1985) in board decision making, in addition to and in concert with the more traditionally accepted use of explicit knowledge and formal, factual, rational analysis. When company leaders make strategic decisions, there is little doubt that sound, thorough analysis and quantitative weighing of options is necessary. It has also been suggested, however, that more subjective intuitive and instinctive processing is a major necessity, especially in high-velocity environments and highly complex environments (Bourgeois, 1985; Eisenhardt, 1989; Eisenhardt and Brown, 1998; Hitt & Tyler, 1991).

The differences between insiders and outsiders will be enumerated and described, but the major focus will be on the contributions made by insider and outsider deliberations and interactions to the overall effectiveness of the board and of the organization. Special note is made of the literature citing the need for decision makers and groups to intertwine and meld the complementary tacit and explicit knowledge bases to craft more informed, more innovative, and more complete decisions (Kleinmuntz, 1990; Nonaka, 1994; Spender, 1993). These authors and others argued that learning can result when this exchange occurs. Many writers over the years, including Barnard (1938), have called for *dual processing* that incorporates left-brain thought and analysis and right-brain intuition (Kirschenbaum, 1992; Kleinmuntz, 1990; Lyles & Schwenk, 1992; Mintzberg, 1976; Mitchell & Beach, 1990; Robey & Taggart, 1981; Spender, 1993; Taggart & Robey, 1981).

Considerable research (e.g., Judge & Zeithaml, 1992; Rosenstein, 1987; Zahra, 1990; Zahra & Stanton, 1988) has found that higher activity and board involvement of the total board in decisions serve to improve decision and deliberation quality. In this study, the level of board activity and strategic involvement is argued to be an important moderator of the relationship between decision style and performance. It seems logical that certain contributions from board members would only be helpful to board and organization effectiveness when the entire board is active enough to perform thorough analysis and review and fully utilize and consider the contributions of other board members.

Insiders and outsiders obviously possess very different knowledge structures, the mental templates that are imposed on information environments to give them form and meaning (Baysinger & Hoskisson, 1990; Fiske & Taylor, 1991; Lyles & Schwenk, 1992; Patton & Baker, 1987). Some theorists have argued that insiders possess more and better information about the intricacies of the company and should be able to contribute much more valuable input to the deliberations. It seems absolutely incumbent on insiders to provide this early sense making interpretation of the decision space. Insiders are argued to have a superior foundation of knowledge and understanding and the cognitive ability to understand the complex causality of the firm's internal and external relationships. Others have called for more outsider representation in board decision processes. The general assumption is that outsiders provide more objective oversight and checks on the strategic decision process than do insiders. Pearce (1983) and Pearce and Zahra (1992) were quick to point out that outsiders are recruited for strategic purposes because of their general expertise as well as their expertise in particular domains important to the firm (as a supplier, customer, or consultant). They note that outsiders are intended to be boundary spanners, and the principal intention of outsider nomination is to increase the firm's environmental awareness and sensitivity. Judge and Zeithaml (1992) added that outsiders provide strategic oversight of and offer experience and seasoning to the reports and opinions presented and discussed by insiders. It seems clear that outsiders are valuable for clarifying, commenting on, checking, and even enlarging and expanding the analysis provided by insiders.

THEORY DEVELOPMENT
AND RESEARCH QUESTIONS

This study's first research question relates to the differences between inside and outside directors. In board meetings, do differences exist between inside directors and outside directors on the degree to which formal reasoning and analysis is used? Are there differences in the degree to which intuitive and instinctive processing is used? Inside directors likely find it incumbent on themselves to report, interpret, and provide understanding on the complex and ambiguous causality and relations among variables. They may also realize that failure to coherently interpret decision-related information could be detrimental to firm success. Hoskisson, Johnson, and Moesel (1994) point out that outsiders lack information about the day-to-day operations of the firm and for them to perform their governance and oversight duties, they need access to rich, detailed information about the company and management's interpretation of the company's interaction with the environment.

How much will insiders use tacit knowledge and intuition in a setting where they are expected to provide the detailed briefing and prospectus on the current situation? Tacit knowledge theorists (e.g. Sternberg, 1997; Wagner, 1987) argued that intuition and tacit knowledge are difficult to express and convey, something insiders are certainly expected to do in the board meeting. It also seems that outsiders, due to their cognitive limitations, lack of knowledge about firm data and information, and their assumed responsibilities of oversight and advising, will rely quite heavily on intuition. What is important to remember, however, is that this intuition and instinct must seemingly be stimulated by a heavy input of formal explanation and interpretation by insiders. The thinking here is that board members should recognize that the deliberation process works appropriately if these information processing roles are played.

For the second research question, it must be asked if the degree to which these roles are played contributes to board and organization success. Does the degree to which inside directors use formal reasoning, analysis, and explanation in board meetings influence the perceived effectiveness of the board and the objective performance of the organization? Also, is the relation moderated by the level of board activity and involvement? Likewise, does the degree to which outside directors use intuitive processing, instinct, and tacit knowledge in board meetings influence the perceived effectiveness of the board and the objective performance of the organization? Is this relationship moderated by the level of board activity and involvement?

Pearce (1983) and Zahra and Pearce (1989) found that an accurate formal and detailed analysis of internal operations on the part of management was related positively to firm performance. Baysinger and Hoskisson (1990) agreed that outsiders are not prepared to delve into and understand the complex causality of the firm and are, at best, only able to make detached judgments about the internal operations of the firm and the quality of decision alternatives. Especially in the industry studied in this research, banking, it appears that insiders will be much more prepared to navigate the detailed analysis of the firm's situation (Bantel & Jackson, 1989). In an effort to provide strategic oversight, outsiders ask good questions. It seems clear that outsiders are valuable for clarifying, commenting on, checking, and even enlarging and expanding the analysis provided by insiders. Outsiders bring a great deal of general knowledge to the table, largely related to the external environment, the ultimate judge of a decision's effectiveness.

Insiders may be bombarded with demands from outsiders for interpretation and information about the company's situation. Bylaws and institutional traditions certainly require lengthy, in-depth reports from insiders concerning the operations of the company, and insiders normally preside over and lead board meetings. Insiders likely feel that outsiders are being paid to listen intently and to comment on the reports being provided. Insiders are likely in a position to demand input from outsiders, asking for their feedback on most issues. Moreover, insiders are asked to set the decision premises, a rough-draft course of action based on considerable information, knowledge, and number crunching. This presentation might be considered a prospectus preliminary decision, a starting point outsiders desperately need to jumpstart their interpretation and consideration of the decision situation. The contribution of outsiders would be considered more perspective broadening input, consisting largely of questions, requests for explanation, broad comments and general opinion, and ultimately approval or disapproval.

As the final research question, it seems necessary to ask whether an interaction exists between the level of insider analysis and level of outsider intuition in influencing the perceived effectiveness of the board and the objective performance of the organization. In other words, does the presence of one enhance the influence of the other? A genuine plethora of literature calls for the efficacy of a dual processing perspective. The bases of these views relate to complementary knowledge, balanced perspectives, and beneficial learning processes. Many researchers, noted earlier, have pointed out the importance of formal analysis in conjunction with experience-based intuition and instinct. Nonaka (1994) argued that the two processing styles are complementary, with the positive outcome being a combination of experience-based wisdom and factual definition of the decision reality. It is this dialogue that drives the creation of innovative new ideas and concepts. Likewise, Huber (1991) noted that one can conclude that more learning has occurred when more and more varied interpretations have been developed. He argued that development and refinement of varied interpretations and explanations change the range of the organization's potential behaviors. A working set of knowledge allows for the incorporation and use of additional knowledge. Cohen and Levinthal (1990) revealed that the ability of a firm to recognize the value of new external information, assimilate it, and apply it to commercial ends is critical to its innovative capabilities. They called this ability a firm's *absorptive capacity* and they suggested that it is largely a function of the firm's level of prior related knowledge. Existing knowledge and perspective allow an individual, group, or organization to see the possibilities and value of new information. March (1991) revealed the values of both exploration (search, variation, risk taking, experimentation, play, flexibility, discovery, and innovation) and exploitation (refinement, choice, production, efficiency, selection, implementation, and execution). March argued that a helpful way to broaden perspective is to get fresh new views from individuals not entrenched or overly familiar with the organization, much like allowing a seasoned copy editor to read an already well-considered manuscript.

This research effort, then, seeks to establish whether differences exist between insiders and outsiders on the level of analysis and level of intuition used in the deliberations process. The authors would also like to determine if decision processing style influences performance and whether an interaction exists between processing styles. The importance of board activity level is also an issue under study here.

METHODS

Participants

Research surveys were sent to a total of 167 board chairs (and CEOs, or both) of independent banks in Alabama for distribution to their respective boards. A board's response was considered usable if 50% of the individual members responded, an amount thought necessary to reflect the general nature of proceedings in a board meeting. Of the 167 boards who received the surveys, 73 responded to some degree (44%). Of these, only 14 boards submitted incomplete responses (less than 50% of the board members responded). Therefore, a total of 59 boards (35%) submitted usable board responses and make up the sample used in this research. Within these 59 complete responses, an average of about 75% of the entire board responded. In this study, the total usable individual board member responses number 359.

Of the 359 usable respondents, 163 were insiders (45%) and 196 (56%) were outsiders. Of the outsiders, 33 were involved in some way in the financial industry, for example as a banker, broker, or insurance agent. Only 13 of the outsider directors had ever been employed as bankers, with 4 of these 13 currently working for a different bank. Ages ranged from 28 years in age to 86, with 75% between 40 and 70 years in age. Of the respondents, 87% (311 out of 359) were male, with only 48 women respondents from the 59 banks. Mean tenure on the board was 13 years, and mean formal education was 16 years (through college).

The responding banks have average assets of around $100 million, slightly smaller than the average assets of all Alabama independent banks. Responding banks grew, on average, 5% to 6% during each of the years 1992, 1993, and 1994, approximately the same as all independent banks in the state. Finally, the average performance level posted by responding banks was almost identical to performance posted by all banks in the state. Banks are highly regulated and bank boards are required by regulators to address the strategic concerns of the bank. In fact, over the last several years, federal regulators have mounted a concerted push for more board involvement in the supervision of commercial banks. Bank boards discuss many of the following issues at many if not most monthly meetings: the economy in general, loan demand, asset management and investments, deposit management, marketing, product and service offering, competition, loan mix, branch issues, human resources and training, loan administration, various policies, trends in banking, loan collection, and quality.

Measures

For purposes of this study, board members were asked to reflect on their cognition and behavior concerning strategic deliberations within the board meeting. The board members were cued by a short scenario deemed as typical of the types of strategic decisions faced by these boards. The items used in this research are included in Table 9.1. Measures of the level of analysis and intuition used by board members were obtained by using self-report items derived from earlier work by Anthony and Daake (1994). Level of analysis was measured using a nine-item measure of the extent to which board members use and are confident with formal reasoning and analysis in making important board decisions (Cronbach's Alpha = .89). Level of intuition –instinct was measured with a five-item measure of the extent to which board members use and are confident with intuition in making important board decisions (Cronbach's Alpha = .76). A measure of board activity level (involvement) was also necessary, with previous research indicating a strong relation between board involvement and board performance. The seven-item scale developed by Judge and Zeithaml (1992) was adapted for this study and included in the board questionnaire (Cronbach's Alpha = .91). The perceptions of board involvement and activity were averaged across all members of the board, producing a board activity score for each board (average of member perceptions). The self-report measure of board effectiveness was constructed by the authors. It represents insiders' perceptions of the effectiveness of the board in dealing with strategic decisions and providing helpful guidance and suggestions to bank management.

TABLE 9.1

Measures

Nine-Item Analysis Measure (Cronbach's Alpha = .89)

I study and use concrete data and facts in my decision processes.

I feel unsure about my decisions unless I can closely study the data and facts available.

I find myself "crunching the numbers" and "putting a sharp pencil to" the reports available.

I study the data intently for clues and answers to the questions that arise.

Even when I have a hunch, I feel the need to study the reports available to me.

The board benefits from my ability to analyze and interpret the data.

Which of the following best describes your level of analysis? (Different levels given)

I rely on staff reports, data, and other information provided for my consideration.

I rely on my analysis and "break down" of the numbers and facts.

Five-Item Intuition Measure (Cronbach's Alpha = .76)

My business sense, knowledge base, and intuitive feel are my guide in board meetings.

I am generally confident with my instinctive reactions and intuitions about the decisions.

The board benefits from my experience and business sense.

The board finds it helpful when I provide my feelings, opinions, and reactions to a scenario.

My initial thoughts, opinions, and reactions are generally accurate.

Seven-Item Board Activity Measure (Cronbach's Alpha = .91)

How vocal, active, and involved is the board?

The board questions and probes management.

How vocal is the board in determining the course of the bank?

Top management is dependent on the board for advice and input.

The board "leaves no stone unturned" when looking for relevant information and answers.

Management is interested in what the board has to say about decisions.

Five-Item Perceived Board Performance (Insider Perceptions) (Cronbach's Alpha = .88)

I am impressed with the performance exhibited by my board in the past few months.

Management and key employees of the bank are given sound guidance by the board.

I would consider this board important to the sound operation of the bank.

The board provides important insight to management.

The board makes the bank and its employees more successful.

Insiders are indeed the consumers of board input and will benefit most from board performance, and their satisfaction with board input and suggestion is a good indication of the quality of board interaction. This measure is included in this study to obtain an alternative acceptable measure of board effectiveness in addition to the more objective, but much broader, organization performance measure. The measure used five items (Cronbach Alpha = .88). Comparison of this board measure with objective bank performance indicated a .56 correlation ($p < .01$), thus providing some indication of validity. Factor analysis and reliability analysis indicated a strong factor with strong correlations among the items. The responses by insiders from each board were averaged, thus yielding a board effectiveness score for each board of directors.

For bank (organization) performance, it was necessary to measure strategic performance over some period of time to reveal a pattern and practice of effective or ineffective board activity (Pearce, 1983; Rosenstein, 1987). It also appears important to utilize a composite measure taking into account many features of performance. For example, strategic performance certainly can not be inferred merely by considering profits. To meet these special needs, this study will use a 3 year average of the 100-point Sheshunoff's Presidents' Weighted Index of Bank Performance, for the years 1992, 1993, and 1994. This index is accepted industry-wide as a standard measure of overall strategic performance. Not only does this index consider profitability but it also factors in capital adequacy (measures taken to ensure the safety and security of stockholder and depositor interests), asset quality (measures taken to ensure the timely collectibility of the asset portfolio), management performance (measures taken to ensure sound operational and strategic management), and liquidity (measures taken to insure sound funds management and availability). This measure is somewhat akin to the five-point capital, asset quality, management, earnings, liquidity (CAMEL) measure calculated by the various bank regulatory bodies (but is confidential), which considers the same factors noted earlier. The weights of each factor in this index are determined by a regular strategic issue survey of many thousands of bank presidents nationwide by the Sheshunoff Company, a well-respected bank research organization.

Following the suggestions of Pearce (1983), it was thought necessary to include two important control variables in the regression equations to preclude the influence of likely extraneous variables. The local state of the economy (current local economic condition) is believed by some researchers to influence the performance of organizations. A weighted average economic score for each county considers unemployment levels, average salaries in the area, retail trade levels, and economic growth. The score was provided by the Center for Business and Economic Research (1995) at the University of Alabama. The number of competitors in the county of operation also was included as a control measure. Please note that these control measures were shown in the study to be nonsignificant in all equations and for purposes of brevity and simplicity will not be included in the results section.

RESULTS

Table 9.2 presents the descriptive statistics and correlations among the variables. The results indicate that objective bank effectiveness, perceived board effectiveness, and board activity level are all fairly high but do not indicate any real differences between responding banks and the other banks in the state.

Board members from each subgroup apparently use fairly high levels of analysis and intuition in the board deliberations and discussions.

Contrasting Decision Styles

Table 9.3 contains the results relevant to the first research question. Before comparisons between insiders and outsiders on the level of analysis were made, a two-way overall analysis of variance (ANOVA) was conducted to test for the effect of member type (insider–outsider), controlling for the organization's effect, information processing differences caused by factors peculiar to the different organizations. In other words, an overall significant main effect associated with subgroup membership would allow for testing of contrasts between the two subgroups of the board. With the nine-item analysis score as the dependent variable, the main effect of board subgroup (insider–outsider) was significant, allowing for a contrast between the subgroups to be considered. A comparison was made between inside directors (bankers) and outside directors (nonbankers) across all boards on the nine-item analysis score. This comparison was made at the individual level, with a sample of 192 nonbankers and 167 bankers for the comparison ($n = 359$). The analysis scores of insiders (bank officers) were found slightly more varied (higher standard deviation) than those of outsiders, which caused rejection of Levene's test for equality of variances. Using the two-group t-test robust to unequal variances, the sample difference of 5.85 was found to be significant, $t(df = 327.26 = -9.34, p < .01)$. It appears that insiders use analysis and explicit information somewhat more than do outsiders. Insiders indicate using analysis at a level approaching *much of the time*, whereas outsiders report using analysis at a level closer to *sometimes*.

TABLE 9.2

Descriptive Statistics and Bivariate Correlations

Variables	Means	SD	1	2	3	4	5	6	7	8	9
1. Bank Performance	59.75	22.5	1								
2. Board Performance	20.98	1.89	.56	1							
3. Board Activity	25.5	2.66	.45	.49	1						
4. Competition	6.32	3.33	-.32	-.22	-.10	1					
5. Economic Condition	62.24	13.77	-.35	-.21	-.15	.27	1				
6. Insider Analysis	35.12	2.91	.30	.30	.49	-.15	-.13	1			
7. Insider Intuition	18.24	1.64	-.05	-.14	-.18	-.02	-.04	-.02	1		
8. Outsider Analysis	29.27	2.47	.10	.11	.36	.01	-.05	.25	.02	1	
9. Outsider Intuition	19.81	1.4	.22	.28	.15	-.04	-.05	.26	.06	.06	1

Note. Italicized correlations indicate *p* < .05.

TABLE 9.3
Analysis of Variance (ANOVA) and Comparison Results

Two-Way ANOVA With Analysis as Dependent Variable Source	Sum of Squares	DF	Mean Square	F
Main Effects	3917.52	59	66.41	2.36*
Insider–Outsider	2027.99	1	2027.99	72.19**
Bank Effect	2237.94	58	38.59	1.37*
Residual	8399.44	299	28.09	
Total	12316.96	358	34.41	

Insider vs. Outsider Contrast on Analysis	Mean	DF	Difference	t
Insiders (n = 163)	35.12 (3.9 per item)	327	5.85	-9.34**
Outsiders (n = 196)	29.27 (3.3 per item)			

Two-Way Anova with Intuition as Dependent Variable Source	Sum of Squares	DF	Mean Square	F
Main Effects	301.69	59	5.11	0.77
Insider–Outsider	60.13	1	60.13	9.07**
Bank Effect	245.07	58	4.23	0.64
Residual	1983.11	299	6.63	
Total	2284.79	358	6.38	

Insider vs. Outsider Contrast on Intuition	Mean	DF	Difference	t
Insiders (n = 163)	18.24 (3.6 per item)	357	1.57	3.55**
Outsiders (n = 196)	19.81 (4 per item)			

*P < .05. **P < .01.

Another two-way overall ANOVA was run using intuition as the dependent variable. The main effect associated with member type (insider–outsider) was once again found to be significant, indicating differences between the subgroups controlling for the effect of the organizational differences. A comparison was made between inside directors and outside directors across all boards on the five-item intuition score. The difference score of 1.57 was significant, $t(df = 357) = 3.55, p < .01$, indicating that outsiders, on average, exercise a somewhat more intuitive decision and deliberation style in meeting.

Effects of Processing Style on Performance

Table 9.4 reveals the results relevant to answering the second research question.

These hierarchical regression equations help to uncover relations between processing styles and bank and board effectiveness measures. A hierarchical regression procedure was performed to control for the effects of other variables before the variable of interest is added into the equation. Two dependent variables are used in these tests: objective bank performance and self-reported board performance. Statistical conclusions are based on resulting partial regression coefficients.

Insider Analysis. The authors suggested a relation between the level of insider analysis and bank and board effectiveness, with effectiveness expected to increase as insiders increase their use of and input of such analysis to the decision deliberation. As Table 9.4 indicates, insider analysis is significantly related to bank performance, controlling for the economy and the level of competition ($B = 1.98, t = 2.01, p < .05$). These results indicate that bank performance tends to be higher when insiders analytically process and report bank data and decision-related information. The relation between the level of insider analysis and board performance was also found to be significant, controlling for the economy and the number of competitors ($B = .18, t = 2.14, p < .05$). The significant regression coefficient indicates that inside directors rate their boards slightly higher in situations when more analysis is offered by their own subgroup. Perhaps insider analysis is an important first step in the effective board meeting.

The next test under the second research question was to see if there was an interaction between insider analysis and board activity level in influencing bank performance. Do higher board activity levels enhance the relation

TABLE 9.4
Hierarchical Regression Results (Research Question 2)

	Variable	Beta	Std. Err.	t	
Dependent variable: *bank performance*	Ins. Analysis*	1.98	0.95	2.01*	$F (dt = 3) = 4.24**$ R-square = .14 Change = .05
Test of Interaction: Insider analysis X board activity	InAnal x Activ* Ins. Analysis Activity	-0.24 8.13 13.34	0.23 3.56 5.13	-1.04 2.28* 2.61*	$F (df = 5) = 5.44**$ R-square = .27 Change = .03
Dependent variable: *bank performance*	Outs. Intuition*	3.22	1.98	1.62	$F (df = 3) = 3.58*$ R-square = .12 Change = .03
Test of Interaction: Outsider intuition X board activity	Out. Intu. X Activ.* Outs. Intuition Activity	.53 -11.61 -7.47	.77 20.23 15.55	.69 -.72 -.48	$F (df = 5) = 4.83**$ R-square = .23 Change = .00
Dependent variable: *board performance*	Ins. Analysis*	.18	.08	2.14*	$F (df = 3) = 2.55$ R-square = .07 Change = .05*
Test of Interaction: insider analysis X board activity	InAnal X Activ* Ins. Analysis Activity	-.06 -0.12 0.11	.14 .83 1.18	.43 .14 .08	$F (df = 5) = 4.03**$ R-square = .20 Change = .00
Dependent variable: *board performance*	Outs. Intuition*	0.37	0.17	2.15*	$F (df = 3) = 2.57$ R-square = .08 Change = .06*
Test of interaction: outsider intuition X board activity	Out. Intu. X Activ.* Outs. Intuition Activity	0.1 -2.21 -1.61	0.06 1.66 1.28	1.51 -1.33 -1.25	$F (df = 5) = 5.53**$ R-square = .28 Change = .03

Note. An asterisk (*) denotes the variable of interest
*$p < .05$ **$p < .01$

between insider analysis and bank performance? The interaction term composed of the two main effects, (insider analysis X activity level) was not found to be significant when entered hierarchically into an equation containing the control variables and the main effects ($B = -0.24$, $t = -1.04$, $p = 0.31$). It appears that the main effects in this equation (both were highly influential) overwhelm the explanatory power of the interaction. With board performance as the dependent variable, the results were similar. Controlling for the main effects associated with insider analysis and board activity level, the interaction term coefficient was once again not significant. These statistical results indicate that within the sample, levels of board activity did not appear to enhance (statistically) the analytical efforts of inside board members.

Outsider Intuition. With bank performance as the dependent variable, the regression coefficient associated with outsider intuition, controlling for the economy and competition, was not significant ($B = 3.22$, $t = 1.63$, $p = .11$). The regression relation between outsider intuition level and perceived board performance, however, was found to be positive and significant ($B = .37$, $t = 2.15$, $p < .05$). It can be reasoned that insiders feel more favorably about the board's interactions when outsiders offer their intuitive input: general thoughts, feelings, instincts, reactions, and intuitions. It was also questioned whether an interaction existed between intuitive processing on the part of outsiders and board activity level, with activity level thought to go hand-in-hand with (and generally enhance) the positive effects of an intuitive outsider group. With both dependent variables, the effect of the interaction term (over and above the effects of the control variables and main effects) was not significant. Indications are that the positive effects of outsider intuition are not significantly enhanced by the board's level of activity. The main effects of outsider intuition and activity level once again accounted for a significant portion of the observed variation in the dependent variables.

Interactions Among Processing Styles

Another set of regression equations was run to test for interactive, complementary relations between the processing styles of the two board subgroups. Once again, the dependent variables of interest were bank performance and board performance. In these hierarchical equations, the control variables were entered first, the main effects entered second, and the interactive term of insider analysis–outsider intuition entered in the final step. None of the proposed interactions were found to be significant.

It was suggested in the final research question that analysis on the part of insiders enhances the positive influence of intuition by outsiders. Vice versa, it is suggested that outsider intuition strengthens and builds on the analysis of insiders. This is the mingling of prospectus and perspective spoken of in the theory building portion presented earlier. The expected outcome of this requisite interaction is improved decisions and improved performance. With bank performance as the dependent variable, the interactive effect of insider analysis X outsider intuition was not significant when controlling for the main effects and control variables. Statistically, there is no evidence that the positive influence of one is enhanced by the presence of the other. With board performance as the dependent variable, similar results were obtained.

The Influence of Activity Level on the Interactions.   Does the expected complementary relation between processing styles only exist in the most highly active boards? In other words, can interactive effects be detected only in situations where requisite discussion and involvement are taking place? To test for this effect, a three-way interaction term should be used. This effect is best explained as follows: the level of one variable influences the interactive relation between the other two. In other words, two variables might interact but only when higher levels of a third variable are present. It has been suggested that the level of activity would enhance the interaction and exchange ongoing among board members. In theory, this suggestion is appealing. From an empirical standpoint, however, this interaction does not appear to exist.

A COMPLETE BOARD MODEL
AND ALTERNATIVE EXPLANATION

The findings thus far tend to demonstrate the utility of processing roles played by the two subgroups, with insider analysis and outsider intuition both related to bank and board performance. One important observation, thus far, is the universal strength of the board activity level variable in influencing effectiveness. The main effect of board activity level generally overwhelmed other effects in many of the regression equations run. As somewhat of an afterthought, it was decided to change the research focus somewhat and try to look at the relative effects of the various processing inputs and board activity level on performance. It seems plausible, given the results thus far, that board activity level is the critical determinant of success and that the processing inputs of analysis and intuition can have positive influences on the level of board activity and involvement in the meeting. It could be that board activity and involvement is an important intervening or mediating variable rather than a moderating variable. A series of hierarchical regression equations were developed to uncover the direct and indirect effects of the processing inputs and the role played by board involvement (activity) in conjunction with the processing styles. In this exploratory research where variables are considered together in regression equations, the authors considered it appropriate to drop the critical significance level to .10, rather than the traditional .05. Also for purposes of exploration, the variables outsider analysis and insider intuition were included.

Before the intervening nature of activity level is assessed, the simple relation between the four processing inputs (insider analysis, outsider analysis, insider intuition, and outsider intuition) and performance should be considered. With bank performance and board performance as the dependent variables, the four independent variables were entered together in the overall regression models. The results of these two regression equations are included in Table 9.5. The goal here was to see which input stood out as most important among all inputs (not including activity level) in an equation predicting performance. The standardized regression coefficients for all variables were run so that all variables could be placed on a comparable, standardized scale. First, bank performance was used as the dependent variable. The largest standardized regression coefficient was associated with the level of insider analysis, the only variable of the four that exhibited significance at the .10 level. With board performance as the dependent variable, the results seem somewhat more substantial. The largest standardized coefficient was outsider intuition ($B = .23, t - 1.8, p < .10$). The second largest coefficient was associated with insider analysis ($B = .23, t = 1.7, p < .10$). These two variables seemingly lead insiders to report satisfaction with the performance of their boards.

The next regression equations were run to test if any of the processing inputs were related to performance when the level of board activity was also included in the equation. Statistically, the effects of the board processing styles are diminished when activity level is also included in the equation. To summarize, the only significant direct effect beyond that of activity level was the effect of outsider intuition on board performance ($B = .21, t = 1.73, p < .10$). The influence of activity level on both dependent variables was compelling. In the bank performance equation, activity level was the only significant independent variable ($B = .38, t = 2.5, p < .05$). In the board performance equation, activity level ($B = .43, t = 3.1, p < .05$) and outsider intuition were the only significant independent variables.

Combined, these results lead one to believe that the activity level of the board is the key influence on performance. The relative effects of the processing inputs on performance were minute when compared to the influ-

TABLE 9.5

Regression Results: Alternative Explanation

Variable	Coefficient	Beta	t
Run 1: Dependent variable, *bank performance*			
Insider analysis	0.255	1.97	1.86*
Insider intuition	-0.051	-0.36	-0.39
Outsider analysis	0.022	0.19	0.17
Outsider intuition	0.151	2.42	1.13
F (df = 4) = 1.73, R-square = .05			
Run 2: Dependent variable, *board performance*			
Insider analysis	0.227	0.15	1.7*
Insider intuition	-0.155	-0.09	-1.24
Outsider analysis	0.041	0.03	0.32
Outsider intuition	0.223	0.31	1.75*
F (df = 4) = 2.56**, R-square = .10			
Run 3: Dependent variable, *bank performance*			
Insider analysis	0.06	0.47	0.42
Insider intuition	-0.125	-1.72	-0.97
Outsider analysis	-0.065	-0.59	-0.5
Outsider intuition	0.136	2.19	1.1
Activity level	0.378	3.21	2.55**
F (df = 5) = 3.46***, R-square = .18			
Run 4: Dependent variable, *board performance*			
Insider analysis	0.01	0.01	0.07
Insider intuition	-0.138	-0.16	-1.11
Outsider analysis	-0.061	-0.05	-0.49
Outsider intuition	0.205	0.28	1.73*
Activity level	0.433	0.31	3.05**
F (df = 6) = 4.75***, R-square = .24			

(Table 9.5 continued)

(Table 9.5 continued)

Variable	Coefficient	Beta	t
Run 5:			
Dependent variable, activity level			
(Influence of information processing inputs on activity)			
Insider analysis	0.416	0.38	3.51***
Insider intuition	-0.193	-0.16	-1.74*
Outsider analysis	0.254	0.27	2.22**
Outsider intuition	0.035	0.07	0.31
F (df = 6) = 6.92***, R-square = .29			

*P < .10. **P < .05. ***P < .01.

ence of activity level. Perhaps appropriate processing inputs are more important because of their influence on activity level and involvement in the meeting. If appropriate processing styles lead to activity level, then this indirect effect on performance is just as important as a direct effect. To test the influences of processing styles on activity level, a regression equation was run with board activity level as the dependent variable and the four processing inputs as the independent variables: insider analysis, outsider intuition, insider intuition, and outsider analysis. In this equation, three out of the four processing inputs demonstrated significance at the .10 alpha level. First, insider analysis had the strongest impact on board activity level ($B = .42, t = 3.5, p < .01$). It appears that strong insider analysis is requisite for the type of board activity necessary for productive and informed decision making. The second most influential variable in the equation predicting activity level was outsider analysis ($B = .25, t = 2.2, p < .05$). Outsider analysis may result in more active boards, or more active boards may possibly allow outsiders to conduct effective analysis. The final significant influence in this equation was the negative influence associated with insider intuition ($B = -.19, t = -1.74, p < .10$). It appears that insider intuition is negatively related to the level of board activity. Although insider intuition can undoubtedly be beneficial in many cases, it could be that insiders who report using high levels of intuition in the meeting are likely hurting the level of activity and involvement exhibited by their board. Intuitive input may provide communication but not of the form needed to stimulate board activity and involvement in the decision process.

DISCUSSION

In this study, the dynamics of the board meeting have been described more thoroughly. The roles played by the two board subgroups, insiders and outsiders, during decision discussions and deliberations have been explored. The ability of the board to generate, enhance, and to benefit from high involvement and activity level has been better elucidated.

Statistically significant differences were found between insiders and outsiders on the level of analysis and level of intuition employed in decision deliberations within the board meetings. It appears that insiders are more inclined to use analysis than are outsiders, although the variability in insiders' analysis scores was higher than in those of outsiders, meaning that some insiders are not nearly as analytical as others. The level of analysis and reporting by insiders would seemingly need to be quite high, for this factual reporting to the board is a major reason for holding a board meeting. Insiders also report using fairly high levels of intuition in the board deliberations, although outsiders reported using intuition at a slightly higher rate than did insiders. The results are somewhat equivocal as to whether outsiders operate more intuitively than do insiders; both subgroups scored fairly high on the intuition measure (per item of 4 vs. 3.6).

Insider and Outsider Contributions

Overall, evidence suggests that in board meetings, it is a paramount responsibility of insiders to bring the directorate in tune with the operations of the bank and in tune with the thinking of management on various issues. Without such a briefing, the outsiders are unable to fulfill their duty (Daily, 1995) as sounding board and evaluator. One of the most important findings was that the level of insider analysis within a board is positively related to board and bank performance. Perhaps just as importantly, it was shown that the level of insider analysis influences the overall activity level of the board. The ability of the management team to stimulate conversation, discussion, and sharing of perspective is related to their ability to bring the directorate in tune with management thinking, and detailed facts and figures are an important part of this. It is conceivable that an outsider will quietly listen and passively approve management suggestions if they do not have sufficient factual information to use in formulating appropriate response. It is likely that the insiders who offer more detailed analysis and explicit information are the managers who genuinely depend on their directorship and who recognize the real value of an informed and active directorate (Daily, 1995). If insiders view outsiders as merely caretakers of stockholder interest and merely on hand to check management, then providing general intuition and conclusions is a likely and convenient choice. This is a possibly a way to meet mandatory reporting requirements without the fear of micromanagement by the outside directorate. The real danger of intuitive reporting is illustrated in the negative relation found to exist between the level of insider intuition and board activity level.

It is recognized that bankers who are more analytical and detail oriented in the board meeting behave this way on a daily basis, carefully considering the complexities of banking. No doubt the scores associated with insiders (managers who also work in the bank on a daily basis) have some degree of additional influence on bank performance. There must be some reflection of everyday style in the scores of insiders. Simply put, the responses of insiders may give some indication as to how business is conducted within the bank daily. Research over the years (Henderson & Nutt, 1980; Nutt, 1993) has agreed that decision style is certainly a part of one's stable personality or personal style. Furthermore, the preferences and styles of a top management group may give some indication as to the style or culture of the entire organization, given the accepted influence of top management on organization culture and style (Hambrick & Mason, 1984). It is therefore quite expected that insider scores will be somewhat more related to bank performance measures relative to those of outsiders. A particularly disturbing possibility is that some bankers are rather intuitive in nature, which was shown to have a negative effect on board activity and involvement. The possible danger of operating intuitively in the board meeting should be apparent, but the notion of a very intuitive banker or a very intuitive banking culture is especially disturbing. The relations with performance must be taken with a bit of caution for they may not reflect board influence alone (Daily, 1995; Hambrick & D'Aveni, 1992; Reger & Huff, 1993).

Quality commentary and reaction by outsiders is a very important component of the effective board. As expected, a large portion of this commentary is composed of intuitive reaction, opinion, and feelings. The level of outsider intuition appears to be a good indicator of how well the board is tapping the experience and professional insights of the outsiders, for these are certainly the desired inputs. Outsider intuition was correlated with insider analysis, indicating that the ability of insiders to inform the board likely related to outsiders' abilities to provide appropriate commentary and reaction.

Combination of Processing Styles: Board Activity Level

The proposed interaction was surprisingly not significant. Despite this, however, exchange processes are no doubt the key to better performance.

The alternative models portion of the results indicate that insider analysis and outsider analysis inputs generally lead to quality board involvement, which is a major influence on bank and board performance. Outsider intuition appears to have direct positive influences on board performance. It appears that through appropriate interaction and involvement, stronger and more complete interpretive representations are built within the parameters of the group level knowledge structure (Daft & Weick, 1984; Langfield-Smith, 1992; Prahalad & Bettis, 1986). In more active boards, there is more opportunity for discussion, questioning, and challenging of assumptions (Bourgeois, 1985). With enhanced discussion and exchange, there is more agreement and enthusiasm due to the fact that different perspectives have been shared and integrated (Bourgeois, 1980; Dess & Origer, 1987).

Board activity level and involvement is indeed a mediating variable rather than a moderating variable. Roles played by board members and the contributions they make lead to high levels of activity that enhance the quality of action taken and the quality of direction and suggestions given to the organization. The intervening effect of board activity is somewhat akin to the concepts presented in descriptions of the learning process in what Nonaka (1994) termed *communities of interaction*. Nonaka explained that different types of knowledge are shared to create additional knowledge, due to interaction and dialogue. The additional knowledge seems to be stimulated in the minds of participants as they listen to and process ongoing discussion. Huber (1991) and Cohen and Levinthal (1990) noted that more learning occurs when more and more varied perspectives and interpretations are developed and shared. The ability to assimilate different information into current problems is a positive attribute.

It is quite significant that this study revealed some of the important determinants of board involvement. In no research thus far have theoretically sound, cognitive processing variables been suggested to improve involvement and subsequently performance. The full models indicate only minimal direct effects of the processing styles on performance but certainly indicate indirect effects, which are likely just as important. This research has thereby given some indication as to how a board can improve their level of involvement and activity and how they can subsequently improve board and bank performance.

This research has strengthened and built on traditional board research through its focus on cognition and decision processes of board members. This certainly appears to be a more theoretically sound and more complex approach to understanding boards of directors. Future research should attempt to further our understanding of board cognition. The traditionally researched issues of composition, control, governance, and performance are rather stale without some notion of the thought processes employed by directors. The flaws of this study suggest opportunities for future research.

The attitudes of insiders toward the directorate appear to be an important variable. Anecdotal evidence and conversations with bankers indicate that the attitudes of insiders determine to a large extent what will be revealed to the board for consideration. This research effort reveals that the ability of the board to do its job is inextricably bound to the willingness of the management team to inform the directorate thoroughly. Researchers should also find out exactly what it is about the facts and figures inherent to analysis that stimulates involvement and further discussion. Researchers should attempt to ask board members exactly which pieces of information are used and which pieces of information are not used.

Overall, strategy research can benefit greatly from systematic application of scientific knowledge on attitudes, information processing, decision making, motivation, communication, and other softer cognitive subjects. The more researchers know about humans within a management system, the more explanation and predictive power can be provided.

REFERENCES

Agor, W. (1986). *The logic of intuitive decision making: A research based approach for top management.* New York: Quorum.

Anthony, W., & Daake, D. (1994). *Measurement of analysis and tacit knowledge in decision making.* Unpublished working paper, Florida State University.

Bantel, K., & Jackson, S. (1989). Top management and innovation in banking. *Strategic Management Journal, 10,* 107–124.

Barnard, C. (1938). *The functions of the executive.* Cambridge, MA: Harvard University Press.

Baysinger, B., & Butler, H. (1985). Corporate governance and the board of directors: Performance effects of changes in board composition. *Journal of Law, Economics, and Organizations, 1,* 102–124.

Baysinger, B., & Hoskisson, R. (1990). The composition of boards of directors and strategic control: Effects on corporate strategy. *Academy of Management Review, 15,* 72–87.

Behling, O., & Eckel, N. (1991). Making sense out of intuition. *Academy of Management Executive, 5*(1), 46–54.

Bourgeois, L. (1980). Performance and consensus. *Strategic Management Journal, 1,* 227–248.

Bourgeois, L. (1985). Strategic goals, perceived uncertainty, and economic performance in volatile environments. *Academy of Management Journal, 28,* 548–573.

Center for Business and Economic Research. (1995). *Economic abstract of Alabama.* Tuscaloosa, AL: University of Alabama Press.

Cohen, W., & Levinthal, D. (1990). Absorptive capacity: A new perspective on learning and innovation. *Administrative Science Quarterly, 35,* 128–152.

Daft, R., & Weick, K. (1984). Toward a model of organizations as interpretation systems. *Academy of Management Review, 9,* 284–295.

Daily, C. (1995). The relationship between board composition and leadership structure and bankruptcy reorganization outcomes. *Journal of Management, 21,* 1041–1056.

Daily, C., & Dalton, D. (1994). Bankruptcy and corporate governance: The impact of board composition and structure. *Academy of Management Journal, 37*, 1603–1617.

Dess, G., & Origer, N. (1987). Environment, structure, and consensus in strategy formulation: A conceptual integration. *Academy of Management Review, 12*, 313–330.

Eisenhardt, K. (1989). Making fast strategic decisions in high-velocity environments. *Academy of Management Journal, 32*, 543–576.

Eisenhardt, K., & Brown, S. (1998). Time pacing: Competing in markets that won't stand still. *Harvard Business Review, 76*(2), 59–70.

Fiske, S., & Taylor, S. (1991). *Social Cognition* (2nd ed.). New York: McGraw-Hill.

Ford, R. (1988). Outside directors and the privately owned firm: Are they necessary? *Entrepreneurship Theory and Practice, 13*, 49–57.

Goodstein, J., Gautam, K., & Boeker, W. (1994). The effects of board size and diversity on strategic change. *Strategic Management Journal, 15*, 241–250.

Hambrick, D., & D'Aveni, R. (1992). Top team deterioration as part of the downward spiral of large corporate bankruptcies. *Management Science, 38*, 1445–1466.

Hambrick, D., & Mason, P. (1984). Upper echelons: The organization as a reflection of its top managers. *Academy of Management Review, 9*, 193–206.

Henderson, J., & Nutt, P. (1980). The influence of decision style on decision making behavior. *Management Science, 26*, 371–386.

Hitt, M., & Tyler, B. (1991). Strategic decision models: Integrating different perspectives. *Strategic Management Journal, 12*, 327–352.

Hoskisson, R., Johnson, R., & Moesel, D. (1994). Corporate divestiture intensity in restructuring firms: Effects of governance, strategy, and performance. *Academy of Management Journal, 37*, 1207–1251.

Huber, G. (1991). Organizational learning: The contributing processes and literatures. *Organization Science, 2*, 88–115.

Judge, W., & Zeithaml, C. (1992). Institutional and strategic choice perspectives on board involvement in the strategic decision process. *Academy of Management Journal, 35*, 766–794.

Kirschenbaum, S. (1992). Influence of experience on information-gathering strategies. *Journal of Applied Psychology, 77*, 343–352.

Kleinmuntz, B. (1990). Why we still use our heads instead of formulas: Toward an integrative approach. *Psychological Bulletin, 107*, 296–310.

Langfield-Smith, K. (1992). Exploring the need for a shared cognitive map. *Journal of Management Studies, 29*, 349–368.

Lyles, M., and Schwenk, C. (1992). Top management, strategy, and organizational knowledge structures. *Journal of Management Studies, 29*, 155–173.

March, J. (1991). Exploration and exploitation in organizational learning. *Organization Science, 2*, 71–87.

Mintzberg, H. (1976). Planning on the left side and managing on the right. *Harvard Business Review, 54*, 49–58.

Mitchell, T., & Beach, L. (1990). " … Do I love thee? Let me count … " Toward an understanding of intuitive and automatic decision making. *Organizational Behavior and Human Decision Processes, 47*, 1–20.

Nonaka, I. (1994). A dynamic theory of organizational knowledge creation. *Organization Science, 5*, 14–37.

Nutt, P. (1993). Flexible decision styles and the choices of top executives. *Journal of Management Studies, 27*, 273–294.

Patton, A., & Baker, J. (1987). Why won't directors rock the boat? *Harvard Business Review, 65*(6), 10–18.

Pearce, J. (1983). The relationship of internal versus external orientations to financial measures of strategic performance. *Strategic Management Journal, 4*, 297–306.

Pearce, J. (1995). A structural analysis of dominant coalitions in small banks. *Journal of Management, 21*, 1075–1096.

Pearce, J., & Zahra, S. (1991). The relative power of CEOs and boards of directors. *Strategic Management Journal, 12*, 135–153.

Pearce, J., & Zahra, S. (1992). Board composition from a strategic contingency perspective. *Journal of Management Studies, 29*, 411–438.

Prahalad, C., & Bettis, R. (1986). The dominant logic: A new linkage between diversity and performance. *Strategic Management Journal, 7*, 485–501.

Reger, R., & Huff, A. (1993). Strategic groups: A cognitive perspective. *Strategic Management Journal, 14*, 103–124.

Rindova, V. (1994, August). *What corporate boards have to do with strategy: A decision-making perspective.* Paper presented at the 1994 Academy of Management Annual Meeting, Dallas, TX.

Robey, D., & Taggart, W. (1981). Measuring managers' minds: The assessment of style in human information processing. *Academy of Management Review, 6*, 375–383.

Rosenstein, J. (1987). Why don't U.S. boards get more involved in strategy? *Long Range Planning, 20*, 30–34.

Spender, J. (1993, August). Competitive advantage from tacit knowledge: Unpacking the concept and its strategic implications. Paper presented at the 1993 Academy of Management Annual Meeting, Atlanta, GA.

Sternberg, R. (1997). Managerial intelligence: Why IQ isn't enough. *Journal of Management, 23*, 475–494.

Taggart, W., & Robey, D. (1981). Minds and managers: On the dual nature of human information processing and management *Academy of Management Review, 6*, 187–195

Wagner, R. (1987). Tacit knowledge in everyday intelligent behavior. *Journal of Personality and Social Psychology, 52*, 1236–1247.

Wagner, R., & Sternberg, R. (1985). Practical intelligence in real-world pursuits: The role of tacit knowledge. *Journal of Personality and Social Psychology, 49*, 436–458.

Zahra, S. (1990). Increasing the board's involvement in strategy. *Long Range Planning, 23*, 109–117.

Zahra, S., & Pearce, J. (1989). Board of directors and corporate financial performance: A review and integrative model. *Journal of Management, 15*, 291–334.

Zahra, S., & Stanton, W. (1988). The implications of board of directors' composition for corporate strategy and performance. *International Journal of Management, 5*, 229–236.

chapter 10

Cognitive Maps of Managers and Complex Problem Solving

K. Unnikrishnan Nair
Indian Institute of Management, Calcutta

Many of the managerial problems are complex, for which there are no ready-made solutions or programmed decisions available in organizations. Making strategic choices, implementing large-scale organizational changes, introducing new products, reengineering work processes, resolving industrial relations issues, or solving any uncommon and not so simple problem in the work context are all examples of this kind. Such situations are often termed as *ill structured* or *complex*. For organizations to be successful, it is important and crucial for their managers to effectively deal with these situations.

How managers deal with ill-structured situations or solve complex problems has been drawing increasing research attention, probably as a direct consequence of the increasing complexity of managerial work and work contexts. For instance, with national barriers being lowered, organizations are experiencing rising diversity in their action domains, as in diverse economic, social, political, legal, and cultural systems of different countries. There is also rising diversity within organizations. The number of stakeholders who can influence organizational functioning is also on the rise, such as regulatory bodies, judiciary (responding to public interest litigation), and a number of interest groups who champion public and consumer rights, plights, and demands of many kinds. All of these add to the complexity of managerial work. It should also be noted that contrary to normal belief, complexity of managerial work is increasing not at the top levels of

211

organizations alone. It is true that top-level managers have to deal with strategic issues that are quite ill structured. However, activities such as technology changeover; new product design, development, and introduction; reengineering work processes, and so on require the active involvement and problem solving of managers at all levels in the organization.

Considering these aspects, it is only logical that, "Problem solving research today is being extended to the domain of ill-structured problems" (Simon & Associates, 1992, p. 52). Although there is increasing interest amongst researchers with different backgrounds and training in the nature of complexity of managerial work and the many different ways in which managers deal with complex situations, they have only made a beginning. VanLehn (1989) echoed this concern: "[Because] research is just beginning in this area, so many of the proposed processes are based only on a rational extension of the basic ideas of routine problem solving" (p. 549).

This chapter presents an empirical study on the complex problem-solving behavior of managers. It specifically looks at how the nature of thought structuring of managers about a complex problem affects the effectiveness with which they solve it. It begins by defining a complex problem and approaches to solving such problems. This is followed by a discussion of research in complex problem solving using computer simulations, leading to the research question. The next section outlines the research design and data collection, followed by analysis and results. The chapter ends with a discussion of the findings.

COMPLEX PROBLEM SOLVING

Complex Problems

Newell and Simon (1972) said that a person is said to face a problem when "he wants something and does not know immediately what series of actions he can perform to get it" (p. 72). Problems may be *well defined* or *ill defined*. A problem is well defined if the initial and final states of the problem are clearly defined, there exist a number of action steps to traverse the gap between the two states, and there are ways of ascertaining if the solution arrived at is the desired end state (Newell & Simon, 1972; VanLehn, 1989). A problem that does not fit well within these characteristics is termed as *ill defined*. Such problems have also been termed by researchers as *complex* (Dearborn & Simon, 1958; Dörner, 1980), *ill-structured* (Ungson, Braunstein, & Hall, 1981) *unstructured, wicked* or *ill-behaved* (Mason & Mitroff, 1972, 1981), *unstructured strategic* (Mintzberg, Raisinghani, & Theoret, 1976), *messy* (Ackoff, 1979), and *nonprogrammed* (Simon, 1957). The terms *complex* or *ill*

structured are used in this chapter. Complex problems are sometimes also referred to as *complex tasks*.

Mintzberg et al. (1976) considered complex problems to "refer to decision processes that have not been encountered in quite the same form and
for which no predetermined and explicit set of ordered responses exist in the
organization" (p. 246). Ungson et al. (1981, p. 120), quoting Simon and
Hays defined complex problems as "those problems in which the problem
solver contributed to the definition and resolution, using information generated from initial unsuccessful attempts at a solution." Ungson et al. (1981)
consider problems to be ill structured due to:

> (1) the ambiguity and incompleteness of problemrelated information, (2) the
> extent to which problems are continually defined and redefined by managers,
> (3) the lack of a program for the desired outcomes, (4) the possibility of
> multi-person influences, and (5) the extended period in which a decision is
> made. (p. 121)

Solving Complex Problems

Solving a complex problem is complicated by its amenability to multiple
problem definitions. That is, there may not be *one* answer to the question,
What is the problem?. The solution could depend very much on how the
problem solver defines the initial state of the problem. What Rittel (as
quoted in Mason & Mitroff, 1972) said with respect to a design problem in
architecture is very relevant in this context:

> They are not well defined: i.e., every formulation of the problem is already
> made in view of some particular solution principle. If the idea of the solution is
> elaborated or even changed during the design process, new aspects become
> relevant and new kinds of information will lead to different questions about
> what is the case in the particular situation and about what is desired or ac-
> ceptable. Since nobody can anticipate all conceivable design possibilities be-
> fore design starts, nobody can list all potentially relevant data in a complete,
> well-defining problem formation. (pp. 479–480)

Secondly, problem solving is also influenced by the goal(s) that the problem
solver sets to be achieved, or defining the desired end state. There is no way
in which one can say with high degree of exactness that any (set of) goal(s) is
superior to another in an ill-structured situation. The goal(s) may guide information gathering and decision making to solve the problem. It may also
influence feedback seeking that, in turn, can enable continuous redefinition

of the current state of the problem and may even lead to redefining the desired end state, if required, as problem solving progresses.

Finally, in solving complex problems, it is also important that there is a defined or declared closure. That is, problem solving must reach an end. This is because the very nature of the problem is such that the desired end state may continuously get redefined as one progresses on the solution and there is no universally acceptable criteria to decide where one should finally stop. Similar to what Rittel (as quoted in Mason & Mitroff, 1972, pp. 479–480) said in the case of architecture design problems,

> There is no criteria which would determine whether a solution is correct or false. These are meaningless labels, which cannot be applied to solutions of design [complex] problems ... there is no rule which would tell the designer [manager] when to stop his search for a better solution. He can always try to find a better one. Limitations of time and other resources lead him to the decision that now it is good enough.

The problem solver may also decide on a closure when he feels that either the goal(s) set have been achieved or the goal(s) are yet to be achieved but the new state is satisfying under a new set of criteria. He may also abandon problem solving at any stage on realizing that pursuing it any further becomes redundant under a new state that has emerged or when he is not able to make adequate sense to solve it effectively.

EXPERIMENTAL STUDIES ON COMPLEX PROBLEM SOLVING

A number of studies have been done on the problem-solving behavior of individuals and groups using computer-simulated complex problems in laboratory settings (e.g., Dörner, 1980, 1990, 1991; see Dörner & Wearing, 1995, and Frese & Zapf, 1994, for review). They have shown that problem solvers exhibit goal-oriented behavior when dealing with complex problems, termed as *action process* (Frese & Zapf, 1994) or the *process of action regulation* (Dörner & Wearing, 1995). It begins with formulation of goal(s) to be achieved. They can be short term– long term, specific–global, or process– end state goals or subgoals arranged hierarchically. The process of defining goal(s) and elaborating on the subgoals is termed as *goal elaboration* (Dörner & Schaub, 1994; Dörner & Wearing, 1995). The individual then attempts to unravel the ill structuredness of the problem through information gathering. He begins to identify the variables in the problem and generates hypotheses about their interrelationships, keeping in mind the dynamism of the situation as a whole. It also involves prognosis. Planning of action, deciding on what to do, and finally implementing the decision(s) follows hypotheses generation. Action results in consequence(s) that may or may not be explicitly visible to the problem solver. Feedback has to be actively sought and the action process monitored and reflected on so as to effectively regulate further action toward goal achievement (Dörner & Wearing, 1995). Monitoring and reflection also enable goal modification(s), if necessary. It is possible that the actual action process may not always be following this sequence.

It has also been observed that many problem solvers tend to deviate from courses of action that are the most desirable in effectively solving the problem. This is termed as *error* (see Frese & Zapf, 1994, for detailed review). Errors happen when potentially avoidable action leads to nonattainment of goals in a goal-oriented action process. Essentially, errors result from undesirable or inadequate action, inaction, or omission by the problem solver.

Effective Problem Solving: Research Question

Laboratory studies using computer-simulated complex problems revealed that some individuals were more successful or effective in solving the simulated problems as compared to the others. This observation lead these researchers to ask the following question:

What enables some individuals to solve complex problems more effectively (or successfully) than the others?

Dörner and Wearing (1995) suggested from a cognitive perspective that the most important aspect for an individual to cope effectively or successfully with the simulated complex problems in their experiments is to build an elaborate network of causal relationships between variables present in the problem. They stated: "The assumption that some subjects are able to construct a differentiated network of assumptions about the system, whereas other subjects only build up simple, straightforward networks, explains many of the empirical differences in subjects' behaviour [while solving complex problems]" (p. 37). That is, an individual attempting to solve a complex problem needs to identify the variables present in the problem and their relationships thereby creating a network structure in mind. The more he is able to go into the details of the problem and build relationships, the more the network becomes differentiated.

However, this assumption raises a few questions. How does problem solving effectiveness vary among individuals as one moves on the network of relations that they create, say, from simple to (very) elaborate ones? Do highly elaborate networks necessarily lead to higher effectiveness in problem solving? Is there some kind of an ideal or desirable level of elaboration that can yield the best results? Some of these concerns were addressed in this study by the following research question:

> How does effectiveness of problem solving vary with elaborateness of the network of relationships that a problem solver develops of the complex problem?

The mental network of relations that an individual makes of the different variables in any problem or context and that guides his information processing is called a *cognitive map* (Eden, 1988, 1992a), *schema* (Bartlett, 1932) or *belief structure* (Fiske & Taylor, 1984; Walsh, 1988). A cognitive map becomes a *cause map* (Bougon, Weick, & Binkhorst, 1977) when the network depicts cause–effect relations between variables.

Cognitive Maps

Tolman first conceived the concept of cognitive map in 1948. In the most elementary form, it is a graphical representation of meaningful sets of words, termed as *concepts*, and relations among them, termed as *links*, that an individual uses to make sense of a problem or situation (Fiol & Huff, 1992). Cossette and Audet (1992) defined cognitive map as "graphic representation of a set of discursive representations made by a subject with regards to an object in the context of a particular interaction" (p. 323). It represents patterns of organized personal knowledge (Weick & Bougon, 1986) and frames of reference (Fiol & Huff, 1992).

Cognitive maps of individuals vary in their content and structure (e.g., Bougon et al., 1977; Calori, Johnson, & Sarnin, 1994; LangfieldSmith, 1992; Laukkanen, 1994; Stubbart & Ramprasad, 1988). Given any problem or situation, different individuals highlight and attend to different aspects leading to variation in their map content. Analyzing the content of cognitive map and its relation to problem- solving effectiveness is a significant research activity but is not the aim of this chapter. Structure of a cognitive map denotes the configuration of the map in terms of its concepts and links—the way they are distributed in the space that the map is. For instance, a map with a number of concepts and most of which are linked will present a dense network as compared to another where the concepts don't have many connections. Accordingly, the latter map would look like a configuration of isolated concepts (or sets of concepts) in the mind of the individual. Thus, it may be possible to think in terms of a simple–complex continuum along which the structure of cognitive maps of individuals can vary. From this viewpoint, the research question was restated as:

> How does effectiveness of problem solving vary with the complexity of cognitive map that the problem solver develops of the complex problem?

RESEARCH DESIGN

Research Site

This study was done in a very large metal processing plant (more than 50,000 employees) in India with high diversity of managerial functions (operations, finance, maintenance, marketing, personnel, legal, medical, etc.), large hierarchy (11 levels, E0 to E10), and managerial strength (more than 4,000). Although this plant is one of the production units under a public limited company, it has been built and operated as an independent unit in terms of all its business functions. With opening up of Indian economy in 1991, the organization at the time of this study was in the process of reorienting itself to remain successful in the changing business environment and facing many novel and complex issues to deal with.

Sample

Size and Characteristics. Cognitive mapping literature is silent on the sample size for mapping studies (Huff, 1990). All studies referred to on mapping in this chapter have used convenient and small samples. Only Bougon et al. (1977) and Hackner (1991) used exhaustive samples in their studies. There are possibly two reasons for this. First, cognitive mapping studies are still in an exploratory stage in management research (Huff, 1990). Secondly, it is very tedious to work with larger samples, considering the volume of verbal data generated in mapping (Huff, 1990; Laukkanen, 1994).

Forty-five managers from 7 hierarchy levels (E2, assistant manager, to E8, general manager) and 6 functional areas (production/operations, purchase/materials management, maintenance, marketing, finance and personnel/human resources development participated in the study. It involved each manager for 5 to 6 hours and the organization had to practically spare him for the whole day. Sample size was influenced by time needed with each manager, consequent organizational constraints, and considerations of statistical analysis (Levin & Rubin, 1994) with allowance for data losses or de-fects. The sample represented 21 of the 82 departments in the organization including most of its core shops. Average age of the sample was 41 years (range: 26 to 55 years). Seven managers were MBAs, 13 postgraduates, and 24 of them also had foreign training on advanced technical and managerial aspects. There was one woman manager in the sample.

Data Collection

Cognitive Mapping Interview.   Cognitive map can be prepared through (un)structured interview(s) with the participant on the problem, issue, or context of investigation. The researcher then maps the discourse obtained, with or without the assistance of coders. In LangfieldSmith's study (1992), the researcher, based on the first interview, identified salient con-cepts that were then presented to the subject to suggest the links between them. In another set of studies (Cossette & Audet, 1992; Hackner, 1991; Laukkanen, 1994), the procedure was more detailed. Laukkanen (1994) for instance, conducted two to three interviews of three to four hours duration each with eight managers from two industries for comparing their cause maps. Some researchers also showed the map they constructed to the sub-ject for validation.

Because any mapping exercise is specific to the problem investigated (Cossette & Audet, 1992; Eden, 1988), cognitive mapping in this study was based on the complex problem Manutex (Schaub, 1988). Manutex was to be simulated on the computer later and the manager had to solve it. The manager was given a write-up (two and one-half pages text plus seven small tables) describing the situation of Manutex. He was told to study the case and intimate when ready for a discussion on that. The case deals with a small scale, readymade garments manufacturing unit called Manutex situated in Malaysia. It employs 37 people in three levels and five departments and is capable of making seven products using three raw materials. The case also gives a brief history of the unit, prevailing work methods, personnel rela-tions, product–market position, inventory level, financial position, and so on of the firm. The manager was required to take the role of its chief execu-tive officer (CEO) and run the unit for two years or 24 simulated time peri-ods (months). On an average, each manager took about 20 minutes to read the case and get ready for mapping interview.

Data elicitation for mapping revolved around the following broad direc-tions/questions.

1. Describe the situation of Manutex as you see it, whatever comes to your mind.
2. State three issues or problems facing Manutex in order of priority and justify.
3. Identify factors in the readymade garments industry that may be critical for the success of this unit, and how do these factors become critical?
4. How do you plan to run Manutex for the next two years, and why so?
5. What goals and objectives have you set for achieving, if any, and on what basis?
6. Any random, wild thoughts … (they may be philosophical, mundane, stupid, etc.)?

Cognitive mapping theory suggests that the interviewer may provide neutral prompts such as *why, how,* and so on to facilitate the discourse. However, if leading prompts such as *competitors, price, seasonality of product,* and so on are provided, then while coding the discourse, the bias introduced by them have to be taken care of (Calori, et al., 1994). In this study, as a general rule, no specific clues or leads were given to any of the managers. Furthermore, at the beginning of the study, it was planned to have first an unstructured interview and then to follow it up with subsequent sittings to elicit the antecedent cause(s) and ensuing effect(s) of dominant concepts that the manager revealed in it. However, after trying this approach with the first three participants, it was abandoned. This decision was based on a review of the process of the author's choice of concepts from their discourse for eliciting further elaboration. It was found that the author was causing a difference in the complexity of the map by selecting a number of concepts that he thought were important in the discourse and asking the manager to elaborate on them further. This approach introduced biases in the number of concepts and links that each manager talked about, whereas, without the author's intervention, all managers gave a discourse to the same number of questions that were asked to them.

Because the aim of cognitive mapping in this study was to examine the effectiveness of complex problem solving in relation to complexity of the map, what was important was to follow a uniform and acceptable approach with all participants. Hence, attempts to elicit very detailed cause–effect relations were abandoned and just the verbal discourse to the questions in the first mapping interview was relied on consistently for all participants. Cognitive mapping studies have been done earlier with one unstructured interview (e.g., Calori et al., 1994). Mapping interviews were conducted with all 45 managers (all of them allowed to record the discourse). However, due to technical problems, only 42 interviews could be finally transcribed. The average discourse spans about 30 minutes per manager.

Presenting the Complex Problem as a Management Game: Computer Simulation of an Organization.

After a brief recess following mapping interview, the manager was formally introduced to the simulation of the complex problem. The situation described in the Manutex case was to be simulated on the computer. Manutex simulation is a total enterprise or top management game (Keys & Wolfe, 1990) or micro world (Brehmer & Dörner, 1993; Senge, 1990) and has been used in previous studies on complex problem solving (e.g., Ramnarayan & Strohschneider, 1997; Ramnarayan, Strohschneider, & Schaub, 1997). A model of Manutex is given in Fig. 10.1 (arrows indicate influences between variables, flow of products, etc.).

The participant had to manage the full affairs of the Manutex firm as its CEO for two years or 24 simulated months, starting from January of a year, within a real time of 2 and 1/2 hours. Manutex simulation is a complex one, with a wide range of information built in it. It also allowed for a wide range of interventions or decisions to be implemented. For instance, the manager could seek information on as many as 53 aspects of Manutex. This information was grouped in seven categories such as products (past production, current target, product quality, scheduling priority, stock, raw material required, etc.), personnel (salaries, satisfaction levels, recruitment, etc.), machine (working condition, maintenance needs, power and accessories, etc.), and money (details of income, expenditure, bank balance, etc.). The manager had to specifically ask for any of this information to be given. He could also take decisions on many of these aspects in each time interval. The author acted as an intermediary (only) between the manager and the computer for gaining information and implementing decisions—as a facilitator.

Once the simulation started, managers used the initial few months to gain understanding of the simulated problem. They did this by asking for information that could give them idea about Manutex—the different aspects and variables in the system, their interrelations, and so on. They also formed hypotheses about the relations among different variables that they identified and tested out some of these by implementing their decisions through the facilitator in the system. Progressing in this manner, it was seen that the managers stabilized on their sensemaking of the problem between the 6th to 8th/9th time period. By this time, they were seen to have either gained a grasp of the problem or not at all. By then, they also stabilized on the pattern of decisions that they took to run Manutex. After this, the general tendency

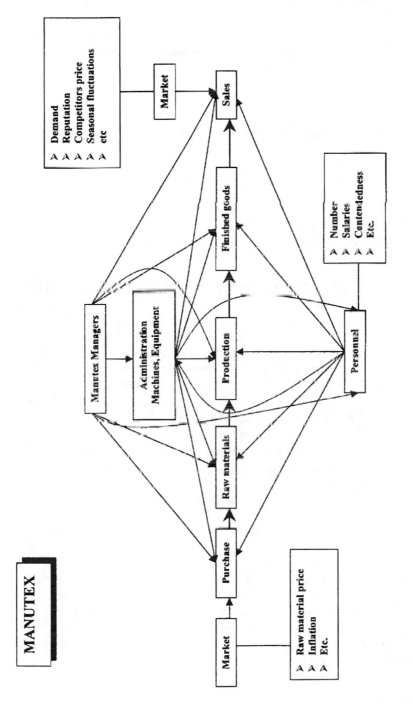

FIG. 10.1 Simplified model of Manutex system. Copyright by Schaub, H., 1988. Reprinted with permission.

was to continue the same approach unless necessitated by crises situations. Of the 45 managers in the sample, simulation could be conducted only with 42. Of these, 5 managers opted out in the initial stages itself. The simulation data of the remaining 37 managers only have been used for further analysis.

The simulation was followed by a reflective discussion with the manager. His experience of solving the problem, the complex nature of Manutex, and its theoretical underpinnings were discussed. His approach to and the process of solving the problem and some implications of these in his work context were also discussed. This discussion took about 30 to 40 minutes.

MEASURES

Effectiveness of Complex Problem Solving: Measures of the Dependent Variable

Evaluating the effectiveness of managers in solving the complex problem is also complex because there is no one measure that can exhaustively and uniquely capture it. This is because different managers give varying importance to different aspects and outcomes of the problem and, accordingly, end up with different solutions that may be satisfying to them and meet their objectives. Hence, multiple measures were needed. In Manutex simulation, solving the problem effectively meant managing the simulated organization effectively. All decisions that the manager took while solving contributed to the state of Manutex firm at any point of time in the simulation. Hence, to assess the effectiveness of managers in solving the complex problem, the author looked at how effectively they managed the Manutex firm. Three dimensions were defined for this: *success, consistency,* and *crises-free nature* of problem solving.

Success in Complex Problem Solving.
Success in problem solving refers to the manager's achievement as measured by different favorable problem outcomes. Managers who solve the problem effectively should show relatively higher levels of achievement as compared to others who are not so effective. Success was measured by the following parameters of Manutex: (a) cash balance and net worth of the firm at the end of problem solving, (b) total production and sales during problem solving, and (c) average values of cash balance, production, and sales during problem solving (all in Malaysian Dollars—M$).

Consistency in Complex Problem Solving.   From an organizational effectiveness viewpoint, some stability is necessary in the operations of any organization even when attempting change, growth, expansion, and so on (Srivastva & Fry, 1992). Extreme fluctuations in production, sales, cash flow, or any other important aspect of organizational functioning can adversely affect employee morale, machine condition, public image, shareholder faith in the company, and so on. Therefore, the variation should not be extreme and drastic but such that it is manageable and within the absorptive capacity of the organization. The extent of fluctuations of different aspects of Manutex such as cash balance, production, and sales during problem solving was assessed with the statistical measure of coefficient of variation (ratio of SD to mean). It is expected to find the coefficient of variation of these aspects to be lower for managers who pursue the problem more effectively as compared to those who are not so effective.

Crises-free Nature of Complex Problem Solving.   Problem solvers may do faulty planning and decision making without gathering all relevant information or with incomplete and insufficient understanding of the complexity of the problem leading to errors in the action process, as discussed earlier. In Manutex simulation, errors result in unanticipated crises for the firm (termed as *alarms* here). Some of the alarms that may appear in this simulation are the store alarm (stock out of raw materials or accessories leading to production halt in the succeeding month), the account alarm (cash balance becoming negative necessitating bank borrowing), and the dismissals alarm (personnel resigning due to low salaries, inadequate social benefits, poor performance of the firm, etc.). A manager who pursues the problem effectively may be expected to face nil or fewer crises as compared to those who are not so effective. Two measures were used to assess the crises free nature of problem solving: the number of simulated months during which managers faced alarms and the total number of different alarms that they actually faced while solving the problem.

Complexity of Cognitive Maps: Measure of the Independent Variable

Preparation of Cognitive Maps.   Data elicitation for cognitive mapping is as given earlier. Maps were prepared as follows. Step 1, the recorded interview with each manager was transcribed verbatim. Step 2, each transcript was taken one by one for mapping. A first reading through the text gave an idea of what its contents were and what the flow was like. In the second reading, the important aspects of the problem that the individual brought out in the discourse were noted. They were put down as concepts on a large sheet of paper forming tentative nodes in the network diagram. Simultaneously, it was also attempted to link them wherever the individual was making explicit connections. The direction of linkage was determined to be causal from one node (concept A) to another (concept B); if A caused B, A preceded B in time, it made logical sense to place A before B, or A was an input to B (Huff, 1990). Furthermore, each of the nodes was considered bipolar. Step 3, a third reading was done to finalize the map by fine-tuning the concepts as well as links between them. Special attention was given to find out implicit links, if any, that emerged over the length of the discourse. The author as the mapper used his discretion to make such linkages. Step 4, reliability checks were then done. Cognitive map of a manager prepared in this manner is given in Fig. 10.2 for illustration.

Reliability of the Maps.   Huff (1990) said that although the application to which a cognitive map may be put is up to the researcher, the reliability of maps has to be ensured. In this study, two types of reliability checks were carried out: intermapper and map-remap reliability. Intermapper reliability is based on the conventional interrater or interjudge agreement measure. A doctoral student of management at the dissertation stage made maps of 5 managers randomly chosen. He was trained in mapping by providing basic readings like Bougon et al. (1977), Eden (1992b), Huff (1990), and Weick and Bougon (1986). The maps were compared for the number of common concepts and links. It was found that there was agreement on (not based on consensus discussion) about 80% of the concepts and about 70% of the links.

Map-remap reliability refers to the agreement between maps made by the same individual at two different points in time. Maps of 5 managers were made by the author twice at two different time intervals separated by about 3 to 4 months. It was found that there were about 90% concepts and 80% links in common between the two maps. The comparatively lower agreement on links in both cases is understandable because many times the managers did not explicitly state the connections between concepts and had to be inferred by the mapper.

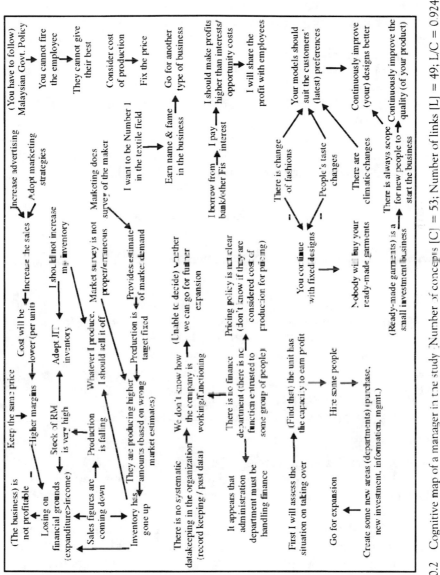

FIG. 10.2 Cognitive map of a manager in the study [Number of concepts [C] = 53; Number of links [L] = 49; L/C = 0.9453).

Measures of Complexity of Cognitive Map.   Complexity of a cognitive map could mean (a) the extent of details or the number of variables of the problem that the problem solver identifies, (b) the number of relations or links that he makes between the variables, and (c) a suitable assessment of the linking of variables (or their networking) in ways that make sense to him. That is, there can be a mass (or quantity) as well as a density (or ratio) dimension to the complexity of cognitive maps. Mass dimension can be measured with C (number of concepts), L (number of links), or their sum (L + C). Because C and L were highly positively correlated to L + C (0.9938 and 0.995 respectively, $p = 0.000$, $n = 35$) and with each other (0.9778, $p = 0.000$, $n = 35$), L + C was chosen to measure the mass dimension (an aggregate or total measure of map complexity). The density dimension was measured by the ratio of links to concepts (L/C).

ANALYSIS AND RESULTS

Cognitive Map Profile of Managers

For analyzing the complex problem-solving behavior, as mentioned earlier, simulation data of only 37 managers were used. Of this, cognitive maps of only 35 managers could be prepared. Figs. 10.3 and 10.4 show the frequency distribution of L + C and L/C respectively. Correlation between L + C and L/C was 0.4297 ($p < 0.05$, 2 tailed, $n = 33$).

Complexity of Cognitive Maps and Effectiveness of Complex Problem Solving

Regression curve fitting was used to relate independently the aggregate (L + C) and density (L/C) measures of complexity of cognitive map with each of the problem-solving effectiveness measures (i.e., cash balance, net worth, crises faced, etc.). This procedure follows simple linear regression, but instead of only finding out the best linear fit, it also estimates if a statistically significant new model (like, quadratic, logarithmic, or exponential) adds any further insights (Norusis/SPSS Inc., 1993). The following procedure was used to select from a number of valid but competing regression models (Goldberger, 1968; Gujarati, 1988; Harman, 1967; Levin & Rubin, 1994; Sen & Srivastava, 1990; Williams, 1959; Wittink, 1988).

First, the overall significance of the regression equation was examined. Models whose F-ratio became significant at $p < 0.1$ were selected. For these

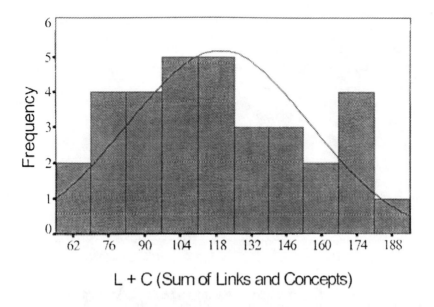

L + C (Sum of Links and Concepts)

FIG. 10.3   Frequency distribution of sum of links and concepts (L+C)
of managers whose complex problem solving behavior was analyzed
(mean = 120, SD = 35.49, n = 33 [2 outliers among the 35 maps],
kurtosis: –0.979, skewness: 0.292, minimum: 63, maximum: 186).

models, the t-ratios and their significance were examined. As one proceeded
from a simple to a complex model (say, linear to quadratic), if the coefficient
of the additional variable in the more complex model was not becoming significant at $p < 0.1$, then that model was eliminated from further consideration. At this stage, if the choice became still difficult, then the one with
highest adjusted R^2 was chosen. Statisticians also emphasize the need to
abide by principles of statistical simplicity and theoretical meaningfulness
(Harman, 1967). Thus, in this study, wherever a linear model became significant, it was chosen unless a more complex model such as the quadratic was
found to explain relatively higher portion of variance of the data.

Effectiveness of Managers in Solving the Complex Problem in Relation to L + C

One of the success measures, cash balance at the end of problem solving,
showed a U variation with L + C ($R^2 = 0.20799$, $F = 3.939$, $p = 0.0303$, $n = 33$). None of the other measures relating to success, consistency, or crises-free
nature of problem solving showed any significant relation with L + C.

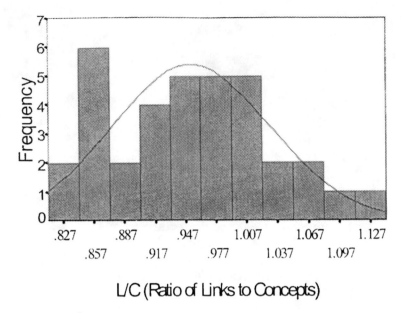

FIG. 10.4   Frequency distribution of ratio of links to concepts (L/C)
of managers whose complex problem solving behavior was analyzed
(mean = 0.953, SD = 0.077, n = 35, kurtosis: –0.511,
skewness: 0.306, minimum: 0.833, maximum: 1.131).

Effectiveness of Managers in Solving the Complex Problem in Relation to L/C

Table 10.1 summarizes the observed relations between various measures of effectiveness of problem solving as the dependent variable and L/C as the independent variable. Some representative relations are plotted (Figs. 10.5 to 10.7). It so turned out that the quadratic model was significant for almost all the effectiveness measures (Table 10.1, last column).

Success in Complex Problem Solving.   Measures such as cash balance and net worth of the firm at the end of problem solving and average values of cash balance and sales during problem solving showed a significant inverted U variation with increase in L/C. That means success of managers in solving the complex problem increased with increase in their map density up to a certain point, after which it began to decline. With increase in map density, managers generated higher cash balances, net worth of their firm increased, and their production levels and sales

TABLE 10.1

Regression Between Different Measures of Effectiveness of Managers in Solving the Simulated Complex Problem and the Density of Their Cognitive Maps (Ratio of Links to Concepts, L/C)

Measures of Problem Solving (PS) Effectiveness (n = 35)	R²	F	Significance of F	t of regression coefficients	Significance of t	Selected Model
Cash balance at the end of PS[a]	0.147 (Quadratic)	2.764	0.078	L/C: 2.145	0.04	Quadratic† (Fig. 10.5)
				L/C²: -2.099	0.044	
Net worth of the firm at the end of PS[a]	0.147 (Quadratic)	2.767	0.078	L/C: 2.321	0.027	Quadratic† (Fig. 10.6)
				L/C²: -2.301	0.028	
Total production during PS[a]	0.11 (Quadratic)	1.973	0.155	L/C: 1.986	0.056	Not significant†
				L/C²: -1.982	0.056	
Total sales during PS[a]	0.151 (Quadratic)	2.844	0.073	L/C: 2.36	0.025	Quadratic†
				L/C²: -2.342	0.026	
Average cash balance during PS[a]	0.189 (Quadratic)	3.73	0.035	L/C: 2.476	0.019	Quadratic*
				L/C²: -2.422	0.021	
Average sales during PS[a]	0.165 (Quadratic)	3.161	0.056	L/C: 2.514	0.017	Quadratic†
				L/C²: -2.513	0.017	
Coefficient of variation of production during PS	0.221 (Quadratic)	4.538	0.018	L/C: -2.792	0.009	Quadratic*
				L/C²: 2.84	.0078	

(Table 10.1 continued)

(*Table 10.1 continued*)

Measures of Problem Solving (PS) Effectiveness (n = 35)	R^2	F	Significance of F	T of regression coefficients	Significance of t	Selected Model
Coefficient of variation of sales during PS	0.169 (Linear)	6.708	0.014	L/C: 2.59	0.014	Linear*
	0.171 (Quadratic)	3.301	0.05	L/C: 0.4	0.692	
				L/C^2: -0.285	0.777	
Number of time intervals with crises during PS	0.137 (Quadratic)	2.536	0.095	L/C: -2.252	0.031	Quadratic†
				L/C^2: 2.248	0.032	
Number of actual crises faced during PS	0.206 (Quadratic)	4.152	0.025	L/C: -2.873	0.007	Quadratic*
				L/C^2: 2.88	0.007	(Fig. 10.7)

[a]In Malaysian dollars, †$p < 0.1$, *$p < 0.05$

230

realization increased. This increasing trend was evident up to a certain point of map density, after which there was decline (Figs. 10.5 and 10.6).

Consistency in Complex Problem Solving.   Mixed results were obtained with respect to consistency of problem solving in relation to map density. Coefficient of variation of production showed a U relation. That is, inconsistency in production decreased with increase in map density up to a certain point and then increased. Coefficient of variation of cash balance also showed a similar but weak trend. However, the coefficient of variation of sales increased linearly with increase in map density, indicating increasing inconsistency in sales.

Crises-Free Nature of Problem Solving.   It was found that the total number of crises or alarms which managers faced while solving the problem showed a significant U variation with increasing map density (Fig. 10.7). That is, as density of maps increased, managers faced fewer crises because of their own actions, inaction, or omission or all three, up to a certain point, after which it began to rise with further in-

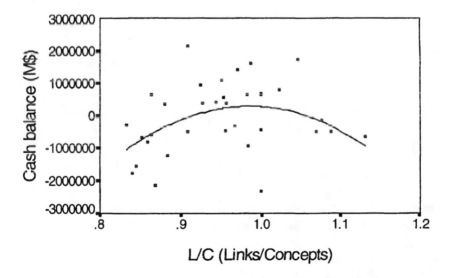

FIG. 10.5   Cash balance (in Malaysian dollars, M$) at the end of problem solving with links to concepts ratio (L/C) ($R^2 = 0.1473$, $F = 2.76387$, $p = 0.0781$, $n = 35$).

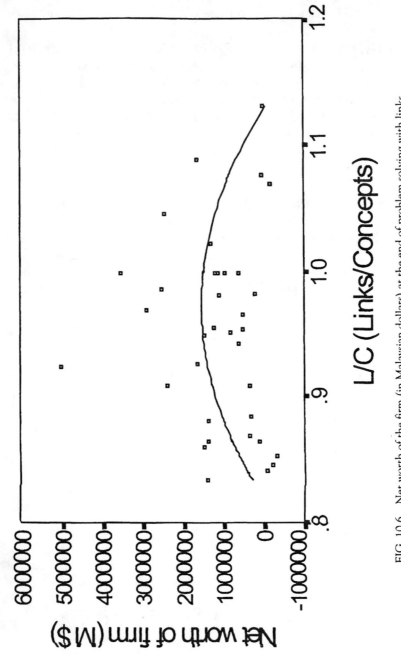

FIG. 10.6   Net worth of the firm (in Malaysian dollars) at the end of problem solving with links to concepts ratio (L/C) ($R^2 = 0.14744$, $F = 2.76705$, $p = 0.0779$, $n = 35$).

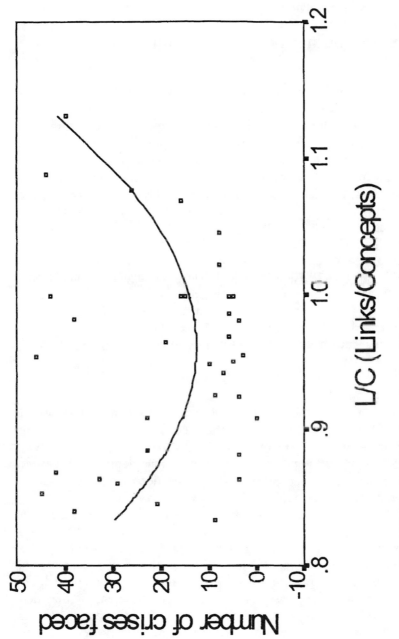

FIG. 10.7   Total number of crises (or alarms) faced by managers during problem solving with links to concepts ratio (L/C) ($R^2 = 0.20602$, $F = 4.15173$, $p = 0.0249$, $n = 35$).

crease in density. A similar pattern was evident for total number of time periods during problem solving when managers faced alarms.

Information Gathering and Decision-Making Behavior During Problem Solving

Information gathering and decision-making behavior of managers while solving the complex problem was analyzed on two dimensions—quantity and diversity. Quantity refers to the amount or total units of information gathered or decisions made while solving the problem. Diversity refers to the number of different or unique aspects of the problem on which the managers gathered information or took decisions. For instance, in Manutex, the manager may identify that taking care of products is necessary to solve the problem effectively. He may then gather information on, say, production plan, past production, product quality, machine hours required, and so on. Each of these aspects when attended to through information gathering or decision making is considered as a unique unit. The number of unique units of information gathered and decisions made by the manager is an indication of his breadth of understanding of the problem and the extent of coverage he gives to solving it. Neither L + C nor L/C measures showed any significant relation with either the quantity or diversity of information gathered or decisions made by managers while solving the simulated complex problem.

DISCUSSION

The findings show that the complexity of cognitive maps measured by their density (L/C) is significantly related to the effectiveness with which managers solved the simulated complex problem. Effectiveness of problem solving increased up to a certain point with increase in map density and then declined. Specifically, with increase in map density, success in problem solving as measured by favorable outcomes increased up to a certain point and then declined. Problem solving became increasingly smooth or free of crises up to a certain point, beyond which crises faced increased. Mixed results were obtained on the consistency of managers in solving the complex problem. Two of the three measures showed that inconsistency of managers decreased up to a certain point with increase in map density, after which it increased. The third measure showed increase in inconsistency with increase in map density. On the other hand, the aggregate measure of L + C did not show any consistent and significant relation with any of the effectiveness measures except one of the success measures. These findings can be explained from: (a) the hypothesis proposed by Dörner and Wearing (1995) based on laboratory studies on complex problem solving, (b) the conceptualization of cognitive maps, and (c) the construct of cognitive complexity.

It was mentioned earlier that researchers who studied problem-solving behavior of individuals using computer-simulated complex problems in laboratory experiments suggested that the most important aspect for their subjects to cope effectively with the simulated problem was to build an elaborate network of causal relationships. Dörner and Wearing (1995) stated:

> Typically our poor subjects reiterate that they have no idea as to what to do ... because they are not able to recognize things and events as special instances of an abstract concept ... they remain isolated for them.... A subject with such a model ... will arrive at a decision well, but it will be a simple decision not connected to other aspects of the system. The subject will not exhibit concerted decision making behaviour, whereas a subject with the network ... [of relationships] will. (p. 37)

Dörner and Wearing (1995) appeared to be emphasizing the unraveling of connectedness of different aspects in the problem as well as arriving at decisions in a concerted or integrated manner. The findings of this study lend support to this hypothesis. With density measure (L/C) of cognitive maps, what is captured is not just the extent to which the individual problem solver is able to identify the many variables in the problem but an assessment of his identifying them in a related or integrated manner to form a network that guides his sensemaking and action.

Secondly, from the conceptualization of cognitive maps, the concepts and links can be hypothetically organized in many ways in the maps of different individuals. On one extreme, the map of an individual can have only concepts, each of which stands in isolation without any linkages. Here, the individual is making disjointed or fragmented sense of some aspects of the problem. There is no integration whatsoever. The other extreme is a map where all the concepts are connected to each other. Actual maps of individuals fall between these extremes. As we move from a map with only concepts to the other extreme, more and more links get added, new concepts come in and some old ones go out or get modified. Some links also can get modified. The different combinations of linkage between concepts help the individual to bring out alternative explanations of the situation. Accordingly, one would expect managers at the higher end of L/C to look into more aspects of the problem, bring out alternative explanations, and solve it effectively. However, in this study, their problem solving was comparatively less effective.

One of the probable explanations for this finding is that managers with higher levels of map density may have come up with a very fine-grained understanding of the problem and followed this by detailed solution strategy(ies). It is possible that they may have found that such high levels of details were not required to solve the problem that was presented through Manutex simulation or that solving Manutex necessitated structuring of their thoughts and actions to match the requirements and specifications of the simulation. These may have led to loss of motivation for these managers to pursue problem solution effectively.

Furthermore, with a very fine-grained map structure, these managers may have also got lost in the nuances of the simulated problem. Negotiating an ill-structured situation is not a one-shot affair. It needs consistent and coherent approach over a period of time involving prioritization of issues, necessary action, and monitoring of outcomes. A fine-grained map with too much details may have put increasing cognitive limitations to this process over time. Forgetfulness (Dörner & Wearing, 1995) and fatigue may have also set in. It is also possible that with a fine-grained map structure, at least a few managers may have been rigid or found it difficult to make alterations to their original maps over time to make it in tune with the evolving scenario of the situation being negotiated. In comparison, maps of managers in the middle range of L/C in the sample are less dense. Openings exist to be filled between concepts, as well as option to add, delete, or modify some concepts and links. It is possible that these managers may have initiated to make necessary modifications in their maps to make it in tune with the evolving scenario of the problem, enabling them to evolve newer perspectives and pursue an effective solution.

Finally, Schroder, Driver and Streufert (1967) identified that individuals possess different levels of conceptual structure that enable them to process information at varying levels. They termed it as cognitive complexity with three dimensions: (a) differentiation—the ability to derive different dimensions to make sense of a problem, (b) discrimination—the ability to distinguish like stimuli on the same dimension, and (c) integration—the ability to combine these dimensions to generate multiple interpretations of the stimulus. Schroder et al. (1967) suggested that rather than higher levels of differentiation, it is the level of integration that is indicator of information processing capability and that is crucial to generating diverse perspectives and explanations of the problem or situation.

Simple conceptual structure is low in integration. It is deterministic and certain and can result in categorical black–white thinking incapable of generating alternatives. The control over behaviour tends to be external because there is no attempt by the self to generate and explore alternatives. As one moves toward higher integration levels, individuals become capable of identifying more dimensions of a situation and generating multiple interpretations.

Even when the individual closes on a particular decision, he is still open to a number of alternative pressures ... He is able to generate strategic adjustment processes, in which the effects of behaviour from one standpoint are seen as influencing the situation viewed from another vantage point. (Schroder et al., 1967, p. 21).

He also becomes self-reflective. From this perspective of cognitive complexity also, it makes sense for the finding that complex problem-solving effectiveness is significantly related to the density of the map because higher density denotes higher integration. However, according to this, one would have expected the effectiveness of problem solving to increase with increase in cognitive complexity, which was not the case in this study, probably due to reasons cited earlier.

In conclusion, this study found that the aggregate of links and concepts (L + C) in the cognitive maps of managers could not explain their effectiveness in solving complex problems. On the other hand, managerial effectiveness in solving complex problems increased with increase in elaborateness of their cognitive maps as measured by the density or ratio of links to concepts (L/C). This increasing trend was evident up to a certain point, after which effectiveness declined with further increase in density. In other words, this study empirically shows that effectiveness of complex problem solving depends not on the number of variables and relationships among these variables that individuals identify in the problem but on their ability to identify the variables with a reasonably high degree of integration. Although ineffectiveness in problem solving was observed at the lower end of map density due to disjointed sensemaking of the problem, managers who built very elaborate or highly dense cognitive maps were also not effective problem solvers. Further research is needed to establish if very elaborate or highly dense cognitive maps lead to ineffective problem solving or is dysfunctional in general.

REFERENCES

Ackoff, R. L. (1979). The future of operational research is past. *Journal of Operational Research Society, 30*, 93–104.

Bartlett, F. C. (1932). *Remembering: A study of experimental and social psychology.* Cambridge, England: Cambridge University Press.

Bougon, M., Weick, K. E., & Binkhorst, B. (1977). Cognitions in organizations: An analysis of the Ultrecht Jazz Orchestra. *Administrative Science Quarterly, 22*, 606–639.

Brehmer, B., & Dörner, D. (1993). Experiments with computer simulated microworlds: Escaping the narrow straits of the laboratory as well as the deep blue sea of the field study. *Computers and Human Behavior, 9*, 171–184.

Calori R., Johnson, G., & Sarnin, P. (1994). CEO's cognitive maps and the scope of the organization. *Strategic Management Journal, 15,* 437:457.

Cossette, P., & Audet, M. (1992). Mapping of an idiosyncratic schema. *Journal of Management Studies, 29*(3), 325–347.

Dearborn, D. C., & Simon, H. A. (1958). Selective perception: A note on the departmental identifications of executives. *Sociometry, 21,* 140–144.

Dörner, D. (1980). On the difficulties people have in dealing with complexity. *Simulation & Games, 11*(1), 87–106.

Dörner, D. (1990). The logic of failure. In D. E. Broadbent, A. Baddley, & J. T. Reason (Eds.), *Human factors in hazardous situations: Philosophical transactions of the Royal Society of London,* B 327, pp. 463–473. Oxford, England: Clarendon.

Dörner, D. (1991). The investigation of action regulation in uncertain and complex situations. In J. Rasmussen, B. Brehmer, & J. Leplat (Eds.), *Distributed decision making: Cognitive models for cooperative work* (pp. 349–354). New York: Wiley.

Dörner, D., & Schaub, H. (1994). Errors in planning and decision making and the nature of human information processing. *Applied Psychology: An International Review, 43,* 433–453.

Dörner, D., & Wearing, A. J. (1995). Complex problem solving: Toward a (computer simulated) theory. In P. A. Frensch & J. Funke (Eds.), *Complex problem solving: The European perspective* (pp. 65–99). Hillsdale, NJ: Lawrence Erlbaum Associates.

Eden, C. (1988). Cognitive mapping: A review. *European Journal of Operational Research, 36,* 1–13.

Eden, C. (1992a). On the nature of cognitive maps. *Journal of Management Studies, 29*(3), 261–265.

Eden, C. (Ed.). (1992b). On the nature of cognitive maps [Special issue]. *Journal of Management Studies, 29*(3).

Fiol, M. C., & Huff, A. S. (1992). Maps for managers: Where are we? Where do we go from here? *Journal of Management Studies, 29*(3), 267–286.

Fiske, S. T., & Taylor, S. E. (1984). *Social cognition.* Reading, MA: Addison-Wesley.

Frese, M., & Zapf, D. (1994). Action as the core of work psychology: A German approach. In H. C. Triandis, M. D. Dunnette, & L. M. Hough (Eds.), *Handbook of industrial and organizational psychology* (Vol. 4, 2nd ed., pp. 271–340). Palo Alto, CA: Consulting Psychologists Press.

Goldberger, A. S. (1968). *Topics in regression analysis.* London: Collier–Macmillan.

Gujarati, D. (1988). *Basic econometrics.* New York: McGraw-Hill.

Hackner, Y. E. R. (1991). *Integrated complexity and profitability* (Working Paper). Cleveland, OH: Case Western Reserve University.

Harman, H. H. (1967). *Modern factor analysis.* Chicago: University of Chicago Press.

Huff, A. S. (1990). *Mapping strategic thought.* New York: Wiley.

Keys, B., & Wolfe, J. (1990). The role of management games and simulations in education and research. *Journal of Management, 16*(2), 307–336.

Langfield-Smith, K. (1992). Exploring the need for a shared cognitive map. *Journal of Management Studies, 29*(3), 349–368.

Laukkanen, M. (1994). Comparative cause mapping of organizational cognitions. *Organization Science, 5*(3), 322–343.

Levin, R. I., & Rubin, D. S. (1994). *Statistics for management* (6th ed.). New Delhi, India: Prentice-Hall of India.

Mason, R. O., & Mitroff, I. I. (1972). A program for research on management information systems. *Management Science, 19*(4), 475–487.

Mason, R. O., & Mitroff, I. I. (1981). *Challenging strategic planning assumptions.* New York: Wiley.

Mintzberg, H., Raisinghani, D., & Theoret, A. (1976). The structure of "unstructured" decision processes. *Administrative Science Quarterly, 21*, 246–275.

Newell, A., & Simon, H. A. (1972). *Human problem solving.* Englewood Cliffs, NJ: Prentice-Hall.

Norusis, M. J./SPSS Inc. (1993). *SPSS for windows: Base system user's guide, Release 6.0.* Chicago: SPSS Inc.

Ramnarayan, S., & Strohschneider, S. (1997). How organizations influence individual styles of thinking: A simulation study. *Journal of Euro-Asian Management, 3*(1), 1–29.

Ramnarayan, S., Strohschneider, S., & Schaub, H. (1997). Trappings of expertise and the pursuit of failure. *Simulations & Gaming, 28*(1), 28–43.

Schaub, H. (1988). *Manutex: Terminology and definitions, operating instructions and introductory text.* Bamberg, Germany: Internal Document of the Institute of Psychology, University of Bamberg.

Schroder, H. M., Driver M. J., & Streufert, S. (1967). *Human information processing.* New York: Holt, Rinehart & Winston.

Sen, A., & Srivastava, M. (1990). *Regression analysis: Theory, methods, and applications.* New York: Springer-Verlag.

Senge, P. M. (1990). *The fifth discipline.* Garden City, NY: Doubleday.

Simon, H. A. (1957). *Administrative behavior.* New York: Macmillan.

Simon, H. A., Dantzig, G. B., Hogarth, R., Plott, C. R., Raiffa, H., Schelling, T. C., Shepsle, K. A., Thaler, R., Tversky, A., & Winter, S. (1992). Decision making and problem solving. In Mary Zey (Ed.), *Decision making: Alternatives to rational choice models* (pp. 32–53). Newbury Park, CA: Sage.

Srivastva, S., & Fry, R. E. (Eds.). (1992). *Executive and organizational continuity: Managing the paradoxes of stability and change.* San Francisco: Jossey-Bass.

Stubbart, C. I., & Ramprasad, A. (1988). Probing two chief executives' beliefs about the steel industry using cognitive maps. *Advances in Strategic Management,* Vol. 5, 139–164.

Ungson, G. R., Braunstein, D. N., & Hall. P. D. (1981). Managerial information processing: A research review. *Administrative Science Quarterly, 26*(1), 116–134.

VanLehn, K. (1989). Problem solving and cognitive skill acquisition. In M. I. Posner (Ed.), *Foundations of cognitive science* (pp. 527–579). Cambridge, MA: MIT Press.

Walsh, J. P. (1988). Selectivity and selective perception: An investigation of managers' belief structures and information processing. *Academy of Management Review, 31*(4), 873–896.

Weick, K. E., & Bougon, M. (1986). Organizations as cognitive maps: Charting ways to success and failure. In H. P. Sims, Jr. & D. A. Gioia, (Eds.), *The thinking organization: Dynamics of organizational social cognition* (pp. 102–135). San Francisco: Jossey-Bass.

Williams, E. J. (1959). *Regression analysis.* New York: Wiley.

Wittink, D. R. (1988). *The application of regression analysis.* Boston: Allyn & Bacon.

11

Cognitive Processes and Decision Making in a Crisis Situation: A Case Study

---

Bénédicte Vidaillet
University of Lille 2 France

Decisions are often described a posteriori as irrational from a normative standpoint. However, it is worth asking whether this apparent irrationality is not strongly related to, and even justified in, the context in which the decision was made. This issue is a critical one when the context is a crisis. In such circumstances, indeed, the human and economic consequences mean that the normal criteria used for evaluating a decision do not seem well suited to judging the relevance of the choices made.

The research presented here aims to analyze the decision-making process during a crisis that occurred in France. This event began with smoke coming from stored fertilizers in a warehouse located on the outskirts of Nantes (France). It was then tackled by two groups of actors. On the spot, the firemen's prime concern was to control the "fire," which produced neither flames nor heat but just stagnant smoke that rapidly became an enormous cloud. In the city, an emergency committee that was never directly in touch with the people on the spot focused its attention on the cloud that was suspected to be toxic and dangerous for the population. The main decision made during this event has been strongly criticized for its irrationality in the

241

French newspapers: 40,000 persons were moved from their homes—it was the largest evacuation in the country since World War II—because they were thought to be at risk from a "toxic" cloud that was later judged to be harmless. However, from the point of view of the main actors involved in the crisis, this decision was guided by a series of judgments that had its own logic and corresponded to a specific rationality.

As a consequence, the author was interested in understanding the cognitive processes that were likely to influence the way the crisis was framed, analyzed, and resolved by the participants. For this purpose, and although it is normally used in experimental research, the behavioral decision theory provided an interesting framework for: (a) understanding how the various actors construct a representation of the crisis; it is argued that the formulation stage is a critical one in the decision-making process and strongly determines its rationality; this is all the more significant, given that a crisis situation is by definition complex and ill-structured and that the decision maker has to structure it while under strong pressure of time; and (b) analyzing the decision-making strategies used by the main decision makers in such a situation.

BEHAVIORAL DECISION THEORY

Economists and psychologists have developed their work on the assumption that people behave rationally. According to the theory of normative decision making, a person makes his or her choice so as to maximize its expected utility. These models of rational choice assume that each decision is based on a stable set of values that the decision maker is perfectly conscious of and the knowledge of which would lead an observer to predict the decision maker's behavior. However, those models seem of little help in understanding real decision phenomena. Decisions are frequently made under time pressure, precluding the sorts of careful balancing and computation the models of rational choice imply. Decisions are made in dynamic, ambiguous, and uncertain environments. Goals or values may be unclear, making notions of known utilities and stable values hard to apply. In a crisis, such factors as complexity, ambiguity, urgency, and perceived risk are far greater than in more normal decision-making contexts, making the model of rational choice even more problematic.

The paradigm of rationality has been strongly criticized (Cyert & March, 1963; March & Simon, 1958; Simon, 1955) on the grounds that it does not adequately describe actual decision-making behavior. Indeed, observed behavior systematically differs from the models proposed by the economists. The limited cognitive capacities of human beings lead them to make satisfactory rather than optimal choices. Since the decision making theory has been challenged, a new field has been developed that tries to describe the cognitive processes underlying human decision making in a more realistic way. This research paradigm brings together interdisciplinary concepts derived from social psychology, cognitive psychology, economics, and so on into a unified behavioral decision theory. For many decades, behavioral violations of rational choice theory have been examined (Einhorn & Hogarth, 1981; Mellers, Schwartz, & Cooke, 1998; Payne, Bettman, & Johnson, 1992; Slovic, Fischoff, & Lichtenstein, 1977).

Studies of individual choice showed that people often use heuristics or shortcuts that reduce complex problem solving to more straightforward decision-making operations. Heuristics are fundamental to inference, making it possible to process information quickly. Usually, using a heuristic will produce fairly good answers, although it can also lead to errors and biases in some situations (Kahneman, Slovic, & Tversky, 1982; Tversky & Kahneman, 1974). For instance, the likelihood of an event is overestimated if it is easy to recall or imagine relevant instances (Nisbett & Ross, 1980; Tversky & Kahneman, 1973). Because this availability is affected by factors such as recency or saliency, it may lead to errors in estimating frequency. It has also been evidenced that individuals adjust their first approximations to an anchor and then adjust it to reach a conclusion. However, the judgment may be anchored by irrelevant details of the situation or reference points (Tversky & Kahneman, 1974). People tend to be overconfident of their ability to estimate the probability of an uncertain event (Lichtenstein & Fischhoff, 1977). They also tend to overestimate the probability of events that actually occur and the extent to which they would have been able to predict past events if they had been asked to do so (Fischhoff, 1975). Other studies examine the ways in which decision makers simplify choices. Incomplete data or multiple alternatives have been evidenced to increase the use of simplifying strategies and to decrease the use of explicit trade-offs (Payne, 1976; Slovic et al., 1977). For example, elimination by aspects (Tversky, 1972) may be one of those simplifying strategies. More recently, other models are being proposed such as the dominance search model (Montgomery, 1989) or rule following (Anderson, 1983; Elster, 1986, 1989; March, 1994). Rule following, which occurs when a rule or norm is applied to a situation, often minimizes effort and provides satisfying solutions that are good enough. Instead of being preference based, the decisions may become generic applications of rules to situations (Mellers et al., 1998). They may express habits or convey a personal, moral, or social identity (Tetlock, 1992).

The concepts of heuristics and decision-making strategies provided by behavioral decision theory seem relevant to understanding some processes used by people for making judgments about uncertain, risky, or complex events. However, because most research in this field is made under experimental conditions, researchers do not know how relevant these concepts are for real decision-making processes. Yet, recent work in the field sheds light on the influence of the context on someone's decision-making strategies. Framing effects, stimulus context, environments and response modes can profoundly shape decisions (Payne et al., 1992). Decision behavior is highly sensitive to a wide variety of task and context factors. For example, time pressure induces coping mechanisms that include the acceleration of processing, selectivity in processing, and shifts in decision strategies (Svenson & Maule, 1993). The effect of different types of context has been studied experimentally (Einhorn & Hogarth, 1981; Hogarth, 1990; Tversky & Kahneman, 1982, 1986). But in reality, events are likely to involve a mixture of components that are studied separately in experiments. Moreover, in real decisions, the individual is not simply assigned prestructured problems (Sternberg & Salter, 1982; Sternberg & Wagner, 1986; Wagner & Sternberg, 1985). He has to formulate it. Work in the field of problem solving and cognition has shown that the way in which a problem is framed or formulated has much to do with the quality of the solutions that are found (Simon et al., 1992; Tversky & Kahneman, 1974). Its formulation determines the nature of the subsequent decision-making process.

This is why it was decided to analyze a real case, a crisis situation involving complexity, risk, uncertainty, and urgency together. In this situation, no clear definition of the nature of the problem was available for the decision makers. They had to formulate it and to establish what they would consider to be the key features of the situation before making choices and acting. The two questions posed in this study were:

How did people construct a representation of the event? How did they formulate the problem?

Which judgmental strategies did they use to decide and act in this context?

THE TOXIC CLOUD CRISIS

Data Collection and Analysis

The research was designed in accordance with the requirements of studying a single case (Bartunek, 1984; Pettigrew, 1985; Yin, 1985).

To establish a chronology of what happened, the author drew on reports made by various people who were involved in the crisis, as well as the work of

C. Gilbert, a researcher who made a thorough investigation during the month following the event (Gilbert, 1990). His chronology of the crisis was used; although it has been criticized by some participants, it is the most acceptable one and is confirmed by this study's investigations.

To analyze the decision-making processes, the 11 main participants in the crisis were interviewed in-depth about their perception of the event, the items of information they received, their interactions with other persons during the crisis, their experiences with crisis-like events, their careers, and the kind of decision making they were used to at that time. The author tried to understand their viewpoints during the crisis. Written notes made by the senior doctor attached to the mobile emergency medical service in the course of action and a written introspective account made one month later by a fireman at the request of researchers from Rennes University's Department of Psychology were used. The transcripts of the interviews that C. Gilbert had with the main participants during the week following the crisis were also used. The main interest was the part of the interview dealing with their perception of the event. It helped limit the effects of hindsight bias (Fischhoff, 1975, 1980) and allowed comparisons with this study's interviews.

Each interview was tape-recorded. The content of the transcripts and written notes was analyzed to restore the participant's point of view during the crisis. For each actor, a story was developed that described his or her experience on that day. Each story followed a time line beginning with the first contact of the person with the event and included all elements mentioned—such as his or her perception, thinking, actions, decisions, and so on. Then, each story was read with the two research questions in mind and patterns in the data were searched for. That search was assisted by taking pairs of stories and listing similarities and differences between pairs. Similarities and differences between the stories appeared and it became clear that the content of the event's formulation was strongly related to the actor's position during the crisis (e.g., the committee members vs. the people on the spot). But, there were similarities in the processes by which the participants formulated the event or decided. In formulating the event (first research question), all the actors used analogies and focused on specific items of information to make sense of the situation. It was interpreted as a way to simplify a complex problem to deal with it. When deciding (second research question), it appeared that their judgmental strategies included anchoring and adjustment processes, risk avoidance, and references to one's professional identities. Comparisons with existing literature in behavioral decision theory were used to sharpen the researcher's insights.

What Happened From the Firemen's Perspective

It is 9:15 a.m. on that October 29. Workers in a warehouse of the Loiret and Haentjens Company, located on the outskirts of Nantes (France) near the River Loire, are trying to deal with smoke coming from stored fertilizers. Seeing that they cannot cope, the person in charge of the warehouse telephones the fire service for assistance. He also gives the product's code (15.8.22) and mentions that the workers are impeded by toxic smoke. At the fire station, the duty chief sends a rescue team to the site and tries to identify the product from a technical manual. Unfortunately, however, the code number has been changed to 15.822 and he does not find it. He therefore concludes that the code indicates danger rather than the product's composition.

The fire captain in charge of the first rescue team tours the warehouse without any breathing equipment and easily identifies the product (NPK fertilizer, used in agriculture). He also locates a stock of ammonitrates and some fuel tanks. He does not think the damage will spread because the ammonitrates, which are dangerous products likely to explode, are stored well away from the NPK fertilizers. Moreover, they are said to be different from the ammonitrates involved in the Texas-City disaster.[1] The tanks are well insulated. What does worry him, however, is the odd nature of the "fire," which produces neither flames nor heat but just stagnant smoke. He does not know what to do. For one thing, indeed, he is afraid of polluting the river by using hoses as the firemen had done at the time of the Sandoz accident in Basel.[2] In addition, the products usually used for hydrocarbon fires prove useless. So, he calls up his field officer, the duty chief at the fire station who had failed to identify the product.

The duty chief thus faces a situation that has already moved on: It has become impossible to enter the warehouse because of the stifling smoke. No further inspection is possible and the products identified by the first fireman can no longer be distinguished. The duty chief remembers what he learned during a recent training session on nuclear risks and is afraid of a major catastrophe. He, too, refuses to use water and fears that the ammonitrates might explode. He asks for the authorities to be warned about a risk of explosion and suffocation for local residents. As he thinks that the event is likely to last some time, he calls the colonel, his superior. He also asks for reinforcements. It is 10:30 a.m.

---

[1] In 1947, ammonitrates exploded in Texas-City causing incalculable damage.

[2] In 1986, the fire of toxic chemical products caused the Rhine River to be polluted. A major crisis occurred under the pressure of the governments and the public opinion of the riverside countries.

When the colonel arrives, the situation is really worrying. He inquires about the measurements taken by the antipollution unit, which show a high nitric acid level (50 ppm[3]) and traces of chlorine above the warehouse. He is confronted with the contradictory advice of two "experts" (who are never subsequently identified): One advocates the use of water in massive quantities, whereas the other opposes this solution. The colonel and some of his colleagues favor dowsing the fertilizers and he asks for further equipment. On his way back from a helicopter reconnaissance flight, he receives the advice of Professor Boiteaux, who has been contacted in the meantime by the antipollution unit. The professor has created the chair of toxicology at Nantes University and is well known for his expertise in this field. He advises using water and thinks the risk of polluting the Loire is slight. From that moment on, everything possible is done to implement this solution. There are some technical problems, but around 4 p.m. the situation is brought under control.

What Happened From the Emergency Committee's Perspective

From 10:30 a.m. onward, an emergency committee has been convened at the prefecture,[4] without any contact with the people at the warehouse. It relies mostly on the items of information picked up from the firemen's radio. The committee is composed of officials used to solving problems of maintaining public order. They take note of the risks of fire and explosion. They consider that it is the firemen's job to deal with those risks while they themselves have to focus their attention on the cloud. It must be emphasized that the emergency committee will continue to have limited contact with the people at the scene although there are numerous means of communication and the deputy prefect has been at the warehouse since late morning. The committee reacts to the news coming in from the firemen but does not try actively to seek further information. Its members focus on the first information they had received, relating to the risk for the population and the length of the rescue operations. They recommend that people living within a radius of 1 km around the warehouse should stay indoors. The committee members are worried about the cloud because they do not know how toxic it is.

---

[3] ppm: unit of measure.

[4] In the French administrative system, the prefect is the person appointed as the local representative of the central government. He is in charge of any question falling within the state's competence, in particular security, transportation, education, emergency plan, and so on. The prefecture is the place where he lives and works.

In the late morning, the prefect takes charge of the committee and still has not received much information. At noon, he has a visit from an expert in water problems, who is the president of a federation of environmental associations; she is immediately alarmed at the risk for the population. At 12:15 p.m., experts from the regional department of industry and research arrive at the prefecture. One of them speaks of his experience in quarrying and mentions the risks of explosion due to the ammonitrates.

At 1 p.m., the antipollution unit and the firemen inform the emergency committee that a measurement made along the main route of the cloud shows a nitric acid level of 5 ppm. From now on, the committee focuses on interpreting this number although all that it has are tables produced by the INRS (National Institute for Scientific Research) giving risk values in case of long-term exposure, not acute exposure as is the case here. The expert at the prefecture becomes alarmed considering that certain population categories may be in greater danger than others (people with respiratory problems, children, and the elderly). The prefect makes a comparison with the poison gas used during World War I. The other experts do not participate much. They do not act as experts but more as informants who have had experience with quarrying. They speak of rules in the quarries that allow exposure up to 25 ppm.

It is worth mentioning that the mobile emergency medical service has meanwhile examined the six workers who were poisoned at the warehouse in the morning and about 50 persons who spontaneously came to the hospital to be examined. At the end of the morning, they conclude that the clinical observations show evidence of poisoning from inhalation of nitrates but not a serious one. According to them, there is no danger for the population at large. However, this highly significant piece of information is not communicated to the emergency committee: The medical service does not try to do so and the committee does not attempt to find it out.

Relying on two main criteria—the risk associated with the 5 ppm figure and good meteorological conditions—the prefect decides to evacuate seven districts (40,000 persons). At 2 p.m., the ORSEC program[5] is launched. The population is informed by the police force, municipal authorities, and local radio stations. An orderly evacuation is made. At 3:30 p.m., an engineer who has been at the warehouse reports that the products involved are NPK fertilizers and not ammonitrates. Moreover, additional measurements made in two districts exposed to the wind show very low nitric acid levels (1 ppm and 0.5 ppm). Then, around 4 p.m., the deputy prefect tells the committee that the fire is almost under control. The meeting is brought to a close. At 7 p.m., the prefect decides to end the evacuation. The ORSEC program is called off the next morning at 7 a.m.

---

[5]Arrangements for dealing with major civil emergencies in France.

THE FORMULATION OF THE EVENT

Differences in the Content
of the Representation

In real decision making, problems are not given preformulated to the actors. A fundamental stage of the decision-making process is to formulate the issue at hand. As people construct a representation of the situation, they may vary in the way that they formulate it. In this case, the way that the participants describe the event differs widely between groups. Each person indeed saw something different depending on whether they were firemen, members of the emergency committee at the prefecture, or the mobile emergency medical service.

For the committee members, their initial representation of the event is based on a few pieces of information, coming from outside, and not supported by direct visual perception. The event soon becomes indistinguishable from the cloud. The main actors—the prefect, his assistant, and the civil protection officer—are informed around 10 a.m. that there is a fire on the outskirts of Nantes without being directly in touch with the people on the spot. The emergency committee is then convened and receives some information about the extent and likely duration of the disaster (the firemen think that it will last a long time) and the products involved (ammonitrates, whereas in fact they are NPK fertilizers). However, the committee considers the fire to be the firemen's job and its own responsibility is the cloud; it therefore takes the first steps to advise local residents to stay indoors. In their interviews, the committee members reduce the problem throughout the day to the cloud—its toxicity and its consequences for the population.

By contrast, the firemen who are at the warehouse describe the event as a *fire*, although it is technically not a fire because there are neither flames nor heat, only smoke. These unusual characteristics of the phenomenon cause the firemen first of all to feel uneasy because they cannot make sense of what is happening. When the cloud becomes so large that its size cannot be taken in with the naked eye, and the firemen's prime concern is to control the "fire," they no longer see the overall situation. "The cloud is not our job." More than ever, the crisis is reduced to its physical aspect on the spot because the firemen are engaged in operational action.

Meanwhile, the antipollution unit, which is responsible for identifying and measuring the components of the cloud, focuses its understanding of the crisis on the cloud and the risks of explosion from a chemical perspective: "What is this cloud made of?"

Lastly, the chief of the mobile emergency medical service stays all day long at the hospital where he normally works. From the outset, he is well aware of the cloud, which he can see from the hospital, but he does not know its cause. According to his written notes, as soon as he sees the cloud he thinks of the Bophal catastrophe. However, after he has concluded from examining the six workers that there is no danger for the population, he forgets the cloud and focuses on the medical tasks (dealing with the people who come to the hospital to be reassured). For him, the crisis is reduced to those who feel they have been poisoned and want to be examined.

These results are consistent with the experiments done in the field of behavioral decision theory, which suggests that the kind of information given to the subject influences the way that the person then formulates the problem (Payne et al., 1992). However, laboratory experiments do not bring out so clearly that the same event may be understood in so many different ways depending on the actor's position. In fact, information is not shared equally and this has a strong influence on the way the crisis is represented.

Similar Processes of Simplification

Although the actors formulate the crisis in so many different ways, it seems that they use similar processes to simplify the perceived complexity of the situation and reduce it to a representation of the problem.

The Need to Stabilize the Representation

In real decisions, people work through the problem by progressively adding, eliminating, and transforming pieces of information. According to Payne et al. (1992), this is how the decision maker copes with the problem's complexity or the conflicting issues. In the Nantes case study, as long as the problem was not fully formulated, the actors felt a sense of anxiety: "aware of time flying by," "sensation of being powerless," "fear of escalation," and "guilt" at being powerless. At first, they had difficulty in grasping the situation, perceived as fuzzy and uncertain: "What is happening?" Then, each one started to make sense of the problem by picking out its most significant aspects. From there, they gradually developed an interpretation. Their representation is strongly related to their visual perception and, hence, to their physical relationship to the event. The actors do not seem conscious of alternative descriptions of what happened: They believe their representation to be the objective description of reality. It should be noted that the representation becomes fixed as soon as the decision makers move into action.

This tendency seems related to the person's degree of specialization and operational involvement. The more someone feels responsible for a specific aspect of the operation, the less he or she tries to restructure the problem. For instance, the firemen in charge of the "fire" rapidly became engaged in action (putting it out) and stayed focused on that aspect of the situation. The mobile emergency medical service organized themselves in accordance with the emergency plan. The members of the antipollution unit concentrated on the cloud's components, thereby losing sight of the problem as a whole—they already had only a partial view because of the way they initially perceived it—and they did not engage in any new analytical processes. A striking example of this inertia is the fireman who perceived the event as a fire although there were no flames or heat. During the operation, while totally engaged in trying to put it out, he noticed new physical clues (water temperature and the consistency of the materials around him) but did not understand them—naturally enough, because it was not, in fact, a fire. Nevertheless, he did not try to restructure the problem. Meanwhile, the prefect—who was not himself engaged in action but who was responsible for making the main decision—tried to sharpen his understanding of the situation, alternating between problem formulation and action. Different problems were tackled in parallel. For instance, the decision to tell people living within a kilometer of the warehouse to stay indoors was taken quickly while the risk of toxicity was still being assessed (experts were being sought).

These results nuance the conclusions of Montgomery (1989). He argued that a person faced with making a decision actively restructures the problem until one alternative becomes dominant, which then makes it possible to make a decision by reducing conflicting options. In this case study, the decision maker in a crisis situation reduces the problem's initial complexity and associated ambiguity by restructuring the problem (incorporating the first items of information, choosing a dominant hypothesis, and stabilizing the representation) until he feels ready to take action. From this moment, the representation is fixed. Further restructuring of the problem (which is still evolving) may indeed challenge the means used to deal with it and lead to paralysis. Although behavior of this kind diverges from normative decision-making theories, it is understandable under special circumstances: A crisis requires decisive action.

Generally speaking, the actors in the Nantes crisis were not only little inclined to reformulate the problem gradually but they also tended to assume that the others involved had a stable understanding of the situation. As a consequence, they felt that it would be superfluous to sound out the same person's opinion at different times. This was all the more noticeable because the emergency committee was not spontaneously informed by the people on the spot and so had to seek information instead of simply taking it in. The people at the prefecture received the first news about the fire and used it in their representation of what was happening but they did not then try to find out more about what the firemen were in fact doing and how those on the spot perceived the problem. This information might have been extremely valuable to the committee members.

The Use of Analogies

Analogies were used by almost all the persons interviewed to get an initial grasp on the problem at the beginning of the crisis. They picked out certain characteristics of the situation and related them to some experience in the past. For instance, one of the firemen referred to a fire in a gardening shop, another to a recent training course on nuclear risks, a doctor saw the analogy with the Bophal accident, the prefect remembered the poison gas used during WWI, others recalled the Texas-City explosion when they heard about ammonitrates, and so on. So, almost everybody uses things stored in their own memories to compare with the situation at hand. The examples have either been experienced personally or come from general knowledge (e.g., Texas-City or Bophal).

Before people can apply prior knowledge to a perception, they have to classify it as fitting into a familiar category. This process of categorization is described by two opposing theories, one based on the exemplar, the other on the prototype. The exemplar view (see Smith & Medin, 1981) suggests that a person categorizes something by seeing whether it resembles a lot of remembered examples from a single category. This process is based directly on personal experience and on instances actually encountered. By contrast, the prototype view of categories describes a category as a fuzzy set centering on a prototype. This prototype is the "central tendency" or average of the category members, and people decide whether a new instance fits the category by assessing its similarity to the prototype. In the study, it seems that people refer to specific instances of crisis-like events instead of referring to a more general, abstract crisis prototype. This result provides empirical support for a hypothesis of Kahneman and Miller (1986): According to them, people are more likely to use examples when they are trying to account for something out of the ordinary. In such cases, the categorization process would consist of comparing concrete characteristics of examples with whatever has to be classified. The main danger of making a categorization by retrieving stored examples is that one's judgmental process is affected by examples that are not relevant to the situation at hand, leading to inappropriate solutions: A fireman thinks of a training course on nuclear risks when the risk is in fact a chemical one; the event is compared to a fire although there are neither flames nor heat, and so on.

The Focus on Visual, Negative and Quantitative Information

As regards the selection of information, experimental studies have shown that the greater the complexity of the problem, the more selective and focused is the decision maker's attention. However, researchers disagree as to the nature of the information selected: Some assert that people ignore irrelevant information (Grether, Schwartz, & Wilde, 1986; Grether & Wilde, 1983), whereas others consider that the judgmental process in complex situations is affected even more by irrelevant information (Gaeth & Shanteau, 1984). Moreover, research in behavioral decision theory indicates that the pressure of time accelerates the process of selecting information and reduces the amount of information taken into account in solving complex problems. In the case studied here, people mostly selected three categories of information: what was visually most obvious (cf previously in this chapter the part on the content of the representation) as well as negative or quantitative information.

This study brings out clearly the differing weights given to positive and negative information. Negative information strongly influences the decision-making process: the advice of the expert from the university who arrived around noon asserting that the situation was catastrophic and could cause deaths; the information that the committee received from the firemen at the beginning of the events relating to the likely duration of the operations (the committee was very surprised to learn in the afternoon that the "fire" was under control). Positive information, on the other hand, was considered to be unhelpful. Hence, the mobile emergency medical service, after they concluded from examining the six poisoned workers that there was no danger for the population, did not realize the significance of this conclusion. As a consequence, they did not try to pass on the news to the emergency committee. They would undoubtedly have acted quite differently if their diagnosis had been that the poisoning was serious.

Those involved pay particular attention to numerical information. Around noon, two members of the antipollution unit decided to take chlorine and nitric acid measurements at places exposed to the wind. Afterward, everyone admitted that this operation was technically very difficult, thus making the validity of the measurements highly questionable: Only one measurement was made, in only one direction, in a closed car, showing a concentration rate of 2 ppm. From this number, the 5 ppm rate was then extrapolated and communicated to the committee as the toxicity level of the whole cloud.

However, during the crisis, nobody questioned its validity, and the seriousness of the situation was assessed with reference to this single criterion. From the moment when the antipollution unit announced this rate, the emergency committee did not look for qualitative information such as the amount of smoke, how it was evolving, or the effects of the rescue operation. Neither did they try to get information about the medical examination although they knew that it had been carried out.

DECISION-MAKING STRATEGIES

Once the crisis participants have an idea of the problem, they use specific decision-making strategies to choose a course of action. The data in the study reveal that people use anchorage as well as adjustment strategies, try to avoid risk, and refer to their professional identity to take decisions.

Anchoring and Adjustment Under Ambiguity

The decision-making problem in the Nantes crisis is characterized by risk and ambiguity. In a high-risk choice, events are uncertain but the likelihood that they will occur is known to the subject— for instance, the probability that a risky event will occur may be 0.4. However, in some cases, even that probability is not properly defined, a situation that is labeled as ambiguous. This ambiguity may prove to be a significant contextual variable in a risky decision-making process (Curley, Yates, & Abrams, 1986; Einhorn & Hogarth, 1985; Hogarth & Einhorn, 1990). According to these researchers, ambiguity is typical of real decision-making contexts and strongly influences decision-makers' behavior—they try to avoid it.

In this case, there was ambiguity first when the cloud's consequences were being assessed and later with regard to the way the risk was likely to evolve. At 1 p.m., the emergency committee was told the supposed nitric acid level of the cloud (5 ppm). What does this number mean in terms of the risk? How does relate it to a toxicity level that will strongly influence the subsequent measures taken for the population? The actors lacked reference points for interpreting the 5 ppm figure. Moreover, less than an hour later, the smoldering fertilizer had generated an enormous thick cloud spreading out over the town. The situation was very worrying. How was it likely to evolve? The longer the fertilizer burned, the more toxic the air was likely to become. The decision makers were concerned about the weather too: What if there were a mist that retained the toxic particles? How would the weather change? At the moment when a decision had to be made, no precise answer could be given to these questions. Hence, there was a dilemma: Decision making is based on anticipating an event, yet there is insufficient information about it to make any predictions. How can one think about the potential danger ahead if one is unable to evaluate the current risk? Moreover, it is even more difficult to get an idea of the risk to the population in the long term. All these elements show the significance of ambiguity—in the sense of Einhorn and Hogarth—in crisis decision making: Risk has to be assessed for the present situation as well as for the future in a rapidly evolving context.

When making judgments under uncertainty, people will sometimes reduce ambiguity by starting with an anchor and then adjusting it to reach a conclusion (Tversky & Kahneman, 1974). In such cases, the main risk is that judgments may be anchored by irrelevant details of the situation or reference points: This is the well-known adjustment bias. Two anchoring processes occurred in the case studied: before and after the toxicity measurement (5 ppm) was communicated to the committee.

Around noon, the expert, a professor at Nantes university and a specialist in water problems, joined the crisis committee at the prefecture. Up to that point, nobody had taken a strong stand on the seriousness of the situation. As to the expert, she was immediately alarmist, considering that people could die. Ex post, every committee member interviewed criticized her for having been too alarmist; one can interpret their reaction as a feeling of having been manipulated. "She placed the bar so high that it was impossible to lower it again." From this moment onward, a point of reference was given to the group, who then used it as an anchor for its own judgment. Consciously or unconsciously, they estimated the risk vis-à-vis this benchmark, which was set at a very high level. The credibility of the source—an expert respected for her knowledge of the question—reinforced this phenomenon.

Another interesting anchoring process appears with regard to the interpretation of the figure 5 ppm. The committee members referred to the only reference point in their possession: the toxicological information supplied by the National Institute for Scientific Research (see Appendix). They compared the level of 5 ppm with the upper limit given there: 4 ppm. However, this anchor was inappropriate to the situation: This number relates to chronic exposure in the workplace and therefore in an enclosed place, whereas the exposure in the Nantes case occurred outside and was acute. The population at risk was a mixture of children, pregnant women, and the elderly, not just workers. It may be asked why the level given by the U. S. regulation (25 ppm, included on the sheet) was not taken into account although it is more than 10 times higher than the French one. Another factor was at work here: The interpretation of the 5 ppm was probably influenced by the initial evaluation of the event, following the first anchoring and adjustment process. As for the prefect, who was the main decision maker, he had decided (but not told anyone) to evacuate the population before knowing of the measurement. So, it was understandable that he should use the measurement as a rational support for his decision and consequently interpret the 5 ppm as related to a strong risk.

Throughout the Nantes example, people used anchoring and adjustment processes to make judgments—and decisions—in an ambiguous situation. The anchoring points came from credible sources (an expert and the National Institute for Scientific Research), which probably reinforced the phenomenon.

Risk Avoidance

The decision to evacuate the population (40,000 persons) is the main decision in the example: It is indeed the most significant decision that an emergency committee can make where there is considerable danger to human life. This decision may be seen as the responsibility of a single actor: the prefect. So it will be examined in detail as a specific decision-making process.

Although it was not announced until 2 p.m., it is clear from the interviews with the committee members that the decision to evacuate the population had been taking shape in the prefect's mind since the end of the morning. This decision was based on only two criteria—such a drastic simplification probably helped the decision maker to cut down the complexity of choice. The first criterion derives from the prefect's confidence that an evacuation would be relatively straightforward. The second criterion was the lack of information relating to the situation and how it would evolve.

> I thought about it well before noon. On the basis of little information. That was the main problem: information. We did not get it when we should have.... In this case, we did not expect either the gas emissions or the toxicity to decrease. I imagined the thousands of possible deaths, the risk of panic. This was a justification for action. Moreover, we could expect toxicity levels to rise again, even in the evening.

This is a criterion of risk, which leads to the problem being formulated in the following terms:

> If I decide to evacuate, I am sure that there is no risk for the population. If I do not, either the cloud is toxic and then there is a risk or the cloud is not toxic and then there is no risk.

In his reasoning, the prefect ignored the probability that the cloud was toxic. He preferred to formulate the alternatives without taking account of probability levels. He chose the option that would minimize uncertainty and provide a guaranteed zero risk, whatever the associated costs—financial, psychological, means employed, and so on. He did not estimate the opportunity cost of an evacuation if the cloud turned out not to be toxic. External observers have strongly criticized the disproportionate scale of the evacuation compared with the probability of risk to the population. However, to the prefect, it was inappropriate to construct different hypotheses about the possible danger and to adapt the course of action according to the likelihood of each hypothesis occurring. In his decision-making process he took only one hypothesis into account—the most pessimistic one—and by so doing removed any ambiguity. No matter how the problem evolved, whatever the level of risk, whatever the level of toxicity, he knew that there would be no risk to the population.

This result is consistent with recent research on managerial risk taking. Decision makers seem to be relatively insensitive to probability estimates when thinking about risk (Lopes, 1994; March & Shapira, 1987; Shapira, 1994). Although theories of choice tend to treat gambling as a situation of decision making under risk, decision makers distinguish between risk taking and gambling. They react to variability more by trying to avoid it or to control it than by considering it as a trade-off with expected value in making a choice.

Rule and Role Following

The accountability theory (Tetlock, 1983, 1992) provides an interesting model for understanding the process by which the prefect is dealing with risk in the Nantes case. According to Tetlock, people with heavy responsibilities, when making a decision with serious consequences, give greater weight to likely losses than to gains, especially where human lives are at risk. Tetlock's work enhances the conclusions of Curley et al. (1986): Decision makers with major responsibilities are more likely to avoid ambiguity because they foresee the difficulties they would have in justifying their choice if the consequences are bad. It is easier to justify an evacuation if it turns out that there was no risk than loss of life if there were no evacuation. Moreover, the prefect refers himself to his responsibility: In the French administrative system, he is explicitly in charge of maintaining security. It has been demonstrated that people differ in the extent to which they focus attention primarily on the worst or best possible outcomes (Lopes, 1987, 1995) depending on what they are concerned with (i.e., in their job). Here, the reference to his professional identity gives the prefect a convenient rule to follow.

This reference to one's professional identity also induces an opportunistic behavior in decision making. The prefect was indeed confident that an evacuation would be relatively straightforward. Right from the morning, indeed, he felt that he had available all that was necessary for carrying out an evacuation if need be: The army had been put at his disposal, he trusted the local police, and so on. Moreover, the weather was good. Did the prefect decide to evacuate because he assessed the situation involved a real risk and the conditions for an evacuation were good or did he judge the situation to be dangerous (and therefore decided to evacuate) because he knew that he was in a position to implement this decision? From the prefect's perspective, the fact that one of the alternatives was feasible and could be implemented quickly was of prime importance. The choice he made corresponds to an opportunistic behavior based on his own capacities: He knew he had the means to evacuate, he had already developed a network of contacts with people in charge of rescue operations, and he had previously experimented such a course of action in his career. Moreover, he was the only decision maker who was allowed to choose and implement such a solution. His decision was consistent with his role and it also reasserted it.

The firemen, the doctors, and the committee members also referred to their professional identities in the decision-making process. The reference to their role provided them a convenient rule to decide what had to be considered as an issue and select the operating procedures.

CONCLUSIONS

The study of a real case provides an opportunity for examining the generalization of experimental results and improving our behavioral understanding of choice. The results provide empirical support for conclusions drawn from experimental research in the field of behavioral decision theory. In an ambiguous situation, the participants to the crisis concentrate on very little information (Grether & Wilde, 1983) and give greater weight to negative possibilities (Curley & Yates, 1985; Einhorn & Hogarth, 1985; Hogarth & Einhorn, 1990). The preference for an option is not unrelated to its feasibility (Klein & Yadav, 1989). Formulating the problem, defining the alternatives, and evaluating them are not separate sequential stages of the decision-making process. They occur simultaneously while the decision is being restructured (Montgomery, 1989; Montgomery & Svenson, 1983). Moreover, the results of such investigation may be a basis for outlining some research issues that may be of great concern for students of individual choice.

The Problem as a Construction of the Decision Maker

A viewpoint that has recently emerged in individual decision research is that preferences are often constructed in generating a response to a judgment or choice task (Payne et al., 1992). The constructiveness of preferences is attributed to the interaction between the limited computational capabilities of decision makers and the complexity of task environments. This constructive view of preferences has lead to a wide variety of studies on the task and context factors that may have an impact on the process of construction. However, it seems that researchers in this field have neglected another issue also related to the context dependence of choices and the limited human processing capabilities. People have to frame the problem of choice and this also corresponds to a process of construction in a specific environment. Because of the omission to study this, behavioral researchers tend to overlook the factors that are key to an understanding of this process such as how decision-making problems come into being and develop in complex situations. These situations provide elements that are drawn on by the decision maker in attempting to formulate problems.

In the Nantes case study, the major variations observed between individual representations of the crisis far surpass the framing effect studied in behavioral decision theory (Tversky & Kahneman, 1986). Laboratory experiments do not bring out so clearly that the same event may be understood in so many different ways depending on the actor's position. This phenomenon is strongly related to the processing of information: In this case, there is a high sensitivity to the order in which information is presented and the type of information received in relation to the actor's position and role in the crisis. Positive and qualitative information is given little weight and there is a tendency to formulate the problem on the basis of negative and quantitative information. The variations between individual formulations of the problem may also be related to the participants' previous experiences and existing knowledge. Decision making involves a search for information in both the external perceptual environment and the internal memory environment, with information from one environment guiding the search in the other. The different ways in which individuals see or frame problems built on prior knowledge limit the search for new options. This phenomenon is highly visible in the Nantes crisis where people used analogies stored in their memory to frame the problem.

Decision Simplification and Sensemaking

Another interesting question is related to the constructivity of decision problems: How and when does the formulation become simple and stable enough as to enable action taking? In this case, as long as the problem was not fully formulated, the actors felt a sense of anxiety. A stable view of the situation was wanted as soon as possible and this stability was linked to action. Decision making is intimately related to sensemaking. Individuals need to make sense of the confusing situation—a crisis—before acting. The Nantes crisis suggests that decision makers use simplifying heuristics to deal above all with ambiguity but also to make sense of the situation. Indeed, the use of heuristics and simplification also has the advantage of reducing the complexities of the situation. It allows the decision makers to construct a representation of it on which they can act and provide a behavioral response—for example, choose a solution that may be efficiently implemented or avoid disastrous consequences. The sensemaking process is related to the decision makers' own capacities and knowledge: The prefect knew he had the means to evacuate and a good knowledge of evacuation due to previous experiences, the firemen focused on controlling the fire, and the doctors focused on the medical tasks. The interest for students of behavioral decision theory in this perspective lies in the linkage between simplification processes and both experience and opportunistic behavior.

Decision Making as Rule and Role Following

Theories of anticipatory and consequential action underestimate the intelligence of another alternative decision logic: the logic of duty, obligation, role, and rules. In the Nantes case, it is, however, clear that decision making is related to this logic. The prefect, the firemen, the doctors, the people from the antipollution unit, and the committee members referred to their professional identities and roles that gave them rules to follow. Rather than evaluating alternatives in terms of the values of their consequence, they focused more on classifying the situation into a category that was associated with their identities and roles and selecting the rules that seemed appropriate to those identities. Their decisions reflected their images of proper behavior. The use of rules and standard operating procedures in routine situations is well known, but the case shows that it is not limited to such situations. The reference to one's identity provides rules about what to do but it also gives rules about the cognitive effort that should be engaged in the decision-making process. It provides rules of good practice and good thinking. For example, for the prefect, a higher perceived level of responsibility (due to his role) implied a stronger cognitive effort and a specific attitude toward risk assessment. He incorporated in his judgments factors such as the awareness of the difficulty of justifying his choices afterward or a sense of accountability. Those factors were strongly related to his professional identity.

Methodological Issues

To conclude, the constructive, contingent, and rule-based nature of decision making has a strong impact on the methodological choices used for studying it. The more we think that decision making is context and rule dependent, the more we should study it in the real world. Extreme cases such as a crisis provide the opportunity to enhance researchers' knowledge of real decision-making processes. Indeed, a crisis offers a special kind of environment, characterized by a mixture of complexity, ambiguity, risk, and urgency. In a crisis, the consequences of the decisions taken for the organization and for individuals are extremely serious, which highlights the responsibilities of the decision makers. Moreover, a crisis deals with problems that are unusual for people. Interesting cognitive processes may occur that make a set of rules, identities and roles matching such a situation and giving behavioral responses. In analyzing those processes, it is therefore essential to describe accurately the context and the role of the individuals in that context.

REFERENCES

Anderson, J. R. (1983). *The architecture of cognition.* Cambridge, MA: Harvard University Press.

Bartunek, J. M. (1984). Changing interpretive schemes and organizational restructuring: The example of a religious order. *Administrative Science Quarterly, 29,* 355–72.

Curley, S. P., & Yates, J. F. (1985). The center and range of the probability interval as factors affecting ambiguity preferences. *Organizational Behavior and Human Decision Processes, 36,* 273–287.

Curley, S. P., Yates, J. F., & Abrams, R. A. (1986). Psychological source of ambiguity avoidance. *Organizational Behavior and Human Decision Processes. 38,* 230–56.

Cyert, R. M., & March, J. G. (1963). *A behavioral theory of the firm.* Englewood Cliffs, NJ: Prentice-Hall.

Einhorn, H. J., & Hogarth, R. M. (1981). Behavioral decision theory: Processes of judgment and choice. *Annual Review of Psychology, 32,* 53–88.

Einhorn, H. J., & Hogarth R. M. (1985). Ambiguity and uncertainty in probabilistic inference. *Psychological Review, 93,* 433–461.

Elster, J. (1986). *The multiple self.* Cambridge, England: Cambridge University Press.

Elster, J. (1989). Social norms and economic theory. *Journal of Economy and Personality, 3,* 99–117.

Fischhoff, B. (1975). Hindsight foresight: The effect of outcome knowledge on judgment under uncertainty. *Journal of Experimental Psychology: Human Perception and Performance, 3,* 349–358.

Fischhoff, B. (1980). For those condemned to study the past: Reflections on historical judgment. In R. A. Shweder (Ed.), *New directions for methodology of social and behavioral science,* (Vol. 4, pp. 79–93). San Francisco: Jossey-Bass.

Gaeth, G. J., & Shanteau, J. (1984). Reducing the influence of irrelevant information on experienced decision makers. *Organizational Behavior and Human Decision Processes, 33,* 263–82.

Gilbert, C. (1990) *La catastrophe, l'élu et le préfet.* Grenoble, France: Presses Universitaires de Grenoble.

Grether, D. M., Schwartz, A., & Wilde, L. L. (1986). The irrelevance of information overload: An analysis of search and disclosure. *South Californian Law Review, 6,* 33–57.

Grether, D. M., & Wilde, L. L. (1983). Consumer choice and information: New experimental evidence. *Information Economics & Policy, 1,* 115–144.

Hogarth, R. M. (Ed.) (1990). *Insights in decision making: A tribute to Hillel J. Einhorn.* Chicago: University of Chicago Press.

Hogarth, R. M., & Einhorn, H. J. (1990). Venture theory: A model of decision weights. *Management Science, 36,* 780–803.

Kahneman, D., & Miller, D. (1986). Norm theory: Comparing reality to its alternatives. *Psychological Review, 93,* 136–153.

Kahneman, D., Slovic P., & Tversky A. (1982). *Judgments under uncertainty: Heuristics and biases.* Cambridge, England: Cambridge University.

Klein, N. M., & Yadav M. S. (1989). Context effects on effort and accuracy in choice: An enquiry into adaptative decision-making. *Journal of Consumer Research, 15,* 411–421.

Lichtenstein, S., & Fischhoff, B. (1977). Do those who know more also know more about how much they know? The calibration of probability judgments. *Organizational Behavior and Human Performance, 20,* 159–183.

Lopes, L. L. (1987). Between hope and fear: The psychology of risk. *Advances in Experimental Social Psychology, 20,* 255–295.

Lopes, L. L. (1994). Psychology and economics: Perspectives on risk, cooperation and the marketplace. *Annual Review of Psychology, 45,* 197–227.

Lopes, L. L. (1995). Algebra and process in the modeling of risky choices. In R. Busemeyer, R. Hastie, & D. L. Medlin (Eds.), *Decision making from the perspective of cognitive psychology* (pp. 177–220). New York: Academic Press.

March, J. G. (1994). *A primer of decision making.* New York: The Free Press.

March, J. G., & Shapira, Z. (1987). Managerial perspectives on risk and risk taking. *Management Science, 33,* 1404–1418.

March, J. G., & Simon H. A. (1958). *Organizations.* New York: Wiley.

Mellers, B. A., Schwartz A., & Cooke, A. D. J. (1998). Judgment and decision making. *Annual Review of Psychology, 49,* 447–477.

Montgomery, H. (1989). From cognition to action: The search for dominance in decision making. In H. Montgomery & O. Svenson (Eds.), *Process and structure in human decision making* (pp. 34–55). New York: Wiley.

Montgomery, H., & Svenson, O. (1983). A think aloud study of dominance structuring in decision processes. In R. Tietz (Ed.), *Aspiration levels in bargaining and economic decision making* (pp. 366–383). New York: Springer-Verlag.

Nisbett, R., & Ross, L. (1980). *Human inferences: Strategies and shortcomings of social judgment.* Englewood Cliffs, NJ: Prenctice-Hall.

Payne, J. W. (1976). Task complexity and contingent processing in decision making: An information search and protocol analysis. *Organizational Behavior and Human Performance, 16,* 366–387.

Payne, W. J., Bettman, J. R., & Johnson, E. J. (1992). Behavioral decision research: A constructive processing perspective, *Annual Review of Psychology, 43,* 87–113.

Pettigrew, A. (1985). *The awakening giant.* Oxford, England: Basil Blackwell.

Shapira, Z. (1994). *Risk Taking: A managerial perspective.* New York: Russell Sage Foundation.

Simon, H. A. (1955). A behavioral model of rational choice. *Quarterly Journal of Economics*, 69, 99–118.

Simon, H. A., Dantzig, G. B., Hogarth, R., Plott, C. R., Raiffa, H., Schelling, T. C., Shepsle, K. A., Thaler, R., Tversky, A., & Winter, S. (1992). Decision making and problem solving. In M. Zey (Ed.), *Decision making: Alternatives to rational choice models* (pp. 32–54). Newbury Park, CA: Sage.

Slovic, P., Fischhoff, B., & Lichtenstein, S. (1977). Behavioral decision theory. *Annual Review of Psychology, 28*, 1–39.

Smith, E. E., & Medin, D. L. (1981). *Categories and concepts*. Cambridge, MA: Harvard University Press.

Sternberg, R. J., & Salter, W. (1982). Conceptions of intelligence. In R. J. Sternberg (Ed.), *Handbook of human intelligence* (pp. 3–28). Cambridge, England: Cambridge University Press.

Sternberg, R. J., & Wagner R. K. (Eds.). (1986). *Practical intelligence*. Cambridge, England: Cambridge University Press.

Svenson, O., & Maule, J. A. (Eds.). (1993). *Time pressure and stress in human judgment and decision making*. New York: Plenum.

Tetlock, P. E. (1983). Accountability and the complexity of thought. *Journal of Personality and Social Psychology, 45*, 74–83.

Tetlock, P. E. (1992). The impact of accountability on judgment and choice: Toward a social contingency model. *Advances in Experimental Social Psychology, 25*, 331–376.

Tversky, A. (1972). Elimination by aspects: A theory of choice. *Psychological Review, 79*, 281–299.

Tversky, A., & Kahneman, D. (1973). Availability: A heuristic for judging frequency and probability. *Cognitive Psychology, 4*, 207–232.

Tversky, A., & Kahneman, D. (1974). Judgment under uncertainty: Heuristics and biases. *Science, 185*, 1124–1131.

Tversky, A., & Kahneman, D. (1982). Judgments of and by representativeness. In D. Kahneman, P. Slovic, and A. Tversky (Eds.). *Judgments under uncertainty: Heuristics and biases* (pp. 84–100). Cambridge, England: Cambridge University.

Tversky A., & Kahneman, D. (1986) Rational choices and the framing of decisions. *Journal of Business, 59*(4), 251–278.

Wagner R. K., & Sternberg, R. J. (1985). Practical intelligence in real-world pursuits: The role of tacit knowledge. *Journal of Personality and Social Psychology, 48*, 436–458.

Yin R. K., (1985). *Case study research*. Beverly Hills, CA: Sage.

APPENDIX

Toxicological File No. 9. Source: INRS Data File

"In France, the Department of Labor has ruled on the recommended maximum exposure to, as well as the average level of, nitric acid that can be allowed in a workshop's atmosphere. These values have been set at 4 ppm, i.e. 10 mg per cubic meter, and 2 ppm, i.e., 5 mg per cubic meter, respectively (...). In the United States, the average maximum recommended exposure to nitric acid has been set at 25 ppm by the ACGIH in 1982."

Commentary:
More Is Not Always Better:
Limits to Managerial Thinking
and Decision Making

Janet M. Dukerich
University of Texas at Austin

The four chapters presented in the Cognition at Work section illustrate the tremendous complexity underlying managerial thinking and decision making in terms of the problems and issues themselves and the methodological issues associated with studying the phenomenon. All four attempt to understand the processes that occur as individuals or groups grapple with ambiguous, unstructured, messy problems. The problems are not insignificant. The chapter by Tamuz considers such problems as near accidents in the airline industry. Bennett and Anthony focus on the deliberations of major bank boards. Nair uses a case describing a manufacturing organization for which the participants assume the role of the chief executive officer. And finally, Vidaillet examines the response to a potential toxic spill crisis. Thus, the phenomenon considered by these four authors set a boundary condition; they do not consider structured or routine problems for which more rational decision-making models can be applied. Rather, the ill-structuredness of the problems allowed for multiple interpretations of the problem itself, the relevance of information, and the appropriateness of various actions, and accordingly, there was a need to use more complex models of decision making.

The methodologies used by the authors also reflected the complexity of the phenomenon and demonstrate how difficult it is to study cognition at work. Tamuz used a qualitative methodology to examine seven aviation safety information systems, whereas Bennett and Anthony relied on a survey of board insiders and outsiders in the banking industry. Nair

265

used an organizational simulation composed of many variables over numerous time periods and attempted to capture managers' cognitive maps, whereas Vidaillet based his conclusions on a case study of decision makers involved in a crisis. Thus, although the four authors share an interest in the phenomenon of ill-defined problems, they differed in how they went about studying the phenomenon. Taken together, the four studies provide a rich description of how managers deal with complex decision making. Considering each one by itself, different facets of the process are illuminated.

The chapter by Michal Tamuz examines how decision-making teams in U.S. aviation safety systems categorize and interpret accounts of potential dangers or near accidents. Following the arguments of Dutton and Jackson (1987), she proposes that decision makers use superordinate definitions of near accidents as *threats* (to rule enforcement) or *opportunities* (for learning). Although this simplification device might help decision makers as they try to make sense of these potentially dangerous, ambiguous events, this categorization has some negative side effects. Specifically, this categorization may "channel attention, shape the construction of information processing routines and thus, by constraining the availability of information, affect the capacity for organizational learning and knowledge generation." In her research, Tamuz observed how the composition of the decision making team affects the categorization of a near accident and how the categorization of potential dangers as threats leads to the use of the data for rule enforcement as well as limits the usefulness of the data for future analysis. Although the benefits of using precise definitions to classify potential dangers would appear to be immeasurable, Tamuz presents a good case that more is not always better. Reducing ambiguity may increase psychological comfort, but turning an ill-structured problem into a seemingly more structured one could impede the learning process.

In their chapter, Robert Bennett and William Anthony (chap. 9, this volume) address the issue of bank board deliberations in an attempt to understand how the use of both intuition–tacit knowledge and analysis–explicit knowledge play a role. A major premise is that the contributions of insiders (employees or former employees of the organization) and outsiders (nonemployees) may be different in the deliberations of boards of directors. As Bennett and Anthony note, researchers have focused on the "correct" composition of boards of directors in terms of insiders versus outsiders (Baysinger & Butler, 1985; Ford, 1988) without analyzing the processes that would affect the ultimate success of the board. That is, the ideal mix of insiders and outsiders is based on the assumption that each type brings in relevant and unique information needed for successful deliberations. Bennett and Anthony argue that insiders provide more formal analysis and outsiders rely more on intuition. Using self-report survey data of bank board members, Bennett and Anthony find that insiders tend to use analysis and explicit information more than outsiders do, whereas outsiders tended to report using a more intuitive decision-making style. The greater use of an analytical process was associated with higher bank performance whereas perceived board performance seemed to be related to outsider intuition level. Although reverse causality arguments cannot be ruled out in this study, a major contribution of the research is that both types of problem-solving styles appear to be critical components of effective board deliberations. Again, more of one kind (i.e., using an analytical process to the exclusion of an intuitive style) does not necessarily lead to the best results.

Experienced managers dealing with a simulated complex organizational problem were the focus of K. Unnikrishnan Nair's research. Nair took on the challenging task of mapping the network of relations that the managers developed as they worked through a complex organizational problem over a series of trials. He argued that the effectiveness of problem solving might vary with the complexity of the cognitive map or the elaborateness of the network of relations developed. The research reported in this chapter differed methodologically from the others in terms of providing a particular problem to a sample of decision makers as opposed to decision makers reporting on problems or issues that they encountered in their day-to-day lives. However, the complexity of the problem itself simulated the ill-defined nature of the phenomenon of interest and the research setting allowed for the observation of the cognitive process as it occurred, rather than being retrospectively reported. Although many of the relations between the managers' cognitive maps and decision making were fairly weak, an interesting result was observed with the inverted U relationship between cognitive map density and success in problem solving. Specifically, Nair demonstrates that increasing the complexity of a cognitive map can lead to more effective problem solving but only up to a point. Too much complexity could lead to cognitive overload. Perhaps ill-structured problems require a certain degree of ambiguity, thus, effective problem solvers should not try to find every link between concepts, rather, they need to focus on the most important ones.

The final chapter in this section examines how different decision-making groups arrived at very different interpretations of the same event, namely, the Toxic Cloud Crisis. This case study of decision makers in France allowed for an examination of the interpretation process as it unfolded over the course of a day (albeit retrospectively) and highlighted the critical nature of the problem formulation stage. Bénédicte Vidaillet provided a consistent application of findings from behavioral decision theory in lab studies (cf., Kahneman, Slovic, & Tversky, 1982) to a real-life crisis. Specifically, she argued that the representation of the problem differed between decision makers depending on the type of information used to label the problem, hypothesis confirming information was more readily accessible and accepted by the decision makers, and anchoring and adjustment was observed that influenced the decision makers' assessment of the risk to human life. One of the more interesting (although somewhat depressing) findings was that each of the various decision-making groups felt that their representation was, of course, shared by all the others. Vidaillet notes that "the decision-maker in a crisis situation reduces the problem's initial complexity and associated ambiguity by restructuring the problem (incorporating the first items of information, choosing a dominant hypothesis, stabilizing the representation) until they feel ready to take action." As noted before, although the reduction of ambiguity may provide psychological comfort, it certainly can impede the learning process. Vidaillet also suggests that the professional identities of the decision makers involved constrained the interpretation process, a finding that has parallels at the organizational level of analysis (Dutton & Dukerich, 1991; Elsbach & Kramer, 1996; Gioia & Thomas, 1996).

Although each of these four chapters provides a different slice of the cognition at work process, both in terms of types of problems considered and types of methodologies used, a common theme may be observed in their implications for managerial decision making. Each of them seems to have something to say about the factors that impede or enhance learning. To be effective in the long run, decision makers in organizations need to be able to learn. However, many of the decision-making tools that emphasize simplifying, focusing, reducing uncertainty, and so on may be quite ineffective when decision makers confront ill-structured problems. The information embedded in ambiguity may be the fodder for future learning, thus increasing problem-solving effectiveness over time. As all of these chapters demonstrate a delicate balance is needed between providing problem categorizations that allow decision makers to proceed and allowing some slippage in such categorizations so that a simplification process does not overwhelm managerial thinking and decision making.

REFERENCES

Baysinger, B., & Butler, H. (1985). Corporate governance and the board of directors: Performance effects of changes in board composition. *Journal of Law, Economics, and Organizations, 1*, 102–124.

Dutton, J., & Dukerich, J. (1991). Keeping an eye on the mirror: Image and identity in organizational adaptation. *Academy of Management Journal, 34,* 517–554.

Dutton, J., & Jackson, S. (1987). Categorizing strategic issues: Links to organization action. *Academy of Management Review, 12,* 76–90.

Elsbach, K., & Kramer, R. (1996). Members' responses to organizational identity threats: Encountering and countering the *Business Week* rankings. *Administrative Science Quarterly, 41,* 442–476.

Ford, R. (1988). Outside directors and the privately owned firm: Are they necessary? *Entrepreneurship Theory and Practice, 13,* 49–57.

Gioia, D., & Thomas, J. (1996). Institutional identity, image, and issue interpretation: Sensemaking during strategic change in academia. *Administrative Science Quarterly, 41,* 370–403.

Kahneman, D., Slovic, P., & Tversky, A. (1982). *Judgment under uncertainty: Heuristics and biases.* New York: Cambridge University Press.

Social and Strategic Aspects
of Cognition

12

Classifying Competition: An Empirical Study of the Cognitive Social Structure of Strategic Groups

---

Vincenza Odorici
Alessandro Lomi
University of Bologna, Italy

Attempts to characterize markets as concrete social structures typically assume that constraints associated with roles are more important in determining individual strategies than either the information or beliefs that decision makers might hold about the specific situation that their companies face (Leifer, 1985; White, 1981, 1988; White & Eccles, 1987). Proponents of this structural approach to markets tend to see roles as regularities in behavior that emerge from a system of equivalencies and differences among competitors in a market. The main analytical focus of this research program is on the reproductive forces behind observed market arrangements (Bothner & White, 2000). However, as Porac, Thomas, Wilson, Paton, and Kanfer (1995) observed: "To identify who competes with whom ... one must capture the belief system that allows these definitions to persist" (p. 204). Hence, the notion of markets as concrete role structures seems to have at its core a series of fundamental assumptions about cognitive processes within and between organizations.

In the business strategy literature— which typically starts from opposite assumptions about the relation between information and decisions—the existence of organized systems of equivalencies and differences among competitors is implicitly acknowledged by invoking notions such as that of strategic group to explain performance and behavioral differences among participants in a market. The notion of strategic group emphasizes the local nature of many competitive processes and the imperfect connectivity of producers' markets. The strategic group construct is based on the conjecture that a direct correlation should exist between proximity and interfirm rivalry, and that within group rivalry and between group rivalry should differ (Cool & Dierickx, 1993; Peteraf, 1993). Because individual producers define their role by comparing themselves only to a restricted number of other reference producers, a substantively important issue concerns how exactly strategic groups are perceived and used to classify competitors.

If shared, these classification schemes assume a taken-for-granted status and become important elements in the institutionalization of competitive interaction and—ultimately—in the reproduction of market structures. When individual producers think of themselves as unique but see others as similar, roles are ambiguous and the corresponding market is likely to be unstable (White & Eccles, 1987). Hence, the view of competition as a process of strategic positioning with respect to competitors and competitive forces also seems to depend critically on the ability of producers to build a shared mental model of their market within which actions are interpretable and meaningful.

This chapter starts from the observation that different perspectives on markets seem to share remarkably similar—albeit implicit—assumptions about how individual actors understand competitive relationships to explore the relational basis of social cognition—namely, of the "individuals' mental representation of the social world, especially of *other* [italics added] individuals and social events" (Pattison, 1994, p. 79). Patterns of competitive relations are analyzed among 18 manufacturers of plants for water treatment located in Italy to address three main questions about the origins and implications of perceptions of strategic similarity among competitors. First, how do individual perceptions of similarity combine to induce constraining roles at more aggregate levels of analysis? Second, how accurately can individual producers reconstruct their own role—or network position—in the industry? Third, how does the structure of competition emerging from the aggregation of individual perceptions differ from the actual structure of competition?

It is believed that these questions are relevant for two main reasons. First, the very notion of market as a meaningful unit of analysis hinges on assumptions about the ability of individual participants to recognize their own role in the market and to identify their competitors accurately. Second, there is a fundamental dualism between markets and organizations. On the one hand, markets are defined by the type and number of organizations that participate in a given set of competitive activities. On the other hand, the type of market context in which individual organizations decide to interact shapes organizational identities and behaviors. For these reasons, it is believed that exploring answers to these questions will improve the understanding of the dual nature of markets both as concrete social structures a well as the result of complex cognitive processes.

Building on Krackhardt's (1987a) model of cognitive social structures (CSS), in this study three-dimensional network data are used to link managerial perceptions of similarity and difference to the formation of strategic groups. Cognitive social structures are three-dimensional arrays of linkages (R_{ijk}) among a set of actors where i is the sender of the relation, j is the receiver of the relation, and k is the perceiver of the relation. The cognitive reconstruction of the links among competitors is then interpreted as the observable counterpart of their mental model of competition in the industry. The chapter analyzes how complex and highly idiosyncratic cognitive representations of competition emerge from the cumulation of individual judgments about strategic similarities among competitors in the industry.

After this general introduction the argument is organized as follows. In the next section, the theoretical background for this work is discussed, and the authors try to link recent results on organizational cognition to the problem of identifying of jointly occupied network positions. The central part of the chapter is dedicated to issues of research design and analytical strategy. In the fourth section, the preliminary results of the study are reported. The closing section of the chapter suggests possible interpretations of the results presented in the light of a number of obvious limitations of the current efforts and outlines possible avenues for future research.

THEORETICAL BACKGROUND

Perhaps two of the most clearly observable aspects of markets are that (a) participants are known to one another and monitor the actions of actual and potential competitors and (b) in formulating their competitive strategies, participants take into account the perceived action only of a limited number of others (Baum & Haveman, 1997; Baum & Mezias, 1992; Carroll, 1985; Gripsrud & Gronhaug, 1985; Hannan, Carroll, Dundon, & Torres,

1995; Lant & Baum, 1995; Leifer & White, 1987; Lomi & Larsen, 1997; Porac et al., 1995).

Both these local information-processing activities are possible only within a *frame of comparability*, or a shared representation of the complex system of similarities and differences among competitors out of which a *market* emerges as a distinct type of social formation with clearly recognizable boundaries (Leifer, 1985; Leifer & White, 1987; White & Eccles, 1987). Frames of comparability orient the practical choices of individual companies indirectly associated with one another through their mutual perception of action and intentions. In turn, these individual choices induce regularities—or *structures*,—at more aggregate levels.

This way of thinking about competition is clearly at odds with generally accepted views of the market as the ultimate decentralization mechanism. How could it be that a decentralized system of individual (possibly profit maximizing) choices induces and sustain the (more or less permanent) roles that are commonly observable in many markets? And, how does each actor contribute to the context perceived by others? Finally, how does market structure emerge from this decentralized system of individual perceptions and interlocked decisions?

To the extent to which individual companies look at similar (but by no mean identical) other companies for reference, comparison, and guidance, the first step toward addressing these question is to understand the origins and consequences of individual similarity judgments, because it is on the basis of these judgments that companies decide how they fit into a specific market, or—in other words—their strategy (White & Eccles, 1987). By linking the notion of cognitive strategic group to that of perceived network position, in the next section it is argued that strategic groups could be seen as a classification device that companies use to express, order, and act on their judgment of strategic similarity.

Cognitive Strategic Groups

How do decision makers in organizations compare competitors and use their judgment of strategic similarities and differences to define their position in an industry, organizational community, or interorganizational field?

Recent attempts to address these questions share an interest in the role of social cognition, specifically, in how individuals and groups within organizations come to form and share a mental representation of the structure of their competitive world (Porac et al., 1995). In this chapter it is proposed that the notion of strategic group could be usefully seen as a classification device used by organizations to classify rivals, namely, to reduce the information processing costs and requirements imposed by complex competitive environments. To be useful in this context, the notion of strategic group ought to be revisited in the light of the cognitive elements underlying any type of classification process (Barney & Hoskisson, 1990). Significant steps have already been taken in this direction (Porac, Meindl, & Stubbart, 1996).

According to Porac, Thomas, and Baden-Fuller (1989), strategic decisions are made in a context of many shared beliefs regarding how and with whom to engage in transactions in the market. Along a similar line, Reger and Huff (1993) tried to identify directly the models used by managers to evaluate similarities and differences between competitors. The cognitive process of categorizing events, objects, and individuals is consistent with the idea of a competitive environment partitioned into, or reduced, to a number of distinct and clearly identifiable groups. However, a cognitive interpretation of the strategic group concept should attempt to go beyond the general tendency to classify and compare competitors on the basis of selected organization-level attributes (Porac & Rosa, 1996). Rather, attention should focus on the heterogeneity of mental representations that a given competitive situation can sustain and on the extent to which conventionally defined (i.e., attribute-based) strategic groups actually bound—and are represented in—the mental models of participants in a competitive arena.

As recently suggested by a number of authors (Bogner & Thomas, 1993; Ketchen, Thomas, & Snow, 1993; Lant & Baum, 1995; Porac & Thomas, 1990; Reger & Huff, 1993; Tang & Thomas, 1992), it is precisely the homogeneity of mental models that is responsible for the reinforcement of organizational similarities, competitive behavior, and responses to environmental changes. Homogeneity of interpretations and beliefs may also induce the inability to respond to actual threats, and—in some case—even to identify potential threats. For example, Reger and Huff (1993) showed that banking industry analysts in the Chicago area perceive competitors in a way that produces very similar and regular groups and that this may create problems for planning and implementing programs of organizational change. Using similar arguments, Abramson and Fombrun (1994) suggested that market insiders rarely are able to change the collective mind-set of an industry. In their study of perceived competitive relations among hotels in Manhattan, Lant and Baum (1995) explored the idea that cognition may be an important source of isomorphism and other institutional pressures on competing firms. Lant and Baum reported evidence of increasing homogeneity and structural isomorphism among members of what Porac, et al. (1989) called *cognitive communities*, namely, a set of companies characterized by shared beliefs about the marketplace.

In this chapter, the problem of heterogeneity in mental models is addressed directly by exploring the extent to which individual judgments of strategic similarity map onto jointly occupied network positions. Block modeling techniques are used to reduce the initial network of similarity ties to a higher level representation of how discrete groups of structurally equivalent producers are related, namely, of their role set (White, Boorman & Breiger, 1976). Building on Krackhardt's (1987a) idea of cognitive social structure, the chapter examines how individual companies perceive the competitive similarities among rival companies and assesses the accuracy of individual perceptions by comparing perceived and actual pattern of strategic similarity. Finally, individual perceptions of similarity are aggregated into a two-dimensional array—called *consensus structure*—that contains information on how many times each dyad has been recognized as similar by all other organizations in the sample. This matrix is analyzed to assess the difference between the actual structure of competition and its collective reconstruction.

DATA AND METHODS

Research Design

The data for this study was collected in 1995 through telephone interviews and questionnaires administered to senior executives in 22 of the major Italian companies involved in the production and commercialization of plants for water treatment. Out of the original 22 companies selected for the study, only 18 returned usable questionnaires.

The questionnaire was designed to elicit both direct similarity judgments as well as indirect—or cognitive—information on similarities among third parties. The question asked was similar to that asked by Lant and Baum (1995) to 43 Manhattan hotel managers who agreed to participate in their cognitive mapping exercise. Lant and Baum (1995) asked managers to indicate relevant competitors whereas our respondents were asked to express a judgment of strategic similarity. Despite the slightly different wording, both data generation schemes are designed to put respondents in a situation in which they are left free to integrate the ambiguous definition of *competitor* and *competition* with their own working definitions. In other words, both studies are based on a realist—rather than nominalist—approach to the collection of relational data (Laumann, Marsden, & Prensky, 1982). The two studies pursue similar learning objectives in that they both attempt to provide a plausible link between macrosocial categories (e.g., strategic groups and markets) and the microrelational cognitive activities. In spite of similarities in the design of the data generating scheme, the current work differs significantly from Lant and Baum's (1995) in terms of analytical strategies. This study asked managers to reflect on strategic similarity among companies in the business under the assumption that similarity judgments have an important role in strategy formulation, particularly when markets are viewed as emerging from a system of equivalencies and differences among competitors (Leifer, 1985; White, 1981; White & Eccles, 1987). Farjoun & Lai (1997) also claimed that similarity is an important organizing principle that individuals use to classify objects, form concepts, and make generalizations. According to Farjoun and Lai (1997), the notion of strategic group hinges on individual similarity judgment.

Direct similarity data were collected by submitting to each respondent a (closed) list of producers of water treatment plants, and by posing the following question: "Among the companies listed below, which do you consider similar to your own in terms of fundamental strategic and organizational dimensions?"

This first part of the questionnaire produced a direct similarity matrix (A) in which the generic cell (a_{ij}) is 1 if company i identified company j as similar, and 0 otherwise. As illustrated by Table 12.1, the direct similarity matrix is square, binary, and nonsymmetric.

Figure 12.1 contains a graphical representation of the direct similarity judgments expressed by each individual company in the sample. The directional structure of the graph clearly highlights the presence of asymmetries. For example, company 13 identifies companies 10 and 15 as the only two companies similar to itself, but only 10 shares this similarity judgment, and reciprocates the similarity tie.

The second part of the questionnaire was designed to elicit information on perceived relations. Based on the notion of cognitive social structure (Krackhardt, 1987a), each respondent was once again presented a list of companies and asked the following question: "Among the companies listed below, which do you think company X would consider similar to itself in terms of fundamental strategic and organizational dimensions?"

This question was repeated for all 18 companies in the sample. The result of this design was a three-dimensional array of size 18 X 18 X 18 (A_{ijk}) where k is the perceiver of the relationship from i to j. Thus the kth slice of this three-dimensional array contains information on actor k's cognitive representation of strategic similarities among its competitors included in the sample.

Finally data on direct and indirect similarities is supplemented with information on more conventional organizational attributes such as age, size (in terms of number of employees and sales amount), form of ownership, origins, and others. To explore differences in observable strategic

TABLE 12.1
Direct Similarity Matrix

Firm		1	2	3	4	5	6	7	8	9	10	11	12	13	14	15	16	17	18
Accadueo	1	0	0	0	1	0	0	0	0	0	0	0	0	0	0	0	0	1	0
Acquenymco	2	0	0	0	0	0	0	0	0	0	0	0	0	0	0	0	0	0	0
Daneco	3	0	0	0	0	0	0	0	1	0	0	0	0	0	0	1	1	0	0
Depuracque	4	0	0	0	0	0	0	0	0	0	0	0	0	0	0	0	0	0	0
Ecomacchine	5	0	0	0	0	0	1	0	0	0	0	0	0	0	1	0	0	1	0
Ecotecnica	6	0	0	0	0	0	0	1	0	0	0	0	0	0	0	0	0	1	0
Elcar	7	0	0	1	0	0	1	0	1	1	1	1	0	0	0	0	0	1	1
Forni	8	0	0	1	0	0	1	1	0	0	0	1	0	1	0	0	0	0	1
Idreco	9	0	0	0	0	0	0	0	0	0	0	0	0	0	0	0	0	0	0
Idro Depurazione	10	0	0	0	0	0	0	0	0	1	0	0	0	1	0	0	0	0	1
Ionics Italba	11	0	0	1	0	0	0	1	0	1	1	0	0	0	0	0	0	1	0
Officina Cami	12	1	0	1	0	0	1	0	0	0	0	0	0	0	0	0	0	0	0
Pircher	13	0	0	0	0	0	0	0	0	0	1	1	0	0	0	1	1	0	0
Polytec	14	0	0	1	0	1	1	1	1	0	1	1	0	0	0	1	0	1	1
Ravagnan	15	0	0	0	0	0	0	0	0	0	0	1	0	0	0	0	1	0	0
Sernagiotto	16	0	0	0	0	1	0	0	0	0	0	0	0	0	0	1	0	0	0
Sida	17	0	0	0	1	0	0	0	0	1	1	1	0	0	0	1	0	0	0
Smogless	18	0	0	0	0	0	1	1	1	0	0	0	0	0	0	0	0	1	0

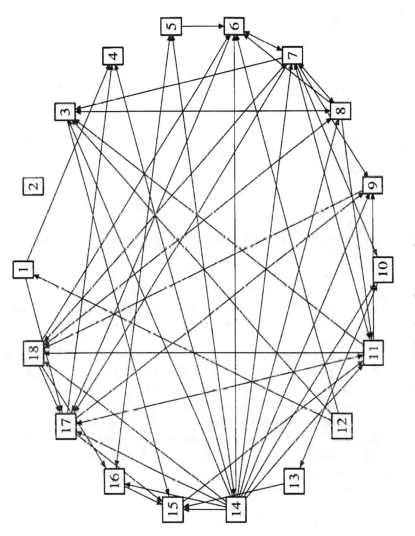

FIG. 12 1 Direct similarity matrix.

behavior, additional information was collected on the degree of diversification and the use of agreements, alliances, and acquisitions as a way of interacting with other companies in the industry.

Italian Producers of Plants for Water Treatment

The empirical part of this study is based on information about the main Italian firms involved in the design, production, and commercialization of plants for water treatment for public and industrial uses and applications. In this chapter, discussion is restricted to the type of companies that operate in this industry and their generic approach to competition. A comprehensive overview of the industry can be found in Boari (1994).

Plants for the treatment of wastewater are designed to deal with pollutants of different nature: biological, physical, chemical, or different combinations of them. Plants for biological processes of water purification are designed to reproduce and accelerate natural processes. The adoption of biological processes is quite common for the purification of public wastewater where the pollution has organic nature. In this case, the aerobic treatment allow bacteria to decompose organic substances thanks to the presence of oxygen. For industrial wastewater, chemical and physical treatment processes are more commonly adopted. Particular substances allow the coagulation of particles in suspension favoring their decantation. Reverse osmosis allows companies to recuperate different elements such as highly polluting metal. These problems are particularly serious for tannery, chemical, pharmaceutical, textile, and related industries. The construction of these plants requires chemical, physical, and biological competencies and a high level of mechanical and civil engineering capabilities.

Since 1976, pollution levels of urban and industrial wastewater have been subjected to comprehensive environmental regulation and control. Approximately 82% of the water treatment plants producers are localized in northern Italy, a geographical concentration mostly due to the higher rate of industrialization and, consequently, to a strong demand for industrial wastewater treatment plants. However, the growth of companies in this business has been driven mostly by investments of local authorities and their consortia in standardized plants for water treatment. Companies large enough to comply with the Byzantine rules established by the Italian public administration law and solvent enough to absorb the financial costs imposed by the unresponsive bureaucratic regime that still characterizes many sectors of the centrally controlled Italian economy have traditionally enjoyed a competitive advantage vis-à-vis smaller and more financially fragile companies. Public investments throughout the 1980s supported the activities of the largest firms in the industry, which in turn acquired resources to develop more sophisticated and creative lobbying strategies. Demand coming from municipal and regional administrations favored firms such as Sernagiotto (ID number 16 in this sample) or Smogless (ID number 18 in this sample), namely, firms with a long history of presence in the business and with a strong reputation. The visibility of these companies is due both to their success in securing governments contracts for the construction of huge public plants as well as their ability to cooperate with their competitors in the context of large projects.

In a sense, the historical development of the water treatment plants field as a recognized and legitimate institutional sector of the economy provides the perfect illustration for Meyer and Rowan's (1977) assertion that: "Organizations that incorporate societally legitimated rationalized elements in their formal structures maximize their legitimacy and increase their resources and survival capabilities" (p. 352). The institutional conditions out of which the water treatment industry emerged in Italy were particularly conductive to the development of bureaucratic organizations designed to incorporate institutional values and conform to rules that are interpreted and promoted as consistent with these values (Meyer, Scott, & Deal, 1981).

Private industrial demand is more differentiated—due to the wide range of pollutants that industrial customers produce—and more dependent on national environmental legislation. These characteristics of the private sector allow for the presence of more entrepreneurial firms with a broader range of organizational and strategic profiles. Daneco (ID number 3 in the sample), Depuracque (ID number 4), Ravagnan (ID number 15), and e Sida (ID number 17) are all firms whose market image and reputation are strongly linked to the competencies of the owner-manager-founder. For these companies, reputation toward buyers depends more on the personal competencies and skills of the entrepreneur than on the existence of legally mandated organizational structures and routines. A third group of firms active in the industry includes a rather large number of young and small firms such as Polytec (ID number 14), Pircher (ID number 13), Idrodepurazione (ID number 10), and Idreco (ID number 9). These firms are typically characterized as niche players and cater to the specific needs of smaller customers. Often, these companies collaborate with larger and more established competitors and with firms specialized on the design of plants for water treatment. The size distribution of companies in the sample is reported in Table 12.2.

TABLE 12.2

Size Distribution of Sample Units

Sales (billion)	1 to 5	6 to 10	11 to 25	26 to 50	50 to 100	101 to 500
Firm ID	12	1, 5, 10, 13, 14, 17	2, 4, 7	3, 6, 11, 15, 16	9, 18	8

Methods

The data collected provide information about direct and indirect perceptions of strategic similarity among producers. The analytical strategy tries to take advantage, as much as possible, of the relational structure of the data. The empirical section of the chapter, starts by analyzing simple locational properties of individual nodes in the direct similarity matrix. Individual degree centrality scores and network centralization indexes are reported to gain a first qualitative understanding of the organizational structure of competition as perceived by the companies in the sample.

Convervence of iterated correlations (CONCOR)—a widely used blockmodeling algorithm—is used to partition the direct similarity matrix into sets of structurally equivalent companies (Anderson & Jay, 1985; Breiger, Boorman, & Arabie, 1975; Breiger & Ennis, 1979; Gerlach, 1992; Knoke & Rogers, 1979; Lomi, 1997; White, et al.,1976). The CONCOR algorithm is based on the observation that after repeated calculation of the correlation coefficient between rows and columns of a matrix, the elements of the matrix will converge to $+1$ or -1. This property of iterated correlation is then used to partition the original matrix into two subsets such that the correlations between items assigned to the same subset (or block) are equal to $+1$, and the correlations between items assigned to different blocks are equal to -1 (Wasserman & Faust, 1994). Because correlation is one of the standard measures of structural equivalence used in social network analysis, companies assigned to the same block are declared structural equivalent. In the specific case under discussion, two companies are structurally equivalent if they see themselves as competing with similar other companies in the sample, namely, if they have similar competitive profiles. It is believed that this analytical construct accurately captures important aspects of the theoretical notion of cognitive strategic group related to the similarity of individual mental representations of competitive ties. If companies represent their competitive environment as partitioned into discrete and disjoint groups, or clusters, then the reduced blockmodel obtained by partitioning the original matrix of direct similarity judgments should be reflexive. To identify the actual bonds (i.e., the nonzero elements in the blockmodel) among structurally equivalent sets of companies the mean density value of the direct similarity matrix is used as cut-off point (White, et al., 1976). This is sometime referred to as the *density criterion for blockmodel fit* (Wasserman & Faust, 1994).

The second part of the analysis starts by exploring how individual perceptions of strategic similarity map onto the actual structure of similarity as expressed directly by each individual actor. This is done by computing the correlation coefficient between each individual slice of the cognitive social structure (A_{ijk}) and the direct similarity matrix (A). The quadratic assignment procedure (QAP) is used to estimate a significance value to the estimated correlation coefficients (Krackhardt, 1987b). Then, all individual perceptions of similarity are aggregated into a single two-dimensional array, called *consensus matrix* (C). The consensus matrix is a reduction of the cognitive social structure where the strategic similarity between firm i and firm j is the result of the vector of perceptions expressed on their relation by all other actors of the network (Krackhardt, 1987a). In this case, the generic element of the consensus matrix is $c_{ij} = \sum (c_{ij1}, c_{ij2}, c_{ij3}, \ldots c_{ij18})$. As before, CONCOR was used to explore the internal structure of the consensus matrix and to evaluate macrolevel representations of the system emerging from the aggregation individual similarity judgments.

RESULTS

On average, each company identified 3 other companies as direct competitors, where competitors are defined in terms of similarity judgments expressed by respondents. Whereas it is possible to think of ways in which the meaning of *similarity* and *competition* might differ, empirical evidence is available that indicates how managers perceive similar others as members of their competitive set (Porac & Thomas, 1990) and how similar organizations compete more intensely (Baum & Mezias, 1992). Empirical evidence is also available that supports the dual statement, specifically, that companies classified as members of the same competitive set are, in general, more similar (Fombrun & Zajac, 1989; Lant & Baum, 1995).

Even if one company identified 13 other companies, 55% of the respondents indicated less than 3 firms as direct competitors and 11% indicated none. Table 12.3 reports the normalized degree scores calculated for every organization in the sample. Because the direct similarity judgments are

TABLE 12.3

Direct Similarity Matrix: Normalized Centrality Scores

	Centrality	
Firm ID	Out-degree	In-degree
1	11.76	5.88
2	0.00	0.00
3	11.76	29.41
4	0.00	17.65
5	17.65	11.76
6	11.76	35.29
7	47.06	29.41
8	29.41	23.53
9	5.88	23.53
10	5.88	17.65
11	29.41	29.41
12	17.65	0.00
13	11.76	5.88
14	76.47	5.88
15	5.88	29.41
16	11.76	17.65
17	23.53	35.29
18	29.41	29.41
Centralization	64.30%	18%

nonsymmetric (i.e., the fact that i claims to be strategically similar to j does not imply, in general, that j considers itself similar to i), both the in-degree as well as the out-degree centrality scores are reported.

The normalized in-degree and out-degree centrality scores are obtained by dividing the out-degree or in-degree of each actor by the maximum possible degree (17 in this case). The figures reported in the in-degree centrality column show that 5 firms have a score of 30 or greater, and the network appears as more concentrated when only the similarity ties sent (out-degree centrality) are considered. Apparently, organizations tend to judge themselves as similar only to a restricted number of competitors. In fact, organizations are typically judged by competitors as similar to a larger numbers of other organizations. Companies 7 and 14 do not conform to this conclusion. Firm 14 indicated 13 other organizations as similar, but it was indicated as similar only by another organization.

The application of CONCOR to the direct similarity matrix yielded the density table and image matrix reported in Table 12.4 and 12.5, respectively. The resulting blockmodel is characterized by the presence of two arcs: one reflexive (2 > 2) and one in (1 > 2). All ties from both blocks (Groups 1 and 2) are directed to one block (Group 2). Thus, at this level of aggregation, no evidence is found for the existence of stable and well-defined strategic groups—a result also found to hold at higher levels of refinement of the blockmodel (not reported). According to this pattern, Group 2 is formed by companies who perceive themselves as strategically similar and that at the same time perceive companies in Group 1 as different. Companies in Group 1 perceive themselves as not similar but claim to be similar to companies in Group 2. This situation combines aspects of cohesion (because of the similarity ties internal to Group 2) and deference (because companies in Group 1, in a way, would like to be similar to companies in Group 2, but companies in Group 2 clearly claim they are not).

TABLE 12.4

Direct Similarity Matrix: Density Table

Direct Similarity Matrix's Density = 0.19

Direct Similarity Matrix's sd = 0.39

	Group 1	Group 2
Group 1	0.13	0.29
Group 2	0.06	0.27

TABLE 12.5

Direct Similarity Matrix: Image Matrix

	Group 1	Group 2
Group 1	0	1
Group 2	0	1

Blockmodels are statements (or hypotheses) about the structure of relations in a network. These statements typically refer to network positions rather than individual units. Because the number of network positions in an exploratory blockmodel is rather arbitrary, the adequacy of a specific network reduction can be assessed in terms of attributes of the actors occupying the positions (Arabie, 1984; Breiger, 1976). If it is possible to characterize the positions in terms of systematic differences among their members, then there would be some external validation of the specific Block modeling solution found (Wasserman & Faust, 1994).

The first three attributes reported in Table 12.6 are helpful to understand the differences between the two groups of structurally equivalent companies identified. On average, companies in Group 2 are 10 years older and are two times bigger (in terms of number of employees) than companies in Group 1. Also, firms in Group 2 tend to fall within sale class number 7 (sales between 26 and 50 billion lire), whereas firms of Group 1 fall on average into sales class 5 (sales between 6 and 10 billion lire). In the light of these results, it easy to understand the attempt of companies in Group 1 to see themselves as similar to the (larger and more powerful) companies in Group 2 while denying internal cohesion. The reflexive tie that characterizes Group 2 seems coherent with the results of other studies about the effects of organizational size on rivalry (Porac et al., 1995). Large firms tend to be perceived as competitors both by other large firms as well as by smaller firms. Firms tend to recognize more similarities with larger firms, probably because of their visibility. A higher incidence of companies that are units of larger corporate groups and a significantly more frequent use of acquisitions as a strategy for growth also may contribute to the higher visibility of companies in Group 2.

Table 12.7 reports centralization measures for each individual slice of the overall CSS. The out- and in-degree centralization scores tell the tendency of individual companies to reconstruct their perceived networks as dominated by a restricted number of alters. If only relations sent are considered, the score would be 100 if only one company was responsible for all the similarity judgment in the sample. The resulting star-like structure would have this one company claiming to be similar to all the others, and n - 1 companies perceiving themselves as unique. Similarly, a score of 100 in the in-degree column would imply that the corresponding company perceives a situation whereby all companies in the sample claim to be similar to the same one company.

According to the figures reported in the out-degree centralization column of Table 12.7, Firms 2, 6, 7, and 14 see a network in which few firms find many similarities with other firms. Organizations 3, 4, and 15 live in a less

TABLE 12.6

Direct Similarity Matrix. Structural Equivalent Groups: Selected Attributes

		Group 1	Group 2	Sample
Firm ID		1, 2, 5, 12, 13, 14, 16	3, 4, 6, 7, 8, 9, 10, 11, 15, 17, 18	
Attributes		Mean (SD)	Mean SD	Mean (SD)
1	Age	26.14	35.64	31.94
		(11.43)	(16.38)	(15.31)
2	Sales	5.28	6.81	6.22
		(0.95)	(1.25)	(1.35)
3	Employees	36.86	71.45	58.00
		(50.51)	(55.92)	(55.15)
4	Change of form	0.57	0.54	0.55
		(0.53)	(0.52)	(0.51)
5	Group membership	0.43	0.73	0.61
		(0.53)	(0.47)	(0.50)
6	Diversification	0.71	0.64	0.67
		(0.49)	(0.50)	(0.48)
7	Origins	0.43	0.45	0.44
		(0.53)	(0.52)	(0.51)
8	Agreements	0.43	0.54	0.50
		(0.53)	(0.52)	(0.50)
9	Ownership	0.57	0.64	0.61
		(0.53)	(0.50)	(0.5)
10	Acquisitions	0.11	0.64	0.44
		(0.38)	(0.50)	(0.51)

Note.
1. Age (years)
2. Sales (classes)
3. Employees (number)
4. Change of form (1 = change; 0 = otherwise)
5. Group membership (1 = part of larger group; 0 = independent)
6. Diversification (1 = diversification; 0 = otherwise)
7. Origins (1 = same sector; 0 = otherwise)
8. Agreements (1 = have been involved in agreements; 0 = otherwise)
9. Ownership (1 = family ownership; 0 = otherwise)
10. Acquisitions (1 = have been involved in acquisitions; 0 = otherwise)

TABLE 12.7

Individual Slices of the Cognitive Social Structure: Centralization Scores

| Firm ID | Centralization | |
	Out-Degree	In-Degree
1	13.971	40.441
2	40.074	26.838
3	11.765	5.147
4	11.029	17.647
5	15.441	15.441
6	66.176	6.618
7	50.00	3.676
8	21.691	21.691
9	20.956	14.338
10	23.529	23.529
11	20.956	20.956
12	17.279	17.279
13	19.118	19.118
14	72.426	19.485
15	6.250	6.250
16	18.750	25.368
17	17.279	30.515
18	27.574	34.191

differentiated competitive world, one in which organizations are all relatively similar to each other.

How do these local differences in perceptions of strategic similarity map onto the actual structure of the network? In other words, how accurately can individual producers reconstruct their own role (or network position) in the industry? To address these questions, the correlation coefficient between the direct similarity matrix and the individual slices in the aggregate CSS is computed. They then relied on permutation methods to establish a confidence interval around the estimates of the correlation coefficients. As Fig. 12.2 illustrates, the accuracy of individual cognitive reconstruction of strategic similarity varies substantially across companies.

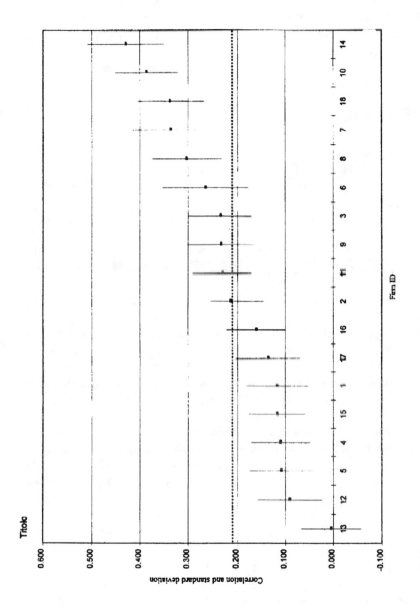

Titolo

FIG. 12.2 Correlation between direct similarity matrix and individual's ices of cognitive social structure (vertical bars are estimated standard errors after 1,000 permutations). Dotted horizontal line is mean value.

Whereas the average correlation coefficient is about 0.20, the estimated values range from 0.005 (company number 13) to 0.43 (company number 14). Note that Company 14 was also the most central in the direct similarity matrix in terms of out-degrees. Figs. 12.3a through 12.3d illustrate further the dramatic differences in perceived strategic similarity among companies.

The final part of the analysis explores the macrostructure of the competition emerging from the aggregation of all local perceptions of strategic similarity. Table 12.8 reports the consensus matrix, the generic cell of which shows how many times the row and column companies were considered similar by the other organizations. For example, Company 3 and Company 8 were judged to be similar 10 times. Company 10 and Company 1 were never judged to be similar. The main diagonal contains only null values. Note once again the asymmetry of this matrix: whereas Company 1 was considered similar to Company 9 one time, Company 9 was never considered similar to Company 1. The mean cell value of the consensus matrix is 1.43 (sd = 1.79).

This value was used to construct the image matrix from the density table obtained by applying CONCOR to the consensus matrix. The two-split reduction produced the pattern reported in Tables 12.9 and 12.10.

The values of the cells on the main diagonal of the density table (Table 12.9) are always greater than the off diagonal values in the corresponding rows. With the exception of element 1, 3, no off diagonal value is greater than the mean cell value of the consensus matrix. These two results imply a rather strong form of reflexivity in the image matrix (Table 12.10). Together, these results suggest that the blockmodel representation of the consensus matrix is consistent with a strategic group-based interpretation of competition among the companies in the sample. Interestingly enough, the analysis of the actual data (i.e., of the direct similarity judgment data) did not reveal the presence of reflexivity and was more consistent with a deferential structure.

As before, it is instructive to analyze how the four blocks of structurally equivalent companies differ in terms of their attributes. As Table 12.11 illustrates, Blocks 1 and 3 contain the largest and older firms in the sample, whereas the two companies in Block 4 are young and entrepreneurial specialist firms still controlled by the founders, which might explain their unwillingness to change form or be acquired by larger industrial groups.

Companies in Block 1 follow the diversification strategy of their parent companies. Units in Block 3, are typically companies with a strong orientation toward growth and are part of larger industrial groups. These companies seem to rely systematically on acquisition as their preferred growth strategy and make recurrent use of agreements with competitors to build

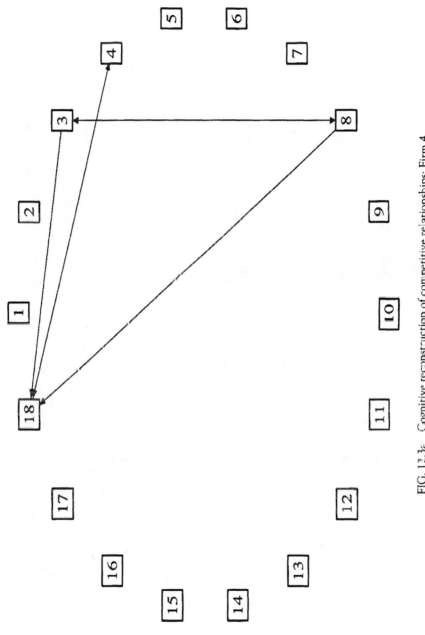

FIG. 12.3a Cognitive reconstruction of competitive relationships: Firm 4.

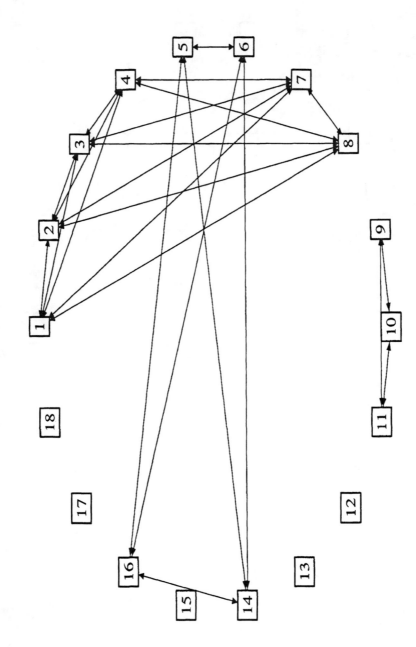

FIG. 12.3b   Cognitive reconstruction of competitive relationships: Firm 5.

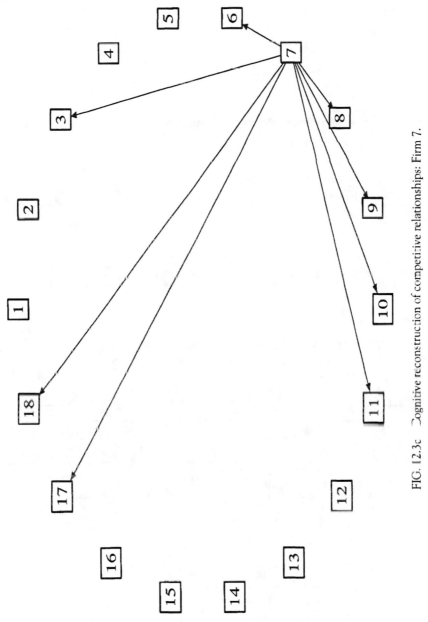

FIG. 12.3c Cognitive reconstruction of competitive relationships: Firm 7.

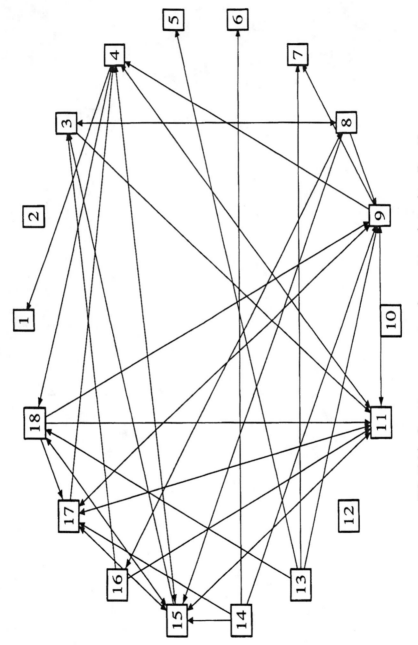

FIG. 12.3d   Cognitive reconstruction of competitive relationships: Firm 17.

TABLE 12.8

Aggregate Consensus Matrix

Firm		1	2	3	4	5	6	7	8	9	10	11	12	13	14	15	16	17	18
Accadueo	1	0	2	3	2	0	2	2	2	1	0	1	2	1	0	0	0	1	1
Acquenymco	2	1	0	1	2	0	0	1	1	0	0	0	0	0	0	1	0	1	1
Daneco	3	2	1	0	1	0	4	2	10	2	0	2	0	0	0	3	2	1	4
Depuracque	4	3	1	2	0	0	1	1	2	0	1	1	0	0	0	3	0	2	3
Ecomacchine	5	0	0	1	0	0	3	0	0	0	1	0	2	0	4	2	4	1	0
Ecotecnica	6	2	0	0	1	3	0	2	5	1	2	2	1	0	1	0	2	3	5
Elcar	7	2	1	5	2	0	5	0	7	6	2	4	0	0	0	1	2	3	7
Forni	8	1	1	9	1	0	1	5	0	3	0	2	0	0	0	1	2	1	9
Idreco	9	0	0	0	2	0	0	4	2	0	2	7	0	0	1	0	1	1	4
Idro Depurazione	10	0	0	1	1	0	1	0	0	2	0	1	0	2	0	1	0	1	0
Ionics Italba	11	0	0	2	1	1	1	4	3	8	1	0	0	0	1	3	1	5	4
Officina Cami	12	1	0	1	1	1	1	0	0	0	1	0	0	0	0	0	0	0	0
Pircher	13	0	0	0	0	1	0	1	0	1	2	0	0	0	1	3	0	1	1
Polytec	14	0	0	1	0	3	3	1	1	3	1	2	0	1	0	3	4	2	1
Ravagnan	15	0	0	2	2	0	0	0	0	0	1	2	0	3	0	0	0	2	2
Sernagiotto	16	0	0	3	0	5	1	2	4	0	0	2	0	0	3	2	0	1	3
Sida	17	1	0	3	4	0	5	4	2	1	2	3	0	0	0	4	1	0	2
Smogless	18	0	1	5	2	0	2	5	7	3	0	3	0	0	0	1	3	3	0

TABLE 12.9

Aggregate Consensus Matrix: Density Table (two split)

Consensus Matrix's Density = 1.43				
Consensus matrix's Standard Deviation = 1.79				
	Group 1	Group 2	Group 3	Group 4
Group 1	2.40	0.30	1.80	0.20
Group 2	0.70	2.17	1.21	0.50
Group 3	1.83	0.64	2.98	0.93
Group 4	0.20	0.25	0.93	2.00

TABLE 12.10

Aggregate Consensus Matrix: Image Matrix (two split)

	Group 1	Group 2	Group 3	Group 4
Group 1	1	0	1	0
Group 2	0	1	0	0
Group 3	1	0	1	0
Group 4	0	0	0	1

large water treatment plants. Finally, companies in block 2 are small and diversified and offer a wide range of products and services. Block 2 contains both independent organizations as well as subsidiaries companies of larger corporate groups.

DISCUSSION AND CONCLUSIONS

This chapter started by arguing that alternative ways of thinking about the organizational structure of markets seem to make surprisingly similar assumptions about how competitors establish—and contribute to the creation of—frames of comparability in the context of which competitive strategies can be crafted and understood.

According to the view of markets as concrete role structures, markets are "social formations which decouple sellers from buyers exactly by turning the

TABLE 12.11

Aggregate Consensus Matrix Structural Equivalent Groups: Selected Attributes

		Group 1:	Group 2:	Group 3:	Group 4:	Sample:
	Firms	1, 2, 3, 4, 8	5, 12, 14, 16	6, 7, 9, 11, 15, 17, 18	10, 13	
	Attributes	Mean (SD)	Mean SD	Mean (SD)	Mean (SD)	Mean (SD)
1	Age	32.40	30.00	34.71	25.00	31.94
		(25.54)	(14.49)	(9.55)	(5.66)	(15.31)
2	Sales	6.60	5.25	6.86	5.00	6.22
		(1.52)	(1.26)	(1.07)	(0)	(1.35)
3	Employees	65.00	51.75	66.71	22.50	58.00
		(77.32)	(66.29)	(43.09)	(3.54)	(55.15)
4	Change of form	0.40	0.75	0.71	0	0.55
		(0.55)	(0.50)	(0.49)	(0)	(0.51)
5	Group membership	0.80	0.50	0.71	0	0.61
		(0.45)	(0.58)	(0.49)	(0)	(0.50)
6	Diversification	0.60	1.00	0.71	0	0.67
		(0.55)	(0)	(0.49)	(0)	(0.48)
7	Origins	0.20	0.50	0.57	0.50	0.44
		(0.45)	(0.58)	(0.53)	(0.71)	(0.51)
8	Agreements	0.40	0.50	0.57	0.50	0.50
		(0.55)	(0.58)	(0.53)	(0.71)	(0.50)
9	Ownership	0.60	0.50	0.57	1.00	0.61
		(0.55)	(0.58)	(0.53)	(0)	(0.50)
10	Acquisitions	0.20	0.25	0.71	0.50	0.44
		(0.45)	(0.50)	(0.49)	(0.71)	(0.51)

Note. 1. Age (years); 2. Sales (classes); 3. Employees (number); 4. Change of form (1 = change; 0 = otherwise); 5. Group membership (1 = part of larger group; 0 = independent); 6. Diversification (1 = diversification; 0 = otherwise); 7. Origins (1 = same sector; 0 = otherwise); 8. Agreements (1 = have been involved in agreements; 0 = otherwise); 9. Ownership (1 = family ownership; 0 = otherwise); 10. Acquisitions (1 = have been involved in acquisitions; 0 = otherwise)

particular persons into occupants of roles" (White & Eccles, 1987, p. 984). According to the view of markets as the crossroads of abstract and disembodied competitive forces, rivals monitor their environment in search of market imperfections and positional rents (Porter, 1980). In fact, both ways of thinking about the organizational structure of competition see individual companies as defining their role (or position) in the market in terms of the similarities and differences that they perceive with respect to other companies. This chapter started from this observation and explored some of the implications of the sociocognitive comparison processes that undergird observed interorganizational role structures in the context of a specific empirical example.

Perhaps the main element of innovation in the current work was the attempt to go beyond an analysis of how competitors perceive their own relative position in the market as a function of selected organizational attributes. The notion of cognitive social structure (Krackhardt, 1987a, 1990) provided the unique opportunity to map out the complex system of perceptions (both direct as well as indirect) within which competitive interaction unfolds and compare individual cognitive representations to an objective structure to assess the degree of overlap between actual and perceived patterns of strategic similarity. Following this strategy, the extent to which actual (i.e., "observed") relational structures constrain and affect individual cognitive representation of competition was cast as genuine empirical problem. In this sense, the current work speaks to one of the most central problems in the study of cognition related to how social actors understand and represent other social actors (Pattison, 1994).

In its current form, the effort to understand the cognitive social structure of strategic groups suffers from two main sets of limitations. The first set involves limitations that, in principle, could be removed or alleviated using the present data in different ways or more effectively. For example, by concentrating on structural equivalent sets of producers, no attention was paid to alternative ways of constructing groups based on cohesion. This was, in part, due to the difficulty of computing cohesion-based partitions (e.g., cliques, k-plexes, etc.) without losing information on relational asymmetries. Also, the operationalization of cognitive accuracy as the correlation between individual slices of the cognitive social structure and the direct similarity matrix is only one of many possibilities (Krackhardt, 1990). Another possibility being explored at the moment involves the analysis of individual slices of the aggregate CSS via blockmodeling algorithms or combinatorial optimization. The idea behind this analytical strategy is to move the first steps toward a sort of ecology of cognition by documenting the convergence of individual mental models to a very small number of alternative aggregate representations of strategic similarity among competitors. In the context of the present work, the full range of company-level information collected has not been exploited. A priori blocks could be computed and compared with the exploratory blocks that have been reported to understand the material basis of cognition, namely, what exactly actors take into account in the formulation of their similarity judgments. As mentioned earlier, this analysis could also be repeated at the level of individual companies. Finally, additional work is needed to arrive at a more substantively interpretable blockmodeling representation of the direct similarity matrix and the consensus matrix. In light of these various considerations, the current results should be considered as preliminary and subject to important qualifications.

The second set of limitations includes a wide range of questions that cannot be addressed in the context of the present sample and that would require a new study and a different research design. One example of this type of limitation is the lack of information on other types of relations in which companies are embedded. In the empirical context analyzed here, multiplexity is important because it is reasonable to expect that the similarity judgments expressed by individual companies are shaped in a fundamental way by other types of interactions such as cooperation, codesign, or subcontracting relations within larger public projects. A second limitation is inherent to the cross-sectional nature of the data collected, which forced the authors to narrow the focus of the analysis to structures (or stocks) rather than processes (or flows), the dynamics of which enerates, changes and dissolves the boundary around observable structures.

Despite these obvious limits, the current efforts might serve as a useful first step toward the understanding of the complex organizational structure of markets, that is, toward a representation of markets both as arenas for strategic decisions processes as well as stable sets of interlocked roles that allow producers to interpret decisions, communicate intentions, and predict competitive behavior.

ACKNOWLEDGMENTS

A prior version of this chapter was presented at the conference Managerial and Organizational Cognition: Implications for Entrepreneurship, Decision Making and Knowledge Management, New York University, New York City, May 7–9, 1998. We are grateful to the participants for their comments and to the editors for their support. Our gratitude extends to David Krackhardt for his help and advice.

REFERENCES

Abramson, E., & Fombrun, C. (1994). Macrocultures: Determinants and consequences. *Academy of Management Review, 19*, 728–756.

Anderson, J., & Jay, S. (1985). The diffusion of medical technology: Social network analysis and policy research. *Sociological Quarterly, 26*, 49–64.

Arabie, P. (1984). Validation of sociometric structure by data on individuals attributes. *Social Networks, 6*, 373–403.

Barney, J., & Hoskisson, R. (1990). Strategic groups: Untested assertions and research proposals. *Managerial and Decision Economics, 11*, 187–198.

Baum, J., & Haveman, H. (1997). Love thy neighbor? Differentiation and agglomeration in the Manhattan Hotel industry, 1898–1990. *Administrative Science Quarterly, 42*, 304–338.

Baum, J., & Mezias, S. (1992). Localized competition and organizational failure in the Manhattan Hotel industry, 1898–1990. *Administrative Science Quarterly, 37*, 580–604.

Boari, C. (1994). Ambito competitivo e gruppi strategici nel settore dell'impiantistica per il trattamento delle acque. [Competitive environment and strategic groups in the plants for water treatment industry]. *Economia e Diritto del Terziario, 2*, 595–617.

Bogner, W., & Thomas, H. (1993). The role of competitive groups in strategy formulation: A dynamic integration of two competing models. *Journal of Management Studies, 30*, 51–67.

Bothner, M., & White, H. C. (in press). Market orientation and monopoly power. In A. Lomi & E. Larsen (Eds.), *Dynamics of organizational societies: Models, theories and methods.* Cambridge, MA: MIT Press/AAAI Press.

Breiger, R. (1976). Career attributes and network structure: A blockmodel study of a biomedical research specialty. *American Sociological Review, 41*, 117–135.

Breiger, R., Boorman, S., & Arabie, P. (1975). An algorithm for clustering relational data with applications to social network analysis and comparison with multidimensional scaling. *Journal of Mathematical Psychology, 12*, 328–383.

Breiger, R., & Ennis, J. (1979). Personae and social roles: The network structure of personality types in small groups. *Social Psychology Quarterly, 42*, 262–270.

Carroll, G. (1985). Concentration and specialization: Dynamics of niche width in populations of organizations. *American Journal of Sociology, 90*, 1263–1283.

Cool, K., & Dierickx, I. (1993). Rivalry, strategic group and firm profitability. *Strategic Management Journal, 14*, 47–59.

Farjoun, M., & Lai, L. (1997). Similarity judgements in strategy formulation: Role, processes and implications. *Strategic Management Journal, 18*, 255–272.

Fombrun, C., & Zajac, E. (1989). Structural and perceptual influences on intraindustry stratification. *Academy of Management Journal, 30*, 33–50.

Gerlach, M. (1992). The Japanese corporate network: A Block modeling approach. *Administrative Science Quarterly, 37*, 105–139.

Gripsrud, G., & Gronhaug, K. (1985). Structure and strategy in grocery retailing: A sociometric approach. *Journal of Industrial Economics, 32*, 339–347.

Hannan, M., Carroll, G., Dundon, E., & Torres J. (1995). Organizational evolution in a multinational context: Entries of automobile manufacturers in Belgium, Britain, France, Germany and Italy. *American Sociological Review, 60*, 509–528.

Ketchen, D., Thomas, J., & Snow, C. (1993). Organizational configurations and performance: A comparison of theoretical approaches. *Academy of Management Journal, 36*, 1278–1313.

Knoke, D., & Rogers, D. (1979). A blockmodel analysis of interorganizational networks. *Sociology and Social Research, 64,* 28–52.

Krackhardt, D. (1987a). Cognitive social structures. *Social Networks, 9,* 109–134.

Krackhardt, D. (1987b). QAP partialling as a test of spuriousness. *Social Networks, 9,* 171–186.

Krackhardt, D. (1990). Assessing the political landscape: Structure, cognition, and power in organizations. *Administrative Science Quarterly, 35,* 342–369.

Lant, T., & Baum, J. (1995). Cognitive sources of socially constructed strategic groups: Examples from the Manhattan hotel industry. In W. Scott & S. Christensen (Eds.), *The institutional construction of organizations: International and longitudinal studies* (pp. 15–38). Thousand Oaks, CA: Sage.

Laumann, E., Marsden, P., & Prensky, D. (1982). The boundary specification problem in network analysis. In R. Burt & M. Minor (Eds.), *Applied network analysis: Structural methodology for empirical social research* (pp. 18–39). Beverly Hills, CA: Sage.

Leifer, E. (1985). Markets as mechanisms: Using a role structure. *Social Forces, 64,* 442–472.

Leifer, E., & White, H. (1987). A structural approach to markets. In M. Mizruchi & M. Schwartz (Eds.), *Intercorporate relations: The structural analysis of business* (pp. 85–108). Cambridge, England: Cambridge University Press.

Lomi, A. (1997). Market with hierarchies and the network structure of organizational communities. *Journal of Management and Governance, 1,* 49–66.

Lomi, A., & Larsen, E. (1997). A computational approach to the evolution of competitive strategy. *Journal of Mathematical Sociology, 22,* 151–176.

Meyer, J., & Rowan, B. (1977). Institutionalized organizations: Formal structure as myth and ceremony. *American Journal of Sociology, 83,* 340–363.

Meyer, J., Scott, R., & Deal, T. (1981). Institutional and technical sources of organizational structure: Explaining the structure of educational organizations. In H. Stein (Ed.), *Organization and the human services* (pp. 151–178). Template University Press.

Pattison, P. (1994). Social cognition in context: some applications of social network analysis. In S. Wasserman & J. Galaskiewicz (Eds.), *Advances in social networks analysis: Research in the social and behavioral sciences* (pp. 79–109). Thousand Oaks, CA: Sage.

Peteraf, M. (1993). Intra-industry structure and the response toward rivals. *Managerial and Decision Economics, 14,* 519–528.

Porac, J., Meindl J., & Stubbart, C. (1996). Introduction. In J. Meindl, C. Stubbart, & J. Porac (Eds.), *Cognition within and between organizations* (pp. ix–xxiii). Thousand Oaks, CA: Sage.

Porac, J., & Rosa, J. A. (1996). Rivalry, industry models, and the cognitive embeddedness of the comparable firm. In P. Shrivastava, A. Huff, & J. Dutton (Eds.) *Advances in strategic management* (pp. 363–388). Greenwich, CT: JAI.

Porac, J., & Thomas, H. (1990). Taxonomic mental models in competitor definition. *Academy of Management Review, 15,* 224–240.

Porac, J., Thomas, H., & Baden-Fuller, C. (1989). Competitive groups as cognitive communities: The case of Scottish knitwear manufacturers. *Journal of Management Studies, 26,* 397–416.

Porac, J., Thomas, H., Wilson, F., Paton D., & Kanfer, A. (1995). Rivalry and the industry model of Scottish knitwear producers. *Administrative Science Quarterly, 40,* 203–227.

Porter, M. (1980). *Competitive strategy—Techniques for analyzing industries and competitors.* New York: The Free Press.

Reger, R., & Huff, A. (1993). Strategic group: A cognitive perspective. *Strategic Management Journal, 14,* 103–124.

Tang, M. J., & Thomas, H. (1992). The concept of strategic group: Theoretical construct or analytical convenience. *Managerial and Decision Economics, 13,* 323–329.

Wasserman, S., & Faust, K. (1994). *Social network analysis.* Cambridge, England: Cambridge University Press.

White, H. (1981). Where do market come from? *American Journal of Sociology, 87*, 517–547.

White, H. (1988). Varieties of markets. In B. Wellman & S. D. Berkowitz (Eds.), *Social structures* (pp. 226–260). Cambridge, England: Cambridge University Press.

White, H., Boorman, S., & Breiger R. (1976). Social structure from multiple networks. Blockmodels of roles and positions. *American Journal of Sociology, 81*, 730–779.

White, H., & Eccles, R. (1987). *Producers' markets*. New York: Macmillan.

chapter 13

Stakeholder Analysis as Decision Support for Project Risk Management

Agi Oldfield
University of Surrey, UK

A major concern in recent years in managing projects has been the continuing problem of dealing with risk and uncertainty. Such concerns are prompted by increasingly severe financial and legal consequences of poor risk management. The continuing budget and time overruns as well as the negative impact of poor project management on corporate image are no longer tolerated by funders (sponsors) or shareholders. When examining high-profile failed projects such as the Channel Tunnel, the British Library, the Heathrow Tunnel collapse, the Channel Tunnel fire, and the Challenger project, it was evident that although sophisticated quantitative risk analysis techniques were used, these still failed to prevent colossal losses.

All these projects were subjected to the most rigorous risk assessment processes utilizing traditional well-recognized techniques, and yet, failures were not prevented. What factors were left out of the equation? Reasons for failure of the projects included issues such as poor estimation, lack of resources, ignoring relevant information, poor management practices, lack of competence, unfounded assumptions, personal agendas and short-term financial and political priorities. If such factors were included in the risk assessment, why did these fail to prompt the decision makers to address these? If not, why were these not included?

LIMITATIONS OF
QUANTITATIVE RISK ANALYSIS

In response to continuing failure to manage project risks, organizations are investing in more sophisticated and "accurate" quantitative risk management solutions. However, many of these techniques still fail to deliver the expected result as evidenced by the earlier examples. The ineffectiveness of traditional quantitative risk analysis to manage projects effectively has also been highlighted by Barnes and Wearne (1993), Collingridge (1992), and Pidgeon, Hood, Jones, Turner, and Gibson (1992), who also confirmed risk factors outside the scope of quantitative risk analysis as a contributory element to failure. It was suggested that for many projects, the major risks are qualitative in nature (Andrews & Jobling, 1992; Berkley, Humphreys, & Thomas, 1989), and this is where increased attention should be placed rather than on the quantitative aspects.

There is strong evidence to suggest that most project failures can be attributed to the impact of people involved in the process. Simon, Hillson, and Newland (1997), argued that 80% of all project risks are human related and thus qualitative, and these are rarely included in the risk assessment process. The reluctance of project managers to include qualitative elements in quantitative risk analysis may be due to the fact that many of the risks associated with people are conceptualized and classified as human resource management or *soft* issues and, as such, are assumed to be outside the scope of quantitative risk analysis (Hastings, 1993). Furthermore, such dimensions are difficult to quantify. Thus human factors tend to be ignored as risk factors. Consequently, a large element of risk is excluded from project risk management (Oldfield 1997, Oldfield & Ocock, 1994).

The interaction between people involved in projects and organizations may be viewed as a social system with multiple and often conflicting goals. Members within such systems are likely to negotiate individual goals and expectations often on a temporary basis (Stamper & Kolkman, 1991) providing another unstable element within the risk calculation. Thus, problems within this kind of system are difficult to define, as they are fuzzy in nature. These are soft systems, and the application of *hard* system methodologies such as quantitative risk analysis, are inappropriate for managing the problem (Checkland, 1981).

Emotions, another ill-defined state of existence, often override logic, and estimation of success or failure will depend largely on the current state of the project and can result in the overestimation or underestimation of intervention impact. As people have a limited capacity to mentally manage diverse information, there is also a tendency to simplify problems to reduce cognitive complexity. Whereas quantitative risk analysis is able to provide accurate estimation of probabilities for success or failure, the project manager, in the end, has to make a subjective judgment about likely outcomes of each option, and this unpredictable factor is not included in the quantitative risk analysis calculation.

The solution to more effective project risk management does not lie in the use of even more sophisticated quantitative risk analysis techniques, which focus on quantifiable risk and avoids unquantifiable risk. Moreover, most of the risks posed by people cannot be assessed using probabilistic techniques (Jobling, 1994). As the majority of project risks are attributable to people, most of the areas of uncertainty thus tend not be included in the quantitative risk analysis process. Nevertheless, managers and decision makers continue to use the same traditional risk management techniques thus repeating previous strategies and consequent risks. In most cases, project managers admit that the last project "did not go according to plan" but "this project is different."

As project management is largely the management of uncertainty and human action, risk management should center on the identification and subsequent reduction of all uncertainties and only then proceed with detailed analysis and assessment. Any problem that is ill defined or unknown represents an area of uncertainty and, consequently, risk for the manager. The available evidence concerning the link between risk and human action underlines the importance of people in the process. So, why do decision makers exclude such crucial information from systematic risk assessment?

RISK IDENTIFICATION

Quantitative risk analysis is an extremely useful tool for assessing risk, but it can only deal with risks that have been identified. There appears to be some confusion between the concept of identification and assessment. In many cases, managers and decision makers assume that if quantitative risk analysis has been carried out then most potential risks have been addressed, and they do not engage in a critical evaluation of the procedure. Although risks identified may have been assessed effectively, what about risks that have not been identified? If a key risk element concerns human factors, then why not include this in the process?

A good example of the lack of awareness of human factors within the risk assessment process involved an organization that dealt with nuclear processing and subsequent storage of nuclear waste. The project concerned the design and development of an appropriate repository for the waste, which had a potential for high risk to society over a substantial timescale. Within the initial phase of the project development at the design and conceptual phase, quantitative risk analysis focused on the failure rate of technological issues. No provision was made for conducting risk assessment on the project team or any other people involved in the process, except in terms of technology. One of the human factor issues related to serious conflict between members of the central project team resulting from misperceptions about roles and objectives of the project. The project manager felt it was his role to determine the nature of the design of the facility, whereas the designer felt that this was his role alone. The resulting conflict hampered the planned progress of the project. The key criteria for decision making relating to the risk assessment process were linked to bureaucratic budgetary issues, which overrode most other risk considerations. When the evident conflict within the team highlighted the necessity for further risk assessment, the decision to conduct further analysis was barred by the financial director (the ultimate decision maker when it involved financial decisions) as the extra cost was not included in the original budget. Therefore, the question of whose rationality is included in the quantitative risk assessment formula may be well worth considering.

This was clearly a structural issue, which not only determined the contents of the quantitative risk analysis but also set a very rigid framework for critical evaluation of the limited risks assessed. The roles and responsibilities of the project team were not defined clearly, neither was the competence of team members to undertake specific tasks determined. Risk associated with people in the process were assumed to be managed through general management techniques and were not considered to pose a risk in the true sense of the word.

Whereas the finance director's main objective was managing within set budget, the project team's was to deliver a safe and effective system. The project was delayed and costs increased substantially, nevertheless, senior management was confident that by conducting quantitative risk analysis relating to technological and financial issues that they had identified and assessed all relevant risks.

Which is the way forward to more effective risk management? It is clear that people are central to the process; therefore, using a framework that approaches the problem from the perspectives of people within the process may be more appropriate in surfacing information concerning the potential for risk.

The influence of people or groups on project outcomes may be usefully explored in terms of the dynamics they bring to the process. Such dynamics concern not only psychological characteristics but also the perceived benefits to such groups or individuals of the outcomes or aspects of the process of the project. People or groups with a vested interest in the project process or its outcomes and who can bring influence on the project can be considered as *stakeholders*, rather that they have a *stake* in the project. When assessing the risks individuals pose to project or organizational outcomes, only those stakeholders who can bring influence to the project need be considered.

Stakeholders' decision making and subsequent behavior may be influenced and shaped not only by the potential gain or benefit but also by their perspectives and perceptions. Individual perspectives can be regarded as *operational lenses* through which people view the project and encourages them to focus on specific elements, often at the expense of other relevant information. These lenses often prevent individuals to see and consider other perspectives as the lenses tend to focus only on their individual issues, thus overlooking other risk factors.

How individuals perceive the project objectives, others? perspectives, the potential for risk, as well a s the level of control they are likely to have over the process will determine their responses. These factors form the basis of key information for decision making.

THE IMPORTANCE OF STAKEHOLDERS

A more robust risk management approach proposed, which takes as its focus the impact of human factors within project risk management, is through the analysis of stakeholders within the process. My definition of a *stakeholder* is "any individual or groups with a vested interest in the project process or its outcomes, alternately; they are people who can bring influence to the project and its objectives."

In taking a stakeholder perspective to risk management, it is necessary to explore why the vested interest of an individual or group may be a key indicator of their likely decision-making processes, which ultimately shape their responses to the process and potential risk. An explanation for trying to understand the importance of the vested interests of stakeholders may lie in decision theory, which states that in making decisions, people choose between alternatives; rather, they select preferences between options. The individual's expected utility or *subjective expected utility* (Savage, 1954) must influence this selection process. At the core of this approach is the way individuals as decision makers maximize their benefits, and thus, the choice is considered to reflect their vested interests or stake within the process.

However, there is a tendency for people to make assumptions about others' potential benefits or utilities. It may be worthwhile to refocus on the subjective element of potential benefits. There is strong evidence to support the argument that people make assumptions about what the other person's goals, objectives, or potential gains are likely to be (Humphreys, Oldfield, & Allan, 1987). Consequently, such assumptions are incorporated into the risk assessment formula, rather than exploring the real underlying expected benefits, which are often masked by stakeholders. Many of the expected benefits may not appear to be rational to others within the project team were they to be brought into the open forum. Therefore, an approach that is likely to surface more accurately such subjective goals and benefits may be more appropriate. Such goals and expected utilities may be better identified through such methods as cognitive mapping (Eden, Jones, & Sims, 1979). Thus, the mental structures or cognitive maps (Eden et al., 1979) with which each person or group operates is an indication of their likely perspectives and perceptions, or rather, their subjective small worlds (Savage, 1954). To determine which choices they are likely to make, it is necessary to surface their underlying perspectives and perceptions and to set these within relevant risk research to help explain why people are likely to behave the way they do.

Analysis of stakeholders' subjective small worlds needs to be carried out on a number of levels of abstraction: firstly at the organizational level to identify structural and cultural influences on their knowledge management process, secondly, at group level to determine the impact of group dynamics on choice between alternatives, finally, at the individual level to determine the individual knowledge structures, perceptions, and perspectives people use to make sense of the world.

To conduct such analysis, it is essential to first identify who are the stakeholders in the process. Managers often fail to identify accurately the range of possible stakeholders and it is only when they are encouraged to take a more systematic analysis of the project plan and outcomes that they might consider stakeholders previously outside their range of exploration. Hence, a first and essential step in the process is the generation of the pool of potential stakeholders.

Adopting a stakeholder approach helps to encourage project managers in particular to cast the net wider in identifying the people or groups likely to have an interest in the project. Taking managers and project teams through a stakeholder identification process has repeatedly resulted in the teams identifying at least five times as many people likely to influence the project than previously considered at the planning stage.

STAKEHOLDER IDENTIFICATION

As project managers identify only a limited number of stakeholders within their project cycle and tend to dismiss many stakeholders outside the organization or project as unimportant or too difficult to control, many of the key players and their potential risk contribution are not considered within the risk analysis process. Understanding the potential impact of, for example, lawyers, media, and building societies in a new development on previously contaminated ground provides useful information for intervention strategies. Limiting the consideration of stakeholder interests limits the extent of risk identification and subsequent risk reduction.

The primary stage in project risk management is the development of a network path analysis, identifying key stages and milestones from project inception to completion. As an integral part of the planning process, all stakeholders, not just those directly concerned with the project, need to be identified at each stage of the project. Stakeholders can be internal or external to the organization. However, people who may be considered at the planning stage as unlikely to be a problem often cause risky events.

As an example, the Jubilee Line Underground project that is due to provide a passenger service for the Millennium Dome at Greenwich was brought to a halt by electricians. This followed the introduction of the European working directive on maximum working hours. The electricians used the opportunity to renegotiate their contracts to meet employers' demand for extra working hours. There was a great deal of publicity surrounding the introduction of the European Directive for more than two years; yet, the project managers did not include the potential risk this legislation would bring to the project. It had been assumed that the electrical engineers would not cause any problems.

Work with a company in the United Kingdom, that was involved in a major housing development project failed to consider stakeholders external to the project organization, among others, lawyers. The managing director's rationale was that local lawyers would have little or no interest in the project process or outcomes. The director's view was that all local people would welcome the project as it would regenerate a rather unpleasant area for the benefit of all. So, why should lawyers be considered as having a stake in the project? However, the development involved building on previously contaminated land. New legislation at the time in the United Kingdom meant that lawyers lost a key revenue generating function, and they were looking for alternative sources of income. Offering their services to the local population who may be affected by the contamination brought the project to halt. The development sponsors withdrew funding for fear of not being able to sell properties and, thus, losing money on the project. It was some time and at a considerable cost before the matter was resolved.

The director of the project failed to establish one of the stakeholder's potential gains in terms of business generation as a result of legislation, which seemed to have no direct link to the project. Through taking a stakeholder perspective, the potential benefit of generation litigation for the lawyers could have been identified.

Thus, when initiating the stakeholder identification process, all stakeholders who may be able to bring influence at any time during the project life cycle need to be included. The network path analysis provides an excellent guide as to who, when, and for how long will be a stakeholder within the process.

Classification of stakeholders will depend on the weighting given to their relevant potential risk contribution to the project. Once these potential contributions are identified, appropriate risk management strategies will need to be developed, which may also mean including these in the quantitative risk analysis process.

ORGANIZATIONAL LEVEL ANALYSIS

At the organizational level, the structure and culture of the working environment can influence stakeholder responses, including the dominant management style, policies, procedures, and communication systems. However, as organizations are made up of people, assessing these dimensions through a systematic stakeholder analysis provides more accurate information about how individuals are likely to respond.

The structure of the organization determines communication patterns, bureaucratic demands, authority of decision making, and most importantly, procedures for ensuring accountability. Also, how roles and responsibilities are allocated, lines of reporting, and monitoring systems can all shape the perspectives and perceptions of stakeholders.

Lack of clarification concerning roles and responsibilities is also a common problem leading to conflict and confusion. In a recent case in a public-funded project, the role of the government-established organization for the dissemination of funds for projects, ranging from minor local initiatives to the development of a leisure complex, was for each project monitor to ensure that projects would be delivered to time and budget according to the laid down procedures. Many of the project monitors were young and inexperienced and most were either unclear about the extent of their responsibilities or misinterpreted these and took on the role of project manager, in many cases, rather than monitor. This confusion placed the organization at risk in terms of accountability. When projects failed to deliver, and the monitor involved acted as a project manager, the burden of blame for failure shifted to the organization rather than the project applicants.

The role of hierarchy has never been taken into consideration in effective risk management, whereby senior managers with hidden agendas may use their role to influence junior staff informally without formal accountability for potential negative outcomes. Such activities are never documented and thus never enter into subsequent risk calculations.

In some cases, responsibility is demanded without the relevant decision-making authority, or decisions are made without accountability. This can best be illustrated by reference to a public sector project for building additional facilities for a local health authority. Whereas the ultimate responsibility for delivering the project to time and budget rested with the project director, it soon became evident that a key member of staff felt very uncomfortable about pressure being placed on him by the chairman of the steering committee to employ subcontractors specified by him. The chairman of the steering committee communicated his expectations in informal settings. When asked about his role within the project, the chairman clearly stated that he had absolutely nothing to do with the project, he was simply there for consultation if and when needed but he would not influence the project in any way. This clearly exempted him from accountability for any problems arising from employing inadequate contractors and architects, yet he was directly involved in the decision-making process. The young member of staff was obliged to follow the chairman's wishes or his career might have suffered as a result of following a rational path. Although the project director had ultimate responsibility for the project, she was completely unaware of the reason for poor project performance. Here is a clear case of influence without accountability and accountability without decision-making authority.

The importance of effective management practices for project risk management has been highlighted by Barnes and Wearne (1993), Collingridge (1992), Hastings (1993), and Lockyer and Gordon (1996) where major concerns center on poor leadership, lack of consultation, lack of provision of necessary resources (especially for project planning), stress, inefficient use of resources, work overload, lack of knowledge of overall project, and lack of decision-making authority.

Allocation of project management roles tends to center on technical capabilities rather than management skills although technical abilities or discipline specific expertise are important, given that project management is mainly the management of people, effective management skills need to be emphasized equally (Lambert, 1994). There is an assumption that if an individual has substantial technical capabilities, then managerial competence is implicit. The competency trap is also recognized by Levitt and March (1988) where favorable performance with an inferior process leads to overlooking knowledge that could lead to more effective processes and outcomes.

ORGANIZATIONAL CULTURE

One of the key factors in how people respond to decision choices is the notion of blame and responsibility, which is culturally embedded in our societal relationships. Risk perception is influenced by the extent to which an individual is likely to carry the burden and consequence of blame for their decision. The influence of diffused responsibility can lead groups to make riskier decisions than individuals, as no one person will carry the blame for negative outcomes (Kogan & Wallach, 1964). Thus, in an environment where the concept of blame is perceived to be prominent, the individual or groups will place undue effort in ensuring their total vindication from any adverse outcomes rather than focus on managing the problem for the benefit of the project.

In a large commercial bank in the United Kingdom it was normal practice for staff to spend considerable time trying to ensure that no blame could be traced back to them in cases of crises rather than channelling their effort into problem solving to protect the business case and manage the attendant risks. This problem has also been highlighted by Pidgeon et al. (1992).

From this premise follows the problem of monitoring procedures, which project managers may put in place to ensure that work is to standard and on schedule. Such monitoring procedures do not always serve the purpose for which they were established. There is often a substantial reality gap between documenting information about activities and actually carrying these out. Individuals may at times manage such procedures to meet their own agendas, thus building up risk for the project. Auditing monitoring information is one way to address such a reality gap, that is, documenting that a task has been carried out does not mean that it has and actually been done. In one organization, a project manager was appointed to beyond his competence level and to cover up his inability to cope with the work, he completed all his documentation although no work had taken place. The project director was confident that on the basis of documentation, the work was going well.

Organizations are established for stability, and senior management often discourages problems, that are likely to destabilize aspects of the structure or culture.

When conducting retrospective analysis, it is often the case that relevant information concerning the potential for risk is available within project teams, but the cultural environment often prevents individual members from offering their expertise. This is not due to group think (Janis, 1977) but rather to a culture that inhibits free exchange of knowledge or information in favor of either positive contributions or rejecting external information, the so called 'Not Invented Here' syndrome. Theories of group dynamics also have to be taken into account when considering effectiveness of project teams, brainstorming sessions, and quality of decision making.

In many cases of project failure, the necessary information concerning risks and problems is available within project teams but is often not acknowledged or sought out by management (Paul-Chowdhury, chap. 6, this volume). Once projects are under way, there is often a feeling of infallibility leading to a collective perception that everything will be fine once activity begins (Collingridge, 1992). At this crucial early stage there is considerable danger of group think (Janis, 1977) whereby the group accepts decisions without critically evaluating outcomes, thinking that they have made the best choices or have good enough solutions. Hugenholtz (1992) and Collingridge (1992) argued for greater opportunity for team members to voice their concerns. As team members adapt to increasing amounts of job stability, they may become less open and receptive to new innovative approaches and procedures, preferring, instead, the predictability of their secure and familiar environments and the confidence, that this brings.

A culture where status is valued will inhibit managers from using all available decision support resources if these are not perceived to be concomitant with the manager's status. Decision support systems that could aid strategic planning are rarely used as most senior managers reject available information technology, considering it to be more appropriate for managers at lower levels of operation instead, they rely on their own expertise to make relevant judgments on the available data. Identification and assessment of these dimensions would aid the project manager's decision making and improve the quality and efficiency of the management process.

THE ISSUE OF KNOWLEDGE MANAGEMENT

To determine what risks each stakeholder contributes to the project, it is necessary to identify not only the stake or vested interest they have in the project but also how they view the project. How each stakeholder or group will behave or act in a given set of circumstances is determined by their underlying values, beliefs and knowledge about their environment, their *perspectives*, how they see the world, and *perceptions*, how they interpret the information. Thus, greater focus needs to be placed on the individual to understand the factors that are likely to direct their focus to specific areas of information, such as individual operational lenses. Each stakeholder or group may have different objectives and may interpret and evaluate the same information and outcomes differently (Levitt & March, 1988) and thus the importance of recognizing the operational lenses through which information is interpreted.

The more the project manager knows about the aims and objectives of the stakeholders, the more information they will have on which to base risk assessment. Individual perceptions and perspectives can be regarded as mental models of the problem that the individual creates about the project to determine the kind of actions and behavior they will adopt. Identifying perspectives enables the development of appropriate intervention strategies to reduce risk and uncertainty (Humphreys et al. 1987).

To ensure common effort to achieving project goals, stakeholders should, ideally, share the same perspectives and perceptions. However, diverse stakeholder perspectives and perceptions concerning the task, roles, and objectives have been recognized as important factors in risk (Pidgeon et al., 1992; Pinkley & Northcroft, 1994; Sawacha & Langford, 1984).

Stakeholder analysis facilitates knowledge acquisition about what may best be described as social processes within an organizational setting, or the interaction between individuals and groups, behavior, vested interests, and other human factors. In effect, the process is about better knowledge management and, thus, more effective risk management.

When attempting to identify stakeholders' views of the world, or rather their knowledge structures, it is useful to note that such knowledge structures are developed through experience, that is unique to each individual, which is referred to as their *subjective small worlds* (Savage, 1954). Mapping such small worlds can reveal the underlying structure, which stakeholders use to represent their information world (Walsh, 1995), and belief value systems, which influences their decision making.

Nonaka and Takeuchi (1995) identified two kinds of knowledge: *tacit* and *explicit*. Tacit knowledge is described as being personal and context specific and present within the individual's mental schema; explicit knowledge is that which is codified and transmittable in systematic language and thus shared. Drucker (1993) considered tacit knowledge as skills that cannot necessarily be explained in words, and the only way to learn this is through experience.

Although knowledge structures are subject to all the biases identified in decision theory, they are nevertheless the ones used by stakeholders. However, much of the knowledge that stakeholders have is tacit. The objective for the project manager is to translate this into explicit knowledge so that it can be shared with others and aid their decision processes through the provision of increased information.

One way of acquiring tacit knowledge is through shared experiences, trust, and mutual understanding (Nonaka & Takeuchi, 1995). This requires an organizational structure, culture, and climate that facilitates rather than impedes this knowledge-sharing process. Organizational knowledge, Wilson (1996) argued, is created when tacit knowledge is codified and converted to explicit knowledge. Nonaka and Takeuchi (1995) proposed that organizational knowledge is a continuous and dynamic interaction between tacit and explicit knowledge.

Drucker (1993) posited that knowledge is generated by individuals from data and distilled into information that can be considered as *data endowed with relevance and purpose* before being converted to organizational knowledge through interactions with systems and procedures. Decision making can be and is a process of managing knowledge. The amount and kind of information determines the level of certainty for the decision-making process. The rational approach would suggest that more information leads to better decision making, however, more information does not necessarily lead to better decisions as the use of such information largely depends on the competency of the decision maker as well as on their vested interests, perceptions, and perspectives.

Marshall, Prusak, and Spielberg (1997) suggested that more information and tacit knowledge alone do not necessarily improve decision making in a risk management environment. Rather, more time needs to be allocated to converting tacit into explicit knowledge, that may be accessible to the organization. Sveiby (1997) proposed that discourse may be an effective means of transferring this knowledge. However, Marshall et al. (1997) again emphasized the importance of the individual's competence in interpretation and transfer of available data.

The importance of subjective small worlds (Savage, 1954) was also recognized by Eden and Harris (1975) in the consideration of bias in the transfer of information based on individual mental models, power structures, and organizational politics. Walsh and Ungson (1997) proposed that use of past decisions can enhance the likelihood of errors, particularly if those decisions are not challenged, and also recommended reflection in terms of motives of individuals transferring information. Whereas explicit knowledge tends to gain greater legitimacy, Jordan and Jones (1997) warned that such knowledge may not be correct and should first be evaluated. Sveiby (1997) also warned that if decision makers wish to look hard enough, they are likely to find information to support rather than to critically challenge their decisions. Strong subjective perception and the value of knowledge further shapes the way information is structured (Drew, 1996).

KNOWLEDGE STRUCTURES

The world of managers as information workers (McCall & Kaplan, 1985) is complex and ambiguous (Mason & Mitroff, 1981) and as problem solvers, they need to make sense of this complex and ambiguous environment. To do this, they use knowledge structures to represent their information world (Walsh, 1995). Knowledge structure can be viewed as a mental template that individuals impose on an information environment and give it some form of meaning (Neisser, 1976). Therefore the template orders the information environment in a way that enables the interpretation and leads to action that is built on past experience. It effectively represents organized knowledge about a given concept (Fiske & Taylor, 1984). This serves as a basis for evaluating information, often in ambiguous or uncertain situations (Gioia, 1986), which is typical of project environments. As such knowledge structures are subjective, or rather, individual specific, clearly they will be specific to each stakeholder, whose knowledge structures guide the focus of their attention (White & Carlston, 1983) and the encoding of information (Cohen, 1981) and thus help interpret experience (Bower, Black, & Turner, 1979). Moreover, it provides a basis for inference about, for example, the project and its objectives, and aids problem solving (Langer & Abelson, 1974, Snyder & Uranowitz, 1978).

However, knowledge structures can also limit the decision maker's ability to understand information domains, through such factors as stereotyping, as managers tend to act on impoverished views of the world by filling gaps with typical but often inaccurate information (Weick, 1979). Moreover, managers also tend to use the same strategies in subsequent situations and thus repeat previous mistakes, and together with inaccurate template matching, may prompt them to overlook or ignore discrepant information that may be important.

The tendency for project managers to be over optimistic at the beginning of a new project, assuming that this project will be different and that they will not make the same mistake again, provides some evidence for the use of well-established strategies for managing. This was evidenced by a major development project that involved the implementation of complex and novel technology on two different sites. Although the first project had failed with colossal financial consequences, the second development was not considered to be risky because the project team would not make the same mistake again, this project would be effective. On closer examination of the key decision maker's assumptions, it soon became evident that the same mistakes were repeated for the second project. The assumption made was that if all the components of the complex information technology system were to be signed off by the project team at the point of manufacture, then once assembled, the system should operate effectively. The previous one did not, but no one felt that perhaps building on the previous cognitive template might not be appropriate. Therefore, it is important to uncover the attributes of a decision maker's knowledge structure and to relate this to consequences for the organization, such as deployment of resources and legal safety blankets.

Understanding and building on stakeholders' knowledge structures and vested interests is an obvious advantage to managing risks. However, the questions as to how to make such knowledge structures available to the rest of the team to serve as a decision support system also has to be addressed by the organization or project manager.

ASSUMPTIONS

Assumptions that individuals make within the project process and outcomes constitute a further risk element (Oldfield, 1998). Such assumptions can be about the level of control individuals may have over the process or outcomes. Managers have a tendency to think that they can control the project process. Introducing rigorous monitoring procedures does not provide effective control over the process as individuals will focus on their own vested interests such as career development, financial reward, maximum gain, and minimum loss. More importantly, they are likely to achieve this covertly. The most popular approach to perceived control is through rigorous contract definitions; however, the fact that litigation can not only cost the organization a great deal of money but can also damage the business case is often ignored in the early stages of planning.

Managerial assumptions concerning shared understanding of objectives are frequently erroneous, as the stated views and perspectives of individuals are often far from their real perceptions and one stakeholder's view of the project is unlikely to match completely that of another's. These assumptions are based on one's own perspectives, which are unique, and subjective as individuals interpret information in different ways (Senge, 1990).

In many cases, individuals do not think through the important aspects of the project process or the outcomes of decisions. Whereas mission statements and clearly defined project aims and objectives go some way to reducing possible misperceptions, the stakeholder's way of looking at the world will still influence individual interpretation. Achieving a shared understanding in problem perception is another essential component of risk management. Adopting an objective approach to understanding others in the process also contributes to risk reduction.

Assumptions that groups as well as individuals will all work toward stated goals and objectives may also be erroneous; many work groups quickly become dysfunctional to the rest of the organization as their own hidden agendas or vested interests become established. This can become crucial once conflicting interests emerge and the focus shifts from effective implementation to mitigating potential losses.

The assumption that individuals make about others' motives, vested interests, capabilities, and levels of control also present further sources of risk. There is often a discrepancy between what is logged on paper and what happens at the "coal-face," problems emerging once it is too late to intervene effectively. People are fallible and may not perform as effectively as presumed by managers.

PERCEPTIONS OF STAKEHOLDERS

Whereas perspectives can be viewed as individual operational lenses, perceptions concern the way the individual interprets information, and what she or he observes.

Conditioned concepts of risk management mean that many contributory factors are excluded from the manager's view of what constitutes risk. How risk is defined and what is defined as risk determines the response of the individual. Risk is often conceptualized as hazard, breakdown (of technology and systems), failure to deliver to time and budget, rather than in its wider terms of lack of certainty about precise outcomes of actions or processes (March & Shapira, 1992). Individuals are thus likely to focus on elements identified as risk rather than consider uncertainties within the project process. Shackle (1983) argued that it is better to view uncertainty as uncertainty rather than risk and therefore shift the focus from probability as it does not support theories of choice in an economic environment.

What individuals or groups consider to be a potential risk also depends on perceptions, mainly based on notions of control. Many of the key risk elements are excluded from consideration as these may not be viewed as risk but simply an area for management; for example, the timing of the transfer of responsibility for specific tasks, where grey areas such as how one defines acceptable standards are not clarified at project planning, or contracting phase. Although this protocol may be available within individuals' knowledge structures, in some cases, these are not initiated at the appropriate time.

Many managers escape into the comfort zone of legal protection through tight contracts, assuming that they have control over the process, arguing that potential problems are managed by threat of legal action. This ignores two realities: firstly the *Huidini* factor, whereby parties may extricate themselves from the contract through effective legal arguments and secondly, that litigation takes time and money and there is little provision for the recovery of the business plan within the project risk management process. In the United States, 20% of all building costs can be attributed to litigation.

Cultural factors also contribute to misperceptions and misunderstanding (Hugenholtz, 1992). Pinkley and Northcroft (1994) considered perspectives as individual lenses through which issues are assessed. Pidgeon et al. (1992) argued that perceptions of stakeholders, which are largely social and subjective processes, cannot be reduced to elements of mathematical models of risk. The stress placed on quantification process fails to prompt a manager to take account of other areas more difficult or impossible to quantify, thus excluding a large element of potential risk. The reluctance of most managers operating at strategic level to use available information technology for improving their decisions also contribute to the effectiveness of their choices.

Empirical evidence concerning risk responses is also often ignored in the risk analysis process. People vary in their estimation of risk so that the same set of circumstances may be evaluated differently by individuals. There is a tendency to overestimate fabulous risk and to confuse probability with consequence (Fischhoff, Lichtenstein, Slovic, Derby, & Keeney, 1983). Thus, there might be a temptation to focus on low probability risk with severe consequences rather than high probability risk with lower potential losses. Evidence suggests that individuals do not understand, trust, or use accurately probability estimates (Fischhoff et al., 1983; Moore, 1983; Slovic, 1967).

Individual factors such as age, previous experience (March & Shapira, 1987), and level of performance aspiration (Shapira & Berndt, 1997), also determines the risk response at the individual level. Stakeholders may become risk seeking in cases of under performance, which could lead to compounded risk

People vary in their approach to risk estimation. Overconfidence about estimation of risks (Moore, 1983) is another factor in how individuals regard risk. There is a tendency to shift preferences of risk depending on the nature of resources available, for example. Also, the age of the executive (March & Shapira, 1992) will influence their response. Managers look for alternatives they can manage rather than accept risk estimates, and this relates to their beliefs about their ability to control the risks through regulation. A manager's previous experience of handling risk also influences their response to identified and quantified risk (March & Shapira, 1987)·

Risk perception is a crucial influence on risk-taking behavior (Sitkin & Pablo, 1992). Overall, individuals are poor assessors of risk. Experience, subjectivity, and the way risk is presented to them play a major role in their perception of risk (Tversky & Kahneman, 1974). Sitkin and Pablo (1992) also emphasized the importance of the link between outcome history and problem framing, arguing that problem framing, how the risk is defined and presented to the individual, determines risk perception and, thus, decision making. How individuals structure or model the problem and the extent to which they consider component parts shapes perceptions and subsequent actions (Humphreys et al., 1987).

The level of perceived importance of decisions also influences behavior and links to consequences of such decisions (Ziegler, Harrison, & Nozewnik, 1996). People often define their problems in ways that cause them to overlook their best options, which may lull them into a false sense of security or ignore difficult areas. In addition, the results are often subjective and biased by the group making the interpretation (Jobling, 1994), including using statistical criteria (i.e., different levels of confidence limits). Many managers ignore data in favor of intuition (Moore, 1983).

Overall, people are poor assessors of risk. Experience, subjectivity, and the way risk is framed play a major role in their perception (Tversky & Kahneman, 1974). Subjectivity is a key factor in assessing risk. Whether a problem is perceived in terms of potential gains or losses are not assessed as a simple mathematical calculation of the problem but as a subjective fear, often linked to consequences of outcomes, leading to poor decision making.

CONCLUSION

If project risk management is to improve, a number of frequently overlooked factors must be taken into account. Definitions of risk should encompass wider issues of risk and uncertainty. Concentrating on quantifiable factors excludes the impact of people or stakeholders who make a major contribution to uncertainty.

The risk assessment process has to recognize the fallibility of humans to assess risk accurately and allow for potential bias in decision making. Understanding stakeholders' knowledge structures and their subjective small worlds is a first step to real risk management.

A process of surfacing tacit knowledge and bringing this into the domain of the project team is essential to provide more reliable information for supporting individual and group decisions. Accurate identification of stakeholder perspectives reduces uncertainty by minimizing the unavoidable assumptions concerning others' views and beliefs and highlighting areas of potential conflict. The identification of possible misperceptions allows the project manager to develop appropriate intervention strategies to avoid or minimize risk.

Risk is best avoided. The earlier the stage at which all project risk and potential for uncertainty is taken seriously, the more likely the chance of ensuring project success at an acceptable price. An understanding of the central role of all project stakeholders in this process makes the largest contribution to this objective. Understanding the process by which managers interpret data and use available tools, techniques, and processes enables the development and application of more robust techniques for using the information available for making more effective decisions.

REFERENCES

Andrews, J. D., & Jobling, P. E. (1992). Addressing qualitative issues and improving decision making through risk management: Theory and practice. Project Management Without Boundaries, Proceeding of INTERNET World Congress on Project Management, Florence, Italy.

Barnes, N. M. L. & Wearne, S. H. (1993). The future for major project management. *International Journal of Project Management, 11*(3).

Berkeley, D., Humphreys, P. C., & Thomas, R. D. (1989). *Project Risk Action Management: Techniques and Support; Transactions.* Proceedings: INTERNET World Congress on Project Management. Atlanta: GA.

Bower, G. H., Black, J. B., & Turner, T. J. (1979). Scripts in Memory for Text. *Cognitive Psychology, 11,* 177–220.

Checkland, P. B. (1981). *Systems thinking, systems practice.* New York: Wiley.

Cohen, C. E. (1981). Person categories and social perception: Testing some boundaries of the processing effects of prior knowledge. *Journal of Personality and Social Psychology 40,* 441–452.

Collingridge, D. (1992). *Management of scale: Big organizations, big decisions, big mistakes.* London: Routledge & Kegan Paul.

Drew, S. (1996). *Managing intellectual capital for strategic advantage.* (Working Paper Series). Henley Management College, Henley, England.

Drucker, P. (1993). *Post capital society.* Oxford, England: Butterworth-Heinemann.

Eden, C., & Harris, J. (1975). *Management decisions and decision management.* London: MacMillan.

Eden, C., Jones, S., & Sims, D. (1979). *Thinking in organizations.* London: Macmillan

Fischhoff, B., Lichtenstein, S., Slovic, P., Derby, S., & Keeney, R. (1983). *Acceptable risk.* New York: Cambridge University.

Fiske, S. T., & Taylor, S. E. (1984). *Social cognition.* Reading, MA: Addison-Wesley.

Gioia, D. A. (1986). Conclusion: The state of the art in organizational social cognition: A personal view. In H. P. Sims, & D. A. Gioia (Eds.), *The thinking organization: Dynamics of organizational social cognition.* (pp. 336–356). San Francisco: Jossey-Bass.

Hastings, C. (1993, June). Soft issues of project management. *Project Management Today, UK.*

Hugenholtz, K. (1992). *Ethic, not efficiency first, decision makers will need new skills: Project managers are the last to know.* Project Management Without Boundaries, Proceeding of INTERNET World Congress on Project Management, Florence, Italy.

Humphreys, P. C., Oldfield, A. I., & Allan, J. (1987). *Intuitive decision making: A five level empirical analysis* (Technical Report, 87–1.) London: Decision Analysis Unit, London School of Economics and Political Science.

Janis, I. (1977). *Decisions making: A psychological analysis of conflict, choice, and commitment.* New York: The Free Press.

Jobling, P. (1994). *Probabilistic or 'possibilistic': Is numerical risk analysis a benefit?* Dynamic leadership through project management: Proceedings of 12th INTERNET World Congress on project management. Oslo, Norway.

Jordan, J., & Jones, P. (1997). Assessing your company's knowledge management style. *Long Range Planning, 30*(3), 392–398.

Kogan, N., & Wallach, M. A. (1964). *Risk taking.* New York: Holt, Rinehart & Winston.

Lambert, A. (1994, April). Association of Project Managers, Project, 6–7.

Langer, E. A., & Abelson, R. P. (1974). A patient by any other name. Clinical group differences in labelling bias. *Journal of Consulting and Clinical Psychology, 42,* 4–9.

Levitt, B., & March, J. (1988). Organizational learning. *Annual Review of Sociology, 14,* 319–340.

Lockyer, K., & Gordon, J. (1996). *Project management and project network techniques* (6th Ed.) London: Pitman.

March, J. G., & Shapira, Z. (1987). Managerial perspectives on risk and risk taking. *Management Science, 33,* 1404–1418.

March, J. G., & Shapira, Z. (1992). Variable risk preferences and focus of attention. *Psychological Review, 99,* 172–183.

Marshall, C., Prusak, L., & Spielberg, D. (1997). Financial risk and the need for superior knowledge management. In L. Prusak (Ed.), *Knowledge in Organizations.* Boston: Butterworth-Heinemann.

Mason, R. D., & Mitroff, I. (1981). *Challenging strategic assumptions.* New York: Wiley

McCall, M., & Kaplan, R. (1985). *Whatever it takes: Decision makers at work.* Englewood Cliffs, NJ: Prentice-Hall.

Moore, P.G. (1983). *Subjective risk termination. In the Business of Risk.* Cambridge, England: Cambridge University.

Neisser, U. (1976). *Cognition and Reality: Principles and implications of cognitive psychology.* San Francisco: Freeman.

Nonaka, I., & Takeuchi, H. (1995). *The knowledge-creating company.* New York: Oxford University.

Oldfield, A. (1997). Managing project risks: The relevance of human factors. *International Journal of Project & Business Risk Management. 1*(2), 99–109.

Oldfield, A. (1998). *The human factor in risk management.* (The magazine for the Association of Project Management), *Project, 10*(10), 13–15.

Oldfield, A., & Ocock, M. (1994). *Risk management: The importance of stakeholders.* Dynamic leadership through project management: Proceedings of 12th INTERNET World Congress on project management. Oslo, Norway.

Pidgeon, N., Hood, C., Jones, D., Turner, B., & Gibson R. (1992). *Risk: analysis, perception and management.* (Report of a Royal Society Study Group). London: Royal Society.

Pinkley, R., & Northcroft, G. B. (1994). Conflict frames of reference: Implications for dispute processes and outcomes. *Academy of Management Journal, 37*(1), 193–205.

Savage, L. (1954). *The foundations of statistics.* New York: Wiley.

Sawacha, E., & Langford, D.A. (1984). *Project management and the public sector client: Case studies.* (Draft paper, 1984, CIB-W-65). Brunel University, Uxbridge, England.

Senge, P.M. (1990). *The fifth discipline.* Garden City, NY: Doubleday.

Shackle, G. L. S. (1983). A student pilgrimage. *Banca Nazionale del Lavoro Quarterly Review. 145,* 108–116.

Shapira, Z. & Berndt, D. (1997). Managing grand-scale construction projects: A risk taking perspective. *Research in Organizational Behavior, 19,* 303–360.

Simon, P. W., Hillson, D. A., & Newland, K. E. (1997). *PRAM (Project Risk Analysis and Management) Guide.* Norwich, England: APM (Association of Project Management) Group.

Sitkin, S. B., & Pablo, A. L. (1992). Reconceptualizing the determinants of risk behavior. *Academy of Management Review, 17,* 9–39.

Slovic, P. (1967). The relative influence of probabilities and payoffs upon perceived risk of a gamble. *Psychometric Science, 9*, 223–224.

Snyder, M., & Uranowitz, S. W. (1978). Reconstructing the past: Some cognitive consequences of person perception. *Journal of Personality and Social Psychology, 36*, 941–950.

Stamper, R., & Kolkman, M. (1991). Problem articulation: A sharp-edged soft systems approach. *Journal of Applied Systems Analysis. 18*, 69–71.

Sveiby, K. E. (1997). *The new organizational wealth.* San Francisco: Berrett-Koehler.

Tversky, A. & Kahneman, D. (1974). Judgement under uncertainty: Heuristics and biases. *Science, 185*, 1124–1131.

Walsh, J. P. (1995). Managerial and organizational cognition: Notes from a trip down memory lane. *Organizational Science, 6*(3), 280–321.

Walsh, J. P., & Ungson, G. R. (1997). Organizational memory. In L. Prusak (Ed.), *Knowledge in organizations.* Boston: Butterworth-Heinemann.

Weick, K. E. (1979). *The social psychology of organizing.* Reading, MA: Addison & Wesley.

White, J. D., & Carlston, D. E. (1983). Consequences of schemata for attention, impressions, and recall in complex social interactions. *Journal of Personality and Social Psychology, 45*, 538–549.

Wilson, D. A. (1996). *Knowledge Management.* Boston: Butterworth-Heinemann.

Ziegler, L., Harrison, J. R., & Nozewnik, A. (1996). *Anomalies in prospect theory: Risk perceptions in strategic decision behaviour.* Paper presented at International Seminar in Risk in Human Judgement and Decision Making, 1996, Leeds, England.

Understanding Managerial Cognition: A Structurational Approach

Laurence Brooks
Chris Kimble
Paul Hildreth
University of York, UK

Business pressures, such as competition and globalization, together with technological developments and the convergence of computer and communications technology to computer mediated communications (CMC) have led to an explosion of new and diverse forms of technology. The nature of information technologies in the office environment is changing. Although electronic mail (e-mail) is perhaps the most high-profile CMC, voice mail, fax, video conferencing, and shared whiteboards, together with traditional media such as the telephone, paper memos, and face-to-face meetings, all provide channels through which work takes place.

Information technologies play a distinct social and interpersonal role in modern organizations. However, when viewed in purely technical terms, all such technology can do is to transfer data or enable it to be shared by a number of users. For machine-to-machine communication this does not pose any particular problems. For human-to-human communication to be successful however there is a need to supply some social meaning, or context, to transform the machine data into human information.

THEORY BACKGROUND

Combining perspectives is the traditional role of the academic researcher. Consequently, it is accepted that examining social meaning associated with technology (i.e., an emergent model of causal agency) can be combined with the concept that outcomes develop over time (i.e., a process theory approach). These ideas can then be linked to multiple analyses taking place at the microlevel (e.g., Markus & Robey, 1988). However, these ideas are difficult to adopt and develop in further research. Orlikowski and Robey (1991) proposed building on Structuration Theory (Giddens, 1990) as way to develop a more practical theoretical framework. In this chapter, Giddens' theory is used in a theoretical framework to investigate how new technology is created, used, and becomes institutionalized within an organization. This chapter demonstrates that the technology is both a product of, and a medium for, human action. Human action is both enabled and constrained by structure.

Clark, Modgil, & Modgil (1990) summarized the core of structuration theory (from Giddens, 1990) in a series of four interrelated points:

1. *Social practices* underlie both individuals and society. Structuration theory does not focus solely on individual actions and experiences or the existence and requirements of a societal totality.
2. Human agents are *knowledgeable*. People know what they do in their daily interactions (whether explicitly or in an implicit/tacit sense), and under given circumstances are able to do it.
3. These social practices are *routinized and recursive* (i.e., ordered and stable across space and time). People draw on "structural properties" (i.e., rules and procedures), which are institutionalized properties of society, to construct the visible patterns (social practices) that make up society.
4. Structure is both the medium and outcome of a process of "structuration." It is activity-dependent, as seen in the production and reproduction of practices across time and space.

The key principle here is the *duality of structure*. Human action is both set up and tied down by structure, but structure is the result of human action. Action and structure presuppose each other, and so, are viewed as a duality (Scheepers & Damsgaard, 1997).

Structuration theory identifies three dimensions of institutionalized social structure—signification, legitimation, and domination (Giddens, 1979)— three key processes of human action during interaction— communication, wielding power, and sanctioning conduct, and three modalities that link these poles of duality—interpretive schemes, resources, and norms (see Fig. 14.1).

Giddens (1979) did not explicitly address the issue of technology, however Orlikowski (1992) did use the structuration viewpoint to examine technology within organizational settings. The assumption is that technology can be viewed as a structural property of organizations. Technology embodies, and therefore represents, some of the rules and resources that make up an organization.

Orlikowski (1992) discussed the *duality of technology*, (i.e., technology is created and changed by human action but is also used by humans to accomplish some action). The other side of the duality premise is that technology is *interpretively flexible*, (i.e., the interaction of technology and organization is a function of the different actors and their sociohistorical contexts).

When looking at Information Systems (IS) in terms of the dimensions identified in structuration theory the following may be identified (Scheepers & Damsgaard, 1997):

Structures of *Signification*: Rules that make up meaning. People draw on interpretive schemes or standardized shared stocks of knowledge that enable (and constrain) communication. In drawing on these schemes, people reproduce structures of signification. For example, in an IS the structures of signification can be seen reflected in the shared meaning of the function of the IS by a group of people.

Structures of *Domination*: The different types and levels of resources people draw on to exercise power. The two main types of resources are *authoritative* (power from having command over people) and *allocative* (power from having command over objects or materials). For example, in

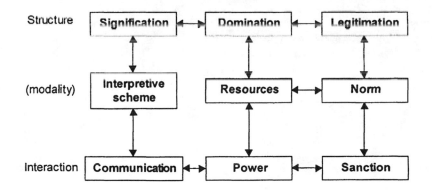

FIG. 14.1 Dimensions of the duality of structure in interaction (Giddens, 1984).

an IS they can be seen reflected in the resources allocated or withheld toward its development.

Structures of *Legitimation*: The norms or rules that individuals draw on to justify their own actions as well as those of others (where norms are the rules governing sanctioned or appropriate conduct). Norms enable and constrain action and through their use in interaction; people reproduce the structures of legitimation. For example, they can be seen reflected in the directives regarding the implementation and use of an IS, in line with the organizational norms (e.g., what information is or is not placed on the system).

What can be seen is that technology is the *product of human action* (i.e., physically constructed by actors working in a given social context [Arrow a, Fig. 14.2]). Because technology is created and maintained by people, it has to be used by people to have any effect. Technology also assumes *structural properties* (i.e., it is socially constructed by people through the different meanings they attach to it and the various features they emphasize and use).

In addition, technology is built and used in a social context that influences it (Arrow c, Fig. 14.2). Human agents act, in an organization, through use of the organizational store of knowledge, resources, and norms (i.e., these organizational structures of signification, domination, and legitimation). Once deployed, technology tends to become *reified* (i.e., seen as fixed and unquestionable). It loses the connection with the human agents who constructed and give it meaning and appears to be part of the objective, structural properties of the organization.

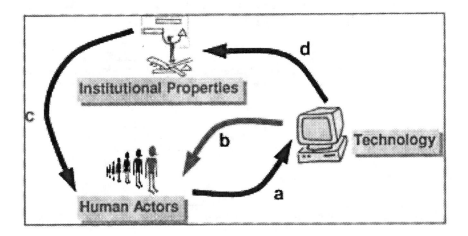

FIG. 14.2   Structural model of technology (source: Orlikowski & Robey, 1991).

However, people and structure are not independent. The ongoing action of human agents in drawing on a technology objectifies and institutionalizes it. If people changed the technology (either physically or interpretively) every time they used it, it could not assume the stability or "taken-for-granted" status necessary for institutionalisation. There are (consequences of interacting with the technology, in particular the ability to influence the social context in which it is used (Arrow d, Fig. 14.2). In using a technology, the human agent either sustains or changes the institutional structures of the organization in which they are situated (i.e. reinforcing or undermining the structures of signification, domination, and legitimation).

Technology is also the medium of human action, that is, when deployed and used in organizations by humans, it mediates (enables and facilitates or constrains) activities (Arrow b, Fig. 14.2). One crucial aspect of human action is that it can be knowledgeable and reflexive. Therefore, agency refers to capability rather than intentionality, although human actions may have intended and unintended consequences. Although the personal action of human agents using technology has a direct effect on local conditions, it also has an indirect effect on the institutional environment in which the agents are situated. The results cannot be guaranteed, even when the actions are directly intended to preserve or change some aspect of the institutional environment.

THE TEMPORAL DIMENSION

Orlikowski (1992) was concerned with how the duality of technology is often suppressed in organizational discourse. The pattern appears to be that a one-sided view of technology arises because one aspect of the duality (e.g., the flexibility of technology is invisible in the organization). Alternatively, dualism may be a recognised, but only one view of technology is emphasised.

Often a technology is developed in an organisation different from the one in which it is used (see Fig. 14.3). Therefore, designers tend to adopt an "open-systems" perspective on technology, whereas users treat it as a "closed system" or "black box."

The time-space discontinuity (shown in Fig. 14.3) is related to the idea of temporal scope. Research can focus on different temporal stages of the technology, and this can influence whether technology is seen as a fixed object or product of human action. Recognising the time-space discontinuity between design use of a technology allows an insight into the conceptual dualism in the literature. Instead of seeing design and use as disconnected moments, or stages, in the life cycle of a technology, the structurational model of technology suggests that artefacts are modifiable through their existence.

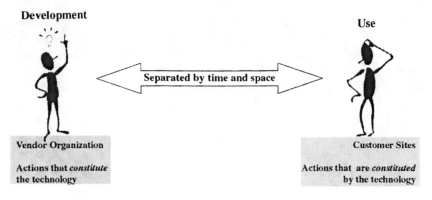

FIG. 14.3   The separation of development and use for technology.

For analytical purposes, it is useful to distinguish between human action that affects technology and human action affected by technology. Human-technology interaction is seen as having two iterative modes: design mode and use mode. Thus, depending on the degree to which users can effect redesign, it is possible to differentiate between design and use of technology.

On the left-hand side of Fig. 14.4, the constructed nature of technology is seen when the focus is on design and development of a technology. Arrow 1 represents the influence of the institutional properties of their organization on the designers of the technology. Arrow 2 represents how the designers fashion and construct a technology to meet managerial goals. These studies are therefore less likely to treat technology as fixed or objective and more likely to recognize technology's dynamic and contingent features (e.g., strategic choice studies).

On the right-hand side of Fig. 14.4, the focus is on examining the utilization of a technology in a workplace. Arrow 3 represents how a given technology influences the users of that technology. Arrow 4 represents how the technology also affects the institutional properties of the organization in which it is used. These studies are less inclined to focus on the human agency that produced the technology and tend not to recognize the ongoing social and physical construction of the technology, which occurs during its use.

It is possible that there is greater "buy-in" by the users, in which they are more involved in the initial development of a technology. However, this should not stop the user from having the potential to change the technology (physically and socially) through their interaction with it. In using a technology the users "interpret, appropriate, and manipulate" it in various ways, influenced by social and individual factors.

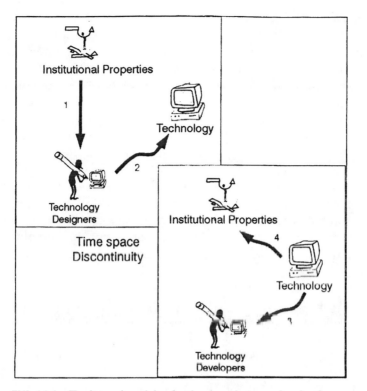

FIG. 14.4   Traditional models of technology design and technology use
(source: Orlikowski, 1992).

However, despite the opportunities for change, there are still often rigid and routinized views of, and interactions with, technology. These developments are a function of the interaction between technology and organizations, not inherent in the nature of the technology. Even the most "black-box" technology has to be understood and actively put to use by people to be effective. It is in such interactions that users shape technology and its effects (e.g., operators routinely deviate from formal, rule-bound operating practices to deal with complex interdependence, unanticipated events).

Depending on the technology, users have a varying capacity to control their interaction with the technology, and hence its characteristics. It is possible that users could exercise control at any time, therefore, according to Orlikowski (1992), the apparent divide of design and use stages is artificial and misleading. Notwithstanding that, the divide between design and use stages is a real social phenomenon. If users do not perceive opportunities to exercise this control, or actively influence the design stage, then this divide has real consequences.

Interpretive flexibility in this framework is taken to be the degree to which users of a technology are engaged in its constitution (physically or socially) during its development or use. Interpretive flexibility is an attribute of the relationship between humans and technology and therefore is influenced by three classes of characteristics: (1) characteristics of the material artefacts (e.g., software and hardware); (2) characteristics of the human agents (e.g., experience and motivation); (3) characteristics of the context (e.g., social relations, task assignment, and resource allocation). There is only finite interpretive flexibility because these factors influence the flexibility of the design, use, and interpretation of technology.

Interpretive flexibility is constrained by the material characteristics of the technology (because technology is physical it is bounded by the state of the art in materials, energy, etc.). It is also constrained by the institutional context (i.e., the structures of signification, legitimation, and domination) and the different levels of knowledge and power affecting actors during the technology's design and use.

Although Structuration Theory cannot be claimed to show a complete analysis of all the factors involved, it is a useful technique for gaining insight in the events that occurred. DeSanctis and Poole (1994) extended the approach by proposing an integration of Structuration Theory and the theoretical concept of *appropriation* (Ollman, 1971). DeSanctis and Poole argued that, "advanced information technologies trigger adaptive structurational process which, over time, can lead to changes in the rules and resources that organizations use in social interaction" (pp. 142–143). Similarly, Guerrieri and Saharia (1996) looked at using Structuration Theory as a springboard for updating Sociotechnical Systems Theory (STS), again for use in IT and organizational analysis.

Walsh (1995) provided a differing and complementary perspective on Organizational Analysis. In his review of managerial and organizational cognition, he presented a framework of knowledge structures split according to individual, group, organization, and industry level. For each level he categorized, according to the representation of the information environment, the use and consequences of that representation and the origins and development of the structure. The importance of this approach is that it allows us to conceptualize the knowledge structures used by individuals within a series of enlarging contexts or environments (e.g., the group, organization, or industry level, while recognizing their historical links).

This chapter draws on the work of Walsh (1995) and Orlikowski (1992). The position it adopts is that the analysis of social meanings associated with an information technology can provide insight in the relationships between group and individual management cognition.

INFORMATION OVERLOAD

The term *information overload* is not new and can be found in the literature of the 1970s. However, in the modern business environment, information has become easy to produce, copy, and distribute without necessarily thinking about the consequences. Although apparently simple, there is little consensus about the meaning of the term *information overload*. Information overload is frequently conceived of as a supply of information that exceeds needs or perhaps more subtly as information presented at a rate too high to process. Although intuitively attractive, this definition has some inherent problems.

Information is not a single object that is added sequentially to some internalized information pile. Information is received, filtered, rejected, interpreted, modified, simplified, and often, forgotten. It may alter or reinforce existing views, it may come from different sources and carry different weight or authority, different degrees of accuracy, and may be more or less timely. This chapter addresses the issue of information overload from the perspective of the social meanings associated with one particular form of information technology (i.e., e-mail).

Stohl and Redding (1987) focused on the internally experienced message. They argued that you have to process a message, or at the very least contemplate doing so, before you can experience overload. What might be useful information to one person is regarded as unnecessary information by another. Similarly, Taha and Caldwell, (1993) discussed the idea of an appropriate level of contact through CMCs only to conclude that it changes with situation and context. This chapter proposes that information overload should be thought of in relation to information expectations, in which expectations are based on information needs.

EMPIRICAL BACKGROUND

This study arose from a letter circulated to British Universities in 1997 by Watson Wyatt Partners (WWP), an international firm of actuarial consultants. WWP identified a problem with Information Overload, specifically with: the number of e-mails received, inappropriate or unnecessary e-mails, and time spent on dealing with e-mail.

The aim of the study was to add to, and improve, the current set of e-mail guidelines. The problem was explored using a questionnaire survey and semistructured interviews. The survey approach was selected to reach a large sample and give a broad picture. The interviews would clearly reach a smaller sample, but it was anticipated that they would provide rich data for comparison with the questionnaire data.

The first phase of the study involved a questionnaire sent to all 1,500 staff in Britain and Europe. This addressed those issues that WWP had outlined in their original description of the problem and those issues that WWP felt were symptomatic of their overload, namely: e-mail bullying (i.e., copying a message to a senior member of staff with the explicit aim of pressurizing the main receiver) and reduction of informal face-to-face encounters.

Based on literature, the survey also sought to identify individual perceptions about the appropriate choice of medium for communication (Rice, 1987; Rice & Shook, 1990). The survey returned 567 questionnaires (a response rate of 37.8%) that was put through a four-stage analysis: (1) frequency distributions for all variables; (2) correlation between ordinal variables; (3) cross-checking between overload factors and level, location, and practice of respondent; and (4) the data set was broken down to identify the worst cases of information overload.

The second stage of the study involved interviews with 22 individuals, selected by WWP, as representative of a range of practices and levels. Of these interviews, 19 were from the head office, the remaining three were from a regional office. The interviews were semistructured aiming to cover similar topics as the questionnaire but allowed other issues to be explored that might have been overlooked in the survey. The interviews were recorded and fully transcribed. A brief summary of the results of the study is included later. More detailed findings can be found in Hildreth, Kimble, and Wright (1998) and Kimble, Hildreth, and Grimshaw (1998).

COMPANY BACKGROUND

WWP is an international management consulting company with over 4,700 professionals in 89 locations world wide. These professionals include consultants, actuaries, lawyers, and other specialists in human resources (HR), healthcare, finance, risk management, communications, and systems. WWP work with a variety of organizations ranging from large, well-know multi-national corporations (MNCs) to public employers and nonprofit organizations.

The alliance between Watson and Wyatt took place relatively in 1995 and led to some cultural conflict as one company was very formal and the other was informal. The organizational cultural difficulties have been largely overcome but are still evident in some areas.

In Britain, WWP have their head office in Southern England and have eight regional offices nation-wide. The different consulting departments, for example, Insurance, HR Consulting and Pensions Administration, are called *practices*. In addition to these departments there are WWP's own support functions, such as internal HR, Central Services (which includes IT support), and Business Development.

TECHNOLOGY BACKGROUND

The main CMC technology in use in WWP is e-mail. The e-mail package currently used is Lotus cc:Mail, with three different versions visible. Voice-mail had recently been installed in the head office with the long-term aim of implementing it in the regional offices. Collabrashare (a Groupware package) had also been installed for use by Account Management. The U. K. Intranet was being implemented during the course of the study.

The technical infrastructure consists of 50 servers Europe-wide with almost 1,500 users, using PC workstations with either Microsoft Windows 95 or Microsoft Windows NT™. The main extension to cc:Mail by the IT department, was the addition of an add-on called "W-List." This allows a mailing list of up to 40 different recipients to be created, therefore enabling greater targeting of e-mails within an group or practice.

SELECTED FINDINGS FROM THE SURVEY

The main survey results suggested that information overload (in terms of volume) was not a major problem for WWP. The only areas in which this problem appeared to exist was with specific managers responsible for implementing the systems and in some parts of the support network. Similarly, for most people unnecessary e-mail did not constitute a large proportion of people's e-mail. In WWP it appeared to be more of an irritation than a problem.

Although most people saw e-mail as beneficial, there was one area in which problems did exist, that of group mailing. The survey and interview findings showed that these problems appeared to arise from contextual conflicts between senders and receivers of messages (e.g., an e-mail message sent as a social invitation might be received as a nuisance or junk message; Kimble et al., 1998). Other highlights from the empirical work concerning media use and preference are discussed in the following sections.

Media Use

Different media have different characteristics and therefore may be more or less appropriate for a task, varying according to context. The survey was used partially to compare and contrast the uses made of the different CMC methods by users across the company. The aim was to explore how users were matching task to medium.

The results clearly show that electronic media in the form of e-mail was widely used in the organization. However, other electronic media, such as groupware, video conferencing, and voice mail, are restricted to a relative minority.

TABLE 14.1

Usage of Electronic Media

	Voice mail	Video Conferencing	Groupware	E-Mail
Sometimes/frequently	42%	3%	6%	97%
Never/rarely	58%	97%	94%	3%

As can be seen in Table 14.1, the organization shows a low usage[1] of other CMCs, and a high usage of e-mail (97%).

The survey also looked at respondents use of e-mail in relation to more traditional media (see Table 14.2). Clearly, e-mail has become well established with 76% of respondents saying that they more frequently use e-mail than any other form for communication.

The results also indicate that e-mail has possibly affected people's reliance on paper, because only 41% said they frequently use paper. Figures for media usage before the introduction of e-mail were not available but comments from the interviews appear to confirm this perception, at least for internal communications (Hildreth et al., 1998).

Media Preference

The aspects liked and disliked by users were also explored. The responses (shown in Table 14.3) demonstrate that e-mail has become an established medium with some useful characteristics. It is interesting to note that there was no feature that was disliked by the majority of respondents. Clearly, there are some aspects disliked by some people.

Finally, the study explored the merits of e-mail relative to more traditional media. Respondents were also provided with 15 different communication scenarios and asked to indicate which communications media they would prefer for each. The scenarios ranged from the impersonal, such as arranging a formal meeting, to the highly personal, such as discussing a personal matter with their superior. Again, e-mail was the most favored means of communication for all but the most personal matters.

ANALYSIS FROM A STRUCTURATIONAL PERSPECTIVE

From the survey a basic set of facts and figures can be derived. However it is clear that these are limited by the inherent constraints of the data gathering

---

[1]Never/Rarely = Low Usage; Sometimes/Frequently = Higher Usage.

TABLE 14.2

Most Frequently Used Media

Medium	Percentage Using Medium Frequently
Face-to-face	83%
Telephone	77%
E-Mail	76%
Paper	41%

TABLE 14.3

E-Mail Characteristics

Characteristics	Like	Neither Like–Dislike	Dislike
Content limited to text.	10%	80%	10%
Slow to compose and enter message.	4%	68%	28%
Easy to terminate exchange.	22%	65%	13%
Easy to ignore a message.	6%	52%	42%
Cannot see/hear partner.	5%	78%	17%
Can make partner seem remote.	5%	82%	13%
Can bring a quick response.	82.9%	16.6%	0.5%
Do not have to be in same place as receiver.	92%	7.5%	0.5%
Can send message without receiver being on line at same time.	92%	6%	2%

method. In order to overcome these constraints and tap a richer vein of data, a series of interviews were conducted. This chapter proposes that, using the different dimensions identified as part of the structurationalist framework, it is possible to gain a greater depth of understanding from this qualitative data. For example the finding about contextual conflict cannot be clearly understood from the conventional qualitative data analysis alone. Although examples could be identified, there was the lack of sufficient framework to understand them.

Structures of Signification

From a structurational perspective it can be argued that there is a strong difference in the approach to e-mail by those involved in managing the technology and those involved in using it, that is, there was a lack of a fully shared mutual signification structure.

From the technology management perspective, e-mail is seen as an enabling and vital system (e.g., "if it is time critical it has to be e-mail"). Whereas from the user perspective it might be seen more as a work around (e.g., "if I can't get somebody on the telephone ... then I will often use an e-mail to say we need to talk about X, can you give me a call, which I don't think is the purpose of it, but I'm afraid I do use it for that").

Although the survey findings showed the perceived general usefulness of the e-mail system, the interviews show a much wider variation in the type and level of interactions. Whereas some individuals use e-mail for communication with clients, others use e-mail for internal communication (e.g., "I think it is quite an impersonal way of communicating and therefore subjectively I would avoid doing it unless I wanted to specifically focus on the clients needs"). In this way, it can be seen that the relative meaning and significance of e-mail technology is still open to interpretation.

Structures of Domination

What appears to happen in the use of e-mail is that the existing power structures within the organization are both reproduced and challenged. An example of this is what is called *e-mail bullying*, whereby a message is copied in some way to more senior members of the organization with the express intention of causing difficulty for a colleague, for example:

> An abuse of e-mail when somebody has an issue and it is a political thing. They will copy in people who they think it is important to impress or if they want to start a political debate. I do see it where an individual has an issue, and they will e-mail that person directly and then copy a senior partner or five just to say, "isn't this person a bad boy?"

Therefore the individual involved is following the norms of the organization, accepting the roles and positions of individuals, and using these structures to reinforce their message. Given that the various structures are inherently linked, the meaning behind copying messages could be courtesy. However the effect could well be one of intimidation and therefore seen as a reflection of a structure of domination.

A final example was of unnecessary e-mail and how a message to the national network resulted in a number of joke replies, which were also sent to the national network. In the end, somebody intervened and effectively "told them off." In this way a domination structure was invoked, to enforce (or reproduce) a company norm, or legitimation structure.

Structures of Legitimation

The most easily identifiable structures are probably those representing the structures of legitimation. Although a number of differing views on the e-mail systems exist, including the degree of usefulness and the levels of security and confidentiality it might include, there were still a number of actions that the technical system was not seen as fulfilling. For example, where a signature was seen as the only legitimate way to confirm an organizational action, the e-mail was printed and signed (e.g., " ... for example a manager might email me and say we are going to increase somebody's salary ... payroll will not accept a change in salary without my signature on it and we don't have electronic signatures, so I print the piece of paper and authorize it or not as the case may be").

In the interviews, a number of respondents indicated that e-mail discipline was a key feature in the perceived problem. The organization now publishes a set of guidelines (i.e., a very clear guide to the structure of legitimation), but there was still a strong feeling was that there was education needed in what was appropriate and inappropriate: e.g.

> Within the guidelines we have within the company, it says don't put things in bold because it sounds like you are shouting, and don't be familiar with people. I think that would depend on who you are communicating with. Some people would like a formal communication, but if you are just communicating with a colleague and you are saying something as if you were talking to them, then you might react in a different way.

Therefore, although the guidelines exist, individuals still maintain their own set of opinions as to how to apply these.

Dynamic Systems

Change is a core aspect of the nature of structuration theory. The main theoretical viewpoint is one based on a dynamic interplay of factors. Therefore, although the current structure of legitimation mediates against being able to authorize electronically, the technology management talked about the changing this. This would involve the introduction of more complex e-mail systems, and more importantly, changing to a view of e-mail as a transport mechanism that could allow the escalation of a form between individuals.

At a more fundamental level, the technology management talked about greater involvement of the business units in the developments to IT (e.g., "we really want the business units to lead IT ideas, not IT staff who have no idea what the use their systems are going to have") .

However, although this intuitively appears a good idea, and definitely a step in the direction of developing the technology to create a better competitive advantage, the manner is still one of the technology management retaining control (e.g., "allowing the business units or coaxing the business units to come up with their own ideas").

CONCLUSION

Overall, structuration theory does appear to provide a good approach for examining and possibly understanding better the complex set of relationships surrounding the use of a specific technology within an organizational context. However, it is equally a difficult approach to use, in that the structural dimensions of signification, domination, and legitimation are closely interlinked. It is therefore unclear how to relate any one issue to any one dimension. For the analytical purposes in this chapter, the examples have been used to support specific instances of the dimensions, but because the structures can only be seen in reflections rather than directly, these could be used in alternative interpretations.

Although structuration theory is shown to be lacking in prescriptive capability, the value arises from the insights in the interaction of human agents, the technology, and the organization. E-mail is commonly viewed as accepted within most organizations, but there are pockets of resistance, or individuals who perceive themselves to be victims at the mercy of information technology. For example in one interview, when asked what was the major problem with e-mail, one respondent replied "paper," the reason being that because they refused to deal directly with e-mail, they had to have their secretary print out all their messages. Therefore, the organization is again in the position of waiting for people to catch-up with the technology. In this way, we can see that the social construction of the technology is a major factor in the effective working of organizations.

E-mail systems, like so many other information technologies, are extremely flexible and have strong impacts on organizational structures, such as those surrounding power, communication, and norms. Therefore, technology implementation must be made in the light of the existing organizational and social structures, in such a way that they are compatible, at least initially.

Whereas the inconsistent structure of signification is shown in the differing views of the meaning of the e-mail system, there was another unvoiced view that the next generation of technology (the nascent groupware and Intranet) would counter many of the problems experienced. However, based on the literature, these more complex technologies involve a more complex set of interactions. In particular the social interactions, or lack of them, between the technology management and the technology users will be a major factor in the successful contribution of the technology toward competitive advantage. What structuration theory might reveal are some elements of the existing social structures. These can then be acknowledged and used to avoid mismatches in future technology implementations, as well as roadmap fruitful areas for extending current systems.

This chapter shows that, not only do organizations need to recognize the implications (both good and bad) of adopting new technology, but also the changes that the technology might trigger in the industry, organization, and the individuals within it. Whereas conventional quantitative analyses provide some level of insight, far richer understandings can be unlocked by the use of a structurational framework for analysis. Essentially the organization needs to recognize and work with the complex interlocking set of dynamic iterative cycles that are its core. Further organizations need to know how to decode these dynamic structures in order to be able to understand the cognitive structures that underpin individuals and by extension, the interaction between organization and technology.

REFERENCES

Clark, J., Modgil, C., & Modgil, S. (1990). *Anthony Giddens: Consensus and controversy.* Falmer Press.

DeSanctis, G., & Poole, M. (1994). Capturing the complexity in advanced technology use: Adaptive structuration theory. *Organization Science, 5*(2), 121–147.

Giddens, A. (1979). *Central problems in social theory: Action, structure and contradiction in social analysis.* Macmillan.

Giddens, A. (1984). *The constitution of society. Outline of the theory of structuration,* Polity Press.

Giddens, A. (1990). *The consequences of modernity.* Polity in association with Blackwell

Guerrieri, J. A., & Saharia, A. (1996). Information technology and organizational structure in the post industrial organization: a modified sociotechnical systems perspective. *Proceedings of the International Association of Management annual conference, Management of IS/IT division, 14*(1), Toronto.

Hildreth, P., Kimble, C., & Wright, P. (1998). *Computer mediated communications and communities of practice. Proceedings of Ethicomp'98,* The Netherlands, Erasmus University, 275–286.

Kimble, C., Hildreth, P., & Grimshaw, D. (1998). The role of contextual clues in the creation of information overload. *Proceedings of 3rd UKAIS Conference,* Lincoln University, 405–412.

Markus, M. L., & Robey, D. (1988). Information technology and organizational change: Causal structure in theory and research. *Management Science, 34*(5), 583–598.

Ollman, B., (1971). *Aliennation: Marx's conception of man in capitalist society.* CUP.

Orlikowski, W. (1992). The duality of technology: Rethinking the concept of technology in organizations. *Organization Science, 3*(3), 398–427.

Orlikowski, W., & Robey, D. (1991). Information technology and the structuring of organizations. *Information Systems Research*, 2(2), 143–169.

Rice, R. (1987). Computer mediated communication and organizational innovation. *Journal of Communication*, 37(4), 65–94.

Rice, R., & Shook, D. (1990). Relationships of job categories and organizational levels to use of communication channels, including electronic mail: a meta-analysis and extension. *Journal of Management Studies*, 27(2), 195–229.

Scheepers, R., & Damsgaard. J. (1997). Using Internet technology within the organization: A structurational analysis of intranets. In S. Hayne & W. Prinz (Eds.), *Group 97: Proceedings of the International ACM SIGGROUP Conference on Supporting Group Work*. Arizona, USA: ACM.

Stohl, C., & Redding, W. (1987). Messages and message exchange processes. In F. M. Jablin, L. L. Putnam, K. H. Roberts, & L. W. Porter (Eds.), *Handbook of organizational communication* (pp. 451–502). London: Sage.

Taha, L., & Caldwell, B. (1993). Social isolation and integration in electronic environments. *Behaviour and Information Technology*, 12(5), 276–283.

Walsh, J. (1995). Managerial and Organizational Cognition. *Organization Science*, 6(3), 280–321.

Commentary:
Strategy *Is* Social Cognition

Dennis A. Gioia
Pennsylvania State University

The story of strategy is a story of social cognition. Yes, I know, strategy can be framed variously as many different stories in many different forms in many different settings, but the essence of all of them at a deep level is a tale of social cognition at the highest levels of the organization.

This observation is pretty basic—perhaps so basic that we almost lose sight of its significance as we roam around in the theoretical ether, ruminating about the complexities of strategy in its many guises. The three chapters comprising this section, despite their differences in domain, focus, and even direct concern with traditional strategic issues, are all testimonials to the essential role of social cognition in strategy. Odorici and Lomi would have readers consider strategic issues in terms of socially-constructed competitive networks; Oldfield prods us to contemplate the importance of listening to more stakeholder voices as a way of improving risk assessment and avoiding strategic disasters; Brooks, Kimble, and Hildreth encourage readers to see technological effects in structurational terms, with a refreshing emphasis on some of the often downplayed cognitive aspects.

Their specific concerns notwithstanding, the features of these chapters that capture my attention are their underlying assumptions, their between-the-lines messages, and their shared themes. As for their more apparent themes, they all employ the notion of mental models for understanding and action and they all have the notion of cognitive schemas (either implicitly or explicitly) as a conceptual basis for the issues they consider. More importantly, however, at a basic level, they are all are demonstrative examples of my longstanding belief that social cognition constitutes the essence of the human experience in organizations.

To me, social cognition really is the distinguishing process around which all else revolves. I fully recognize and appreciate that Weickian views of sensemaking give justifiable prominence to action as a trigger for cognition and that Giddensian structuration-like approaches, of course, do a more comprehensive job of explaining the relations of cognition, action, and structure over time, but at the center of all of it is social cognition. Meaning that when you look for an essence of the human personal experience, you find it in social cognition, and when you look for an essence to the human organizational experience, despite all the attendant complications, you find that also in social cognition.

Yes, the processes involved are all messy and they all encompass recursive loops: perception–interpretation, interpretation–action; action–structure; structure–outcome and all their interdependent permutations, and so on, so understanding people in organizations is never simple (and I actually prefer it that way). But, some degree of clarity comes from simply understanding that the core of the whole business is human social–cognitive construction. And no, I am not dissing, discounting, dismissing, or demeaning action, structural, or ecological issues; they are all critical and, over time, even dominant processes that can make cognitive phenomena recede into the background and thus seem of lesser importance. What I would like to dramatize, however, is that taken to first principles, social cognition is implicated at the most basic levels of all organizational processes—not only at the most intimate, personal levels but also at the most far-reaching levels of strategic thought and action. Understanding social cognition dynamics enables the deeper understanding of virtually every other important organizational process, action, and structure (See Gioia & Sims, 1986, for a now aging early statement of this stance in organizational study).

A loose analogy dramatizes this simple but significant and perhaps provocative point. The belief in emphasizing social cognition in all the debates about cognition–action–structure relations echoes the concerns of all those devoting extraordinary effort to understanding what happened in that first microsecond of the Big Bang that created the universe. Researchers know a great deal about the state of the universe and planet Earth afterward, so why all the fascination with that microsecond of creation? Why are so many of the best minds in astronomy, cosmology, and astrophysics so taken with that instant? In one sense, it hardly matters because it apparently does not much affect people's lives in the present. Yet, understanding that defining moment tells us quite a lot about how we got here (and at some more abstract level could conceivably give us some hope for insight into *why* we might be here). The same is true of the efforts to get at the nature and processes of social cognition as we try to understand how it relates to action, structure, and meaning in the upper reaches of an organization. Of course actions and structures matter. A lot. But, if you want to understand how structures originated and subsequently enable and constrain how strategists act, then look at that moment that created the structures. Social cognition is the essence of that Little Bang.

In the larger vein, that is why there are such energetic voices engaged in the study of social cognition. That also is why there are an increasing number of scholars studying cognitive processes in the strategic domain. Social cognition is key to the origins of action, structure, and perhaps most importantly, meaning at the organizational and even interorganizational level. From a slightly different perspective than they adopted in portraying their own work, this is what I see Odorici and Lomi doing—tracing the origins (the Little Bang) of perceptions and interpretations that produced a putative structure for continuing action among a group of competitors. I love their third question: "How does the structure of competition emerging from the aggregation of individual perceptions differ from the *actual* [italics added] structure of competition?" I am always reminded of the enduring wisdom of W. I. Thomas' observation (quoted in Volkart, 1951) that "If men define situations as real, they are real in their consequences" (p. 5). (Readers should forgive the dated sexism in the framing of the observation). Precisely the same thing is going on in this study. Note that the actual structure matters little; what matters for thought and action is the social construction of the structure. Odorici and Lomi are exactly correct when they note that strategic competition is essentially a product of the tendency of competitors to construct some shared interpretation of a competitive arena within which strategic thinking and action becomes meaningful.

At a tacit level, Oldfield"s work recognizes that this social construction process is best construed as a bona fide collective enterprise (not one confined to a small collection of like-minded individuals). Inviting more stakeholder voices into the organizational conversation about risk assessment enlarges the social scope of social cognition and turns it into a practical advantage. The surfacing of tacit interests and tacit knowledge are both key to the construction and execution of adequate action and structure. Understandably, one of Oldfield's main concerns is with migrating that barely accessible knowledge into useable form so that it might actually be employed by decision makers to avoid or minimize risk. Predictably enough, the conversion of tacit into explicit social knowledge is itself a social process—one intended to circumvent the many human decision-making foibles, including insidious competency traps that tend to mask risky situations.

Brooks, Kimble, and Hildreth enter the process a bit farther downstream from the concern in this commentary with the cognitive origins of action and structure. Nonetheless, they have done a laudable job of pointing out the prominent role of cognition in their structurational view of technology—a view that too typically gives prominence only to structure and action. I view technology as a malleable concept, one that is created and altered by people and one that is used by organization members to set the stage for further thought, action, and possible structural alteration. I of course agree with the authors that people tend to reify technology, morphing it into something ostensibly tangible so that it appears to exist independently of the people who created it out of meaningful thought and action. Indeed, in the modern era, technology is arguably the most important factor in the workings of an organization, but we must not lose sight of the sometimes difficult-to-grasp notion that the technology matters less than the social construction of the technology. The meaning and impact of technology is, at essence, rooted in social cognition, even if the technology is created to gain strategic advantage

Taken together, all three of these chapters serve as entré points into some key notions in social cognitive approaches to studying organizations and the strategic orientations that guide them. In their own ways, they are all dealing with mental models of organizational situations. In their own ways, they also are noting that organizational life, in its many aspects, is a schematized life. Most importantly, however, they all, in varied fashion, demonstrate that social cognition is at the core of the organizational experience. When we consider these three views as dealing, in one way or another, with issues that have strategic implications, it is not a very long reach to discover that the tracings of strategic action, structure, and meaning all lead back to social cognition. No matter the varied ways we might characterize strategy, social cognition is implicated in every aspect. And that is why I chose the emphatic and demonstrative shorthand to characterize this stance: At its essence, strategy *is* social cognition.

REFERENCES

Gioia, D. A., & Sims, H. P., Jr. (1986). Introduction: Social cognition in organizations. In H. P. Sims, Jr., & D. A. Gioia (Eds.), *The thinking organization: Dynamics of organizational social cognition* (pp. 1–19). San Francisco: Jossey-Bass.

Volkart, E. H. (Ed). (1951). *Social behavior and personality: Contribution of W. I. Thomas to theory and social research.* New York: Social Science Research Council.

The Past and Future of Organizational Cognition Research

CHAPTER

15

Is Janus the God of Understanding?

William H. Starbuck
New York University

The Roman god Janus had two faces that allowed him to review the past while he anticipated the future. This chapter suggests that the past of cognitive research gives a context in which we can better appreciate today's challenges.

SCIENTIFIC PSYCHOLOGY EMERGES AND A CONTROVERSY DEVELOPS

Scientific psychology began as the study of perception, a concern that was stimulated by the observational problems of physical science. Because scientists had to depend on their bodily senses for observational data, they had to place great importance on sensory accuracy. For example, in 1796, an assistant astronomer named Kinnebrook at the Greenwich observatory was dismissed from his job because his estimates of transit times differed consistently from those of his superior. (His superior seemingly had no doubt that the less accurate observations had been Kinnebrook's.) Such differences led Karl Gauss, in 1809, to study the distributions of errors in human senses, with the result that Gauss proposed the Normal distribution as a description of the errors. In 1823, the astronomer Friedrich Bessel demonstrated that individual people exhibit consistent differences in reaction speeds and in estimates of short time intervals.

351

Psychologists usually credit Ernst Weber with being the first person to dedicate himself to psychological studies. In 1831, he formulated Weber's Law to describe humans' perceptual accuracy. Weber's Law states that a change in a stimulus that is just barely large enough to notice—a "just-noticeable difference"— is proportional to the stimulus intensity:

$$dR = C \times R$$

In 1860, Gustav Fechner reformulated Weber's observation in terms of a hypothetical cognitive concept—"sensation." Sensation, asserted Fechner's law, increases with the logarithm of the intensity of the stimulus:

$$dS = C \times dR/R$$

$$S = A \times \log R + B$$

Wilhelm Wundt (1873) followed Fechner insofar as he focused on people's reports about their sensations. He innovated by creating, in 1874, the first psychological laboratory. Wundt argued that psychic states have to be explained in psychic terms and that introspection provides accurate data about psychic states. One of Wundt's students, Edward Titchner, introduced scientific psychology to the United States in 1898. Titchner contended that conscious elements and attributes are sufficient to describe a mind. Like Wundt, he relied on introspection. He believed that introspection provides direct, immediate contact with a mind. Thus, in the United States and much of Europe, nineteenth-century scientific psychology was a science of perception that relied on introspective evidence.

However, other intellectual currents flowing in the nineteenth-century challenged the usefulness of a cognitive-introspective psychology. For one thing, developments in science and engineering highlighted physical and chemical processes: Biologists sought to explain the behaviors of organisms in mechanical and chemical terms; for instance, Jacques Loeb traced some behavioral changes to chemical changes that were caused by sunlight, heat, or electrical fields. For another thing, speculation about evolution implied that laws derived from animal behavior might apply to humans. Ivan Pavlov's famous experiments, which began in 1889, demonstrated the roles of conditioned reflexes in the behavior of dogs.

In 1913, John B. Watson became the leading spokesman for a rising movement in psychology. Watson declared the cognitive psychology of Wundt and Titchner a failure. "It has failed signally ... to establish itself as a natural science" whereas it ought to be "a purely objective experimental branch of natural science." Watson blamed introspection for psychology's failure. Before it could become a science, he asserted, "psychology must discard all reference to consciousness;" (p. 163); it should "no longer delude itself" that it can observe mental states. Introspection describes only what is conscious, and this description cannot be verified. "What we need to do is to [make] ... behavior, not consciousness, the objective point of our attack" (pp. 175–176).

Watson (1913) and those who agreed with him called their approach behaviorism. Behaviorism's "theoretical goal is the prediction and control of behavior." "The behaviorist ... recognizes no dividing line between man and brute. The behavior of man ... forms only a part of the behaviorist's total scheme of investigation" (p. 158).

BEHAVIORIST VERSUS COGNITIVE INTERPRETATIONS OF ANIMAL BEHAVIOR

The behaviorists' attack framed cognition and behavior as methodological and philosophical competitors. In the United States, behavior won more support than cognition for forty years. Emphasis shifted to control of behavior rather than observation of mental processes–e. g., B. F. Skinner. The great majority of American psychologists looked at introspection as an imperfect or irrelevant source of information, but few of them wanted to proscribe introspection totally.

The longstanding controversy about the relevance of cognitive processes can be symbolized by the contrasting Edward Tolman's rats with Edwin Guthrie's cats. Fig. 15.1 diagrams a very simple apparatus with which Tolman, Ritchie, and Kalish (1946) gave preliminary training to rats. Of course, the rats soon learned to run across the table and into the walled alley, which led them indirectly to the lighted food box. Then the experimenters modified the apparatus by blocking the walled alley and adding many additional exit alleys, as shown in Fig. 15.2.

When confronted by this modified apparatus for the first time, the rats chose different alleys, with the frequencies graphed in Fig. 15.3. Thirty-six percent of the rats chose Alley 6, which ran in the direction that would have led directly to a point four inches in front of where the food box had been during the preliminary training.

In a famous article that popularized the idea of "cognitive maps," Tolman (1948) interpreted this preference for Alley 6 as evidence that some rats had "acquired not merely a strip-map to the effect that the original specifically trained-on path led to food but, rather, a wider comprehensive map to the effect that food was located in such and such direction in the room." Tolman

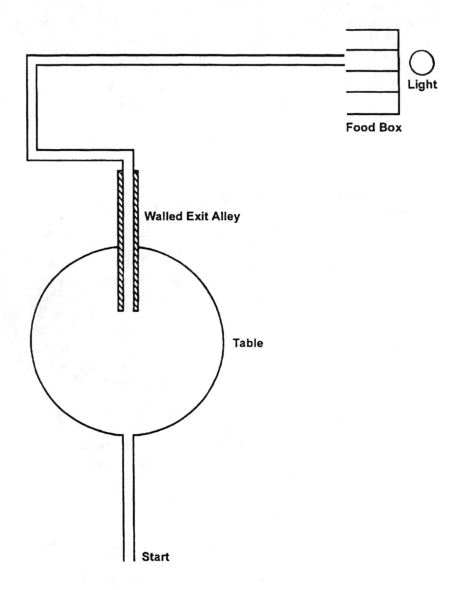

Light

Food Box

Walled Exit Alley

Table

Start

FIG. 15.1   Apparatus used in preliminary training (adapted from Tolman, 1948).
354

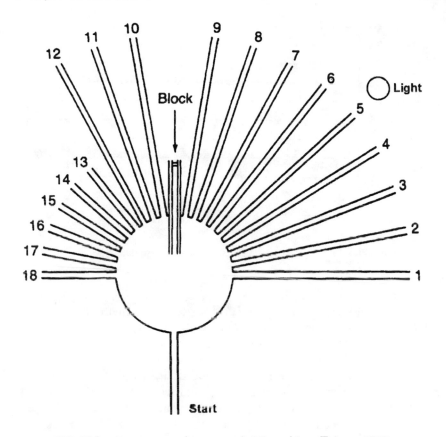

FIG. 15.2 Apparatus used in test trials (adapted from Tolman, 1948).

identified four "conditions which favor narrow strip-maps and ... those which tend to favor broad comprehensive maps not only in rats but also in men" (p. 205). Tolman then contended "that some, at least, of the so-called 'psychological mechanisms' which the clinical psychologists and other students of personality have uncovered as the devils underlying many of our individual and social maladjustments can be interpreted as narrowings of our cognitive maps" (p. 207).

Since the 1890s, psychologists had studied cats' learning as they repeatedly escaped from boxes. Guthrie and Horton (1946) argued that speculation about the cats' thought processes was unnecessary:

We were, in the first place, seeking a description in terms of behavior rather than in terms of consciousness. We do not at all deny that the cat undoubtedly has experience analogous to ours. But it appears to us highly desirable to

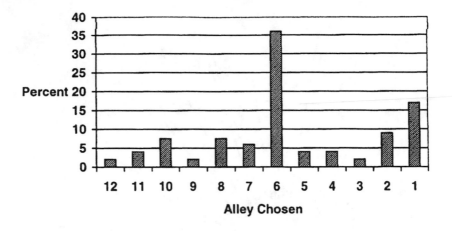

FIG. 15.3   Percentages of rats choosing alternative alleys.

find an adequate description of the cat's behavior without recourse to such conscious experience as it may have.... If we lean too heavily on conscious ideas in explaining behavior we may find ourselves predicting what the cat will think, but not what we can observe it to do. (p. 7)

Guthrie and Horton (1946) watched 800 trials in which 52 cats escaped from a box—by tilting a pole, by pushing a cardboard tube, or by blocking a light beam. The apparatus photographed the cats at the instants they triggered the release mechanism, and the report by Guthrie and Horton included schematic drawings produced from these photographs. Figure 15.4a shows Cat K at the instants when it tilted the release pole on trials 46 through 51. Cat O first experienced 25 trials in a box where release depended on blocking a lightbeam, and then 25 trials in a box where the release trigger was a pole. Figure 15.4b shows this cat on trials 22 through 24 with the lightbeam, and Fig. 15.4c shows it on trials 48 through 50 with the pole.

Guthrie and Horton (1946) concluded, "The cat learns to escape in one trial" (p. 41). The second time a cat entered the box, it repeated its behaviors during the preceding trial. "In a large number of instances a long and complex path about the box was repeated on the second trial" (p. 37). Cats behaved differently over time only because of differences in the way they entered the box or because of "accidental distractions, which may deflect the behavior from its former sequence" (p. 41). Because distractions do occur, "the most stable response is the one which ends in release from the box. In some instances this is a comparatively long series of movements ending in exit" (p. 41). Guthrie and Horton ended their report by expressing:

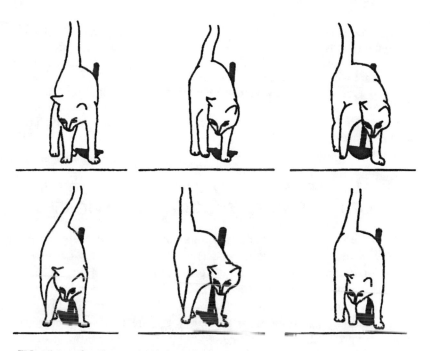

FIG. 15.4a   Cat K on trials 46 through 51 (adapted from Guthrie & Horton, 1946).

FIG. 15.4b   Cat O blocks lightbeam on trials 22 to 24
(adapted from Guthrie & Horton, 1946).

FIG. 15.4c   Cat O tilts pole on trials 48 to 50
(adapted from Guthrie & Horton, 1946).

our conviction that human behavior shows the same repetitiousness of manner and means as well as of ends. The chief difference lies in the greater repertoire of movements of manipulation possessed by men and in the human capacity for maintaining subvocal word series somewhat independent of posture and action. Thought, which is language in use, is itself as routinized as the movements of the cat. But the fact that thought routines are not completely dependent on action enables them to exert their direction and interference at new points, and men in a quandary may discover the exit while sitting still or during irrelevant action. (p. 42)

COMPUTER SIMULATION ALLOWS MODELS OF ROUTINIZED THOUGHT BEHAVIORS

In 1956, Allen Newell and Herbert Simon proposed the use of computer programs as models of thought processes. This novel idea captured the imagination of many, and since computer programs are plainly mechanistic, it allowed cognition to be regarded as mechanistic behavior. Furthermore, Newell and Simon's methodology emphasized introspection. They asked problem solvers to describe their thoughts as they solved problems, then they created programs that could generate approximations to these "protocols". One key idea was that problem solving depends on "heuristics," which are rules of thumb that abbreviate search.

Early studies by Newell and Simon and those they influenced produced models of such diverse behaviors as students solving problems in mathematical logic (Newell and Simon, 1956), chess play (Newell and Simon, 1958), people making predictions about series of binary events (Feldman, 1961), department-store managers' decisions about prices and quantities (Cyert and March, 1963; Moore and Weber, 1969), accident investigations (Braunstein and Coleman, 1967), and production scheduling (Hurst and McNamara, 1967). However, the early enthusiasm for "simulation models" has waned.

Some strengths and weaknesses of computer-simulation models are apparent in the efforts of John Dutton and myself (Dutton & Starbuck, 1971) to model the behavior of a production scheduler named Charlie. We spent six years studying the routines this man used when performing his job, including one year in which we ran nearly 600 experiments that focused on his rules for estimating run-time. Our models could make run-time estimates that Charlie was unable to distinguish from estimates he himself had made. Figure 15.5 compares our estimates with Charlie's for one of two production lines. However, our models did not attempt to imitate Charlie exactly: Our models calculated machine speeds whereas we inferred that Charlie had memorized a large database of machine speeds that would occur in different situations; we estimated that this database contained between 5000 and 20,000 entries.

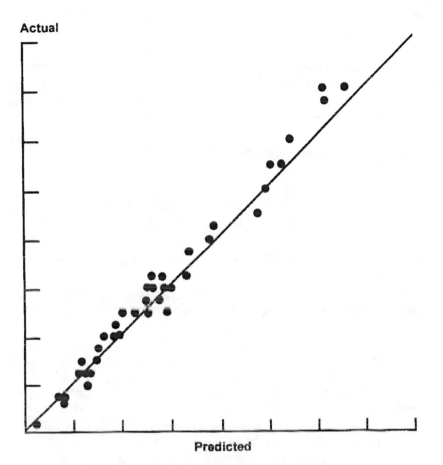

FIG. 15.5   Actual versus predicted estimates of run-time
(adapted from Dutton & Starbuck, 1971).

We also learned to distrust Charlie's oral reports of his cognitive processes. For instance, he said that he calculated machine speeds, not that he
looked them up in a memorized table. Initially, Charlie's reports about his
though processes were erratic; they jumped inconsistently from one topic to
another, and we could not make sense of them. Then, we withheld all information until Charlie asked for it. This revealed the sequence in which Charlie used information, a sequence that was quite consistent. Charlie's
estimation procedure was consistent with Dreyfus and Dreyfus' (1986)
claim that human experts do not rely on generalizations but remember tens
of thousands of specific instances.

We did succeed in modeling Charlie's routinized behaviors with great accuracy. However, this achievement had a considerable cost in time and effort, and we only modeled behaviors that Charlie performed at least daily. To model innovative behavior in this fashion might be impossible. Further, we demonstrated to our own satisfaction that oral reports of cognitive processes could be very wrong. Charlie's oral reports were consistent with Nisbett and Wilson's (1977) inference that introspections are not insights but common-sense theories, and with Argyris and Schön's (1974) observation that people may be unaware that their espoused theories of action are incompatible with their theories-in-use.

COMPUTERS GIVE COGNITION
MORE PROMINENCE

Robins, Gosling, and Craik (1998) made an empirical study of the visibility in the United States of four schools of psychology: behaviorist, cognitive, neuroscientific, and psychoanalytic. Figure 15.6 interprets their data about citations appearing in four flagship psychology journals: For 1967 to 1976 and 1997, Fig. 15.6 shows the relative frequencies of key words corresponding to each school of psychology. For 1977 to 1996, Fig. 15.6 averages the frequencies of key words in citations with the frequencies of citations to each school's leading journals.

The main changes since 1967, obviously, have been a dramatic increase in citations to cognitive studies and a corresponding decrease in citations to behaviorist studies. During the late 1960s, citations to studies in the behaviorist school occurred about twice as often as citations to studies in the cognitive school. By the mid 1990s, there were 5 times as many citations to the cognitive school as to the behaviorist school. Robins et al. (1998) attributed these changes to the availability of computers:

> Computers provided scientists with a new metaphor for conceptualizing how the mind works, one based on information processing and associated concepts of storage, retrieval, computational operations and so on. Perhaps equally important, computers paved the way for the development of new methods for the scientific measurement of mental processes (for example, highly controlled presentation of stimuli, reaction times, dichotic listening, simulations of cognitive processes and brain-imaging techniques). (p. 312)

Although Robins et al. did not measure these frequencies, it seems that there has also been increased emphasis on human beings and less attention to other animals.

Forecasting research has shown that trends are much, much more likely to continue for a few more periods than to shift dramatically. Thus, the trends shown in Fig. 15.6 will, more than likely, continue, with cognitive studies becoming even more dominant.

THE DIALECTICS OF THEORETICAL DEVELOPMENT

Cognitive theories can explain phenomena that behaviorist theories cannot. In particular, it is difficult to explain with a behaviorist theory people's efforts to create desired environments for themselves. Consider, for example, a debate in the *Journal of Management Inquiry*. Dunbar et al. (1996a) asserted that managers should help their organizations' adapt to their environments by managing the organizations' acquisition of sensemaking

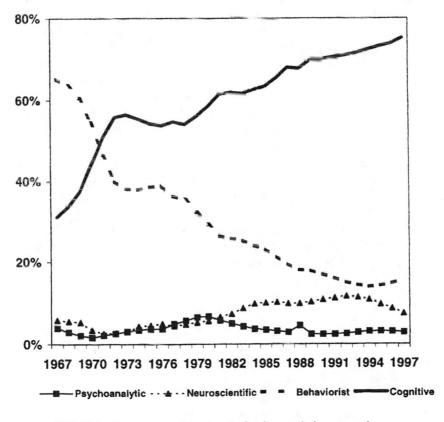

FIG. 15.6   Frequencies of citations in flagship psychology journals.

frameworks. Thus, Dunbar et al. were advocating that managers should try to make their work environments more effective. Porac and Rosa (1996) contested the need for such efforts on the ground that organizations are able to succeed without adapting to their environments: "A [sensemaking] frame's fit with the external environment is largely irrelevant," they claimed, because an organization can impose its frame on its environment (p. 35) "Success," Porac and Rosa, (1996) said, "is more a function of energy and persistence than of the repeating cycles of belief and discrediting proposed by Dunbar et al." (p. 40). Thus, Porac and Rosa were saying that organizations can create environments they prefer. Dunbar et al. (1996b) replied that merely adhering to consistent strategies without attempting to adapt leaves survival up to natural selection, implying that adaptation itself makes an environment more desirable.

As well, behaviorist theories can explain phenomena that cognitive theories cannot (Starbuck & Hedberg, in press). Consider, for example, the implications of research about errors in people's perceptions of their worlds. Our studies as well as those of other researchers show that many people have grossly erroneous perceptions (Starbuck & Mezias, 1996; Mezias & Starbuck, 1999). When we asked managers to tell us about the revenues of the business units they managed, only about one third of their estimates were close to measured values; over one half of the estimates were off by more than 75%. In another study, 40% to 80% of the managers replied "I don't know" to questions about product and process quality in the business units they managed. If one assumes that cognitions strongly influence behaviors, it is very difficult to explain the success of people who are so ill-informed. Of course, most of these people's competitors are equally ill-informed, so the competition may not be severe most of the time. But a significant fraction of our respondents do have accurate perceptions, so the potential exists for the well-informed to out compete the ill-informed, and we have found no evidence that ill-informed managers or their business units do poorly. On the other hand, behaviorist theories can explain how people succeed despite faulty perceptions and ignorance. These theories say that people can behave effectively although they misunderstand their worlds. In particular, if people behave like Guthrie and Horton's (1946) cats, nearly all of their behaviors follow precedents. As long as their environments do not change suddenly and drastically, people can repeat their past behaviors and achieve results that resemble their past results. The behaviors that produced success in the past are likely to produce success in the present.

Obviously, cognition does sometimes guide human behavior; only a few of the most radical behaviorists denied that this is so. But there are several reasons to infer that the influence of cognition on behavior has to be loose or highly variable. First, the theories that people derive from experience are often very wrong; if people really relied on these theories, they would make gross errors. Second, behavior reflects many influences besides cognitive ones; external forces compel some behaviors. Third, people sometimes imitate without understanding; they do what appears to produce success for others. Fourth, people behave habitually and organizations follow routines without repeatedly reevaluating the appropriateness of these behaviors (Starbuck, 1983). Fourthly, various research studies indicate that actions may diverge from preferences; for example, subordinates' actions toward their leaders do not correlate with their judgments about these leaders (Kerr and Slocum, 1981). Finally, there is substantial evidence that people's cognitive processes often, perhaps almost always, diverge from their own perceptions of these processes.

There are also reasons to infer that the influence of behavior on cognition is often strong. When Paul Nystrom and I (Nystrom & Starbuck, 1984) reviewed the research findings about the effectiveness of efforts to change organizations, we concluded that, in general, behaviors exert stronger influence on cognitions than cognitions exert on behaviors. We recommended: "Change beliefs by changing peoples' behaviors rather than by ideological education, propaganda, or structural interventions. Focus on behaviors as causes of beliefs rather than the other way around" (p. 384). Leon Festinger (1962) formulated the issue of behavioral dominance versus cognitive dominance as a trade-off between the difficulty of changing cognitions and the difficulty of changing behaviors. Some behaviors are easy to change and others hard to change; and likewise, some cognitions are easy to change and others hard to change. Human behavior, he hypothesized, adopts the easier alternatives.

Researchers may someday be able to integrate behavior and cognition into an encompassing framework that shows how they represent alternative interpretations of the same phenomena. A distinction between cognition and behavior has to be an abstract one, as they are not separate in the realities of daily life. Behaviorists have long maintained that cognition is only a subcategory of behavior and subject to the same laws as other behavior. Cognitive theorists can certainly agree that cognition is behavior, although many of them would argue that the laws arising from behaviorist studies do not describe cognitive behavior effectively. Certainly, behaviorists have had little success in demonstrating that behaviorist theories explain complex cognitive behavior, and behaviorist psychology has not subsumed cognitive psychology.

Over the long run, researchers make progress by framing issues as conflicts and then convincing themselves, gradually, that the conflicts do not exist. But researchers should not pursue integration aggressively, as they should not integrate intellectual traditions too rapidly. Researchers need contrasts as much as they need consistency. Theoretical competition can be fruitful: Contrasts help to clarify concepts, and juxtaposition and specialization spur development. At present, both behaviorist and cognitive studies add to our understanding, and researchers are likely to make sounder progress if the behaviorist and cognitive schools continue to compete.

REFERENCES

Argyris, C., & Schön, D. A. (1974). *Theory in Practice: Increasing Professional Effectiveness*. San Francisco: Jossey-Bass.

Braunstein, M. L., & Coleman, O. F. (1967). An information-processing model of the aircraft accident investigator. *Human Factors*, 9(1), 61–70.

Cyert, R. M., & March, J. G. (1963). *A behavioral theory of the firm*. Englewood Cliffs, NJ: Prentice Hall.

Dreyfus, H. L., & Dreyfus, S. E. (1986). *Mind over machine*. New York: Free Press.

Dunbar, R. L. M., Garud, R., & Raghuram, S. (1996a). A frame for deframing in strategic analysis. *Journal of Management Inquiry*, 5, 23–24.

Dunbar, R. L. M., Garud, R., & Raghuram, S. (1996b). Run, rabbit, run! But can you survive? *Journal of Management Inquiry*, 5, 168–175.

Dutton, J. M., & Starbuck, W. H. (1971). Finding Charlie's run-time estimator. In J. M. Dutton, & W. H. Starbuck (Eds.), *Computer simulation of human behavior* (pp. 218–242). New York: Wiley.

Feldman, J. (1961). An analysis of predictive behavior in a binary choice experiment. *Joint Computer Conference, Western Proceedings*, 19, 133–144.

Festinger, L. (1962). *A theory of cognitive dissonance*. Stanford, CA: Stanford University.

Guthrie, E. R., & Horton, G. P. (1946). *Cats in a puzzle box*. New York: Rinehart.

Hurst, E. G., & McNamara, A. B. (1967). Heuristic scheduling in a woolen mill. *Management Science*, 14(4), B-182–203.

Kerr, S., & Slocum, J. W., Jr. (1981). Controlling the performances of people in organizations. In P. C. Nystrom, and W. H. Starbuck (Eds.), *Handbook of Organizational Design*, (Vol. 2, pp. 116–134).

Mezias, J. M., & Starbuck, W. H. (in press). The mirrors in our funhouse: The distortions in managers' perceptions.

Moore, C. G., & Weber, C. E. (1969). A comparison of the planning of sales by two department store buyers. In C. E. Weber, & G. Peters (Eds.), *Management action* (pp. 19–40). Scranton, PA: International textbook Co.

Newell, A., Shaw, J. C., & Simon, H. A. (1958). Chess-playing programs and the problem of complexity. *IBM Journal of Research and Development*, 2(4), 320–335.

Newell, A., & Simon, H. A. (1956). The logic theory machine, a complex information processing system. *IEEE Transactions on Information Theory*, IT-2(3), S-61–79.

Nisbett, R. E., & Wilson, T. C. (1977). Telling more than we can know: Verbal reports on mental processes. *Psychological Review*, 84, 231–259.

Nystrom, P. C., & Starbuck, W. H. (1984). Managing beliefs in organizations. *Journal of Applied Behavioral Science*, 20(3), 277–287.

Porac, J. & Rosa, J. A. (1996). In praise of managerial narrow mindedness. *Journal of Management Inquiry*, 5, 35–42.

Robins, R. W., Gosling, S. D., & Craik, K. H. (1998). Psychological science at the crossroads. *American Scientist*, 86, 310–313.

Starbuck, W. H. (1983). Organizations as action generators. *American Sociological Review*, 48, 91–102.

Starbuck, W. H., & Hedberg, B. L. T. (in press). How organizations learn from success and failure. In M. Dierkes, A. Berthoin Antal, J. Child, & I. Nonaka (Eds.), *Handbook of Organizational Learning*, Oxford University.

Starbuck, W. H., & Mezias, J. M. (1996). Opening Pandora's box: Studying the accuracy of managers' perceptions. *Journal of Organizational Behavior*, 17(2), 99–117.

Tolman, E. C. (1948). Cognitive maps in rats and men. *Psychological Review*, 55, 189–208.

Tolman, E. C., Ritchie, B. F., & Kalish, D. (1946). Studies in spacial learning: I. Orientation and the short-cut. *Journal of Experimental Psychology*, 36(1), 13–24.

Watson, J. B. (1913). Psychology as the behaviorist views it. *Psychological Review*, 20, 158–177.

16

New Research Directions on Organizational Cognition

Theresa K. Lant
Zur Shapira
New York University

The role of cognition in organizations has been seen differently, depending on whether one views organizations as systems of *information* or systems of *meaning*. This book is a collection of the latest theoretical and empirical research on cognition in organizations from an international group of scholars. The work presented in this volume has its roots in two prongs of cognition research: the computational and the interpretivist perspectives. We did not charge the authors with the task of integrating these two perspectives. Thus, it is especially noteworthy when viewing this collection as a whole the extent to which it helps to reconcile these divergent approaches. We believe this is significant for the future of organizational cognition research because these chapters represent a sample of the latest work in this area; as such, they provide a window into the next phase of organizational cognition research.

This book tackles the special significance of cognition in collectives such as organizations. Much work in social cognition assumes that collective cognition can be reduced to an aggregation of individual cognition. Others, however, argue that once we move to the collective levels of analysis, cognition goes beyond individual minds (Glynn, Lant, & Milliken, 1994; Sandelands & Stablein, 1987; Walsh, 1995). An important related issue is how one should view organizations as repositories of knowledge (Argote, 1999). Is knowledge (i.e., previous cognition) simply encoded in rules and routines? Or, is knowledge in organizations somehow recreated and reinterpreted with use? Walsh (1995) argued that "our understanding of managerial and organizational cognition is limited because we have been held captive by the computer metaphor of information processing" (Walsh, 1995, p. 307). Garud and Porac (1999) also noted the "shift from viewing organizations as information processing to knowledge generating social systems" (p. xiii). We concur with the need to move beyond viewing organizational cognition as the simple aggregation of individual cognition (Lant & Phelps, 1999; Walsh, 1995). Yet, organizations can be characterized by decision-making systems that process information according to targets set in light of chosen criteria.

Is there a major difference between the information processing and knowledge generation views? The debate is reminiscent of the attempt to distinguish creative problem solving from programmed decision making that surfaced both in artificial intelligence and in psychology. Psychologists have looked for a long time at learning as being associative; even animal learning was conceived as the creation of associations among elements in the nervous systems. New developments in studying learning suggest that the association metaphor may not be essential to learning that can be conceived as computational; however the cognitive–association models may provide a heuristic for conceptualizing the learning process (see also, LeDoux, 1996).

A similar debate rages on also in the field of artificial intelligence. Arguments that machines can think when circuits in computers are modeled on the brain (Churchland & Churchland, 1990) were met with vehement opposition by Searle (1990) who invoked the Chinese room experiment to demonstrate that computers, by their nature, are incapable of true cognition because they do not create and attribute meaning to the symbols that they manipulate.

These debates are echoed in the literature on organizational cognition where ideas about computation versus interpretation are the focus of debate. We believe that these two aspects should be seen as complements rather than rivals. As March (1997) noted, decision making in organizations can be viewed at times as rational and computational in nature and as retrospective sensemaking processes at other times. Indeed, these two aspects are interwoven in discussions of organizational decision-making processes (Shapira, 1997) as well as risk-taking processes in organizational settings (Shapira, 1995).

An additional aspect that needs to be mentioned is the fact that cognition in organizations should not be viewed as the mere aggregation of individual cognition (Lant, 1999; Lant & Phelps, 1999; Walsh, 1995). The interaction among individuals may lead to higher (or lower) levels of knowledge creation, as is the case in group problem solving where interactions among individuals may lead to either synergism or groupthink phenomena (Maier, 1967).

We hope that this volume has provided a deeper understanding of the interactions and interdependencies of actors in complex systems. By looking closer at the interface between actors and systems, the contradiction between computation and interpretation fades, as both activities are seen to go on continuously as actors interact with each other and with organizational systems.

We have suggested that organizations can be viewed as systems of information or systems of meaning. Our intent is not to erase this distinction, because doing so would lead us to blur the distinctive qualities of each perspective that provide us with insights into different aspects of cognition in organizations. If one focuses too much on organizations as information processors—getting more information and finding more efficient ways to process it—then one will lose site of the importance of creating meaning around what is found. If one focuses too much on how meaning in created in organizations, one will lose sight of the importance of knowledge as a critical resource that needs to be managed in organizations. Organizations will always face both the dilemma of *ignorance* and the dilemma of *ambiguity* (March, chap. 4, this volume). Neither dilemma can be subsumed under the other. Our position is that systems of meaning can not be reduced to systems of information processing and vice versa. Although we recognize the utility of modeling organizations as symbolic representational systems (Vera & Simon, 1993), we agree with Searle (1990) that the manipulation of symbols is not sufficient to explain the meaning that these symbols connote to actors. We also differ from those who would argue that symbols mean whatever one wants them to mean. Bougon (1992) suggested that "there is no underlying or deeper reality to be discovered. The socially constructed reality of a system of cognitive maps ... is the social reality" (p. 381). We take the position that *social* reality is constructed, but also that the symbolic representation of basic rules and mechanisms is important. We suggest that symbolic representation and meaning creation are interdependent, not mutually exclusive.

One needs meaning and interpretation to set goals; determining what types of outcomes are important is an interpretive process. One also needs meaning and interpretation to make sense of the outcomes and events that occur (e.g., is this a normal event or a cause for concern?). To take volitional action, however, actors must, at least for certain periods of time, fix their goals and decide on a certain interpretation of outcomes. Without momentary certainty of this kind, it seems that purposeful action would cease. Given a set of goals, one can gather information to one's advantage, leverage it, create knowledge, and disseminate knowledge so organizations are more effective. Organizations and their actors move in and out of these different processes continually by asking questions such as: How did we do? What should we do? How best to do it?

Section II of the book provides a framework for thinking about the roles of information processing and interpretation processes in organizations. Jim March's chapter (chap. 4, this volume) strikes at the heart of the issue of organizational level cognitive processes: Organizations must simultaneously manage the dilemmas of ignorance and ambiguity. Ignorance is a problem of *computation*. Intelligent action requires information and prediction. In a world where information is difficult and costly to obtain, and future states are uncertain, intelligent action is problematic. However, as Vasant Dhar (chap. 2, this volume) points out, given sufficient data, theories about cause and effect, and a well-defined payoff matrix associated with uncertain outcomes, this problem boils down to one of computation.

Ambiguity, on the other hand, is a problem of *interpretation*. To assess the intelligence of actions, one has to know what outcomes are desired and know when outcomes have been achieved. The definition of preferences turns out to be a very sticky problem and one that, in organizations, is played out in a social domain. As Ocasio (chap. 3, this volume) explains, organizations are dynamic social systems that structure and regulate the situated cognition of organizational participants. Sitkin's commentary shows how the dilemmas of computation and interpretation relate to the dilemmas of exploration and exploitation in organizations (March, 1991). In Sitkin's (Commentary, this volume) view, exploration and exploitation are complementary, rather than contradictory, processes. As March has reminded us on many occasions, organizations need to manage both processes in the pursuit of intelligence. Similarly, Sitkin reminds us that organizations need to manage both computation and interpretation. These processes do not need to be opposing world views about the nature of phenomena. Even Dhar, whose approach is to develop ever more sophisticated computational methods, suggests a set of boundary conditions under which computational approaches are feasible and desirable and can replace human judgment and when they can merely serve as support systems. Similarly, Ocasio shows how both the computational and the interpretive perspectives are crucial to an understanding of cognition at the organizational level of analysis. Organizations need to search for, store, retrieve, and transmit knowledge. However, as both March and Ocasio point out, these information processing activities are embedded in situations that influence the meaning attached to knowledge.

The chapters in Section III illustrate empirically how knowledge and decisions in organizations are influenced by the structures, routines, and processes within which they are embedded. Rulke and Zaheer (chap. 5, this volume) found that the intelligent action of the grocery stores they studied was influenced by the extent to which managers had useful mental maps that helped them locate and retrieve knowledge in their organization. Paul-Chowdhury (chap. 6, this volume) also tackled the issue of the location and dissemination of knowledge in a very different type of organization—a financial institution. She found that the transfer of lessons learned from performance feedback in one subunit of an organization was inhibited due to barriers such as organizational structures, reward systems, and pressures toward conformity. These barriers were reduced, to some extent, by the direct communication of leaders in the bank.

These two field studies, in two very different industries—retail groceries and banks—illustrate common challenges for organizations trying to solve the *ignorance* dilemma. For organizations, taking more intelligent actions is not simply a matter of gathering and processing more and better information. Knowledge in organizations is subject to significant barriers to its transfer and use. One part of this problem stems from institutional barriers that discourage the flow of knowledge. The structures and routines of organizations are often designed for purposes other than maximizing the flow of information, such as maintaining authority and control. Another part of the problem lies in the interface between organizational storage and retrieval mechanisms and human actors who use these mechanisms. As Paul-Chowdury finds, the creation and use of these mechanisms are not value free. Motivations and power relations can influence the type of information that is stored in organizational memory, who has access to this information, and how this information is used. In her commentary, Sutcliffe points out that there are elements of social construction even in the findings of the studies on the flow of knowledge within organizations. This is due to the process by which knowledge is disseminated through stories, conversations, and speeches. These communicative acts are also acts of interpretation. For instance, Paul-Chowdury finds that when poor performance outcomes are communicated within the frame of a normal occurrence, very different knowledge is created and shared within an organization than if these outcomes are framed as deviations from normal events.

The Murphy, Mezias, and Chen chapter (chap. 7, this volume) is a study of goalsetting in a financial institution, similar to Paul-Chowdury's setting. Their findings have implications for the *ambiguity* issue raised by March. They suggest that the setting of goals is a decision that frames performance feedback as either positive or negative, thus influencing the interpretation of this information. This work extends the behavioral decision theory work on framing of decisions (Tversky & Kahneman, 1981) from the laboratory to complex organizations. This chapter shows how simple decision rules, such as how aspirations adapt in response to feedback, can have a powerful effect on the goals that are set by organizations. This is significant for the ambiguity dilemma because goals determine which outcomes are considered important, what the organization wants to achieve, and how performance is interpreted. Their findings also resonate with those of Paul-Chowdury in terms of how performance outcomes are interpreted. Outcomes are framed in terms of their deviation from goals. When goals are lowered following poor performance, discrepancies are dampened and outcomes are interpreted as normal events. Thus, although one might think of the comparison between performance and goals as a matter of computation (an arithmetic fact), Sutcliffe reminds us that the meaning attributed to this comparison is a matter of interpretation.

The chapters in section IV illustrate that the framing and categorization processes that precede information processing influence how information is used in ambiguous situations and, thus, the decisions that are made. These studies use four different methods, including qualitative and quantitative methods, in four very different contexts. Still, the consistency in their findings is striking.

Through the examination of aviation records and interviews with managerial teams involved in designing these record-keeping systems, Tamuz shows how the categorization of ambiguous events, such as aircraft *near misses* (an interpretation process) influences if and how knowledge about these events is generated. Thus, interpretations influence the computational processes of retrieving and storing information. Like the lessons we learned from the Paul-Chowdury and Murphy et al. studies, categorization and framing processes (is this normal or a deviation?) influence the knowledge that is generated in the organization. Tamuz (chap. 8, this volume) shows how these interpretations influence not just current decisions but the storage of information. Thus, the stock of knowledge that an organization can draw on to make future decisions (a computational process) is influenced by interpretive processes. Specifically, she shows how "classifying … events affects the allocation of attention and the construction of information processing routines, which, in turn, influence the availability of data that the organization can transform into knowledge" (Tamuz, chap. 8, this volume). She finds that the past experiences, goals, and positions of decision makers influence how they will interpret and categorize ambiguous events. Thus, again, one finds that the computation question is not a simple one.

The knowledge base used for computation has been influenced by interpretive processes somewhere along the way.

Bennett and Anthony's (chap. 9, this volume) study of inside and outside boards members suggests that, similar to Tamuz's findings, a director's role and experience influence how they categorize and interpret events. This study also reflects March's (chap. 4, this volume) notions of exploration and exploitation. Learning is facilitated by the interaction of different perspectives among outsiders and insiders on boards of directors. More active boards engage in more interaction, which results in better learning and performance.

Nair (chap. 10, this volume) finds that it is not enough for managers to have substantial knowledge to make complex decisions. They need to have a cognitive map that links pieces of knowledge together in a meaningful and complex way. We liken this to the usefulness of a road map; to be useful, maps must provide connections between locations, not just locations. Although this is a study of individual level decision making, the findings are similar in pattern to those of Paul-Chowdury's (chap. 6, this volume) study of banks. Unless there are connections linking pockets of knowledge in the organization, knowledge is not shared.

In Vidaillet's (chap. 11, this volume) inductive study of the decision-making processes surrounding a hazardous material incident that occurred in France, she finds that before information about the incident could be processed, the actors needed to frame and categorize the incident. Each set of actors constructed a representation of the crisis and then processed information and acted accordingly. The context of the actors—their background, job, and physical location—all influenced their framing of the incident. As we saw in the Tamuz (chap. 8, this volume) study, interpretive processes seem to precede computational processes. The interpretive stage is influenced by the background and role of the decision maker.

These four chapters illustrate how important the interpretive processes of framing and categorization are to actors faced with ambiguous issues. In all these examples, this interpretive process is a precursor to information processing. The interpretations of managers are influenced by their context—their prior experiences, their social context, and their location in time and space. This common pattern of findings is striking because these studies use different methods in different types of organizations and different types of decision making. The implication is that if one only examines decision making after goals, preferences, and problem definitions have been set, one will see decision making as largely a computational, information-processing exercise. To do so, however, misses half of the story. Defining problems and determining preferred outcomes are interpretive processes that serve to reduce ambiguity and allow information search, retrieval, and processing to ensue. As Dukerich (Commentary, this volume) points out, the similarity among all these studies is that they explore how decision makers deal with ambiguous, unstructured problems. She suggests that it is the ill-structured nature of these problems that allow for multiple interpretations of the problem, diverse opinions about the relevance of types of information, and differing judgments as to the appropriateness of various actions. The diversity of interpretations that results from ambiguity may actually enhance learning, however. The same dilemma for managers that was raised earlier is seen. To proceed with information processing and decision making, problems need to be categorized and goals need to be set. However, if ambiguity is reduced too soon or too completely, computational energy may be focused in the wrong direction. One may process information about the wrong problem.

The chapters in Section V explore the nature of socially situated cognition at three levels of analysis: interorganizational, organizational and intra-organizational. Odoroci and Lomi (chap. 12, this volume) examine interorganizational cognition by studying how managers of water treatment plants in Italy categorized their competition. They used managers' judgments of strategic similarity to build a map of the cognitive social structure that exists among the group of competitors. They found that managers from different firms often had different assessments of the degree of similarity among the competitors. They also varied in their accuracy with respect to similarity judgments. Assessments varied depending on the manager's perspective. Managers tended to judge their own firms to be similar to few other firms, whereas they judged other firms to be similar to a large number of firms. Managers' idiosyncratic knowledge of their own firms may make the differences between themselves and others more salient, whereas these differences would not be as salient when they judged the similarity between other firms.

Oldfield (chap. 13, this volume) examined many incidents of failed large-scale projects in Britain. She discovered that these projects often fail because the framing of problems associated with these projects systematically excludes information that would help assess project risk. She finds evidence that the relevant information for predicting negative outcomes is often available within project teams but that this knowledge is not shared effectively throughout the organization. This occurs because the interests of certain stakeholders are routinely excluded, resulting in an overly narrow definition of problems. This issue is seen as well in Section IV, where framing and interpretation can lead to computation about the wrong problem. Section III demonstrated that interpretive processes often hinder the flow of knowledge throughout an organization.

Brooks, Kimble, and Hildreth (chap. 14, this volume) propose that knowledge is constructed within organizations through its use in specific contexts. They use structuration theory (Giddens, 1984) to explore the processes by which an information technology is created, used, and institutionalized within an organization. They show how technologies are not just used by actors in an organization but, rather, are created and institutionalized by the process of actors using technologies. Information technologies, as Dhar (chap. 2) suggests, are supposed to aid in the computational problems of organizations. However, the use of these technologies is influenced by interpretation processes.

At all three levels of analysis, one can see the role of the interaction of actors in creating the interpretations of situations that guide action. In all three cases, one sees how features of organizational life that on the one hand seem to lend themselves especially well to computational approaches—the definition of strategic groups, assessment of risk, and application of technology—are all influenced by interpretive processes. Gioia (Commentary, this volume) suggests that these chapters illustrate that social cognition is the fundamental principle underlying interorganizational, organizational, and intraorganizational action, structure, and meaning.

Starbuck (chap. 15, this volume) refers to the two-faced Roman god Janus to remind readers of the essential duality of cognitive processes. This duality has been seen throughout this book—the tension between stability and change, and the simultaneous challenge of ignorance and ambiguity. He also reminds readers that although the integration of different perspectives is a noble goal, there is value in facilitating debate that clarifies the concepts and assumptions of the perspectives. We have similar goal for this book. Although integration of the computational and interpretive perspectives in the long run is sought, variance, contrast, and debate at this stage of the game is encouraged.

REFERENCES

Argote, L. (1999). Organizational learning: Creating, retaining, and transferring knowledge. Boston, MA: Klawer.

Bougon, M. G. (1992). Congregate cognitive maps: A unified dynamic theory of organization and strategy. *Journal of Management Studies, 29,* 369–389.

Churchland, P. M. & Churchland, P. S. (1990). Could a machine think? *Scientific American, 262*(1), 32–36.

Garud, R., & Porac, J. F. (1999). Kognition. In R. Garud & J. F. Porac (Eds.), *Advances in managerial cognition and organizational information processing* (Vol. 6, pp. ix–xxi). Greenwich, CT: JAI.

Giddens, A. (1984). *The constitution of society: Outline of the theory of structuration.* Berkeley, CA: University of California Press.

Glynn, M. A., Lant, T. K., & Milliken, F. J. (1994). Mapping learning processes in organizations: A multi-level framework linking learning and organizing. In C. Stubbart, J. Meindl,

& J. Porac (Eds.), *Advances in managerial cognition and organizational information processing* (Vol. 5, pp. 43–83). Greenwich, CT: JAI.

Lant, T. K. (1999). A situated learning perspective on the emergence of knowledge and identity in cognitive communities. In R. Garud & J. Porac (Eds.), *Advances in managerial cognition and organizational information processing* (Vol. 6, pp. 171–194). Greenwich, CT: JAI.

Lant, T. K. & Phelps, C. (1999). Strategic Groups: A Situated Learning Perspective. In A. Miner & P. Anderson (Eds.), *Advances in Strategic Management* (Vol. 16, pp. 221–247). Greenwich, CT: JAI.

LeDoux, J. E. (1996). *The emotional brain: The mysterious underpinnings of emotional life.* New York: Simon & Schuster.

Maier, N. F. (1967). Assets and liabilities in group problem solving: the need for an integrative function. *Psychological Review, 74,* 239–249.

March, J. G. (1991). Exploration and exploitation in organizational learning, *Organization Science, 2,* 71–87.

March, J. G. (1997). Understanding how decisions happen in organizations. In Z. Shapira (Ed.), *Organizational decision making* (pp. 9–32). Cambridge, England: Cambridge University Press.

Sandelands, L. E., & Stablein, R. E. (1987). The concept of organization mind. In *Research in the Sociology of Organizations* (Vol. 5, pp. 135–161). Greenwich, CT: JAI.

Searle, J. R. (1990). Is the brain's mind a computer program? *Scientific American, 262*(1), 26–31.

Shapira, Z. (1995). *Risk taking: A managerial perspective.* New York: Russell Sage.

Shapira, Z. (1997). *Organizational decision making.* Cambridge, England: Cambridge University Press.

Tversky, A., & Kahneman, D. (1981). The framing of decisions and the rationality of choice. *Science, 211,* 453–458.

Vera, A. H., & Simon, H. A. (1993). Situated action: A symbolic interpretation. *Cognitive Science, 17,* 7–48.

Walsh, J. P. (1995). Managerial and organizational cognition: Notes from a trip down memory lane. *Organization Science, 6,* 280–321.

Author Index

A

Abrams, R. A., 261
Abramson, E., 277, 302
Ackoff, R. L., 212, 237
Adcock, S., 158, 159, 182
Agor, W., 186, 207
Albert, S., 40, 58
Allan, J., 323
Allison, G. T., 54, 58
Allport, F. H., 5, 10
Anderson, J., 243, 261, 284, 302
Andrews, J. D., 306, 323
Anthony, W., 8, 185, 191, 207, 265, 266, 267, 373
Arable, P., 284, 288, 302
Argote, L., 84, 100
Argyris, C., 18, 19, 21, 26, 36, 360, 364
Ashkenas, R., 104, 117, 122
Audet, M., 216, 218, 238

B

Bacdayan, P., 78
Baden-Fuller, C., 277, 303
Baker, J., 187, 208
Bandura, A., 129, 144
Bantel, K., 188, 207
Barnard, C., 186, 207
Barnes, N. M. L., 306, 313, 323
Barney, J., 277, 302
Bartlett, C., 83, 99, 100
Bartlett, F. C., 216, 237
Bartunek, J. M., 244, 261
Batra, B., 104, 123, 126, 145, 152, 153
Baum, J., 146, 275, 276, 277, 278, 279, 285, 302, 303
Baysinger, B., 185, 186, 187, 188, 207, 266, 268
Beach, L., 186, 208

Begeman, M., 20, 36
Behling, O., 186, 207
Bendor, J., 181, 182
Bentham, J., 71
Berger, P., 3, 10
Berkeley, D., 323
Berndt, D., 321, 324
Berry, D. C., 86, 99
Bettis, R., 206, 209
Bettman, J. R., 262
Billings, C. L., 166, 189
Binkhorst, B., 216, 237
Black, J. B., 323
Blau, P. M., 56, 58
Boari, C., 282, 302
Boeker, W., 186, 208
Bogner, W., 277, 302
Boorman, S., 278, 284, 302, 304
Bougon, M., 216, 217, 224, 237, 239, 369, 375
Bourgeois, L., 186, 206, 207
Bower, G. H., 148, 153, 318, 323
Bower, J. L., 54, 58
Braunstein, D. N., 212, 239
Braunstein, M. L., 358, 364
Brehmer, B., 220, 237, 238
Breiger, R., 278, 284, 288, 302, 304
Brown, J. S., 75, 78, 102, 103, 104, 122, 186, 208
Browning, L. D., 75, 79
Bruner, J., 4, 10
Burns, T., 104, 121, 122
Butler, H., 185, 186, 207, 266, 268

C

Caldwell, B., 335, 344
Calori, R., 216, 219, 238
Campbell, D. T., 43, 58
Cardinal, L. C., 75, 78
Carlston, D. E., 318, 325

377

Subject Index

Printed in the United States
110548LV00002B/315/A